Published Writing

1976 – 2021

Eric Wiberg

Island Books

for **Prof. David A. Northrup**

by the same author:

Bahamas in World War II
Mailboats of the Bahamas, U-Boats in the Bahamas
U-Boats off Bermuda, U-Boats in New England
Tanker Disasters, Tankers East of Suez
Drifting to the Duchess, Drifting (script with Paolo Pilladi)
Travel Diaries, Yacht Voyages
Surviving St. George's & Scars
Sea Stories & Swan Sinks
Published Writing & Juvenilia
Round the World in the Wrong Season
First Fifty in Fifty
Napoleon's Battles (with Felix Wiberg)
*Åke Wiber*g (with Mats Larsson)

ISBN 978-0-9843998-6-4, 0-9843998-6-0
E-Book ISBNs: 978-0-9983759-6-0, 0-9983759-6-9
Library of Congress Control Number: 2009914213

layout by Abdul Rehman Qureshi: writingpanacea@gmail.com
Island Books, Boston, MA, USA
1st Edition Boston, May, 1992, 2nd Ed. Newport, May, 2003, 3rd Ed. Norwalk, Dec. 2009, 4th Ed., New York City, May, 2017, 5th Ed., Boston, April, 2021.

All editions, Island Books
Printed in the United States of America

Table of Contents

Self Portrait, 1987

Education

Education means coming to a place you've never seen.

At the Farm

On March 2nd 1978 we went to the farm. We saw cows get milked by machine. First about 7 cows were milked then one by one they went out. Then the washed ones were milked. Then we went to the calves. There were 8 there. We fed them. They sucked our fingers. They thought they were their mother's teats. The mothers do not give milk for two months if they are getting a baby. They save the milk for the baby. The baby comes out from the back of the cow. There were 300 cows and 30 more were coming by plane from Canada. The most it can give is 50 pounds [of milk].

Tall Tales of Eric Wiberg

Once I saw a man blowing a horn towards the sky. I said, what are you doing? Freezing the sky was the reply. That night I heard from the sky the sound of cracking ice and then it stopped, then I heard the sound of rain on ice. Then suddenly something broke through the ice Then rain fall on my roof. But before I knew it had stopped. All through the night this happened. And even in the morning I woke up and to my amazement the sky had frozen! And about three miles higher rain was falling on the frozen ice above.

Just then my dog Greta barked at me and I told her to rest again for she was having puppies that day. He's quick as lightning I got my mountain climbing stuff. I tried to get my anchor to hitch a piece of ice and at last I did, quickly I climbed up swift through the air. I was about a mile high and was very tired. Suddenly I got a brain wave. I looked round only to see clouds. I climbed on to one and sat there for a moment. I just saw a little brown hairy thing in the cloud.

I pulled it up to hear an "ow" from the man who froze the sky! For 4 minute I sat and talked to him (not really retiring that such a thing was happening). But he suddenly fell through the cloud. Down through the air he went. Just then I heard a thump! He had

2

gone down my chimney. I found my rose that was now frozen. It was easier for me for I had just to slide down and in five minutes was on the ground. When I got down, I heard a puppy cry. I looked at Greta, she had had her five puppies, but there was something unusual about them there were eggshell near her.

Thinking she had got them from the garbage I came closer to spank her. But one egg was unopened and rocking. I picked it up but it cracked and out ran a playful little male puppy, I was cold and hungry and had no time to waste. So I patted them all, let them in, fixed dinner, dog t a batch, cut some wood for a fire and placed the first log in the fireplace to suddenly hear an "Ow!".

I looked around and then to the fireplace. I lifted a log up so see a dirty foot. And as you should know it was the man who froze the sky. We made friends. My information from him was his name was Bob the Vagabond. I gave him one of my puppies and now we are famous for having an egg-laying doge. We also have a report on the happy past. Sand we live happily together....... Bob, Me, Greta, my dog and her five puppies.

Stuff:

Forest fires blaze with it,
James M. Wiberg plays with it,
Fire - I like that stuff.

Grouper roam in it,
Boats foam in it,
Sea - I like that stuff.

Columbus sailed in one,
Captain Hook failed in one,
Ships - I like that stuff.

Cows feed in it,
Corns seed in it,
Fields – I like that stuff.

Soldiers die in it,
Bombs fly in it,

3

War – I like that stuff.

People lie in them,
Ladies cry them,
Graves – I dislike that stuff.

Birds soar in it,
Planes roar in it,
Air – I like that stuff!

May, 1981, Stuff, St. Andrew's School *Yearbook*, Class 6 Harding, Nassau, NP, Bahamas

The Straw Market

The unending hustle and bustle of the growing crowds reached its prime as the day peaked. The stampeding crowd drew clouds of dust from under foot. There was neither a breath of air nor a droplet of rain to answer the prayers of those in the market on this scorching hot day.

Things had come to life. "Come to life" is putting it mildly as scores of jittery crowds streamed into the marketplace. From the docking cruise ships, there came a steady flow of tourists; from the gangplank into the ready-waiting taxis they went, making a beeline for the inevitable, eager for an exciting day of browsing and shopping.

There stands the market: rows of shanty, makeshift stalls, heavily laden with the exotic commerce extracted from the islands. Foregrounding the scene, almost dominating it, is the misty blue water of Nassau harbor, on which the fishing smacks, full of talkative natives, lie gently swaying stop the incoming swells. Every new swell reveals the head of one of the native lads, out for a day of coin diving, then envelops it and replaces it with the head of yet another. As they occasionally dive, vanishing into the murky depths, their slippery dark-skinned bodies fade gently into the indigo sea.

Restricting this endless mass of water are the massive concrete walls, the crust of the granite piers, gratified and dented. Atop these veteran clifflets rest the ragged wooden stalls, laden with

4

turtles, fish of all colors, and other fresh seafood, conch, rainbow-colored sea-fans, and straw, handmade hats and baskets with intricate and colorful designs for the passing tourists. The spicy conch and freshly gutted fish fill the air with the smell of a pier, while the necklaces of beads and shells cannot be heard rattling above the noise.

Although the natives, blasting their reggae, roam in this nomad's land freely, tourists are the populace of the market, satisfying their virgin eyes with the scenery of the unwavering palm trees, statues in all their grandeur, and sparkling fountains silhouetted grey against the clear azure sky.

Above the honking taxis, blaring music and bargaining tourists, one might hear one of the many crate-ridden old vendors shouting endlessly about the quality of his work or shouting vain curses from his toothless mouth at the back of one of the less-vulnerable tourists, only like everything else in the market, to be swallowed up in the turmoil of loud noise and ever-flowing crowds. There seems never to be enough havoc wreaked in this marketplace.

A Day at Sea

As we lugged our heavy gear across the sparkling golden toward the beached dinghy, Frank and I knew nothing of our forthcoming adventure. Having attached the anchor, motor, and cooler to the small dinghy, we shoved off, headed in the general direction of the jagged shoal. We had with us our spears, masks, snorkel, fins, and various other gear. The boat belonged to Frank, a fourteen-year-old friend of mine. His German ancestry showed clearly through his golden hair and azure eyes.

After a five-minute voyage across the glassy bay, we reached the shoal. From the surface it was brown, orange-spotted blot in the turquoise water. It was abundant with life; lobster, sharks and fish roamed freely through the gently swaying sea-fans and rainbow-colored coral heads. Our first dive below surface, brief as it was, put us in a world of ecstasy and thrilling adventure, a world of colors blending and fading gently into each other, the yellows, reds and purples of sea-fans blending smoothly in with the orange of the coral heads and bluish-green of the gently swelling water, engulfing the diver in a flurry of color.

After ten minutes, Frank speared the first fish of the day; a parrotfish, its colors matching the bird it was so cleverly named after. Soon after that, Frank spotted the two heavily crusted objects lying fifteen feet apart on the hazy seafloor, roughly thirty feet below us. It was I who took the first curious plunge. Almost breathless at the bottom I stopped, aghast. There, but five feet ahead of me, lay two large cannons, both heavily crusted in weeds and shells. Beside the first lay a large black-tip shark. Tempted as I was, I refused myself a closer look, for my lungs, by now bursting, were clawing desperately for air. I spent most of my remaining strength stopping Frank from a quick look.

One Rainy Day

I was not surprised on such a day, with the cold, enshrouding mist clinging to us, that we were the only team trudging toward the murmuring group of coaches. Their whispers and suggestions grew slowly more audible as we completed our silent trek across the soft, green grass. The soccer players had not come into the cold that day; instead, they were comfortably and warmly snuggled inside, probably watching "Mr. Bill," James Bond, or something of the like.

A shrill whistle pierced the thick, dank air, but before the coach could accompany it with, "Take a lap!" we had all started the tiring chore.

The 'click-clack' of our heavy pads and the 'squish-squash' of fifty pairs of cleats pounding a muddy puddle interrupted the tranquil silence. The dew clung to my skin, and I could see my breath as I rounded and bend and headed downfield. I floated in the crowd.

Silently we congregated before the coaches, panting, spitting, and leaning on one another, like a team. Occasional thuds, and shouts drifted toward us from across the field, where the Junior Varsity players were completing their practice. We could hardly distinguish their numbers as they ran into the distance, into the fog. Away. All was silent.

Gentle raindrops began to splatter on my helmet while others fell, muffled, to the wet grass. I started to drift off. A sunny day on a warm beach. No work.

Suddenly I shivered, snapped back. The coach yelled my name, but I just stood staring through him, mouthpiece dangling. He sighed, and, placing his hand on my helmet, positioned me on the flank of the offensive line. My mind raced: "Me? Starting flanker?" No, I was still second string. The first string began forming the starting defense. Then I knew why he had put me in.

I looked toward him. He was organizing out defense, and I noticed that the shoulders of his sweatshirt were splattered with rain, turning them dark blue instead of grey. The other coaches called the scrubs together, but I was busy trying to figure out why they believed that it could never rain on a football field.

Coastline

The coastline, dividing land and sea,
Where nature's conflicts prevail.
The truest of all rivalries,
Their lulls and stings entail.

The land is great defense,
Oceans pushing forth their waves,
The two each other's limit,
Remaining neither's slave.

Land blessed with immobility,
The ocean blessed without,
These battles of infinity
Is continued bouts.

Beckoned from the ocean's depths
Surge the strengthened waves,
Pushed against the waiting coast
Into its growing caves.

Along the frontal battle line
The strong grey cliffs arise.
Firm against the waves they stand,
Echoing their cries.

As men in turmoil now are trapped,
These elements are caught,
But even if our turmoil ceased,
The coastal wars would not.

How long has such a conflict lived?
To be with us today?
As long and for much longer than
We humans here shall stay.

Big, Dead, Headless

On a Saturday in November 1986, I was one of the first persons to discover the corpse of a 900-pound Leatherback turtle, the largest of sea turtles, on Newport's Second Beach, the very sine qua non of our view from St. George's. The corpse weighed some 900 pounds and was six feet, ten inches in length. Leatherback (or Trunkback) sea turtle such as this are capable of traversing the Indian, Pacific, and Atlantic oceans. It is possible that this Leatherback was killed in an attempt to ensnare itself from a fishing net. The left forepaw of the turtle was badly lacerated. My second visit, on Sunday, revealed that the Leatherback had since suffered decapitation.

The leatherback, well known for its eight foot, fifteen-hundred-pound potential size and for its ability to probe virtually all of Earth's warm-water oceans, also played a role in World War Two. During the Pacific conflict of the 1940s the tracks that female Leatherbacks left after laying their 60 to 150 eggs were mistaken for the tracks of enemy mini-tanks!

Swedish Countryside

I am stationary –
Sitting on the train.
Outside my windows
The quiet greens
Of a Swedish countryside
Are moving past -
Behind us,
Scene after scene
Of postcard-perfect scenery
Are presented
Before they swallow
Up our wake.
I shall not say that
"The countryside is rolling by"
Because that is the common tact
Of poets and the likes.
To me it seems that
We are staying quite still and
A countryside is being pulled
From behind
As wrapping paper across a table -
Cur down the center.
They say wheat
Moves not unlike an ocean
In the winds.
It does.
It is as though the train
Is an anchored sloop
And the ocean – windswept –
Is persisting against us.
An ocean of wheat passing by –
Sliced only by our prow.

I imagine that on this train
You pay for the minutes
During which the countryside
Unravels itself.
Perhaps.
Sitting here –
Not moving.
Watching a plane of Swedish countryside
Being pulled beneath us.

Quotes

"There is still room in the round table of philosophy for those thinkers of the late twentieth century free of the yoke of television."

"A situation wherein the proletariat are satisfied to spend the majority of their non-working hours in submittal to the television sustains (and eventually becomes the weapon of) the bourgeois. The situation fosters the growth of mute, passive, and dependent working masses which America's 1776 Revolution were not."

"Life is the creation of nostalgia."

Swimming: Whittemore-Wiberg and the Water Wonders

The sport here has gone through some dramatic changes, and as the 1988 season plows onward the enigmatic institution keeps improving. This season we are pleased to welcome many talented new swimmers, returning lettermen, a new coaching staff, as well as several changes and reforms. There are two elements to our swim team, the coaches and the pool, that make and have made the sport standout since 1925. In the past three years the team has had as many coaches, and this year, with two experienced new coaches sat the helm, the turnout is higher than ever. After the 1986 season the responsibility of head coach went from Mr. Montgomery to Mr. Greenwood, who can be credited for having kept the program going for the 1986-87 season. This year S.G.S. swimming is grateful to have with us veteran coaches Mr. and Mrs.

Evans, our head coach, was at one point an All-American swimmer at the North Carolina State University, and both have swum competitively before. Although we have only one senior this year, the talent is strong and varied, and there is much hope for the future. We have been training since late November and the two-and-a-half mile practices are being replaced by a consistent string of swimming meets. Although for the first time ever a separate girls' squad attended the meet, both practices and meets are still co-educational. Of a record squad size consisting of thirty-five persons, there are twenty-six varsity competitors, including returning lettermen Jenna Cook, Kerry Connell, Laura Stack, Anne Smythe, Colin Born, Morgan Farrell, Jesse Pasco, Eric Wiberg, and co-captain / senior, Josh Whittemore. Out of many talented swimmers joining us this year, several stand out: Michele Minihane, Bethany Wenner, Kirsten Keenan, Allison Leboeuf, Eleanor Lucas, Oliver Brooks, Brent McClean, and Manning Unger. Indeed, there are many other freshman and sophomore squad members about whom you are bound to hear more. For many new swimmers this is a first time on a swim team.

Over the years the pool and program have experienced several changes, and this year has been a renaissance of sorts, with a lot of assistance from the maintenance squad. An element of "pool pride" has grown. Last year we lost our final meet against archrival Portsmouth Abbey by one point in the closing relay, yet more successful meets are on the horizon! This year the tradition of open-pools for student use during free hours several times weekly was re-instituted and has thus far been a success. Often the lifeguards are certified students. For practices the group is divided into two groups so that one swims with others at the same level. En masse the training lasts from 3:00 to 5:45, when swimmers re-energize in King Hall. Practices take an hour and a half for one group and an hour for the next. Coach Evans is not the only one pleased and optimistic about the Swimming program here. When interviewed he sounded positive: "I am pleased with the enthusiasm on the team.

The more experienced swimmers are very enthusiastic, and it's infectious. The younger team members catch onto that feeling and want to do better; each individual improvement helps the team." A motto, which seems very relevant to our team states "pain can be fun." Swimming is not an easy sport when you take it seriously and though it is taken painfully seriously at St. George's, the swimming team here manages to make it fun.

Memories of WWI

I never wanted to be there - I was drafted.
Even the voyage of France sucked - seasick often.
There were no parades or women on arrival -
We were sent directly to the lines.
When I saw the faces of the veterans in the trenches I felt virgin.
I wish I could have stayed that way.

It all took place pretty quickly - the war.
We lived and fought in another world: a world of cold stone, wet mud...
I read about our conflict now - about the 'heroes' of the war.
Men with pieces of tin on their chest.
I suppose they expected heroes of us,
But I know that I was never one.

I sued to cry - silently to myself - kneeling in the trenches.
Alone, not accepted even in war, my tears rolled down.
Sometimes I would watch the moon
Or try to understand French.
I would carefully think out letters
(To people that I loved...or hated)
And never write them.

The earth was wet and cold - puddles formed in the trenches.
Our coats saved us from neither the mud nor the gas.
I had never been violent by nature,
And when Malcolm, on that late fall morning,
Rolled back from our dawn bayonet attack
(Snapping ice crystals with his body)

And settled into the trench where I crouched, trembling,
Something within me tore.

In the quiet lulls we heard the Germans –
They were never far away it seemed.
On clear evenings we would exchange cigarettes
For their dark chocolate - tying them to stones for throwing.
Sometimes we would hear the enemy 'singing':
"...*Ja wohl, ja wohl, ich liebe alcohol* –
Ich liebe kiene wasser, ich liebe alcohol, ja wohl, ja wohl..."
Though they were rare, these were the nights I remember.

I was quite alone after Malcolm was taken - I had been before.
Hearing them singing, I wondered that the Krauts weren't
The army is so unemotional.
War is so confused.

I never really understood why we were doing it.
Why we lost Malcolm.

Why I was there.
Why then.
Somethings I knew all too well:
Through my own tears and broken faith and what I'd seen
And still I have never understood war.

I heard late in the war about the Russians to the East -
Walking home toward their own lives.
Unafraid, they walked away from death.
I started moving back from the front then.
I've been moving ever since.

*In memory of William Boulton Dixon, St. George's class of 1911.
He was killed in an artillery barrage at Thiacourt, France on
October 17, 1918.*

Evenings

The day is just done,
Evening just begun.
A farm day's till from dawn
And an estate dinner from dusk.
In from the sweat
And then out for the socializing.
The only non-parent (or even non-grand-parent!)
At an estate dinner.
Clearing the dishes
Of the Swedish Dukes and Barons.
A farmer's skepticism
And a tired lady's inability to impress
Are both yours for the evening.
The company is good –
Young for a change (two-score years)
And with a zest for life
Effervescent.
The wine is fine –
Partridge superb,
The coffee post-meal
A savior.
The smoking room;
Coffee, soft chair, and a lamp.
Reading poetry
As they watch T.V.
The poetry is good,
And nothing like your own,
Yet the author is unknown.
Insignificance like rust
Attacks your steel defenses.
And swims among
Your powers stored –

Destroying them.
The walk outside
After goodnights
Would not repair depression.
Aided by the 60's Port, realizations
That – unlike sunshine –
Are too gaudy a grey to soak
Permeate a solitary soul.
The elk and deer ignore again
Your evening walk from the lake.

The Boot

One winter's day while walking
Among coastal stones,
I found a boot sun-soaking,
And pondered it alone.

A sailor's shoe, I saw it,
And watched it where it lay;
I hoped that in its moldy fit,
A foot had lodged – and stayed.

Many dead had cleansed that coast,
And leg or foot, or toe I sought,
But, thought I dreamt a limb to boast,
I looked and there was naught.

Within the boot there was no foot,
No shin, no toes, no ankle.
Vacant lay the tattered shoe –
I left it there quite baffled.
I gripped it well and flung it far
Into the sea from whence it came.

Standing back, I pondered then
How foolish I had seemed.

I hoped, though, for the boot's return
Filled high with hopes and dreams.

Excerpts from Chapel Dreams

During solemn chapel worship
I gaze dreamily
Upon her quiet countenance.
Her innocent pink and white frocks
Floating silkily - unconcealing,
Across her bosom.
They whisper over the smooth,
Round curve of her hip.

My thoughts are evil
For such a consecrated hall,
But how can one EDIT that which,
As hail is buffed by the winds and enlarged,
As the snowball rolling down the winter slope
Grows grander –
Vibrantly propagates within my soul?
I CANNOT and WILL NOT curb my thought.
The id is NOT every-conquering!
The soul, in black-ice purity
Is NOT affected!

...Across from me
Sits the object of my thoughts;
My secret, evil, and fornicative desires.
Strong as steeds are they, and,
Hooves clattering across the sacred marble,
I send them clattering onward:
Wild, shrill bays and whinnies!
Echo silently within by being.

She sits across the way from me:
Six pews...

And a universe between us.

I sit behind my mask,
My costume,
My ROLE
Of indifference.

Ignorance Epigram

Ignorance as a product of laziness is not unlike insistence upon drinking only from, and swimming only in, a stagnant puddle on a tiny island. Meanwhile, vast oceans of clear, fresh waters surround the island and horizons of knowledge stretch invitingly beyond any human comprehensions. These oceans may go unnoticed by those who wade in the pool of satisfaction – those without any inclination towards inquisition.

A Swimming Paragraph

Congratulations team – indisputably a good year for St. George's Swimming. Season score 2-3-1; not bad at all. We are history makers; largest squad ever; yes, a real girl's meet; great new coaching staff; eight records broken; and the best is yet to come! Hopkins and Mo Brown going DOWN next year! Thanks for all the diving points, Betsy. Six dual meets for Varsity, three team meets for everyone (we'll have a Dragons vs Saints shoot-out next year!), and, of course, the New Englands. Everyone improved - a success!

End of season: does anyone know if they're in Red practice or White? Don't ask Eric! A1 – you'll get that dive yet! Jesse goes streamlined with the cap over the goggles. Good job, Red group; looking at you next year. Go get 'em, Ollie! Meets: we'll get you a megaphone next year, Jenn. Hoods on, everyone; yes, Steve, even if we look like monks! We'll get the 'ripsaw, buzzsaw' better next year: maybe even the "ONE, TWO, THREE, St. George's, St. George's, St. George's..." as well! Open Pools: head for the social lane. Lockers removed and hey, we can see the bottom of the pool! White group: Laura's lane pulls ahead of the guys for one more practice. Memories of Dragons vs Saints and Boys vs Women. New false start rule gotta learn the hard way. Loved our new caps and especially the T-Shirts! Pool Pride. Team dinners – a new tradition.

New England's: tapering at the YMCA and recovering from fifth form ski weekend. No mohawks this year – we'll get you one next year, Morgan. Swimming with the big teams; congratulations Michele and Laura for breaking those records. Snowy Boston driving up to the Carriage House Motel.

Tough practice November through March (on and off). We could have swum to the Bahamas by now! Can pain be fun? "Just swim a couple of miles but sure, we'd love to swim a few no-breathers!" Somehow the meets and the spirit helped to make it worth it. A fine season it was. We'll miss Captain Josh (the 'Whittemore-Water-Wonder'), and Romina next year. So many thanks go to this year's coaches; Mr. and Mrs. Evans. You really made it all fall into place. Until next year.

Sinking Sailors

"Do you know," I asked, standing upon the boulder and ocean-gazing, "That enough sailors will drown this winter and sink a ship?"

Her hair ran away from – slithered and whipped in – the wind. She turned her face toward me but her eyes stayed upon the sharp green horizon. Her lips moved deliberately in the cold.

"No," she said, "Enough ships will sink this winter to drown many sailors."

The wind.

That Day

The Caribbean dawn was brilliant. Late in the morning I bicycled the ten coastal miles into town alone. There, as I rested in a pub, the cold front came in over the harbor. I had finished my fish and my back was turned to the big window overlooking the harbor when the golden beer into which I stared turned grey. So did everything else in the room. I turned around on my stool. The storm was coming in from the northwest, looking like a squall.

Already the placid waters were frothing, and the boats had begun their constant rocking. I knew that the sun was gone for the rest of the day and that there was another pub closer to home that had a pool table. I thought that with the rains coming it would be better to take the stretch back home before they hit.

"'ave a nice day," I said, putting two dollars onto the bar.

"Will do," the bartender replied.

The grey wind slammed the door of his quiet pub closed as I began the ride to the next village, nine miles down the coast. About the second mile it began to pour. A wet hour later, I pulled into the pool/bar and, putting my coin down the last pool table, sat down on a bench I the far corner. By the third game the day's winner came to my table.

"You wa' shoot?" He probed.

"Yeah, I ga' shoot," I replied.

"Rack," he commanded. I racked. Ten minutes later I had won. The muscles of his black face were tense when he left the bar – the big ones in his jaw near his ear ripples back and forth.

My unexpected victory discouraged my departure, and an hour or so later the same local 'pool shark' returned. He brought with him two solemn companions. I swigged from my Becks, and a game began afresh. He won, and I eyed my bike longingly. His companion, a taller, quiet one, stood up. I had lost, and should have been free to leave, but that was not his intention.

He told me to rack. I didn't argue. He beat me in that game fast. The third Bahamian was a short smiley fellow, and I disliked him. He stood up, and I racked. I sensed what they were planning. They were going for the clean sweep. All three had come to beat the white boy. The short one won, and not without smiles.

"We only give cut ass hea'," he told me.

"I didn't come to win," I lied. Sinking my fourth Becks, I pushed my bike into the dark rain and began to pedal home.

Egyptian Adventure

For most students it would have been a dream come true: an excursion through Egypt in the middle of February. Well, this winter the Newport Art Museum offered architecture teacher Richard Grosvenor and his wife Margot the opportunity to go on a two-week investigative tour along the Nile River. Mr. Grosvenor, who has long been the architecture teacher at St. George's, has since returned and been very busy sharing his observations and travel tales. He has presented slide shows, given talks, and displayed sketches, which he painted in Egypt. I was able to discuss his adventures with him earlier in April.

Mr. Grosvenor and his wife arrived in Cairo on the eighth of February, along with twenty-five other members of the Art Museum who constituted their travelling group. The party was led by Egyptologist Lynn Holden, who had worked with the Boston Museum in the past. They spent four days at the Mena House in Gizah, where they stayed only a quarter of a mile from the pyramids and the great sphinx! From there, they continued to Memphis, once a cultural and religious center, and the city where Alexander the Great was anointed Pharaoh in June of 322 B.C. The Grosvenor's then flew via EgyptAir to Luxor, which is some two hundred miles to the south and also along the Nile. Among the ruins of Luxor, Thebes and Abydos, they saw two magnificent temples, the largest being Karnak, where the Holy Procession once took place. Karnak featured a Sacred Lake (for Priests to bathe in) and huge obelisks. At the New Kingdom Temple, which dates back to 1500 B.C., the pillars are thirty-six feet in circumference and almost seventy feet in height. Some of these structures even retain their original paint in the dry Egyptian atmosphere.

After a visit to the Valley of Kings and the tomb of Tutankhamen, the party moved south in a 180-foot passenger ship. Entertained by diverse passengers, the Grosvenor continued up the Nile to Aswan and Lake Nasser (which was created when Soviets and Egyptians constructed the controversial Aswan High Dam). From Swan, the group visited Abu Sunbul before returning together to Cairo, and then to Boston. Mr. Grosvenor was especially pleased that the Egyptian people, though few of them spoke English, were hospitable. He fondly recalls Captain Ali, who singlehandedly operates a tourist- laden 'felucca', or Egyptian river-boat. Captain Ali's boat had a steel hull and a 30-foot lateen rig. In order to land, the skipper would simply run directly ashore! On another occasion a Cairo taxi driver gave the Grosvenor's an unforgettable rip though the city trying to understand English road directions. Like many other Egyptians, he does not drink, and was a very coordinated driver.

During the fortnight of intense travelling within Egypt, Mr. Grosvenor made several architectural observations, as well as many watercolor sketches of the Nile. He reflects that pyramids as old as five thousand years are precisely proportioned. The sides tend to be one half the length of the bases, and seem to relate to the later Greek concept of a "Golden Section". At Sakkara, there is evidence that the Egyptians experimented with advanced concepts as many as twenty-six hundred years ago! The architects experimented with "circle radius" and "pie" and later Greek concepts. It is known that Pythagoras and Herodotus, among other, studied in Egypt.

Mr. Grosvenor was also impressed that the tombs were actually and not terribly somber, but colorfully decorated. This stems from the polytheistic religions of Ancient Egypt, and the belief that deities like Ammon Ray (Sun-God), and the Goddess Isis, would voyage onto another existence (hence burial ships). Like many before him, and (pollution permitting) many more in the future, Mr. Grosvenor left Egypt with a profound respect for their advanced accomplishments and the artistic flavor of the culture, which he and his companions experienced.

Having returned to St. George's and resumed teaching, Mr. Grosvenor acknowledges the indispensable assistance of his colleagues at school. He is grateful to Mr. Harman for permitting the journey, the Newport Art Museum for sponsoring it, and Mr. Harrison, Miss Boocock, Mrs. Buehler, and Miss Minor for taking over his many classes while he was absent. I got the feeling during the interview that Mr. Grosvenor came away from his Egyptian Odyssey intellectually rejuvenated. Now let's see...first I would have to get sponsors...a ticket for Cairo...one way...

Alexander the Great East of The Indus: 327-325 B.C.

Having defeated Darius III and secured the conquest of Egypt, the Mediterranean East Coast, and Persia, Alexander the Great of Macedonia embarked, in 327 B.C., upon an invasion of India. This expedition, which culminated at the Battle of Hydaspes, marked the climax of Alexander's military career and imperial conquest; it concluded historically the most dramatic of imperial campaigns then known. At the Beas River in the Indian Punjab region, Alexander finally met his limit. The expedition brought Greek civilization to several regions for the first time and combined Eastern cultures with the Hellenic to create a Hellenistic Empire. Alexander's actions east of the Indus River are of vital historical importance; they exemplify his attempts at racial fusion, and naval and military exploration, and secured him an enduring legacy of tremendous impact

Alexander III, born a Leo in the summer of 356 B.C., inherited Macedonia, all of 2Greece except Sparta, and the Balkans. In only thirty-three years he conquered all of Persia, Egypt, and Southwest Asia, His father was Philip II of Macedonia, and his mother was Olympias, Princess of Epiros. Raised in Pella, the capital of Macedonia, Alexander was tutored first by Leonidas, a renowned scholar and the uncle of Olympias, and later by Aris-totle, whom he preferred. He especially liked to study Natural History. As a young man, he was noted for having subdued the fierce black horse Bucephalus ('ox-head'): "noticing that the horse was afraid of its own shadow, he maneuvered the horse so as to have it face the sun. Once the shadow was behind it, the horse calmed down and could be handled with ease." He showed little interest in either men or women, a security among certain intimates, and despite the failure of relations between his parents, a strong affection for his mother.

At the age of sixteen, Alexander became Regent of Macedonia, and his first military exploits began when he was eighteen, when he was given control of Philip's Companion Cavalry. At Chaeronea, on the Boetian Plain, his forces were victorious over Athenian and Theban forces under Demosthenes. In 336 B.C., Philip was killed by Pausanias, and Alexander acceded to the throne and eliminated his opposition.

Alexander was a militarist from an early age; he possessed the admired inclination towards 'philotimia,' or love of honor. In his devotion to Homer and his idol (and perhaps relative) Achilles, Alexander slept with a knife and a copy of the *Iliad*, under his pillow. Unfortunately, Philip left his son with debts up to eight hundred talents, the equivalent of four million, eight hundred thousand drachmas. 2 In part to make up for this debt, Alexander called together the League of Corinth in late summer, 336 B.C., and was selected to lead a campaign against Persia. The leadership of Persia, after several rapid assassinations and successions beginning in 359 B.C., had gone from Artaxerxes II to Artaxerxes III, his son Arses, and finally, in June of 336 B.C., to the mild Darius III, Alexander's Persian rival.

Alexander began his invasion of Persia against Darius III in the spring of 334 B.C.. It was the first such expedition since Xenophon and his Ten Thousand escaped through the fingers of Artaxerxes in the 380s B.C., and was partly intended as a revenge for Xerxes' invasion of Greece. Alexander left Antipater in control of his Greek empire, and crossed the Hellespont for the last time at the age of twenty-two. He and General

Parmenio controlled a force of thirty-seven thousand infantry and cavalry, with which they routed several Persian satraps at the Granicus Torrent, near the Sea of Marmara. In 333 B.C., at Gordium, Alexander performed the cutting of the Gordian knot, which promised him the conquest of Persia.

Between 333 and 332 B.C. he routed Persian forces at Issus and Tyre. He wintered in Egypt between 333 and 332 B.C. He was anointed Pharoah of Egypt in Memphis on June fourteenth, 332 B.C., and in Siwa he was praised as the son of Zeus-Ammon. In 331 B.C. he founded the city of Alexandria along the southern shores of the Mediterranean Sea. In the fall of that year, Darius fled, offering Alexander all of Persia and its treasures. Alexander and his army proceeded to cross the Euphrates and Tigris Rivers from Northern Syria 3 in pursuit. In October, his Greek and Thracian force of forty thousand soundly defeated Darius' vastly larger army at Gaugamela, north of Arbela. Darius, however, retreated east again. During the winter of 331/330 B.C., Alexander was welcomed by Babylon, in the heart of Persia, and took control of Susa. Asimov relates that:

He went on to occupy Persepolis, the capital city of Xerxes a century and a half before. The story told is that, after a drunken feast of celebration, he ordered Persepolis burned in revenge for the Persians' destruction of Athens in Xerxes's time. He then made ready to pursue Darius, who was in Ecbatana, the capital of Media. Satraps under Bessus murdered Darius in mid-330 B.C., and left his body near Heacatompylus for Alexander to find. For the next two years, Alexander ranged over the eastern reaches of the Persian Empire, fighting satraps and wild tribesmen...Alexander was never beaten, by anyone or at any time... (he) was beginning to assume the airs of a Persian King... to see himself as a universal monarch.

In the spring of 329 B. C., Alexander crossed the harsh Hindu Kush mountain range through Kush-Khawak pass **5** towards Bactria and the new 'Great King,' Bessus. The size of his force, including families, mercenaries, etc., is liberally estimated to have been one hundred and twenty thousand. Bessus retreated across the Oxus River into Soghdiana and was followed by Alexander in June. In late 329 and early 328 B.C., he was betrayed by Spitamenes and "placed on the roadside where Alexander and his troops would pass, naked, bound to a post..." **6** The army wintered at Zariaspa, Bactria's capital and birthplace of Zoroaster, and spent 328 and 327 B.C. campaigning against Spitamenes, Alexander's most serious rival since Memnon of Rhodes.

Spitamenes successfully distracted Alexander's forces for two seasons, but, in early 327 B.C., harassed by Coenus, he was betrayed into surrendering Massagetaens, and the territory north of the Hindu Kush fell safely under Alexander's control. In 328 B.C., during a drunken feast in Maracanda, there took place an embarrassing episode between Alexander and Cleitus the Black. When Cleitus criticized Alexander for being a braggart and taking the credit due Philip and the Macedonians, Alexander ran him through with a spear. Though consumed by guilt, he mustered his forces and began a campaign southwards through Soghdiana and

Bactria and towards Taxila and the Punjab region. Meanwhile, many of Alexander's finest veterans and Thessalian

volunteers, still infuriated over Alexander's murder of Parmenion in 330 B.C., and a restless four thousand miles from home, revolted and had to be pacified and sent home. Many other soldiers died of dehydration, over-drinking, and possibly cholera. As a result, Alexander "took a gamble," and, for the first time, recruited local 'barbarian' auxiliaries on a large scale."

Dramatic changes overcame Alexander and his forces as they neared their second crossing of the Hindu Kush mountains and the Indus River, over which no Greek had crossed before. Gradually, Alexander and his entourage became more Persian, and all but the Greek soldiers began a massive fusion of Greek, Persian, and Indian cultures, which was to survive indefinitely and ultimately affect Eastern Mediterranean societies. Cities were erected in the eastern lands, Alexander adopted Persian dress, Buddhism and Hinduism were investigated, and inter-racial marriages took place.

One of the most dramatic events of this new era was the marriage of Alexander to a Persian princess named Roxane. In the spring of 327 B.C., while on his way southward, Alexander and his army came upon a tower of rock called the 'Rock of Soghd,' or 'Soghdiana,' whose tribal inhabitants, under Uxiart, a Bactrian, taunted them to sprout wings or go on their way. Writes historian Harold Lamb:

The challenge nettled (Alexander)...(climbers) were to climb the rock at night, across ice surfaces, where apparently it could not be climbed..some thirty of them fell...the survivors reached the summit after sunrise...and the Bactrians beheld armed men waving banners...and the Rock of Soghd surrendered...it was the last refuge of the mountain folk, and Alexander climbed the approach to inspect it...a girl came out, not prostrating herself before him. She had long braids as light as new wheat twisted back from her head...her name was Rushanak, (Roxane), or "Daughter of Light' She became Alexander's first wife. Marriage ceremonies exemplified his quest for racial fusion; during the spring of 324 B.C., in Susa, Alexander married the daughter of Darius III and supervised the marriages of some nine thousand Persian women to Greek soldiers.

In spite of Alexander's efforts at cultural fusion, such as the foundation of several Greek cities (like 'Alexander Khodzenhent,' or 'Alexander at World's End') in Persia, his friendship with Kalanos, a Buddhist ascetic (who later immolated himself), **9** his preference for "comfortable Iranian dress of embroidered jacket and trousers (over) the Greek tunic and plaid," **10** and the installation of 'hyparchoi,' or 'subject-rulers,' many conservative Greeks still despised Persian mores. Wrote Green: "Nothing better exemplified the fundamental division in court circles than the matter of 'proskynesis,' or obeisance." Enraged, Callisthenes, a powerful Macedonian general, refused to bow. His actions inspired several young soldiers, under one Hermolaus, to rebel in a 'Pages' Conspiracy,' and Callisthenes was put to death as a result.

While introducing and enforcing his new cultural policies, Alexander began to amass a major army from what remained of his seven-year-old Greek campaign and the Persians he could muster. That same year, Lamb tells us, he began to instruct "some fifty thousand eastern youngsters, training them in the Greek language and use of weapons...the army itself ceased to be Macedonian." With this strengthened force, Alexander re-crossed the Hindu Kush using the Rushan Pass, in the summer of 327 B.C., despite tribal resistance and fierce weather. They passed through the Dionysaic village Nysa, under Acuphis, and spared it simply because it grew ivy, perhaps left by previous Persians! They were not so merciful against Aomus, or 'Birdless Rock,' a town situated seven thousand feet above the Indus River (It was later rediscovered by Sir Aurel Stein). **13** In early 326 B.C., after splitting with them at Kabul, Alexander's forces rendezvoused with Hephaestion's army in Attock, on the banks of the Indus River. After burning all unneeded supplies, they crossed the two-to-five-mile-wide river (from which, in the words of Curtius, *"India tota ferme spectat orientem..."* (all of India looks east). By thus venturing farther east than had either Cyrus the Great or Darius I, they had invaded India.

Perhaps relying on accounts by the historians Scylax, Herodotus, Periplus and Ctesius, Alexander had anxiously anticipated the invasion. It may have been inspired by gifts of pearls, rubies and twenty-five elephants sent with a plea for help from, Ambhis, the King of Taxilas. Tales of banyan trees, tigers, sapphires, indigo dyes, monkeys, peacocks, and shrines helped to spur on the men. However, the modem historian Peter Green believes that: "Alexander's main impulse in invading this mysterious wonderland was sheer curiosity, coupled with a determination to achieve world dominion in the fullest sense. " His ultimate ambition was to go as far east as the Ganges River and possibly into Eastern Asia to a fabled 'Endless Sea' at the end of the world, but these plans were ill-supported and fell through. Alexander's crossing of the Indus, however, was of tremendous strategic and historical importance.

Bums tells us that "time and chance had wrought many changes in the army that had crossed the Hellespont eight years before... the men famous later as the great successors of Alexander had come to the front: Perdikkas, Ptolemy (son of Lagus), Lysimachos, later King of Thrace, and Seleucus 'the conqueror. " Crateros, Menidas and the powerful Hephaestion are others mentioned. Bums estimates the force at forty thousand strong, as well as five thousand Indians under the King of Taxila. They moved east towards the Punjab, 'region of five rivers,' as the treacherous monsoons began. On the banks of the Hydaspes River, in March 326 B.C., Alexander and his invading forces met the Paurava Rajah, called Poms, and there engaged in his final all-out battle.

The opposing force, said to have three to four thousand cavalry, fifty thousand infantry, two hundred war elephants, and three thousand chariots, greatly outnumbered his own, but Alexander was able to employ his superior cunning and strategy to his advantage. Facing Poms across the Hydaspes, Alexander managed to baffle and exhaust the Indians in preparation for attack. The Greeks would move forces loudly along the river, rousing all of Porus' army, and then rest for the night. After many days of such tiring, vain pursuits, Poms assumed that Alexander would wait out the eternal monsoon torrents before attacking. Here he had misjudged his opponent. Alexander had noted a long, thickly wooded island, (called Admana) at Jalapur, seventeen miles north of the camp, which was at Haranpur, and there planned to make a massive crossing.

Arrian, a historian, who also, according to Collier's, "governed northeast Asia Minor and inspected the Black Sea coasts under the Roman Emperor Hadrian (r. A.D. 117-138)," uses accounts given by Ptolemy and Aristobulus (one of Alendander's engineers) to describe the start of the ensuing Battle of Hydaspes.

The decision once made, Alexander began his preparations openly. Craterus was left in charge of the original position...his order s not to attempt a crossing until Porus had moved from his position to attack Alexander...(thus) Meleager, Attalus and Georgias were posted...just before dawn rain stopped...and the crossing (of Alexander, Hephaestion, Perdikkas, the Companions, Demetrius, Seleucus, Ptolemy, half of the Guards, Lysimachus, Bactrians, Scythians, and Soghdians) began – screened by the island...(but), the second crossing completed...Alexander gave orders for his infantry, nearly six thousand strong , to follow in order of march, while he (with five thousand cavalry), moved forward rapidly...Porus' son had with him two thousand mounted troops and one hundred and twenty chariots when he reached the spot...the Indians, seeing Alexander there in person ...broke and fled...Porous decided to move in with force against Alexander.

What followed when Porous turned his force of thirty-five thousand men, creatures, and weapons toward Alexander and left only a small rear-guard against Craterus is a tribute to both leaders, though especially to the ingenuity of Alexander and his forces. Against the Indian line of battle, which was perhaps four miles long, Alexander attacked Porus' left wing with the Companion Cavalry and several other divisions of fierce cavalry. This drew Porus' right-wing cavalry away, and gave the opportunity for the Phalanx to march into the enemy left and center. The Indian right flank was thus exposed, and cavalry under Coenus and Demetrius swung behind the army and attacked their right near flank. Also, Craterus and his forces in Haranpur crossed the Hydaspes and supported the flanking motion. The Indian infantry, stung from forward and behind, fled to the protection of the elephants.

The elephants were a particular horror to the Greek infantry and horses, who had never contended with such beasts. Writes Green:

The real nightmare facing the phalanx - one that haunted them for the rest of their days – was that row of maddened, trumpeting, furious elephants. (Yet Alexander's men would) encircle them, let the archers pick off their mahouts, and then discharge volleys of javelins and spears into the most vulnerable parts of their anatomy. The infantrymen, meanwhile, slashed through their trunks with Persian 'scimitars ', or chopped at their feet with axes...some Macedonian soldiers were caught up with their trunks and dashed to the ground. Others found themselves impaled in the great beast's tusks...

Alexander's forces managed to surround the Indians and butcher as many as twenty thousand of them. Unlike Darius III, Porus bravely led a final charge before he was wounded in his right shoulder and forced to retreat. Alexander's first embassy of peace, under Ambhis, was a diplomatic *faux pas*, and was attacked by Porus. The second, under a friend of Menos, enabled Porus to inform Alexander that he wished to be treated "like a King." When Alexander asked if his respected prisoner required more, Porus is said to have replied, "everything is contained in that one request."

Porus was to remain a loyal ally for as long as he lived. The Battle of Hydaspes, climax of Alexander's eastern campaigns, was won, and the lands of the Jhelum and Punjab essentially secured.

The Battle of Hydaspes was the high-water mark of Alexander's campaign. Its aftermath, all the way to Alexander's death three years later, was anti-climactic. Bucephalus died of an injury received early in the battle; the city of Bucephala was founded and named in his honor. He was nearly thirty years old, and had never been ridden by anyone but Alexander. Nicaia, 'city of victory' was also founded in celebration of the battle. There still persisted tribal resistance from the Malloi and Oxydrakai, however, and Alexander's army crossed the Chenab and Ravi Rivers to the East, encountering fierce opposition and crushing some thirty-seven obstinate hamlets.

At Sangala, on the Beas River, in July of 326 B.C., the soldiers in Alexander's army refused to go any further. At that point, despite his ambitions to proceed as far as the Ganges and the Great Sea, Alexander's geographers began to doubt it was possible. The soldiers had been battered with problems of rust and mildew, caused by the monsoons for months, and heard only of dreadful snakes, crocodiles and forces of thousands of loathed elephants (Chandragupta later amassed six thousand of them). Along the Beas, they stopped marching and fell silent. A meeting of the officers was called, and Coneus, son of Polemocrates, and one of the most respected veterans, responded to a fine speech of Alexander, which encompassed past glories and future goals (they were only a twelve days' march from the Ganges). Coenus, says Bum, spoke:

...Not for the officers present, but for the men. He thought it was time to stop. Few were left of the original army...death in battle, discharge from wounds, sickness most of all, had taken their toll...Let the king go home in triumph...he could make another expedition with a fresh army, either to India, or the Black Sea, or to Carthage.

The emperor was, for the first time, unable to convince them to go on with him, despite powerful speeches, and days of pouting. The campaign east, eight years old and undefeated, came to a halt Alexander conceded, was cheered by the men, and organized major altars and sacrifices to be make in honor of the twelve deities. In early November of 326 B.C., after giving Coenus an honorable burial, Alexander chose Nearchus of Crete to lead the navy, and marched south along the Indus to Patala, leaving Craterus and a large force at Shikarpur. Nearchus left the new harbor at Patatla on a historic, rigorous voyage along the north shores of the Arabian Sea and the Persian Gulf, accompanying Alexander's forces west. He was the first Greek known to make this voyage. Meanwhile, through early 325 B.C., Alexander waged a fierce campaign against Brahmins, marked by several massacres.. He received a serious lung wound during a singularly brave assault against the Malloians. The retreat continued across the waterless Gedrosian Desert in September, during which many hundreds of men fell victim to dehydration, as well as many of the families of the weaker men, who, while sleeping on a dry river-bed were drowned in a freak flash flood. Nevertheless, the march continued.

Desertion raised its ugly head as the remnants of the campaign struggled west, and Harpalus, treasurer, took some six thousand mercenaries and four thousand talents and returned to Greece, where he was later murdered. As a result of revolts, three thousand mercenaries roamed Eastern Asia, and the Purge of Satraps began in 325 B.C.. Craterus' army reinforced Alexander's forces and Nearchus' exhausted sailors at Salmous. In 324 B.C., they returned to Persepolis war-weary and thin in numbers. Alexander, after visiting Cyrus the Great's tomb, settled in Susa from February to March, during which thirty thousand trained Persian 'Successors' returned. **23** Towards the end of 324 B.C., under the 'Exiles' Decree,' he dismissed a majority of his remaining Greek forces despite protests, and sent them home under Craterus, the Regent after Antipater. He ended the year in deep lament of the death of his great friend, comrade, and (possibly) lover, Hephaestion, in Ecbatana. After a brief campaign against the Cossaeans, he returned to Babylon, where he died in 323 B.C.

Alexander dedicated his life not only to self-indulgent conquests, but-to fusion of races, languages and religions; to increasing the empire and the honor of Macedonia, and to actions over words. As a result, Greek and Eastern Mediterranean culture evolved from the 'Hellenic' into the Persian influenced 'Hellenistic;' a world more open to different art and literature, rituals and deities. After Alexander, there rose the empires of Ptolemy in Egypt, Seleucid's from Babylon to the Mediterranean Sea and the Persian Gulf, Parthia (which gained independence in 260 B.C.), Bactria (in 225 B.C.), and in Greece, the Antigonid, Aetolian, and Achian Leagues. Alexander's outstanding military and cultural legacy prevailed over the Mediterranean Sea and Persia up until the evolution of the Roman Empire more than three hundred years later, in the first century A.D.

There is unlimited speculation as to what Alexander could have accomplished had he continued east of the Beas or simply lived longer. Chandragupta, leader of the Punjab region in India after

Alexander, apparently said that "Alexander had been within an ace of seizing India, because its king was so hated and despised..." Indeed, Alexander had striven to maintain (as is demonstrated by naval explorations in the Persian Gulf) consistent ties with eastern lands, yet it may also be argued that by staying west of the Euphrates, he could have more easily consolidated his empire. At any rate, this is speculation, and "Alexander's achievement to wipe out the Achaemenid Empire changed the political map of the whole area, and accelerated that Greek cultural penetration of Southwest Asia which lasted down to and even after the age of Muhammad."

Whether one prefers to delve into the potential of his campaigns or the actual achievements of his life, Alexander the Great of Macedon has become an idol of western civilization and an example of individual success for all people since. His campaign east of the Indus is especially significant because it incorporated both his ideals and conflicts and saw them put into practice. The Battle of Hydaspes in 326 B.C. was the military climax for the man whose feats are remembered here by the historian W.W. Tam, in Volume VI of the *Cambridge Ancient History.*

He lifted the civilized world out
Of one groove and set it in another;
He started a new epoch; nothing
Could again be as it had been.

Curtains

Curtain's dangle, pull the wind;
Beckon minds, seduce and win.
Curtains capture, tease our gaze,
Induce our thoughts to yearn and craze.
Curtains, cloth, whose bottoms are
Arms that, severed, point afar.

For Kerouac

...And it's been strange – vapid flashes like thunderclaps of memory; no coherence, chains, or links. Understand this. This prosperity - beginning perhaps with the sounds of boots on gravel, and leading to Santas on children's laps... to a man trying to drink the ocean – not from the shore, with his head into the sea, but with his whole body submerged. Leading onto trees without leaves; to revelations of loneliness and beautiful girls (hair pulled back) – but that is plain.

We spent the afternoon in a sudden city. They all gave excuses - then they left me. "Lewis," they said, "we have to go hunting." Or maybe "shopping," or "eating," or (most insulting); "studying." Study me! But no. I drove then; that afternoon. My radio told me where the accidents were - where to avoid, like a receding hairline. I did just the opposite. I was about five accidents; fender-bender first (a disappointment); then a overturned "Blood Bank" truck, its cargo flowing paint-like across hot tar. Fire department hosed down all the donated plasma. Then there was the scooter accident: an architect scooting along pedestrian walks near the park (in a rush for a board meeting perhaps?) hit a pram with two Asian twins. First one took a long time to die (bones nearly flexible). Other one shaken. Mother dramatic – ashen face.

Came evening, I wore my Vladimir Lenin shirt into a seedy bar. Barman looked from shirt to me, then away. Some guy told me he dug Lenin. Had hair on his wrist and all behind his ears. I left. Took my glass with me. Barman came out and grabbed it. It was half-full. Three dollars' worth of Guinness Stout gone, and me left alone on the curb.

Slowly, someone began to pull the sun away – what was her excuse? Enslaved by the universe? I wanted rain. Wanted the skies to spread and drench me. I get none. I trod along a warm shore. Tried to swim to a parasail float, but my clothes were too heavy, so I quit. My tabs of acid got wet, so I dropped one more.

Mink had returned from survey in Siberia. Visited her apartment. She made me stand in her tub till I was drier, and then fixed me a hot-buttered rum. I fished out a candle from a pocket. Romance. It had been a long time. She looked marvelous, half of her hair (her left, my right) was blonde; the other side dyed black.

I didn't ask why. It made her look like a wonderful eclipse; like a zebra.

"Lewis" she whispered. Again. The "isss" sounded like a deflating tire. I didn't mind. When she fell asleep, I left her. No kisses on the forehead. Outside. Collar up, socks damp. Took a bus to the airport. Gave a wad of cash as Desk A and boarded at Desk B. on board, I stole two min-bottles of gin, bought a third, and stole a can of tonic. Felt good, only not twist of lemon. Sucked on two crushed, bent cigarettes. Non-smoking flight. Rubbed my chin and looked around. College girl with Walkman on set in the aisle seat, and a Spanish-American sat on my left. I read Ginsberg. We landed, spilling gin on a copy of War and Peace. It was warmer when we deplaned at dawn. Caribbean Island. Oh.

I walked (using hand- rails) to a car rental desk. Drove a rented car onto a beach. Slept. Was woken by hunger early in the afternoon. Some brats nearby were roasting hot dogs. When they went snorkeling, I took one, and their mutt gave me a hard time.

Dark threatened. Drove into the town, got a cheap boarding-house room. It had a verandah across from a church, littered with butts. Lonely. Slept again.

In the morning I bought some 'Stoli.' Drank vodka and orange juice for breakfast. Rolled the bottle in my sleeping bag and put it in the car trunk. I was determined to meet people. Where? Didn't find an English pub till after several native ones. Was beaten in pool. At the "Wayfaring Goose" I enjoyed lager on tap and watched Brit sailors. One – his jaw was perfect.

Lasses in the corner. I met them in the early evening. They took me late to a dance club. There, we listened to Caribbean music; emotional, listless coos, bouncing drums. The music was soothing, lively 'soca.' I danced with one of the women: she was not slim and not tall, but damned attractive. She smelled like trodden flowers; like raspberries freshly picked. There they left me. Swallowing my last Guinness, I walked home. Had a cigarette in the verandah. Slept. Then…

Untitled

Now, if you were to listen
To tales of passion and adventure,
Perhaps you might understand
Some of the *pressures* which pervade
This strange little existence
(Which is debatably the fast lane of life, love,
And the pursuit of happiness)
On Planet Earth.

Sometimes, imagination overbears body and mind.
Thus am I merely a bleeding concept –
A figment of my own imagination, which is free.

Now, were poetry a form of art,
Then perhaps I would be an artist (or a lunatic)
For being more than me - for being time.

Now, were I your grandmother, you would hate me.
For that. For being your root.
But I am not your kin
(Exclamation marks)
I am me. Whom?
I do not know.

History says:
'When whites arrive and refuse to depart,
It is time to leave.'

A simple boy with unquenchable yearnings
(Denied, granted, and taken for granted)
Also has lived, but has witnessed a death of sorts –
A strangling creativity;
The victory of guilt and SHAME.

...Were I a songwriter, I would write songs.
Were I a sailor, I would sail,

But I am student - a PREP school student –
So for now, that is that.

Weeb's Final Adieu

It didn't happen suddenly; the ban was enacted over a period of years. The students at Nasti Grogee's School who protested it were graduated or expelled before each of its successive stages. There is still uncertainty about its exact origins, though most agree that the parent generation was simply rebelling against their 'bleeding liberal' youth – you know: The Sixties. The administration sought medical backing for their decision and found it. Repulsive articles detailing students' degeneration toward caffeine addiction (and the resulting loss of limbs) were smeared over campus walls. Though in days of yore, students and faculty at Nasti G's had drank it openly, coffee was banned in the faculty room, and students needed parental permission to stand outside and sip their vice.

In an ensuing moral outcry against the 'caffeinated' special interest groups like M.A.C.C. (Mothers Against Coffee Craze) petitioned the President to install a coffee minimum age. Fearing the loss of their votes, and acting on the advice of his aides, he gave states the 'option' to enforce a minimum age of 19 on coffee purchasers. Of course, the states which refused had their highway funds cut. Soon fake I.D.'s were circulated around campus, and older students made supply-runs into nearby Wetnorp. Coffee-drinkers (yes that evil tribe) were driven underground. Athletes, fearing for their letters and varsity standing, tried to quit. "Senior Tea' became a thing of the past. There were those who 'did' coffee, and there were others who overcame its allure. Factions among students grew.

Most exemplary of the building conflict were the interactions between 'busting' faculty and 'busted' students. Coffee machines became a school-wide fire hazard, and because most students were now legally under-age, caffeine and its paraphernalia became strictly outlawed. There were cases where scholars were nabbed for having filter papers. Form letters were sent home to the sinners' parents. Even in assembly students heard that:

"The Discipline Committee convened to discuss the case of – (the animal!), who was seen drinking on such-and-such roof. When addressed from the ground by a faculty, the student panicked and jumped off the other side of the building. He was apprehended while limping away, and has been suspended..."

Social coffee-chugging clusters became the mode in Kcut Shop. They would sneak to the wall in pairs or groups, oblivious to the infrared binoculars that were often trained on them. Restless 'busters' with dogs and flashlights patrolled campus during social hour. They learned to follow the extension cords, which snaked through the grass from hockey-rink sockets to inevitable coffee machines and caffeine chefs. Students with breath, which reeked of cocoa beans, provoked scenarios of uncertainty from which they almost always emerged the guilty party. Yet life on the 'hilltop' continued. Now about all this candy the students are eating...

A Summer Under Sail for Eric

Eric Wiberg, 19, heads off to Boston College, Boston, Massachusetts, in the fall, where he hopes to study journalism. He has spent much of his summer preparing and then competing in, a sailboat race from Marion, Massachusetts, to Bermuda.

SAILING AWAY: Eric Wiberg, 19, was a boat-boy aboard the 'Tempo,' a 39-foot sailboat that sailed alongside 163 other vessels in a race from Marion, Massachusetts to Bermuda. Before the three-day long race started on June 23, Eric helped prepare the 'Tempo' in Newport, Rhode Island.

This June, the thirty-nine-foot ocean-cruiser 'Tempo' crossed the starting line off Marion, Massachusetts, with a Bahamian crew-member aboard, and set a course for Bermuda.

Around midday on the June 23, the seventh biennial Marion-Bermuda race began, and though the following four days brought thrill and victory to our boat, they also brought thrill and victory to our boat, they also brought wreckage and death to others.

A record 163 boats, some as long as 60 feet in length started the Marion –Bermuda race that was begun by David Kingrey in 1977.

Kingrey was frustrated that the Newport- Bermuda race begun in 1906 has become too competitive. So, the cruising yachts that compete hold amateur crews and are not permitted to raise spinnaker racing sails or use satellite navigation.

Cruise, instead must use, sextants and star-sightings to navigate more than 625 nautical miles from Buzzards Bay, New England, to Saint David 's Light then on to a rendezvous at the Royal Hamilton Amateur Dinghy, which, along with Marion's Beverly Yacht Club and the Royal Bermuda Yacht Club, sponsors the race. As newsmen from "Cruising World" and Bermuda's "Royal Gazette" observed, the yachts made their way offshore by nightfall of the first day.

'Tempo' found herself drifting at midnight in light winds — she is a two-ton sloop-rig, and flounders without wind. However, by the race's first dawn, the Crew of six had 'Tempo' moving at six knots in conditions which would last us the race: winds 15 - 25 knots and seas 4 - 7 feet.

Among the 800 participants, I was the only Bahamian. Although the race was my first real introduction to offshore or "blue-water" sailing, 'Tempo's' crew had sailed 30 Bermuda races among them.

Our skipper, Dr. Fischer, and his son Ted, had long since mastered their ship. Richard Goennell, my watch-captain, had raced to Bermuda more than 20 times; and a fifth crewmember had made 'Tempo's' sails, so I felt in safe hands.

My, position of boat-boy this summer entailed preparing 'Temijo' in Newport, Rhode Island, and crewing aboard her to and from Bermuda.

I held watch between midnight and 4 a.m. (graveyard watch), 8 a.m. till noon, 4 p.m. to 6 p.m. (dog Watch), then a switch. I was also responsible for cooking and general cleaning and up-keep.

The work was often exciting and, always varied. Though our ages ranged from my teens into the sixties, our crew amicably gathered over pre-cooked dinner, salad and sandwich lunches, porridge, and snacks.

As 'Tempo' sailed ^through her second day, all attention focused on achieving maximum speed: I either steadied the helm, used my weight to steady the ship, or busied myself setting and striking as many as three sails.

With the wind behind us, we sped along at up to nine knots with the mainsail to starboard, and two huge light headsails. By the third day we had overtaken several boats, and a few had come very close upon our stern before veering off. Even at night vessels were never far off, sometimes trailing our lights at intimidating distances.

Our only mishaps included a snapped vang (which supports the boom from the mast), and a loss of lights and speed gauge equipment. However, 'Bellatrix' was not so fortunate: the 44-foot Canadian yacht broke its rudder on the night of the 25th. Shortly thereafter, the preventer -snapped, and the swinging boom killed crewmember Dr. Donald Hill, a 52-year-old Vancouver neurosurgeon. The Russian research vessel 'Akadenik Dernadshry' towed 'Bellatrix' to New York.

Meanwhile, aboard 'Tempo', we knew nothing of the tragic mishap, and by the third day were crossing I the Gulf Stream, where we sighted whales, porpoises, sargasso weed and sharks. The weather warmed and the water temperature shot to 80 degrees as we neared Bermuda on the evening of the third day.

Although plastic debris hinted land, we didn't sight St George's, Bermuda, until dawn of the fourth day. Tail birds welcomed us as we 'cruised across the finish line past the 'Pirate' off St David's Light in North East Bermuda.

When 'Tempo' and her crew pulled along the "winners' wharf" of the Royal Hamilton Amateur Dinghy Club, we had been ranked 123rd overall in 'D' class, had crossed the line 53rd, and had placed with a corrected time (with handicaps) of eighteenth!

The crew received a trophy and various souvenirs for placing. Bermudian Warren Brown's ship 'War Baby' won line, honors and New York Yacht Club Commodore; Frank Snyder's 'Chasseur' won 'A' class. 'Yukon Jack,' an O'Day 34-footer won corrected, time. About 20 boats withdrew in the finishes' light winds or earlier on in the 30-knot gusts.

As for me, I enjoyed my first visit to Bermuda - which was wonderfully similar to the Bahamas - before the week-long return to Newport. 1 only hope that I am not the last Marion-Bermuda Bahamian.

Memorial Orchestrated

The orchestra played for a departed comrade, the conductor premiered his solo violin composition, and the son of the deceased energetically filled the church with virtuoso violin artistry between appraisals of his father's, many accomplishments last Wednesday. So evolved the moving performance by the Boston College Symphony Orchestra, conducted by Neal Hampton and with guest violinist Jun-Ching Lin. After a service in St. Ignatius Church dedicated to the memory of Dr. Jeong-Leong Lin, the evening's presentation began with Franz Josef Haydn's "Symphony No. 99," and ended with the BCSO's rendition of Felix Mendelssohn's "Violin Concerto in E Minor."

The emotional implications of a memorial concert for a longtime dedicated Boston College professor, a member of the BCSO, and a family man, aside, the music was tremendously presented. The caliber of performance and the quality of the pieces seemed to improve as the concert progressed. Haydn's No. 99 was at times difficult, to follow. However, the lively minuet and trio, which deserves particular attention for Haydn's deviation from convention, spirited the performance up before moving into the finale in a vivace tempo. The finale was firmly presented, with the violins getting emphasis in deep, driving, closing notes. The E-Flat Major performance matured into entertaining coherence from its more temperamental beginnings. The spacious stone concert area amplified the sound well, providing all among the large audience with clear sound.

Following an intermission and a short speech by Academic Vice President Neenan, who commended Dr. Lin's active life and introduced Neal Hampton's "Lament," Jun-Ching Lin, son of the deceased and assistant concertmaster of the Atlanta Symphony, took center stage. Lin stood before St. Ignatius' large wooden sculpture of Jesus and, with the bow of his violin, quickly, dispelled the emotional suspense so prevalent in the crowd. Lin began with the conductor's interpretation of initial shock, which begins

"Lament." The stages represented in "Lament" - "initial shock... numbness... sorrow... reminiscence of happy memories...anger and rage - leading to an arrival at a place of peace and acceptance," were emotionally rich and moving, perfectly appropriate for the occasion. Without a focus on the poignancy of the work the piece might have seemed, strangely unsubstantiated, never fully ripening – only nearing full con-junction before embarking on another tangent. Perhaps this- is the intended ' effect, or the effect a modern composition has in contrast to Haydn's, from the 18ᵗʰ century.

The concert progressed after several words on the life of Professor Lin, into a lively and inspiring rendition of Felix Mendelssohn's "Concerto for Violin and Orchestra in E Minor, Opus 64." Here Jun-Ching Lin shone through as an energized virtuoso violin soloist. His performance, free from the overwhelming pressure he must have felt in the previous piece (lamenting his father under the very hands of the composer) was envigo-rating. Mr. Lin and the Symphony Orchestra flung themselves into a joyous finale "allegro molta vivace," heavily supported or replied to by the strings, bass, winds, or brass. Certainly, it was a positive and appropriate performance to end the concert on - the musicians deserved the standing ovation that they received for such a closing to what was a rewarding and well-orchestrated concert.

Armed Robbery Occurs at Local Li'l Peach

Li'l Peach at the Boston College T stop, was the scene of an armed robbery on September 15.

An armed man robbed the Li'l Peach convenience store at the Boston College MBTA stop on 2195 Commonwealth Avenue on Saturday, September 15, at 10:25 pm, stealing an estimated $200 in cash before fleeing down Lake Street on foot. No one was injured in the robbery.

So far, Brighton Police have not made any arrests in connection with the incident. Investigation involving security camera coverage on the theft is underway.

According to Brighton Community Service Officer, Joe Parker, the assailant used an antique-looking black revolver with an eight Inch, barrel.

The suspect was described as being black in his twenties, about 5'8" tall, 155 pounds, of medium build, and having 'full facial hair'. He was wearing a black jacket with an 'Adidas' logo with a white stripe across the back. He also wore a black baseball cap and dark jeans. His companion, who waited outside during the heist, was described as a black male in his twenties.

The convenience store was closed for the rest of the night while police investigated the incident and interviewed several possible witnesses. Some students spent up to half-an hour assisting the investigation.

A Li'l Peach official expressed appreciation for the rapid response of the Brighton Police. He said that the store has been taking additional security precautions, with the help of representatives from the company, which operates 75 Li'l Peach stores out of Billerica, New Jersey. Security cameras inside the store recorded their robbery. The film evidence is currently being reviewed by detectives.

Anyone who has any information concerning the incident may telephone the Brighton Police Department at (617) 247-4256.

Faculty Discusses U.S. in the Mid-East

Four Boston College professors presented a panel discussion on the current crisis in the Middle East last Thursday evening Higgins 304.

Professors Ali Banuazizi and Benjamin Braude of the History Department, and Professors Donald Haffner and David Deese of the Political Science Department led the discussion, with Setti Warren, UGBC Lecture Series Coordinator, mediating, The panelists provided the audience of over 100 people with historical, political, cultural and economic perspectives on United States involvement in the region, focusing on recent developments in Iraq and Saudi Arabia. The floor was then opened up for questions.

Professor Banuazizi, a social psychologist who teaches a course on modern Iran, began the debate by outlining four of the reasons Iraq has cited for their August 2 invasion and subsequent annexation of Kuwait, on the Persian Gulf. One justification which Iraqi President Saddam Hussein has used is historical. Banuazizi pointed out that in 1921 the British "pieced together various parts of the Ottoman Empire," allotting Kuwait the port of Basta and rendering Iraq virtually landlocked, except river deltas. He compared Iraq's annexation to Argentinian action in the Falkland Islands and People's Republic of China's impending re-possession of Hong Kong, summarizing that Iraq's annexation is "not a novel problem."

Banuazizi further cited that Iraq had been at war with Iran for a decade after 1980 and "badly needed petrol and money." He pointed out that Kuwait was producing up to forty percent more oil than Iraq desired them to, lowering the price per barrel from a possible $20 to between $13 and $14. Before invading, Iraq had apparently given repeated warnings to the Kuwaitis to comply with its requests to slow down production. Thirdly, Banuazizi cited the 'Robin Hood' argument, which Iraq has used, claiming that United Arab Emirates and Saudi Arabia possessed a "disproportionate amount of Arab land." In contrast to this altruistic claim, the "audience was reminded that most Iraqi money has gone toward their war with Iran."

43

The second speaker was Professor Deese, who teaches international politics in the Political Science Department. Deese began by emphasizing how this recent crisis has brought international politics into a "hopefully peaceful" change mode. The United Nations and its five-member Security Council, he said, are playing a fundamentally stronger role, the closest to being cohesively effective since the 1946 U.N. Charter was drawn up. However, he did not think that sanctions could be entirely effective in controlling Iraq and Hussein, even when the newly proposed air embargoes are put into effect.

Deese went on to propose a possible solution to the crisis. Iraq must relinquish its claim of ownership of Kuwait and that Kuwaitis offer "permanent lease and effective control of islands in river mouths and some of the fields" to the Iraqis. Deese said that war is "in nobody's interest, especially the U.S.," and that with the escalating price of oil, many nations, including Third World Countries, are economically weak and "can't afford a real land war in Kuwait."

Third to the podium was Professor Haffner, whose specialty is international politics and national security policy, with an extensive background in energy and security. Haffner began by saying that he felt President Bush's decision to send U.S. troops to Saudi Arabia were "a good idea." He went on to describe how, with troops in place, Americans are anxious for a quick resolution.

Haffner then analyzed the role of U.S. troops in Saudi Arabia, saying that their role is to bring about "negotiation rather than domination." He looked at the comparative military forces of the United States and Iraq, reflecting on the fact that Iraq is "an entrenched enemy in its home territory," with an army of one million, many of whom are veterans. The traditional ratio required to be a victor in such a situation is that the invader dominate3 to 1. In contrast, the U.N. forces amount to about 125,000 to 250,000 troops, 1200 tanks, and 800 aircraft.

Professor Braude of the History Department, whose specialty and current field of research is the Middle East, Arabia and the Persian Gulf, was the fourth panel speaker.

Braude called Hussein and his government "well-skilled in stifling and quelling its enemies and dissidents." in the past ten years, they have weathered war with and attempted uprisings by Iranians, as well as coups. Speaking on Arabs in general, Braude expressed anxiety that an Arab disaster, such as the fatal collapse of a tunnel in Mecca, or the burning of sacred Arab documents by a Westerner, might unify them and cause waves of sympathy. He closed by saying that he felt that the "likelihood of war is very great."

Braude's was the final panel presentation before Warren opened the floor to questions.

A Sailing Devotee Shares his Love of the Sport

To the Editor:

At noon on Saturday, September 15, 25 sailors set-off from Newport, Rhode Island, racing down Narragansett Bay and around the world in the l 990 BOC Challenge Around Alone race. The commencement of their historic 27,000-mile voyages (which features stops in Cape Town, South Africa, Sydney, Australia, and Punta del Este, Uruguay), passed relatively unheralded. While American Mike Plant led the way to Africa, violence, inebriety, and theft raged at the tailgating of a BC football game.

For those readers who appreciate the endurance, technical and tactical knowledge, and courage, which these men and women are presently undergoing, there are few venues through which to keep updated on the race. Having escorted the skippers to sea at the start of the race, I returned to Boston College seeking to enlighten and be enlightened: the essence of University, no? Instead, the article which I wrote on the race was not printed by The Heights, and my attempt to find any sailing periodicals (Nautical Almanac, Wooden Boat; Cruising World, Sail, or Ocean Navigator) in O'Neill Library proved fruitless. Hence this letter.

Rather than rave about these shunnings, I shall herein accept the excuses provided - that my article had no pertinence to BC, and that O'Neill is an academic, (and thus selectively informative?) library. I will concentrate on providing a brief synopsis of offshore sailing. Starting with American Pioneer Joshua Slocum's first-ever solo circumnavigation at the turn of this century, single-handed sailing has been rapidly evolving, with this year's BOC Challenge setting new standards.

There have been two previous BOC Challenges, (1982/83 and 1986/87). Frenchman Phillipe Jeantot won both, setting a record of 134 days, 5 hours, 23 minutes, and 56 seconds. He went on to create, from the patio of the Marina Pub in Newport, the Globe Challenge- a solo non-stop round-world race that finished last spring. In those three races alone, almost twenty boats and one sailor were lost, and in this year's BOC-only a fortnight told - Irishman Enda O'Coineenhas been dismasted by a fishing ship. Yet this did not daunt Isabelle Autissier of France or Jane Weber of Canada, who are the first women to participate in the BOC Challenge.

The racers, (who range in age from 28 to 62, and are from 10 countries and various backgrounds) are divided into 3groups; sponsored 60-footmonohulls in Class 1, shorter boats in Clasp 2, and unsponsored in the new Corinthian Class. Mike Plant, the first American to race around the world, and a Newport favorite, told The *Newport Daily News* (Sept. 14) that "the start is extremely critical. It's extremely important to get off the blocks and go like hell." And go like hell he did. With 24 adversaries and a fleet of well-wishers behind him. Plant plowed 'Duracell' across the starting line mere seconds behind the gun. With a whoop of joy arid a leap in the air, he set off alone across the North and South Atlantic Oceans.

That was two weeks ago. By calling the race headquarters in front of the Museum of Yachting's Singlehanded Sailor's Hall of Fame at Fort Adams in Newport, I learned that Frenchman Alain Gautier (age 28) is winning, with Plant coming in sixth. They are due into Cape Town at the end of October. The racers should start returning to Newport in late April and May of 1991. Meanwhile, more than 20,000 students and almost 500 schools around the world are tracking their progress. BC (you may have guessed!) is not. The race sponsors, British Oxygen Corporation (BOC) are offering $250,000 in prize money and donating sales proceeds to the World Wildlife Federation. Skippers are radioing information on pollution to the WWF, as well as saving their refuse.

As an offshore sailor with comparatively few (5,000) offshore miles experience, I have the utmost respect for these often-unsung pioneers. Any readers interested in the sport can subscribe to the above-mentioned magazines, or support the BC sailing team. For information on the BOC Challenge standings, one may call the headquarters in Newport at (401) 848-0910 or (608) 221-3904. On Tuesday, October 2, ESPN will show coverage of the Newport start (I'm aboard the 60-foot 'Colt International' in the spectator fleet!).

BC Unable to hold Mass. Audubon Society Conference

The Massachusetts Audubon Society will not hold its proposed seminar to promote recycling on Saturday, November 10 at Boston College as a result of BCs inability to guarantee the necessary facilities in time for Mass, Audubon's Labor Day deadline.

According to David Early, Assistant Director of BC's Bureau of Conferences (B.O.C.), the B.O.C. approved the seminar, but buildings like Robsham Theater 12 requested "breakout rooms" could not be reserved for before the school year began and before he received the Office of the Registrar's complete list of schedules.

The Massachusetts Audubon Society, one of the oldest Audubon Societies in the world and the largest in New England; is dedicated to "conservation, preservation, research, and advocacy." The society, a branch of the National Audubon Society and the publisher of *Sanctuary* magazine, is "a voluntary association with a common concern for preservation of an environment that supports both humans and wildlife".

The approval indicates that Mass Audubon is welcome, and leaves their attendance up to whether or not the facilities can be made available. In this case the deadlines which the Society had for printing material on the seminar forced them to withdraw Society their application in July.

Ellen Dougan, Senior Functions Coordinator at BC, anticipates future correspondence with Mass Audubon and "looks forward to other program proposals of a different nature," such as smaller conferences; with less building space required.

Early noted that the application came at "a tough time of the year," and that with some 10,000 and applicants and more than a hundred student clubs vying for space in the fall, certain facilities had to kept open. The seminar does not cater exclusively to students, though the focus is environmental and recycling efforts on campuses all over the state. The policy, according to Early, is to charge only for the necessary maintenance work.

"It was just a question of logistics and guaranteeing facilities for 400 people... the B.O.C. was extremely cooperative; there was no animosity," said Robert Coleman, who corresponded with the B.O.C. from Mass. Audubon's Lincoln office. Coleman described BC as "an ideal site, within close proximity of Boston." He regretted having to withdraw the application, but described the B.O.C. as being "helpful and apologetic".

Coleman also expressed admiration for the recycling efforts at BC under the Environmental Action Center (E.A.C.) and Eleanor MacLellan. "We would really like to come to BC... it is at the top of the list because of the administration's understanding of the issues," he said.

MacLellan, who spoke with, both Coleman and the BC administration about the seminar, said that the E.A.C. is "having to struggle to establish a recycling movement here." Comparing the volunteer-operated recycling effort at BC to better administration-run programs, at Tufts, BU, and Stanford, she said, "the [BC] University isn't taking over."

Judy Kuszewski, A&S '91, of the E.A.C., who alerted The Heights of the seminar's withdrawal, expressed fear that "the B.O.C. consciously thwarted what would have been a major coup for the E.A.C.," reflecting on the success of last year's Earth Day at BC and the number of students who may have been brought into firsthand contact with the recycling movement by the seminar.

Both Early, and Coleman responded that it was a matter of logistics and not of any effort to stymie the seminar, which prevented its being held at BC this year. While most of the correspondences have been either recycled or thrown away since the summer, it appears that they would not reveal anything, which the correspondents themselves do not recall.

The seminar is Mass. Audubon's largest annual gathering. Each year it is held at a different academic institution, with a focus on a specific environmental issue.

Last year a seminar on watershed features were held at Clark University, and this year's seminar on recycling will beheld at the University of Massachusetts' Harbor Campus.

Many of the seminar attendee are Massachusetts citizens, and Coleman noted that the area around Boston College "has a heavy concentration of members." Students are welcome to participate, and are given a discount on participation dues. Dennis Hayes, who founded Greenseals Incorporated of California, and who helped begin the first Earth Day in 1970, will be the keynote speaker, focusing on solid waste. He was featured in a recent Life magazine article on 100 outstanding Americans. Other special guests are slated to speak, and the prestigious "Aubudon A Awards" will be presented to environmental leaders in teaching, volunteer work, media, business, and citizen action. Anyone interested in attending the conference may call Mass. Audubon in Lincoln at 259-9500 or contact Patricia at Extension 7501.

The International Influence of Sailing

In the ever-evolving sport of ocean racing, there are several outstanding sailors and organizers who are creating history as you read; and shattering not only records, but also sometimes damaging preconceptions of the sport. Among them is audacious 33-year-old Frenchwoman Florence Arthaud, who recently broke the West-East trans-Atlantic sailing record - the first woman to do so. Finishing on August 3, 1990, Arthaud skippered the 6G-foot trimaran "Pierre Ler" from Sandy Hook, New Jersey to Lizard, England in nine days and 21 hours. Her new record is two days and 7 hours faster than the 1905 record set by the schooner "Atlantic".

Writer John Marchese, in an article featured in this month's "Sail" magazine, called her "one of the world's most famous female sailors..., the femme fatale, of sailing...an icon among the international sailing set..." Having raced solo trans-Atlantic at age 21 and participated in many races including last year's Whitbread

Round the World Race, Arthaud hopes to skipper the 60-foot trimaran, "Pierre Premier" to Victory in the singlehanded Route du Rhum race from France to Guadeloupe (which began on November fourth). She tried to convey her "relationship with the ocean to Marchese. "The ocean brings you back to the essential things in life... a solitary voyage allows you to clear your brain of all the ugly things you find on land." On her role in the sailing world, she reaffirms that "it is not a profession that is closed to women... and then, you can't be the type that scares easily". Arthaud's accomplishments speak for themselves.

Another pioneer in the sailing world, Bill Pinkney, age 54, set sail from Boston on August 5, 1990 for a year-long solo circumnavigation dedicated to the teaching of underprivileged children. From aboard his 47-foot sloop "Commitment", he will send grade students radio messages, newsletters, and games. Michael Tamulaites interviewed Pinkney for "Sail" magazine's October issue, citing Pinkney's motivation to "be a positive role model for underprivileged children, especially minorities." Pinkney was told as a child in the South Side area of Chicago that single parent, low-income children like him didn't have a chance. But he didn't listen. A sailor for 25 years, Pinkney describes himself as "a student," saying "this journey will push me." With thousands miles ahead of him and as many eager eyes following his progress, Pinkney will be for many the mediator between the oceans and the land-locked.

International camaraderie and shared environmental concern have also become more founded in the sailing world, though sometimes with political resistance. The Soviets have for the first time become involved in yacht racing, starting with participation in 1989 the Block Island Race Week, and continuing with their entry of "Fazizi" in the last Whitbread Around the World Race. Although their skipper killed himself in South America during the rate their yacht and crew set quite a precedent. For the first time, the Soviets have entered a 65-foot yacht in the 1992 America's Cup race. However, "Time" magazine reported in their November 12, 1990 issue that "the (U.S.) federal Port Security Committee, invoking a 20-year-old anti-spying policy, has barred the Soviets from San Diego Bay," the intended site of the next America's Cup.

This injunction is not expected to deter the Soviet team from participating.

Environmentally, the competitors in this year's ongoing BOC Around Alone Challenge has offered to monitor evidence marine life and human waste (a major contributor to ocean-floor sediment) and to save sometimes weighty-trash during the voyage. By not throwing their waste overboard, they are doing more than most United States Navy offshore vessels. Sales proceeds from the race will go towards the World Wildlife Federation through their newly created Oceanwatch Program. "Sail" magazine editor Patience Wales, (Nov.'90 issue) declared that the magazine's newly created "Environmental Outlook and Political Tacks will run regularly in (the) Sailing News section." An article in the same issue focused on the Lexus International Sail Challenge in Newport, in which, "through Sail Newport, an organization devoted to sailing instruction and competition in Newport, nine teams of physically challenged Sailors" raced in custom Freedom Independence 20s and the Performance Handicap Racing Fleet. Along with the Shake-a- Leg Regatta, such races are "designed specifically for physically challenged sailors".

Meanwhile, innovators like Jeff MacInnes and Mike Beedell (who sailed the Northwest Passage in a Hobie catamaran), Newport, Rhode Islander Ned Gillette (who rowed with a crew from Tierra del Fuego, South America to Antarctica), author/solo circumnavigating record-holder Tania Abei (who will speak in Boston in January) and this year's BOC. Around Alone race participants (Isabelle Autissier and Jane Weber among them) continue to further integrate and set new standards for the sport of sailing. Those who ply the seas of the world, weather their undulations, and continue to push oceanic adventure and exploration to extremes offer an encouraging message of constructive progress to a world in which mega-powers find themselves increasingly ensnared in political, racial, and religious conflict.

Durrell Captured "The Complexity of Human Relationships": An Appreciation

Lawrence Durrell, renowned author and poet, died in Sommieres, France, on Wednesday, November 7, at the age of 78. Born in India to British and Irish parents in 1912. Mr. Durrell's chose Mediterranean settings such as Egypt, Greece, and Cyprus as places of residence and settings for much of his prose. An obituary in the *New York Times* on November 9 accredited Mr. Durrell as "a sort of prophet of the sexual revolution, though his vivid descriptions, erudite perceptions, and insightful travel writing were as provocative as his delving into sensuality

Although his most heralded works, namely *The Alexandrian Quartet and Bitter Lemons,* were written in the late 1950s and early 1960s, Mr. Durrell was hardly obsolete at the time of his death, which was apparently due to emphysema. *Caesar's Vast Ghost: A Portrait of Province,* his most recent compilation of more than thirty publications, is being distributed in the United States by Arcade Publishing this winter. It is a non-fiction account of the region in France where Mr. Durrell has lived and worked.

Mr. Durrell's association with the author Henry Miller, about whom Anais Nin wrote in her autobiographical *Henry and June (a controversial new film)* played an important role in Durrell's early development as a writer. *A Private Correspondence (with Henry Miller)* was published in 1962. As Miller's *Tropic of Cancer* was considered pornographic and suppressed, so was Durrell's The Black Book of Argon, published first in 1938 and later in 1960. T.S. Eliot highly of this work, in which Mr. Durrell wrote that he "first heard the sound of (his), own voice."

Among his works, which began with the *Pied Piper of Lovers,* published in 1935, and Panic Spring (1937), *Prospero's Cell, Stiff Upper Lip,* and the verse-drama *An Irish Faustus* (1963), represent Mr. Durrell's broad spectrum of literary talent. Without doubt, however, the novels *Clea, Mountolive, Balthazar,* Mr. Durrell's accounts of and *Justine,* which, compose the *Alexandrian Quarter* brought him the most acclaim. The quartet is a bold attempt to depict simultaneously the perceptions of Egyptians and expatriates in Alexandria. In it, Mr. Durrell challenged conventional concepts of dimension, time, reality, and the correlation (or lack thereof) between sexuality and sincerity.

Prolific in his writing, this work set the precedent for Mr. Durrell's Avignon Quintet (f975-1985). Mr. Durrell, who received his early education in India and Great Britain, lived not only in France, Belgrade, Yugoslavia and on the islands, of Rhodes, Corfu, and Cyprus in the Mediterranean. He married three times, and is survived by a daughter and brother Gerald, who wrote *My Family and Other Animals*. For many years he served on the British Foreign Service and as a press officer. The time he spent living in Cyprus, endowed with this diplomatic instinct white the Turks battled the Greeks, provided Mr. Durrell with a point of departure for *Bitter Lemons* (1957), which was named for one of his poems. Truly a magnificent work of travel writing and cultural perception, it is written in Mr. Durrell's floridly poignant and descriptive style,

Mr. Durrell's accounts of establishing himself in Cyprus and constructing his home on a mountainside harken to Thoreau in all but his interactions with the villagers. Prose scenes of drives through - or meetings among – the fields of the Mediterranean island stand up to the most spectacular landscape scenes in the film *A Room With a View*. Mr. Durrell combined in his narrator the colonial objectivity of a British observer with the indigenous sensitivity characteristic of the likes of the Greek poet C. V. Cavafy. In this sense his accounts can be aligned with those of Forster's *A Passage to India*, only more like passages within India, or, be it as it was – *Cyprus*.

Each of Mr. Durrell's numerous settings were vividly portrayed and given depth through, as the Times obituary said, his "notable sense of place and concentration on the complexity of human relationships." Lawrence George Durrell weathered both praise and criticism during his self-establishment into a modern and progressively international literary era.

Government Blamed for Inner City Violence

On Wednesday, November 28, Boston City Councilor, Rosaria Salerno, addressed the ongoing struggle to bring equity and justice to all Boston residents in a lecture entitled "Violence in the Inner City - How We Can Help."

Salerno, a founder of the Boston College Coalition for Peace and a member of the BC Chaplaincy for nine years until 1988, wasted no time in addressing the needs of Boston's inner-city communities, which she described as "effective combat zones." "The federal government is out of touch with its citizenry," she said. "This country is very sick, and has very strange priorities," she added.

Before sharing her proposals and possible solutions, Salerno expressed concern that the United States government "doesn't have a commitment to public education (or) the war on drugs." She pointed out that although "there are some very bright people in our government," it "doesn't know how to run a peace-time economy," and many of the problems which inner-city communities face persist. "The courts are backed up, the jails are full, and the police force is inadequate," Salerno said.

Salerno described her recently proposed "Boston Peace Plan" in which she emphasized the importance of life ethics, community responsibility, and sector integrity. Since the Mayor and Police Department of Boston reviewed the first draft last year, Salerno stressed that more than a hundred people have been killed in Boston's inner city. She pointed to recent examples such as the murder of Kimberly Harbor and the death of Hector Gonzalez. She mentioned that as a city councilor she had met with the X-Men, a gang in which Gonzalez was a member, in Eagleton Square.

Among possible ways to assist inner city residents, Salerno cited the building of recreational parks, an "increase of cells for people who commit 'anti-people' crimes," separate cells for young detainees who need detoxification, and an increase in the time that courts are open. She proposed Sector Integrity so that certain police officers would train in and consistently patrol a given area so as to enhance community trust and cooperation. Life ethics refers to the community's responsibility to provide moral

54

education for its youth, ideally from kindergarten on, and to diminish illiteracy.

The emphasis said Salerno, is upon community assistance. "If you have a cocaine problem, and you are in my community," she said, "then I've got a problem."

Salerno has had first-hand experience with the violence in the inner city. She has patrolled in police cars, met with citizens, and counseled prisoners. She expressed concern over the harassment not only of prisoners, but of those who visit them, as well as persistent fears often dealt with by residents of the inner city.

Besides her peace plan and responsibilities as a city councilor, Salerno discussed her attempts to bring a much-needed 36 million dollars to support the programs. If for no other reason, she said, citizens should work against violence in the inner city in order to combat "the long shadow over the future," which a high murder rate and economic social security burdens create. For her efforts to obtain this money through parking taxes, she said that she had earned the dubious title of 'Attila the Hen.'

While she spoke, and during more informal meeting-style talks afterwards, Salerno involved the audience in an open discussion of issues such as stop-and-search tactics, proposed curfews, prison treatment, and the difference between 'suburbanites' and those for whom life in the inner city is a daily struggle. Members of the audience were able to pick up copies of her "Boston Peace Plan," described as "a comprehensive Anti-Drug and Violence Plan for the City of Boston."

At the closing of her talk and discussion, Salerno was presented with a shirt reading "Justice Do It" by Urban Immersion Program volunteers Ray Vaillancourt, A&S '91, Gabriel Lamazares, A&S '92, and Mario Allonzo A&S '93.

Vaillancourt, saying that he and his friends had heard Salerno speak and worked for shelters and food banks with her before, described her as "a real dynamic personality."

Salerno said afterwards that her return to Boston College was "like coming home," and that she was pleased with her warm reception and the turnout.

The University Chaplaincy and the Coalition sponsored the event for Peace.

BC Recognizes the Seriousness of AIDS

Boston College recognized the worldwide AIDS crisis on Monday, December 3, with a lecture and a film presented by the American Red Cross and UGBC Social Awareness.

The efforts of the Red Cross, UGBC, Resident Assistants, and sociologists to bring heightened awareness of HIV/AIDS on this day brought less response than was expected. Although the official day of recognition-was Saturday, December 1, Monday was selected as the weekday when presentations could, be made in the workplace and in educational institutions. The lecture and film on HIV (Human Immuno-Deficiency Virus- the root of AIDS) and AIDS (Acquired Immune-Deficiency Syndrome) were presented by Red Cross volunteers Lynne Marlor and Jody Bangs in O'Connell House at 7 pm.

Marlor and Bangs, who are certified American Red Cross HIV/AIDS facilitators, and who have both been Red Cross volunteers in Massachusetts for several years, focused on the concept of prevention, and emphasized the maxim "better safe than sorry."

The lecture was enhanced by the use of a dozen, large diagrams, the first of which outlined the basic principles of their HIV/ AIDS presentation. Five points were the touchstones to the lecture: 1) HIV includes more than AIDS. 2) You can protect yourself. 3) If you do not have sex or share needles with an infected partner, you greatly reduce your risk. 4) You cannot get HIV through casual contact. 5) You cannot get HIV from giving blood.

Mahlor, who described the Red Cross as an organization dedicated to offering help in times of crisis, emphasized that the AIDS/HIV disease "is the most depressing crisis facing us now. The AIDS epidemic is growing at tremendous proportions," she said. "The only thing we have now is education."

Though trained in the medical terminology, the volunteers presented their lecture in "layman's terms," and the diagrams presented medical concepts in the form of simple illustrations. Bangs described how AIDS can grow from HIV after a "window period" of 6-8 weeks or into full blown symptoms of AIDS any time in the following 5-10 years. As of yet, there is no cure for the fatal AIDS virus.

Bangs, who had worked on HIV/AIDS awareness at University of Massachusetts-Amherst, presented statistics from an AIDS surveillance, report published by the Center for Disease Control in Atlanta. In the United States, 54,917 cases of AIDS have been confirmed, and 6-8 million worldwide.

The report indicates that Massachusetts, which has the Tenth highest national AIDS death rate, has seen 3,183 residents die from AIDS since 1981. Boston is ranked 12 in a list of AIDS casualties within U.S. cities. Reports also estimate that up to 40 percent of intravenous drug users in Boston have AIDS.

In the follow-up film Dr. Anthony Fauci, MD, credited HIV and AIDS as having "the ability to attack the cell which is responsible to protect the body. The immune system's purpose is essentially to act as the defense department of the body".

Among modes of transmission, the, sharing of needles or participation in oral, vaginal, or anal sex with infected persons are the primary causes of catching HIV and AIDS. Though infected breast milk is a transmitter, blood exposed to air and secretions such as sweat, tears, and saliva are not modes of transmission. Blood transfusions are said to be responsible for a total of only 6 AIDS cases but of all 120 million units taken since 1981. Since those cases, the Red Cross has screened the blood more meticulously, examined donors more closely, and provided donors with the option to confidentially withdraw the donation after giving blood.

Besides abstinence from intercourse and intravenous drug use, the volunteers described the use of latex condoms with nonoxynol-9, also used in spermicides, as being the most effective form of AIDS prevention during intercourse.

The Volunteers also emphasized that college communities are not free from the-threat of AIDS. A study at UMass revealed that as many as 1 in 500 college students have HIV or AIDS, and that "drugs and alcohol may promote the chances of having unsafe sex."

Marlor and Bang closed the presentation by thanking the attendants and emphasizing the importance of continuing awareness of the growing problem of HIV and AIDS. They made it clear that they are "willing to come back again," and that seminars and workshops to train HIV/AIDS awareness volunteers are programs "which all colleges ideally should have."

In response to the sparse awareness to the HIV/AIDS attendance, Scott Sellers, UCBC Vice President for Social Awareness, said he had distributed more than 150 flyers and contacted the School of Nursing. Last year, he said, no one attended the lecture.

In another effort to bring awareness to the HIV/AIDS diseases, Walsh Hall Resident Assistant Heather Roche, CSOM '91, sponsored sociology graduate student Glyn Hughes to lead a student discussion of AIDS in the Walsh third floor lounge on Monday at 8 pm. Hughes brought the issues into a daily perspective by allowing students to discuss how, when becoming become inebriated and acting promiscuously, they put themselves at risk of acquiring AIDS or HIV. A volunteer for the   National AIDS Hotline in Washington D.C., Hughes warned of the potentially fatal ramifications of irresponsible sexual behavior in any environment. The volunteers encouraged students to use AIDS Hotline numbers. The numbers are 1-800-342-AIDS or 1-800-342-SIDA.

Aebi Details Her Solo Sail Around the World

Community Boating Center, Boston, Tuesday night. A woman in her early twenties sits complacently in the lobby. A crowd of nearly fifty people linger nearby, some sipping coffee. They are hoping that their names will be called from the waiting list to hear her speak. A gentleman timidly approaches asking her to sign his book. He reminisces wonderingly on her feats. "What's done is done," she says. He is speaking with Tania Aebi, the youngest person and the first American woman to circumnavigate the globe alone.

The book is *Maiden Voyage*, coauthored by Bernadette Brennan of Cruising World magazine and ' published in 1989. It is an account of 27,000 miles of challenge in the face of immense natural adversity, of triumph and despair. Miss Aebi doesn't talk about triumph and despair though. She talks about her voyage her genuine feelings, and why she set out from New York in her 26 feet J.J. Taylor Contessa sloop "Varuna" at the age of 18.

A New Yorker originally from Switzerland, Aebi's straight talk and sharp wit belies her warm recollections and sensitive writing. While sharing nearly 156 slides and a detailed account of the voyage, Miss Aebi kept the capacity audience laughing or sighing compassionately.

The voyage and the circumstances which brought it, about were wrought by emotional and physical hardships and punctuated by spectacular landfalls and close friendships made along the way. Between her departure from New York on May 28, 1985, and her triumphant return on November 6, 1987, Miss Aebi suffered a knockdown and a collision. She lost her mother and a friend and she gained a husband, Olivier, who was single-handedly circumnavigating the world searching for exotic shells and emeralds.

Miss Aebi had different motivations for embarking. Her father, a Swiss artist who was "always of a mind to travel," had skippered her and her kin across the Atlantic. She had graduated from high school and was searching for a direction. Finally, her father gave her the option of attending college or sailing alone around the world. Though at first skeptical, Miss Aebi agreed to set but and learned "that it's not so easy to quit something once you get started."

Miss Aebi went on with a comprehensive illustrated account of her complete circumnavigation. Between every thirty or so slides, the viewers followed Miss Aebi's progress on large projected maps. Sailing from Bermuda, Miss Aebi continued to St. Thomas, Virgin Islands, through the Panama Canal, and to Cairns, Australia via the Galapagos, Marquesas, Tahitian, Samoan, and Vanuatu Islands.

Her companions during most of the voyage were cats. For giving a friend an 80-mile 'lift' from one Pacific isle to another, someone threatened anonymously to 'tell the world'. Insulted and angry, spirited Miss Aebi decided, "I'm not going back." In doing so, she forsook the world record as the youngest person to circumnavigate alone. By then she had crossed about half of the world, tattooed her ankle, battled with storms, lice, and her mother's agonizing death. She had also met Olivier.

During her longest crossing, between the Galapagos and the Marquesas, Miss Aebi celebrated her 19th Birthday. She shared a diary excerpt from that day in *Maiden Voyage*. "The most beautiful, yet sad Birthday... I miss my home and family... when I return it will all be so different... My ship is so small and the Ocean so immense. I am content with the rush of water, the wind, and the leaks. Both rugged sailor and sensitive writer, Muss Aebi defies the singlet-hander's stereotype for being anti-social.

Both in her book and in the manner with which she spoke, Miss Aebi conveys the overwhelming strain which upwind sailing, frequent partings with friends and immense pressure from deadlines that her father placed on her.

Having lost nearly 20% of her body weight and a bit of her temper, Miss Aebi described what a struggle it was to set off across the rugged North Atlantic after two years at sea. Yet set off she did arriving in New York on November 6, 1987 after a mammoth 50 days at sea.

Nearly four years later, Miss Aebi, holder of the Cruising World Medal for Outstanding Seamanship; is spending less time at sea and more with her husband Olivier in New York. Last summer, the couple crossed the Atlantic together in their new 38-foot sailboat. They plan additional ventures in the future.

Students Lend a Hand in Ecuador and Haiti

During January, two student pilgrimages organized by the Boston College Chaplaincy visited Haiti and Ecuador in order to provide aid, companionship and spiritual warmth to the malnourished and poor.

Greg Zlevor of the Chaplaincy Officered a group of 12 students to Duran, outside Guayaquil, Ecuador, a South American nation of. 9 million, persons situated between Columbia and Peru. It was BCI's first such contingent to Ecuador.

Father Robert Braunreuther, SJ, led 21 students on his eighth pilgrimage to Port Au Prince, Haiti, a nation of '5,2 million Creolle-speaking people in the Caribbean between Puerto Rico and Cuba.

While the Haiti expedition was jeopardized by political turmoil and a Coup d'Etat, which endangered their stay and departure, the Ecuador contingent experienced no such difficulties. "I was glad it worked well," said Zlevor, who worked with the Faith, Peace and Justice program at BC in organizing the trip.

Though Braunreuther said he was uncertain if the Haiti pilgrimage could continue after two consecutive trips have been beset by political unrest, he also said he felt fulfilled by the work, which the students were able to do through Mother Teresa's organization of community aid.

Zlevor travelled to Ecuador for the first time with his wife, Anne, and 12 students of all years, including a graduate student of Nursing and several Spanish speaking students. The group lived from January 2 to January 12 in the town of Duran, across the Guayas River from Guayaquil. The students stayed in an old mission house called Santa Marianita on the "cerro," or hill above Duran.

The villagers among whom BC students lived "are poor. There is no plumbing, little electricity and poor roads," Zlevor said.

Speaking of the conditions of living there, he said that it cost around seven U.S. dollars a day to feed 14 people. Running water was available for 15 minutes a day, and had to be boiled, he said.

The group worked with young and teenage students at the Nuevo Mundo school. Their primary role was to "meet and live with the poor, to understand them, and to provide companionship," Zlevor said. A Father Gorge from Guatemala worked with them. The students visited the local market daily and went into Guayaquil for a day.

Speaking of his cero impressions of the recent trip, Zlevor emphasized the children. "There were children everywhere," he said, "we would play and sing and visit with them, every day, dawn to dusk."

Zlevor noted with pain that as many as 50 percent of the infants die before the age of five. Whole families live in sugar cane huts, he said, "on the dirt floor they do all the cooking, washing, eating and sleeping."

Mr. Zlevor's most poignant image was of a woman who came to the door of a shack, which he was photographing. It was decorated with a paper Santa Claus and decorations, which had been found in the dumps of Guayaquil. The woman dispelled Zlevor's uneasy embarrassment by asking him to photograph the matron and her husband in the doorway. The group hosted a party for the children on the night before they departed. After the piñatas and food had been enjoyed, he said, the same father with whose children the students had been playing told him, "my home and my heart are always open to you." Mr. Zlevor was moved and encouraged.

Father Braunreuther's group's stay in Haiti was between January 3 and 11. They were strongly influenced by political events which all but paralyzed activity in Port Au Prince, the capital of Haiti. The Chaplaincy group's stay began with a visit to their host convent by Haiti's interim President Madame Ertha Pascal Trouillot. Within a few days however, an attempted coup d'etat disrupted power and communication and made travel within the city dangerous.

Despite the upheaval, however, the group of 21 mostly female students, along with Dr. Sandy Thompson and a nurse from Boston, were able to accomplish most of what they set out to do. "All the things that needed to go right went right," Father Braunreuther said.

The group made visits to The Home of the Destitute arid Dying, the Home for the Abandoned and Malnourished Children (both run by Mother Teresa's Mission), and the Methodist Tuberculosis

Home. Sister Monique hosted them in a convent about three miles outside of Port Au Prince.

The group visited some of the nearly 200 schools run by Father Bohnen of Haiti. BC students provided Companionship and consolation to the sick. They played games with and provided toys for the children. Father Braunreuther felt that the students were exceptionally open and spent much of their spare time playing with children around the convent in which they stayed.

Father Braunreuther had the tremendous responsibility of safely administering his group, many of whom "didn't realize the seriousness of the situation." Enemies of the people were being killed in the streets. One nun greeted the group by asking, "what are you doing here?" After a daylong struggle to secure seats on the only plane to the U.S. in a week, the group returned to Boston, relieved and tired.

Though the future of the Haiti program is uncertain and both trips required a certain amount of fund-raising; Mr. Zlevor and Father Braunreuther expressed optimism and hope that the pilgrimages would continue in the Spirit of humanitarian and religious fellowship.

Democratic President Elected in Haiti

On February 7, Father Jean-Bertrand Aristide, Haiti's first democratically elected president, was inaugurated in Portau Prince, the nation's capital.

Several Boston College students and teachers experienced first-hand the January 6 attempted coup d'etat; a final effort to usurp interim President Ertha Pascal-Trouillot's democratic rule.

Aristide is described by Howard French of The New York Times as "...a 37-year-old Roman Catholic priest who rose from the obscurity of a small parish to help lead the battle against the Duvalier family dictatorship." (2-8-91)

In the same article, former U.S. President Jimmy Carter, who along with almost 1,000 others monitored Haiti's only successful free elections in the 186 years of independence, said, "What has been achieved by the Haitian people is momentous in history."

Between Aristide's popular election by 65 percent of the vote last December 16, and his taking of office on February 7, supporters of Haiti's exiled dictator Duvalier attempted to overthrow the interim president arid have raided orphanages to which they consider Aristide sensitive.

Early on Saturday, February 2, "...perpetrators widely believed to be members of Tontons Macoute, the militia that terrorized the country under the Duvalier family's 29-year rule. "They set fire to one of the orphanages, which Father Aristide had helped begin, and supported. There were nine casualties; four burned to death. Though he conceded that "...they aimed at my heart," Father Aristide also declared that "...the reign of the (Tontons) Macoutes is over." (The New York Times 2-7-91).

Between Sunday, January 6 and Monday, January 7 of this year, Duvalier's (who was exiled five years ago) supporters under Tontons Macoute leader Lafontant tried to overthrow interim President Ertha Pascal-Trouillot. Among those who witnessed these events and turmoil, which wracked Port au Prince, were a contingent of 21 Boston College students and three leaders, including Father Robert Braunretheur, S.J.

Encountering political unrest in Haiti was not new to Father Braunretheur, who had made eight pilgrimages there. Last year, the group's return was heralded by a Heights article by the McCafferty headlined "Students Caught in the Middle of Revolution." (March 19, 1990).

This year, the expedition underwent similar unrest, but for very different reasons. Last year the dictator Avrill was being pressured to resign; this year Lafontant was trying to overthrow a popular president.

Pierre Barreau is related to former President Trouillot, and was with her in Port au Prince up to her abduction by Lafontant. Mr. Barreau, an American for years, is a sextant at Saint Ignatius Loyola, and teaches choreography at Boston College. He explained that at around 9 pm on January 6, Lafontant arrived at Trouillot's residence and abducted her in an armored vehicle. By threatening her and her children, Lafontant and his group coerced Trouillot into resigning, on Haiti's national radio at around midnight. However, Trouillot did not simply state "I resign;" as wished,

Rather, she told the Haitian public that she was being "forced to resign."

This brought the Haitian public, wary of such a move on the eve of their first democracy, to their feet and into the streets. As Neal Amaral, Ana F. Garcia, and Karen Olson, Boston College students who were in Portau Prince at the time, related, "Beatings and killings broke out while the people looted and burned tires in protest of the governmental overthrow" (Heights 2-4-91). According to Father Braunreuther, the tires were being placed around the necks of suspected Tontons Macoute and set afire.

According to Barreau, who was in contact with President Trouillot during the attempted coup d'etat, Lafontant declared himself the new leader of Haiti and invited his Tontons Macoute supporters to join him at the Presidential Palace. The bitter Haitian people were in the streets with machetes, sticks, and tires waiting for them, within 24 hours, it became obvious to Lafontant that his coup d'etat was neither popular nor successful. In a notable shift, General Abrams of the Army cast his support behind Trouillot, who was reinstated. Lafontant was incarcerated by late January 7, said Barreau.

In the street violence surrounding the incidents, 37 people were reportedly killed. Sanon Lezeau, CSOM '92 is a student at Boston College from Aux Cayes, Haiti. His mother, who was living in Port au Prince during the coup d'etat, believes that there were more likely "over 200" killed during the unrest. "The news doesn't really give you anything," he said. "Houses were burned with people in them... it's not like you call the 911 when someone is missing," Lezeau and Barreau are two of forty to fifty Haitians affiliated with Boston College, and-a sizeable Haitian community in Dorchester, Boston. Both of them (expressed optimism and hope for Haiti's future.

Ultimately, they would like to be able to safely return, and that Haitians can fulfill their ambitions there. Though he didn't advocate revenge, Lezeau stressed that "Haitian people are not so gullible anymore," and anticipated sustained democracy there.

The United States has been guarded in their response to Aristide's election, "because of the priest's criticism of American foreign policy and his liberal ideology" (The New York Times 2-8-

91). Barreau and Lezeau were wary that Haiti become dependent on the U.S., or that an industry like tourism would dehumanize Haitians or bring over-development. "Haitians are told not to go on their own beaches when tourists are there," Mr. Lezeau pointed out.

With the turmoil, which launched Aristide to power finally subsiding many Haitians, wait hopefully. As Lezeau said, "He has made a lot of promises. 1 would like to see them fulfilled."

Sandel Argues for 'Substantial Moral Discourse'

"The justice or injustice of laws against abortion and homosexual sodomy depends, at least in part, on the morality or immorality of these practices;" said Michael J. Sandel, professor of government at Harvard University, in a talk titled Moral Argument and Liberal Toleration; Abortion and Homosexuality, given last Friday.

Sandel's lecture was based upon an article of the same title, which appeared in the California Law Review, of May 1989 (Volume 77:521, pages 521 to 538).

Sandel reminded the audience that he does not argue, "The morality of immorality of a practice is the only relevant reason in deciding whether there should be a law against it." He outlined conceptions of how laws should be neutral; relativist, utilitarian, voluntarism and minimalist. Sandel advocates "a keener appreciation of the role of substantive moral discourses in political and constitutional argument." Substantive moral discourse; or the inclusion of moral perspectives in law making, was the touchstone of Sandel's argument.

The theology and political science departments sponsored the lecture. Dean White of the Graduate School of. Arts and Sciences introduced Sandel to a near capacity audience composed primarily professors and graduate students.

Sandel was elected to the Board of Trustees at Brandeis University while he was a *Summa Cum Laude* undergraduate student. As a Rhodes Scholar at the University of Oxford he earned his doctorate in politics and philosophy, Sandel presently teaches Justice at Harvard, one of the university's most popular courses.

In his lecture, Sandel outlined; "two arguments against antiabortion and anti-sodomy laws." He stated that primarily these practices are "morally permissible." Secondly, that, "Without reference to the moral status of the practices... individuals have a right to choose for themselves."

Sandel argued against this liberal toleration on the grounds that they "bracket" or set aside "controversial moral and religious conceptions for the purpose of justice." Sandel made clear his intentions to "defend the claim that you can't separate morality and law."

Sandel referred to legal decisions of Louis Brandeis in 1890 and more recently- of Supreme Court Judges Stevens, Blackmun and White. Sandel discussed several legal cases, including *Griswold v. Connecticut* in 1965 (which "recognized a constitutional right of privacy") and *Eisenstadt v. Baird* in 1972 (which "protected the freedom to engage in certain activities without governmental restriction"). For his analysis of laws concerning abortion, he referred to the 1973 Roe v. Wade case in which the Supreme Court declared that they "need not resolve the difficult-question of when life begins."

In his investigation of the legality of sodomy, Sandel referred to the 1969 case of *Stanley v. Georgia*, which "upheld the right to possess obscene materials in the privacy of one's home." Sandel noted the different perspectives of homosexuality expressed by the Stanley decision, which deals with obscenity, and the Griswold decision, which deals with almost sacred interpersonal and private relationships.

Sandel also recounted the 1980 case of *People v. Onofre* in which "the New York Court of Appeals vindicated privacy rights for homosexuals."

Sandel concluded his lecture by saying that, "The justice or injustice of laws against abortion and homosexual sodomy may have something to do with the morality or immorality of these practices after all."

Sandel was challenged, by members of the audience to take a political or philosophical stance on the issues, to which he responded that to do so would be inconsistent with the premise of his argument. When accused of refusing to go beyond the bounds of objectivity, Sandel replied, "What bounds would you have me pulled across?"

Jim Nedved, a doctoral candidate in politics at Boston College, believed that, "the audience was pushing for a moral stand" from Sandel. Nedved felt that Sandel, in dealing with a voluntarism perspective, strayed from the determinism of natural law. "There, is a discontinuity between voluntarism and natural law," he said. "The Constitution is in agreement with Locke."

Jerry Kleven, who is pursuing his post-doctorate degree in the Bradley School of Theology, felt that, "In staying away from the actual issues, he (Sandel) helped to clear the ground" for more concise analysis. He felt that Sande's argument was "right as far as it went."

Further questioning by members of the audience led to discussion of previous legal cases such as the Dred Scott decision of 1857, and an 1856 debate between Stephen Douglass (a liberal tolerant, according to Sandel), and Abraham Lincoln (a proponent of substantive moral discourse).

As a "live issue," slavery was compared to abortion and homosexuality.

CBS PoWs Return from Iraq

On the afternoon of Sunday, March 10, two of four CBS newsmen who were captured by Iraqi soldiers on the Iraq-Kuwait-Saudi border on January 21 arrived in Miami after 40 days of captivity. Roberto Alvarez, 37, and Juan Caldera, 29, a Miami-based freelance camera and sound crew, were greeted at Miami International Airport by family, friends and fellow journalists.

On January 23, less than a week after the outbreak of war, the crew, led by Bob Simon, 49, CBS News Chief Middle East Correspondent and Peter Bluff, 47, CBS News London Bureau Chief, was reported missing. On January 22, a Saudi Arabian military patrol discovered their abandoned Toyota Land Cruiser with $6000 in cash and television equipment.

The crew had ventured into no-man's-land in order to "check out movements" on the front. Alvarez described how the men, "never went on a (government censored) press pool." Caldera said that they were "being journalists, going-right up to the lines—up the road." He recalled previous experiences in Columbia and his native Nicaragua.

Both men have had extensive experience covering events in South and Central America, where Caldera had been held, unharmed, by contras in 1986.

Of the 40 days following their capture, the crew spent the first night in Basra, eight days in a camp outside Baghdad, 24 days in solitary, confinement at Iraqi intelligence headquarters, and a week in a prison outside of Baghdad. They were released in Baghdad on March 2, 22 pounds lighter and fully bearded. They spent the following week in London undergoing medical tests and giving interviews before returning home in Miami.

On the first day of captivity the crew underwent interrogations, and were "slapped around." Alvarez said that though the interrogation was, "a hell of an experience," his Cuban lineage might have spared him from serious torture. The routines in solitary confinement consisted of daily rations of two slices of bread, water and soup. Daily activities included pacing their 7-by-14 foot cells, and talking to themselves. Alvarez described becoming, "an entity, a person with yourself, each day coming closer to the war's end."

The most immediate danger befell them on the 33rd day of captivity, when three allied bombs fell directly on the massive Iraq intelligence headquarters in Baghdad.

Alvarez described the destruction when he said, "There was shattered glass, the cell was completely torn, [and] the door caved in." Caldera, whose ankle was injured and his body bruised by the rubble, described that "you could see the sky" from within his bombed cell. For the first time in 24 days, Alvarez and Caldera were able to see Simon and Bluff, as well as meet captured allied pilots.

Within a week of the bombing, the four prisoners were freed, and returned to the luxuries and family companionship, which they had longed for while in captivity.

When asked by reporters what they had planned for the future, Alvarez and Caldera asserted that for the time being it was more a question of what they were not going to do and where they were not going to go.

During intermission, journalists just back from the Persian Gulf, region shared photos and stories while Alvarez and Caldera responded to questions from friends and colleagues.

Consuls Night Opens Doors to Students

International Consuls representing as many as fifteen countries gathered in BC's Greycliff Hall on Thursday evening, March 21, to participate in the eighth 'annual Consuls' Night.

Consuls from Brazil, Chile; Ecuador, France, Germany, Italy, Korea, Monaco, Pakistan, Portugal, Spain, Sweden, and Venezuela shared conversation and a buffet dinner with international students and teachers.

"This is the best Consuls' Night I've ever seen," commented Tanya Norman, A&S '91, who is a minor in Germanic Studies and will study in Germany next year under a Fulbright scholarship. She described previous Consuls' Nights as "meager" in comparison. Isabelle Ollier, a Greycliff R.A. and French tutor from Paris, said, "it is very important that everyone is here. The students are very excited."

A motive behind hosting the Consuls was to allow students an opportunity to speak and practice other languages and to expose them to various nationalities. Professor Harry Rosser, chairman of the romance languages department, thanked the Consuls for "helping to change the myopic view in the United States that the rest of the world should speak English."

He reminded the audience that "what we cannot say can hurt us." Citing the number of language students at BC, he referred to "a renewed interest foreign languages and literature."

In closing, Rosser thanked Professor Enrique Ojeda and Professor Emeritus Vera Lee, the founders of Greycliff.

Lee commented that attitudes towards Greycliff have become "a lot better = more serious."

She emphasized the importance of students sharing meals together, which they do five evenings a week. Father Allen S.J.

spoke, encouraging students to develop an appreciation for art and other people.

Greycliff Hall, BC's international house hosts several classes in Spanish and French during the week. Ollier described the students as "enthusiastic to speak French - I always begin back magazines and books from France for them." Greycliff R.A. Vladimir Mathieu, A&S '92, who is form Haiti, described Greycliff as "the only dorm where the community aspect stays."

Mark Wike, A&S '94, is a freshman living in Greycliff. He feels that, while the dorm "may not be for everyone," he has enjoyed "the interaction with other students and the good food."

Several graduate students live in Greycliff, which Wike described as "a little community-like home."

Nancy Vallencourt, CSOM '91, said that she "wouldn't live anywhere else." Vallencourt, who transferred to BC, "didn't study Italian until she lived in Greycliff."

This summer she will participate in an advanced Italian seminar at Middlebury College. She feels that "The School of Management, doesn't stress language enough," and that "business is interaction between people" in which language be very important.

Andreas Seigel, press attaché for the German Consulate in Boston, said that at universities in Germany events, such as Consul's Night, were not available. Seigel was impressed by "the enormous effort put into Consuls' Night" and said that he would gladly return.

The event was organized by Greycliff R.A.s Michelle Miller Isabelle Ollier and sponsored by Dining Services and the Housing Department.

Earth Week Plans Underway on Campus

Preparations for Boston College's Earth Week (April 22 to 26) celebrations and environmental awareness presentations are currently underway.

Last Wednesday, representatives from various campus groups met to discuss the agenda and plan their displays, which are to be presented on the Dust bowl. "Every group on campus has been contacted. Earth Week participants are by no means exclusively environmental or social action groups," said Scott Oberstaedt, CSOM '93, who handles Earth Week information and publications.

"It was basically a forum through which group leaders shared ideas," said Elizabeth Dees, A&S 93, who is an Earth Week volunteer assisting in public relations. The events will be sponsored by BC's Environmental Action Center (E.A.C.) and The Recycling Effort at Boston College (T.R.E.E.), the UGBC Social Awareness, and the Activities Funding Committee (A.F.C).

BC's Earth Week begins with Earth Day, which is recognized globally on April 22. Earth Day was initiated in 1970 by environmentalist Dennis Hayes, founder of Greenseals Incorporated of California. Earth Day 1991 will unofficially kick off in New England on Saturday, April 20 with a massive concert in Foxboro. The concert, organized by Concerts for the Environment will feature the Indigo Girls, Ziggy Marley, 10,000 Maniacs, Jackson Browne, Willie Nelson, Billy Bragg and Bruce Hornsby, to name a few. Other events will be held along Storrow Drive in Boston.

BC's Earth Week festivities this year will be University oriented, and will no longer be directly affiliated with other environmental organizations such as MassPirg (Public Interest' Research Group), Mass. Audubon Society or Greenpeace.

Earth Week activities will include group displays, music, and food on the Dustbowl, speakers, a film and a Cafe Night. The purpose of Earth Week and Earth Day is to share environmental concern and "take different issues and make them salient to people at BC, in Boston, and around the world," said Oberstaedt.

There are a number of environmental issues on which Earth Week intends to address and provide information. Among them,

72

Oberstaedt, who is organizing a publication of related articles for the event, cited "nuclear disposal, the Bush administration's Energy Policy, pesticides, insecticides, recycling, the James Bay Two project in Canada, deforestation, and deterioration of the Ozone Layer."

Oberstaedt conceded, "It is obviously going to take a long time to solve some of these problems. Our goal is to get the issues out to a lot of people. If everyone acts, the problems become less overwhelming, and each person really does make a difference."

Reflecting on the upcoming Earth Week activities, Elizabeth Dees commented. "It is wonderful that our school is involved; I think that every school should be. As well as celebrating Earth Week, our concern for the environment should really be a focus all year long."

Frenchman Wins '90-'91 Sailing Challenge

After sailing his 60-foot sailing sloop "Group Sceta" more than 2700 miles around the world alone, French skipper Cristophe Auguin crossed the finish line of the BOC Challenge in Newport, Rhode Island at 1: 11am on Tuesday, ApriL29. Auguin, who is 31 years old, set the race record sailing around the world in 120 days, 22 hours, 36 minutes, and 35 seconds, and won $100,000 in prize money.

A close finish, a suicide, dis-mastings, collisions with other boats and icebergs, run-ins with storms, and seven withdrawn entries marked the race.

Auguin, who had slept only six hours of the previous 72, was unshaven and exhausted, with hardly enough energy to raise a magnum of champagne. After celebrating on Newport's Coat Island, he gave a press conference in his native language of French. Auguin conceded that, "the most difficult parts of the voyage were the icebergs in>the Southern Ocean," though, 'the three last legs were very tiring." Auguin, who was making more than 12 knots coming into Newport, explained that, "Yesterday my mast was touching the water. One wave was stronger than the other."

The sailors made stops in Cape Town, South Africa, Syndey, Australia and Punta del Este, Uruguay. During the course of the mammoth race, Auguin also encountered storms and hit a whale. When asked by a reporter if he felt confident enough to compete in the upcoming Globe Challenge, a solo race nonstop around the world, Auguin, who has sailed since he was a child, replied. "To go in that race, you have to be foolish. No marks are necessary."

During Tuesday morning's press conference. Auguin was still uncertain whether he or Alain Gautier had won the race. Gautier, a 28-year-old Frenchman, aboard 'Generali Concorde' held a lead of 21 hours over Auguin going into the final leg from Uruguay.

The race is considered the closest ever, and only poor weather and misfortune held Gautier from winning. Gautier was penalized 16.5 hours for arriving late for the suit. Though he was the first racer to arrive in Cape Town, and set a record for the first leg of the race, the penalty put Auguin in the lead.

Only days before arrival in Newport, Gautier had his mainsail torn in two by 50-knot winds west of Bermuda. Adding insult to injury, light winds plagued him while Auguin pulled into the lead with a superior set of sails, one of which measured 150 meters square. Gautier arrived in Newport on Thursday afternoon, April 25, 38 hours behind Auguin, who won.

French skipper Philippe Jeantot, 38 years old, was the third boat across the line on. Friday, April 26, at 2:34 am aboard 'Credite Agricole.' Jeantot won the only two previous BOC races and set the 125-day record. By April 22, American Mike Plant, Frenchwoman Isabelle Autissier, and Australians David Adams and Kanga Birtles were vying for places. They are due into Newport between Sunday April 28 and Tuesday May 1.

Competitors from the Division II and the unsponsored 'Corinthian Class' are also due in. The only American in Division I competitor, Mike Plant aboard 'Duracell' began the race with high expectations, expressing his goal to 'go like hell' and hoping to win the race. Unfortunately, Plant was beleaguered during the first leg by a faulty generator and lack of fresh water. During the start of the second leg, he was rammed by another competitor in Cape Town's Table Bay. Though Plant suffered a two-foot gash in his hull, he refused to turn back for repairs. As a result, he spent most of the second leg bailing out water and attempting repairs himself, which cost him a chance at victory.

Of the 25 yachts that began the BOC Challenge Around Alone 1990-1991, sponsored by the BOC Group and presented by I8M, only 18 are expected to finish.

One boat, 'Allied Bank,' skippered by South African John Martin, sank after colliding with an iceberg in the Southern Ocean. Martin was rescued from a life, raft after three days by fellow South African Bertie Reed aboard 'Grinnaker.' Australian David Adams, aboard 'Inn keeper,' was knocked overboard in a 40-knot gust of wind, but managed to struggle back on board.

The only woman in Division I, Isabelle Autissier of France, suffered a broken mast near Tasmania, and several boats, including Hungarian Nandor Fa's 'Alba Regia,' experienced dangerous knockdowns. The sailors rounded Africa's Cape of Good Hope and South America's Cape Horn, battling seas known as 'the roaring forties' to sailors because of 50-mile-an-hour winds.

Skipper Yukoh Tada of Japan, in fear of capsizing in the treacherous Antarctic seas, killed himself in Sydney Australia. Tada had begun to doubt the sea worthiness of 'KodenVlll,' which he made himself, and had withdrawn from the race halfway around the world.

His death is a poignant reminder of the dangers faced and discipline of mind and body required to complete a race as demanding as the BOC Challenge.

Log of Yacht Chebec's Trans-Atlantic Voyage
[Duplicate, Manchester College Oxford, 1992, & BC Stylus, 1993]

Down to the Sea in Ships: The Crossing - Logbook

"We must sail and not drift, nor lie at anchor."
Oliver Wendell Holmes, from The Autocrat at the Breakfast Table, 1858

Date: Sunday, 12 May 1991 -15:45

Position: Aboard *Chebec*, tied Nelson's Dockyard, English Harbour, Antigua

Weather: Winds 10-15 knots South/Southwest

Events: My first night in Antigua I walked to a large sailboat named *Chebec* and. asked for Yves, the Belgian skipper. "Come aboard!" Off with the shoes, hat, and beer, and up the gangplank I went. His back was to me, his face in the shadows, like Brando playing Kurtz in "Apocalypse Now."

Yves: "Yes?"

Me: "Do you want help going across?"

Pause.

"Yes. Welcome."

Disbelief. Pause.

To Yves: "I have five thousand miles."

"I've known fools with a hundred thousand miles. Welcome. Where is your beer? Have a Polar."

I drank the cheap Venezuelan beer, dizzy with excitement.

"Where to?"

"Belgium."

"How?"

"Direct."

"When?"

"Two days. When I get money."

"Who with?"

"Me, you. Loco, and Captain Splash."

Fear: "Aren't you the skipper?"

"This is Kapitan Splatz."

My new skipper held up a kitten and smiled.

"You're welcome. Move your gear aboard tomorrow."

I did.

Date: Tuesday, 14 May - 08:00

Aboard: *Chebec*, English Harbour, Antigua.

Weather: Calm, warm, humid, pace slow and languid.

Event: Now it is only Yves and I crossing the Atlantic. Loco, a poor Venezuelan, left for a wage on another boat. *Chebec* is a 19.5-meter (165 foot) ketch (2 masts). Her teak deck was laid in Taiwan (strikingly beautiful when clean). She is wide, deep, and heavy, strong and seaworthy, as is Yves. *Chebec* has survived some 16 Atlantic crossings, and Yves almost as many.

On Mother's Day I called home and told my mother that I would cross the Atlantic virtually single-handed. The last time I tried that, I ended up on her doorstep after three weeks in the middle of the night; malnourished, bleeding, and barefoot. We sail for St. Maarten tomorrow.

Date: Friday, 17 May - 01:00

Position: *Chebec*, moored off Philipsburg, St. Maarten, Dutch West Indies

Entry: I am now First Mate of *Chebec*; the second in command. There were nine of us, including Splash the cat, on our first voyage. All but four sailors and one passenger have left us here.

Leaving Antigua: Dragging anchor towards coast. Midnight. No skipper. With moments to spare, Yves returns to *Chebec* with an entourage of well-wishers in dinghies. Songs are sung, farewells said, the anchor and sails hoisted, and off we set. Yves has convinced two Antiguan employees of the Galley Bar, Paula and A., to join us (Yves, I, Splash, and Mark, a New Zealand backpacker who'd shown up earlier) all the way across. We bid Antigua farewell under the midnight moon. Yves sets a course and recedes below, not to be seen again until before we make St. Maarten. I pull night watch, trim sail for a dawn squall, and plot course to St. Maarten.

Date: Tuesday, 21 May -10:40

Position: Road Bay, Anguilla, West Indies (Anguilla means "serpent")

Weather: Winds 10-15 knots, gusts to 25, seas choppy outside bay, rain

Entry: Arrived 18:00 Sunday 19 May. Took on water, air for diving tanks, cleared customs. I have my own spacious cabin, forward of the salon (where Paula sleeps). Intended for charter guests, it has lockers, bookshelf, two bunks, access to the head (toilet), and hatch leading to the foredeck. Yves in aft cabin, A. in port, Mark in forepeak. The large transom at the stem end of *Chebec* holds our gangplank, the cat's litter box, our fishing gear, and the inflatable dinghy. The four sailors hold six hours of watch alone per day. We are forever on call — dishes to be done, boat cleaned, sails set and altered. Even at anchor we spent the windy night fending off an abandoned ship.

Change of plans. Shall set sail for Bermuda later today.

Date: Friday, 24 May - 09:35

Position: Longitude 62 West, Latitude 23 North

Weather: Kicking up a good 20-35 knot winds S./S.W., following seas

Entry: On starboard tack heading 15-20² N.N.E.. Brisk sail. Offshore at last!

Date: Monday, 27 May -10:00

Weather: Placid, windless, calm, humid

Entry: We missed Bermuda! We finally have St. David's Light within sight. Were due to have sighted land by dawn, after nearly a week at sea. SatNav (satellite navigation) is down. Stayed up all night; A. and Paula alert as their first real passage nears its end. Seas flat calm. Under power. Failed to hail an aeroplane overhead. Bermuda Radio telling us to be at work on time. At 8:00 Yves altered course to W.S.W. — wise decision. An eerie arc in our wake for only distant whales to observe. A. devastated when we told him we were missing Bermuda and heading straight for England. Bad joke. Cat prancing with smell of land. Startled by tiger shark, which hit us twice. I was sitting on rail and almost toppled. Bermuda long tail dove circled our mast, and then led us directly to land. I help

Yves guide us ashore, having transited Bermuda six times under sail. We're all nervously excited, and toothbrushes and combs surface after days of misuse.

Date: Sunday, 9 June - 23:00 (radio: man lost overboard to S.: drowned)

Position: Lat. 37 N., Long. 62 W. - c.300 miles North of Bermuda

Entry: Just narrowly avoided a collision with a Bulgarian merchant ship. It passed less than a mile from our port side. We lingered in St. George's, Bermuda, for ten days. Ships and crews rot in port. Someone asked me if *Chebec* was my 'yacht'. No, not mine, and not a 'yacht.' *Chebec* is a sailboat. I help to sail her. Loophole and Stormy Weather (1936 yawl) alongside us. Paul, captain of Stormy Weather, sailed north into the ice packs on the way to France just to chip an iceberg for iced gin and tonics!

Departure at 20:00 on Thursday, 6 June. On stormy departure, Loophole's First Mate caught his jacket on *Chebec* while pushing off from quarantine dock and was stuck with us. We gave him back, which is just as well. He spent 14 weeks at Cambridge. Mark performed the Kiwi All Black Maori war dance in full volume on the foredeck. We blew our horns. Loophole's crew mooned us.

Put on our running lights, and headed through the channel. Few times in my life have I been so profoundly moved. Scared might be the word. I'd left that harbor for Portugal the previous summer and never made it. Somberly I tied up our ensign, dug up the safety harnesses, and prepared for at least three weeks of very trying, very true, sailing. It has proved a grueling voyage. Separated by Loophole within hours. Never saw her again.

Date: Monday, 10 June-21:06 POSITION: Lat. 38 N., Long. 61 W.

Entry: Today is the glorious celebration of Yves' 35th birthday. We put on the autopilot and engine. The sun shone, and sea spread before us as flat as our pancakes at breakfast. by which time we'd drunk a bottle of Gosling's Black Seal rum, and were savoring Mark's infamous Gin and Tangs. Sumptuous. Mark and I brought Yves drinks in hammock, tidied up, read.

Date: Saturday, 15 June - 05:00 POSITION: Lat. c.42 N., Long. 46 W.

Weather: Entry explains itself ENTRY: 1,120 n. miles N./N.E. of Bermuda, 1,900 miles from Bishop's Rock, Scilly Islands, England.

North Atlantic. Waters cold and grey. Paula understandably queasy. Captain Splash doesn't know what to make of it. Her litter box washed overboard. *Chebec* running downwind under bare poles, with only the Yankee and Mizzen sails up. We are making 8-12 knots; at times all 35 tons surf down the waves at 15-17 knots! The wind is blowing a steady 40 knots, with gusts as high as 60. The seas are blown in sheets of spray against us. On the Beaufort Scale, we are experiencing the worst weather: Force 10-11. Yves reports that they were blowing 67+ earlier this morning. This is hurricane force wind.

Date: Sunday, June 16 -19:00 Local, 21:00 GMT (Greenwich Mean Time)

Position: Lat. 44:15 N., Long. 39:50 W. on *Chebec* headed for Bishop's Rock

Entry: Today has to have been one of the shit days of the voyage. I'm afraid, after 11/2 months and 2,500 miles. During my shift from 6-8 A.M. Yves and I discovered that we had: 1) blown the Main halyard — the sail was whipping on deck, not lashed; 2) blown (tom) the Stays'l; 3) blown the Mizzen and Main preventers; and 4) flayed the awnings and the covers for the varnished rails.

Wore safety harness once — changing sails on the bowsprit, clinging half-submerged to doused sails. (Took them 45 minutes to find Jim. He was comatose. He lived. Lucky.) Many a time do I rest with a knot in my stomach. Many a time must I lay

down for ten minutes in full gear, thinking about the coming hours on watch. All I can do is put full body weight on the helm, hoping she doesn't turn towards the waves (fatal). Shoulders ache. Hands swollen. We didn't expect the cold. A. wears paper bags on head, hands, and feet. Have an infection festering on my left foot from a scratch in Anguilla. Have not braved a look at it. Too c-c-c-cold to take off boots and socks.

Date: Sunday, 23 June -16:50 GMT POSITION: Lat. c.48 N., Long, c.12 W. c.300 n. miles S.W. of Bishop's Rock, 65 n. miles from final destination: Nieuwpoort, Belgium. ETA June 27.

Entry: Am reading Kundera, Marquez, Hesse, Conrad. We listen to tapes of Bee Gees, Gypsy Kings, Santana, Jacques Brel, Paul

Anka, Peruvian music. Stereo lashed down. Couldn't afford to "top up" on provisions or fuel in Bermuda. Only second week and completely out of: eggs, milk, butter, sugar, coffee, oil, crackers, meat, veggies — of course no smokes or booze. For 23 hours after dinner at c.21:00 we are rationed to two slices of Yves' homemade bread with whatever we find. Rarely anything. Dinner normally pasta or rice.

Accosted A. (26-year-old ex-smuggler and addict) when he came off morning watch and took huge bites from our daily loaf of bread. I called him a thief. Shouldn't have. He drew kitchen knife from the rack and held it to my throat saying he was going to cut me, kill me, poison me, cut my eyes out. I looked up from my book, which had become a blur, and told him to put the knife down. Began to 'read' again. Highly agitated, he pressed throat harder. I looked up at him and told him with surprising honesty that if he drew my blood, I would kill him. On the spot. With my own hands.

Paula intervened, shrieking. Grabbed his arm. Stephanie's parting reminder: vessels alter course for Bermuda to drop off bodies of murdered crew and imprison killer. Never have my hands shaken so much at the helm of a boat as when, moments after A/s attack, I climbed the companion way and relieved Mark for two hours.

Date: Tuesday, 25 June - 20:00 POSITION: day 19; Long. 7 W., Lat. 50 N.

Entry: LAND HO! Just after my 14:00 watch began, deciphered through the fog and drizzle faint trace of an outline of land (Bishop's Rock, England). Strained as they were, my eyes did not deceive me. For a few moments laughed to myself. My smile would have made a Cheshire cat envious. Slid hatch to Yves' cabin open:

"Yves?"

"Yes?"

He was sleeping.

"I think I've sighted land."

Pause.

"What makes you think so?"

Pause. I think to myself.

Can't resist: "Because I am looking at it, Yves."

Still three days of sailing.

Today has truly been one of the happiest days of my life. When we unfurled our moldy Antiguan flag, its golden sun seemed to bring out the real sun from behind the clouds. After two weeks of grey, we welcomed the warm sunshine as a long-lost friend. Tonight, we whisk past the dark silhouettes of merchant ships, peacefully gliding along the Cornish coast, savoring the womb-like presence of land around us.

Date: Wednesday, 3 July -12:00

Position: Train from London to Oxford

Entry: We arrived aboard *Chebec* in Nieuwpoort, Belgium, at c.18:00 GMT+2 on Thursday, 27 June, after almost exactly 3 weeks at sea (21 days virtually to the hour). Captain Splash had a run-about on *terra firma*, and we made our way to warmth, Duivel beer, and Belga cigarettes in the KNYC: Royal Yacht Club at Nieuwpoort. Though can't honestly say that in my state its 'Royalty' meant a damned thing to me, we were treated hospitably. Yves fed us well.

The Stats: 4,000 nautical miles sailed. S. to N. 35 lines of Lat.; 2,000 n.m. W. to E. 30 lines of Long., 3,000 n.m.: 6 time zones, 3 layovers, 7 weeks, 30+ days at sea, 100+ watches each. Innumerable tears, pain, and longings.

Date: Saturday, 16 November, 1991 -18:33

Position: Crouched in front of the computer, Manchester College, Oxford

Weather: Exceedingly grey and foggy — dangerous weather to bicycle in.

Events: Epilogue: Hurricane Grace ravaged Bermuda earlier this month. Several boats were dismasted. Anna Christina (95 foot) lost. *Chebec* with Yves, Paula, A.(?), and Captain Splash crossing Atlantic back to Antigua presently. Kapitan Splatz I'm sure sorely missed by fellow-feline in English Harbor. Neither spoken to or heard of any crew of *Chebec* or Loophole. They now live in a sphere distinct from my own. It is a sphere into which anyone is welcome, but which one only attains by being there. By living in it.

"Dream dreams, then write them. Aye, but live them first!"

Samuel Eliot Morrison, Sailor Historian, 1887-1976

From a statue on Commonwealth Avenue, Boston, MA

Eric Wiberg '89 spent the 1991-92 academic year at Manchester College, Oxford.

Log Of *Chebec* Voyage

DUPLICATE, see *St. George's Bulletin*, summer 1992 *Chebec* Atlantic Crossing Down to the Sea in Ships, also Harris Manchester College Oxford *Mancunian*, 1992

Australian Tall Ship 'Young Endeavor'

Resembling a large bird with its wings tucked at its sides, the Australian training tall ship, "The Young Endeavour," welcomed a young Nassuvian aboard at Port Canaveral in Florida last week in preparation for its voyage to the Bahamas.

A gift from the United Kingdom to the people of Australia in 1988 in honor of their bicentennial celebration, the 44-meter (145 foot) brigantine has just begun the third and final leg of its first voyage around the world in commemoration of the voyages of discovery made by Christopher Columbus and J James Cook.

The 'Young Endeavour" is a traditional tall ship equipped with modem safety and comfort features. The actual sailing is still done manually. The crew consists of 24 select young men and women from around Australia led by a competent staff of eight Royal Australian navy crewmen and Commander Frank Allica. Due to arrive in Sydney, Australia, by Christmas, they have already sailed across the Indian and Atlantic oceans; often accompanied by other tall ships.

Thanks to an invitation from the Australian High Commission in Kingston, Jamaica, and Captain Allica, I was able to join the crew in Florida on Thursday, August 13. I was "hands-on" of their tallest mast, with its traditional "square-rig" yards.

Blue and white, with all its flags aflutter, the "Young Endeavour" is a beautiful and sturdy ship. Its decks are rich teak and its ten sails are a complex "web of power" hand hoisted by the crew.

The crew's smiles and genuine reception belies the strenuous job that they must perform onboard. On Friday morning, the crew

83

gathered for breakfast at 7am. After cleaning their bunks, all 33 hands and staff met for a briefing at 8am. The white Australian naval ensign was hoisted and the national anthem sung, followed by talks by the captain, navigator and executive officer.

We then spent an hour or more scrubbing, polishing and dusting the brass, wood, gallery and all. At 10am, with uniforms on and inspection complete we pushed off from Port Canaveral, Florida, for the Bahamas.

On Friday the vessel cruised south along Florida's East Coast, against the crew set sail and steered eastward across the Gulfstream for Grand Bahama. AH Friday night we sailed and by dawn were rearing Grand Bahama's West End light, making the North West Providence Channel.

"Young Endeavour's" crew spent Saturday setting and striking her massive main gaff topsail, and foresails according to the winds. We paused in the afternoon between the Berry Islands and Abaco's Hole to celebrate two birthdays — the captain and crew dined on ice cream and cake in the warm Bahamian sun.

By Saturday night we were passing massive cruise liners and heading south for Nassau. Sunday morning was brilliant and clear. Under full sail we plied the clear blue waters, hailing western New Providence on the horizon late in the morning.

After a peaceful religious service led by Commander Allica, complete with guitars

and songs, we began to "tack" along the Nassau Coast towards. All hands were on the deck to heave the sails and keep us off the reefs.

By 2:45pm all the sails were "doused" and tied up, and the brass was all shining. With the crew lining the tall yards of the square sails, we entered Nassau Harbour docking at the Prince George Wharf at 3pm, in Navy style.

There to greet us were the Australian High Commissioner and staff and the Dean of the Consular Corps and family members - one of whom (yours truly) was granted the highest mast perch!

"Young Endeavour's" crew have since performed a sea chanty pantomime for children at the Ranfurly Home and received dignitaries aboard. The ship welcomed visitors between one and

5pm daily, on Thursday, August 20, it left Nassau and sailed home to Australia via |he Caribbean and the Pacific. From their Bahamian hosts, "bon voyage!"

Harbour Island Visitor Gives First-Hand Account of Storm

By sundown on Sunday, August 23, Hurricane Andrew was just withdrawing its venomous barb, leaving Dunmore Town, Harbour Island, and the local inhabitants who had resolutely remained, to stagger in dismay through the strewn streets of the hurricane's first landfall.

"The island gone!" a passerby coming from the waterfront called up to my brothers and me as we huddled atop what was once the roof of Whale Villa, a wooden eighteenth-century Loyalist cottage near the waterfront.

The four or so hours of the hurricane's peak (from 3 to 7 pm) were marked in the mind's eye of a survivor by children held to the ground by their mother, chickens and roofs flying, windows shattering, barricades being torn free.

Venturing outside at the height of the hurricane to get the full story, my brother, John, 23, and I were regrettably caught in the midst of full winds and negative visibility. In the rescue of: a dog stranded in storm surges up to 20 feet high, we lashed ourselves and the dog to a wooden thatch umbrella dug into the sand.

If the hours before the hurricane had been marked by unspoken tension and barometric pressure so low that you had to struggle for air, then those hours following it were at once a sigh of relief and a shudder of dismay. In the feeble light of the fading sun, a tour of Harbour Island in the wake of the worst hurricane the oldest of the inhabitants could remember revealed the extent of its destruction.

The darkness of the first night was punctuated by lone flashlights and wailing women - marked by people walking arm in arm, silently, and others emerging from the wreckage calling names in the hope of joyous reunion.

Aside from the wailing wind and surf on either side, the only sounds came from a man in a fireman's hat hammering dosed, the provisions room of the Tip Top store from looters. Electricity, water, telephones, and provisions were all out.

What is most striking about Harbour Island after Hurricane Andrew is the almost complete' absence of foliage. The skyline of the island and of North Eleuthera in the distance is marked by a skyscape of shattered limbs and twigs groping towards the grey sky. The appearance is as much like the remains of a bomb blast as one can imagine; "more severe than New England in the dead of winter" one witness said. "I'll never see 'Briland in quite the same way" commented another, using Harbour Island's affectionate nickname.

From the water tower the panorama of destruction is complete. Many of the community's primary buildings were severely damaged by the winds, rains, and flying debris. The three primary churches each lost all or most of their roofs. At the peak of the hurricane, the commissioner's building was marked by its Bahamian flag, shredding in the wind.

Homes on the hilltop over the harbor lack windows and roofs.

Visible across what were once ornate gardens and groves of trees, however, most buildings remain standing. All that; visibly remains of Gusty's bar, on the hill overlooking the sand banks nuts: side the harbor, is its sole pool table, bereft of years and walls full of graffiti.

Surprising, considering the damage, is that apparently none of Harbour Island's 1300 or so residents were killed by the blast of winds gusting up to 200 mph. "It'll take more than that to kill off we 'Brilanders," exclaimed an elderly inhabitant.

Whale Villa, which my two young brothers, John and James, 19, were sent to defend with me, was bestrewn with wreckage. Gone were large sections of roof, an entire verandah, gates, fencing, ail coconut trees. The interior was splayed with chips of leaves and trees, ankle-deep in water, the ceiling seeping with water and leaving brown puddles of termite refuse in neat circles.

Beyond the villa, the damage was worse. Except for a few sheltered houses only partially damaged, most homes and the shoreline were critically struck. At points, more than half of Bay Street had been churned up and swept to sea. Open boats and sailing yachts alike were cast high above the water line. Tire island's fishing and ferry fleet lay scattered up the street, some in yards and on verandahs.

What had been Valentine's Marina was marked by lone poles, dockless, poking out of a soupy grey sea. Only the bottoms of overturned vessels marked a once busy fishing and diving haven. A propeller spun wistfully through the air behind a Boston Whaler on its side against the pilings.

The concrete government dock had been swept clear of awaiting cargoes; its gasoline pumps severed. Some 6,000 gallons of diesel were reported seeping from ruptured tanks into the historic harbor of the Bahamas' former capital. Every pier and dock on the island had been shattered to splinters and torn away. As during the days before Hurricane Andrew, after visitors and residents fled by air and sea, Harbour Island was completely cut off.

Though certainly no boats remained afloat on Harbour Island, and few places remained for vessels that visited late on Tuesday, the islanders were pleasantly surprised late Monday morning by the arrival of a Royal Navy helicopter. From the town's empty water tank high up a ladder, my brothers and I witnessed its tiny form enlarge and its rotors become audible as it swept from the East.

HMS Cardiff, Royal Navy Frigate with 280 sailors and commandos, had arrived to assist Harbour Island and North Eleuthera. The captain confidently anchored her outside the narrow cut off Whale Point, and the helicopter serviced the region with medical supplies, blankets, advice, and damage assessment before sending in teams of Navy personnel on landing craft.

Some of the commandos, men and women, actually emerged from the water in diving gear not far from Whale Villa, while we were at work clearing debris from the roof. Their assistance was much appreciated, especially as it was Harbour Island's only contact with the world beyond. This much we gathered when 'Brilanders outside

Vickhum's bar, mistaking Nassuvians for British sailors, asked us, "What can your country do for our little country?"

A cosmopolitan community inhabited by an international set during much of the winter, the island's residences from bungalow to seaside estate were equally hit. As one local 'Brilander put it, "the Big People get hit"

Along the island's famous 3- mile Pink Sands beach, the portly estates only just avoided being swept to sea by storm surges of up to 18 feet which lapped 100-feet and more up the shore, taking trees and debris and reportedly at least one dog. Their vacated homes were marked by shattered glass and highbrow books and framed paintings scattered along the shore.

Willie's Tavern sustained structural damage, as did Vickhum's, whose proprietor, nicknamed Hitler, could be seen doing repairs. Testament to the resilience of these islanders, Vickum's remained open virtually throughout, and what remains of Gusty's bar was opened by Tuesday evening.

BC Student Meets Hurricane Andrew in the Bahamas

Less than a week before I was due back at Boston College, my brothers and I faced the worst of Hurricane Andrew on the very site of its first landfall — Harbour Island, off the east coast of North Eleuthera, in the Bahamas.

Caught by surprise while on a weekend get-away, the three of us, all college students, secured our parents and sister on the last seats of evacuating airplanes home to Nassau. All boats had already fled. The island was cut off.

Harbour Island, the former capital of the Bahamas, is a small town of roughly 1,000 residents where a cosmopolitan set from North America and Europe assemble in the winter months. Resigned to our fate, we retreated into the quaint 150-year-old wooden cottage, which we were meant to defend.

By Sunday, August 23, Hurricane Andrew, which is now known as the costliest hurricane to hit North America, was bearing down on us at a rate of up to 18 miles an hour. In preparation, we sealed most windows and doors with sheets of wood and stockpiled candles, water jugs and what food we could find. Then, we waited.

Winds were predicted at 150 mph and seas surged to 18 feet. The island was astir with fear. The sound of hammering shook residents from Sunday morning sleep.

In the deathly calm before the storm, the three of us wandered through the town to the east side of the island, famous for its natural pink sand beach, a full three miles long. There, with a stray dog for company, we watched a sickly confused sea, awash with sand for miles from the shore.

The troughs of the waves were so extreme that gnarled tops of reefs were epodes to the air as though fangs were being bared. Nursing a jug of rum punch, we watched the hurricane heading directly for us and rolling in from the North Atlantic Ocean.

By mid-afternoon we were being lashed with rain and gathering winds. We retreated into the cottage as trees began to sway and the first of the debris began to fly. Within an hour the hurricane had begun to pummel the settlement with its full force. During a telephone interview with the Bahamas Tribune newspaper, telephone lines, electricity and water were all out.

Hurricane Andrew arrived sooner than expected. Though the sky had become a dusky grey, daylight remained. Thinking it was yet to grow, my older brother and I ventured outside and across the island to witness the destruction first hand. Lashing ourselves together, and wrapped in plastic garbage bags, we weaved through streets already strewn with tree limbs, bricks and planks of wood.

As the hurricane gained velocity, we staggered across the island to the coast. There the ocean's devastating surge became apparent, In walls of sea over 20 feet high, storm surges swept 100 feet across the beach and up into the dunes, grasping foundations of seaside homes and tearing away clumps of earth, trees and anything in the way.

It was along the treacherous shore that we witnessed the same stray dog, a mutt, struggling anxiously to regain the dunes from the beach, where it had been swept by the surge. Lashing himself to a wooden piling, which once held a thatched roof umbrella, my brother struggled into the surf to rescue him. I stayed ashore, managing a photograph.

With the dog in tow, we made our way back to the harbor, evading toppling trees as we went. By then, chickens were being swept away by the wind; coconut trees were leaning almost horizontally.

A woman struggling from her shattered home had to hold her children to the ground. Later she was overheard attributing her children's lives to her matronly obesity!

By the time we made it to the harbor, our "excursion" left us with one desperate option – we had to struggle to return to the cottage, which our younger brother was trying to hold together.

The route was not an easy one. The local marina was being lashed with salt spray, the seas had risen above the docks and were tearing them apart.

Of the half dozen or so boats not brought ashore, all had torn their moorings, and three were being battered relentlessly against what remained of the docks. All that was visible of one, on its side half submerged, was its propeller spinning wistfully in the wind.

Gathering up the dog, we virtually crawled along the harbor road, ducking behind barricades as sheets of wood and roof came hurtling through the air, threatening to dissect us. We were knee deep in tidal surge, with half of the road swept out to sea at a crucial section before our cottage. We pressed onto the cottage.

From the cottage, the three of us, and our adopted dog watched the hurricane reach a pitch. The beautiful garden was uprooted and swept away. Whole trees – coconut, mango, and lime alike were flattened and uprooted.

The gate to the cottage was smashed down, its awnings and fencing torn away, the balcony and verandah sent into the neighbor's lawn. Ultimately sections of our own roof were ripped off in chunks, leaving us staring at either grey sky or a ceiling fan undulating as the wind sucked at the house.

Windows were blown in and rain pelted the cottage's interior through cracks at all angles. Puddles of water formed around our ankles as we struggled to hold the place together, finally retreating to the smallest, most secure room, with water, candles and fruit. Few or no houses in the Bahamas have basements, and so this was not an option for refuge.

By midnight Hurricane Andrew was withdrawing its venomous barb, heading west across the Bahamas towards Florida. Exhausted, we slept.

The chop of helicopter motors awoke us the following morning. The British Royal Navy Frigate HMS *Cardiff*, with 280 sailors and a support vessel, had come up behind the storm to bring relief supplies.

They had clocked the wind for 10 seconds at 240 mph, and sent a chopper laden with medical supplies and body bags. But, as one elderly resident told me, "It'll take more than that to kill we 'brilanders'!" (A nickname for Harbour Islanders – tough and resilient island people).

Although as many as six persons died in North Eleuthera as a result of Hurricane Andrew, all Harbour Islanders amazingly survived.

The same cannot be said of the historic town. Every dock and pier in the harbor had been submerged, the wood smashed to splinters. The concrete government dock had its gas machines swept away, and form a nearby marina, 6,000 gallons of diesel seeped into the harbor. The view across the water was marked lone poles and wrecked boats poking out of a soupy grey sea. Across the island, houses and churches, roofless, stood stark against a steely blue sky.

In the wake of the worst hurricane, at least in living memory, Harbour Island is virtually barren of foliage – "worse than New England in the dead of winter," commented one visitor of a vista that had once been tropical gardens cloistered around villas and lit up by the turquoise blue sea.

Around the portly-estates of winter-residents, high-0brow books, Caribbean paintings, board games, furniture are scattered. Harbor Island and one dazed BC student will never be the same.

Amid the wreckage of the hurricane, however, are signs of recovery – Bahamian style.

Though all that remains of one-half of Gusty's Seaview bar is an exposed pool table on a concrete slab, the proprietor, Gusty, could be found inside selling beer while he cleaned up.

Vickhum's the local 'hang' resiliently remained open throughout. The running joke, in the days following Hurricane Andrew as we were all cut off entirely from all but British sailors and commandos, who would be the first to print the T-shirt reading, "I got blown by Hurricane Andrew!"

BC Admissions Thrives Despite Recession

Records indicate that the 2,215 incoming students of the Class of 1996 are Boston College's most diverse freshman class, with a record of 20.6 percent AHANA students and 3 percent international students registered, just below the national average.

John L. Mahoney, director of Undergraduate Admissions, expressed satisfaction with the number of applicants and their national diversity.

At a time when many colleges are struggling to attract applicants, 12,283 prospective students applied to BC, which is seven percent more than applicants last year. This statistic is approximately six times the available spaces for students.

Attributing the strong number of applicants to the "very aggressive recruiting practices'" of him and his staff, Mahoney cited a strong network of BC admissions aids who operate nationally and with youth, programs in urban centers.

"Geographically, we received a very good response," Mahoney said, noting that regions such as Florida, California and Texas are-represented especially well.

Mahoney cited BC's growing national reputation, spread in part by nationally televised sporting events such as football, as another contributing, to the University's popularity.

"Our business is promoting BC. You can't buy that publicity," Mahoney said of the football exposure.

Academically, Mahoney felt that the caliber of incoming students is "as strong if not stronger than in past years."

On the scale commonly used, the range of SAT scores for the middle 50 percent of the incoming class is between 1140 and 1270 out of a possible 1600. At least 25 percent of the incoming, freshmen received scores above 1270.

Mahoney, also cited the infusion into BC of approximately 100 transfer students annually, which he saw as a positive grafting of university experiences.

Referring to the high percentage of incoming AHANA students, Mahoney said, "This is the first time in BC's history that we have reached the 20 percent mark."

Mahoney stressed that BC's graduation rate is very high compared to that of other universities.

Both Mahoney and Richard Escobar, director of International Admissions, acknowledge that BC must continue to diversify in order to keep up with an increasingly diverse and multicultural America.

While having witnessed tremendous progress towards diversification during his 14-year tenure, Escobar conceded that Boston College is not yet demographically equal with the rest of the country.

"It doesn't mean that we can rest on our laurels," Escobar said. While "excited" by the diversity of incoming students, Escobar expressed concern over a drop in international student enrollment. Sixty-six international students from 32 nations, however, join the Class of 1996.

The progress could be as strong as with AHANA student admissions, Escobar said, if international admissions were increased.

Escobar noted that, unlike many other colleges and universities, BC does not attend international recruitment fairs.

While this fall the admissions staff, including Mahoney and Escobar; will be roaming the United States promoting BC, the University has no active international recruitment policy. Currently it is handled almost entirely through "word of mouth."

On the national front, however, Mahoney is intent that he and his staff "will continue our aggressive tactics of recruit-ment."

Editorial on the L.A. Riots [Missing]

This article was published in fall 1992.

Studying Abroad Heights

This fall, approximately 200 Boston College seniors returned from a semester of Junior Year Abroad in countries as varied as France, Nepal, England and Australia. Having participated in a number of programs through Boston College's Junior Year Abroad Office, now the Foreign Study Office, students returned to BC. Some students are relieved to be "home," while others still miss life "abroad." "Many of the students come back [to BC] determined to return to their host country, if only to visit," said Veronica Jijon-Camaano, A&S '93, a spokesperson for the Foreign Study Office. The FSO, in Gasson Hall, is operated by Professor James Flagg and Margaret Ramirez. Jijon-Camaano studied for a summer in Kenya and during her junior year in Cork, Ireland. She summarized that 89 students spent the full academic year of 1991-92, while more than 100 spent at least one semester abroad.

In contrast, only 44 juniors have gone abroad for the entire academic year 1992-93. Junior year has traditionally been a popular time for students to study abroad, due to constraints on housing at BC during junior year. Jijon-Camaano said that after spending time abroad, students who return as seniors must readjust to campus life. Boston College offers several programs of its own, in Cork, Ireland, Leuven, Belgium, Oxford, England, Japan, Strasbourg, France and now Tokyo. Many students, however, arrange their studies through other universities or organizations such the Institute for European Studies, and the Institute for Asian Studies, which includes Australia.

According to Jijon-Camaano, the most popular destinations have been France, Spain, Italy, England and Ireland. However, seniors have returned from Lithuania, Czechoslovakia, Austria, Kenya, Nepal, Bali, Korea and Australia. This year there are BC students in Columbia, Argentina, Costa Rica, South Africa, India, Greece and Scotland. Traditionally, students receive full or at least partial credits at BC for their academic work overseas, if previous preparations were made.

While the study of a foreign language is often an integral part of an education abroad, it often incorporates a variety of interests. Linguistic, cultural and historical studies are often a premise;

However, students also tackle a variety of topics, from theology to ecology and wildlife management, which Lauri Maher, A&S '93, Shannon Moore, A&S '93, Susanna Gaunt, A&S '93 and Jijon-Camaano studied in Kenya, East Africa. "A lot of what one learns from living abroad happens outside the classroom," Jijon-Camaano said. "Many students cherish their time abroad, especially those who might otherwise have not left the U.S." Concerning admission to FSO programs, she stated that "It is not as difficult a process as they might have thought." Another integral part of being abroad seems to have been travel, with many students spending their vacations "Eurailing" through Europe or around the host country. Others, like Richard Walsh, A&S '93, and Thomas Lacy, A&S '93, who were both at Oxford through BC's Honors Program, spent vacation time traveling through more exotic places. Lacy visited the Middle East and Walsh traveled to South East Asia.

In Europe, and especially in cultural hubs such as Paris or Madrid, BC students were often able to get in touch with one another. Some, like Stephen D'Alessandro, A&S '93, Julie Fish, A&S '93, and Devon Sheldon, A&S '93, who studied in France, became so immersed in the foreign culture that they did not want to return. While D'Alessandro found it difficult to return to BC and surrender the independence he savored in Paris, Fish and Sheldon experienced more of an immediate "culture shock." They spent second semester together in Aix-en-Provence, a "temperate, reasonably small European city" in southern France, walking, hiking on Mt. Saint Victoire. "We appreciated the daily details, the food and wine, the easy-going ambiance," Fish said.

In contrast, their return to the U.S. was characterized by aggressive officials and lost luggage in the turnstiles at New York's JFK airport. While Fish had most of the summer to readjust to American life, she returned to BC somewhat "disillusioned" with the contrast in education in the U.S., missing the less structured French environment. "Everything seemed to work itself out and I questioned students' motivation in the U.S. in comparison," Fish said. In contrast, Jijon-Camaano felt that her classes in Cork, Ireland were larger and included less student participation than at BC. "I didn't like BC as much during my first two years, but after

Junior Year Abroad, it definitely makes it better to be back here," said Steve M., A&S '93, who returned from a year at Manchester College, Oxford. John Carroll, A&S '93, spent his junior year at BC and studied abroad at Leuven, Belgium during the summer. "Although while you are living there [in Europe] and traveling, you feel that it's the greatest, but it's always nice to get back to the life you missed," he said. "I mean, no one in the world lives as well as we do here." Many students who studied abroad felt a "bond" established with others who studied abroad. "It's not a conspicuous bond," Fish said, "but it's definitely there." Though certainly not an exclusive experience, BC students who ventured out around the world during their junior year bring back a whole range of impressions from months of cultural fusion. Flagg and Ramirez of the Foreign Study Office expressed pleasure and relief that last year's students have all returned safely, and have shared in welcoming those returning to BC.

Eric's Guide to the Jitneys

Jitney buses are if not the most convenient, then certainly the cheapest (75¢) and most uniquely Bahamian way to move between Nassau, Cable Beach, and Paradise Island Bridge for visitors to Nassau. "Jitney" is a broad term for the large white buses which dash between destinations on the island, often to the beat of calypso or reggae.

Jitney-buses are almost all Nissan Civilian in make, white with trim, privately or company-owned (with meters) and have been recognized or subsidized and organized by the government and traffic wardens, and are seen as a more efficient and safe option than costly cabs or rental cars.

In Nassau. the Jitney driver will send agents onto the streets to encourage visitors aboard. It's alright to follow them, as the standard fare cannot exceed 75¢, 50¢ for children. Note, however, that the driver is not allowed to give change. Times during which Jitneys are allowed to run are be-tween 6 A.M. and 8 P.M. daily. There is no set time schedule, however, and the wait can vary.

There are many bus stops scattered along routes, dropping visitors at nearby attractions such as Adastra Gardens, Coral

World. the Queen's Staircase, and the Bacardi Rum distillery plant on Inichael Road. To get to the resort and casino area of Cable Beach about five miles west of downtown Nassau, visitors can meet a #10 Jitney at Navy Lyon Road, directly beneath the Sheraton British Colonial Hotel (the massive pink building at the end of Bay Street). Between Nassau and Cable Beach, Jitneys will make various stops along the way, dropping visitors off at the hotel of their choice. They then turn around and carry visitors back to town along the same, or slightly longer, route behind town. The return route is often more interesting to visitors, as it carries them through parts of Nassau they would not otherwise normally see.

Visitors hoping to travel inexpen-sively between downtown Nassau and the renowned resort casino and beach area of Paradise Island can just step aboard a Jitney bus on Frederick Street, which is just off Bay Street in downtown Nassau. The buses labeled Kemp Road (#6) and Carmichael Road carry passengers to the base of Para disc Island Bridge.

Eric's Guide to Mailboats

It can seem difficult to believe, when visiting the Bahamas, that Nassau and Freeport are but two of more than two thousand Family Islands in the Bahamian archipelago. Many beautiful and rustic islands are within a day's voyage by the cheapest and most unique Bahamian way; by mailboat. These sizeable freighters, complete with galleys and cabins for passengers, depart from Potter's Cay Dock, beneath the Paradise island Bridge, in Nassau, on a daily basis. Voyages tend to last from 2-3 days and cost roughly. $20 per person.

A fleet of 25 mailboats Service some 50 islands and almost 100 settlements. Mailboats are still as rustic and alive with [1] local color as ever, while retaining a very liveable and comfortable shipboard environment. Cabins with cleaned bunks are [1] customary on overnight voyages, and often three hot meals are served per day to all passengers.

The overall cost of mailboat travel is what may draw many travelers. An overnight or day-long passage, for example, will rarely exceed $20 in cost; an extra $5 guarantees a bunk. You may choose .to voyage from Nassau to another point for several days before returning, or follow the full mailboat route at one go, a gratifying excursion. Prices for such excursions can Often be worked out in person with the captain of the ship. Because the primary function of mailboats is delivery of freight, goods, and people (a choir, for example - or pews!) among settlements, the traveler is allowed to savor a certain genuine independence.

To procure yourself a 'berth' on a mailboat, start by reading the schedule in *What's On*. You can call the Dock Master's office at 393 -1064 or stop in there for information; it is a yellow building to the right of the bridge on Potter's Cay Dock, under the Paradise Island Bridge (approachable from Nassau by Jitney). You may want to familiarize yourself with the boat and captain you choose. They are often accessible, friendly, and informative.

The experience of voyaging by mailboat in the Bahamas is a memorable and often uplifting one. After all, there's nothing like leaning over the bow of a vessel laden with bricks, boats, cars, fruit, goats and mail, gazing at starfish or plankton, to the sound of gospel hymns being sung!

Eric's Guide to the Paradise Island Ferry

Because Jitneys cannot deliver passengers through the toll-booth on the Paradise Island side of the bridge, some visitors may prefer to take the more direct route to the beaches there. This is possible by the Paradise land Ferry system, which ferries from Nassau to Paradise Island every 20 minutes from dawn till dusk (6A.M. to 8 P.M.) at a cost of $2 per person.

The Paradise Island ferry service carries passengers from along the Prince George Wharf behind the Straw Market across Nassau Harbour to two destinations on Paradise Island. The two docks are beside the Club Med estate, a short walk from the Paradise Island beach and cove, and further down at the base of the Paradise Island Bridge, nearer the casino.

These ferries, which operate under tantalizing names like "Paradise Express", "Grand Adventure", and "Rainbow Snapper", and "Blanche Louise" (Capt. Willie Brown) are skippered by competent Bahamian ferrymen, who may also provide guitar music while you wait. Besides merely ferrying passengers, they offer a scenic route across the historic harbor, around the Sheraton British Colonial Beach, under the cruise ships, and past the shipping piers.

Harbour Island Recovers from Andrew

Nearly five months after Hurricane Andrew lashed ashore at Harbour Island, North Eleuthera, and lay waste to 60 years of relative tranquility in fewer than 6 hours, all but one of the town's resort facilities are back in operation. Though all major—facilities except the Pink Sands Hotel were re-opened by Christmas, the island and its people - especially the fo ge, are still in a long process of ecovery.

As-Clayton_ugmen, a local schoolteacher and leader of the Harbour Island Hurricane Relief Committee put it - "basically we suffered a very bad storm which hurt the island aesthetically, but hasn't destroyed it. Harbour Island offers what it offered before in every category." While power, water and telephone service has taken some residents up to four months to regain, access to and from Harbour Island was restored almost immediately after the hurricane.

The airport on North Eleuthera, which services the worst-hit settlements of Current, Spanish Wells, and the Bluff as well, was reopened within days of the

Hurricane. The ferry service from the airport to Harbour Island was also restored. Mailboat and shipping freight service is also fully restored, with four vessels departing at 7 A.M. Thursdays to service the region.

Of equal importance in terms of access to Harbour Island are the number of slips available to visiting yachts. Although virtually every dock on the marina except the government pier was shattered in storm surges of 18 feet, the primary docking facility at Valentine's Yacht Club and Inn is scheduled to have a capacity 39 slips completed within 6 weeks.

Hurricane Andrew plowed across Dunmore Town, Harbour Island, former capital of the Bahamas, on August 23, 1992.

Harbour Island, or Briland for short, lies East of North Eleuthera. The island sustains a permanent population of roughly 1,500 residents. Its economy is based primarilly on a winter influx of tourists and land-owners, and profits from a small fishing fleet.

The August hurricane destroyed most docks on the harbor and damaged virtually every property on the island. Most of the small boats have been back in operation for months, however, and repairs to buildings continues. Last December, a large fleet of yachts and vessels called in at Briland during Christmas and New Year. Fewer, however, than usual.

Yet as the work to restore Harbour Island continues, as the people and On 11 January Valentine's dockmaster Peter Anderson affirmed that 8 slips were in use, with 14 larger ones due to have power within a week. "We are ope and running, alive and well," affirmed Anderson, who contracted marine ngineers under Hi s of Spanish Wells to effect repairs to the renown marina and dive shop! ather than simply repair, Anderson plans to upgrade Valentine's with 3-phase, 100-amp. power and become "the onl marin in the Family Islands with this capability."

Valentine's has also strengthened the new docks and anticipates a strong showing this spring, when large fishing yachts base themselves there. "From May to August we'll be hard-pressed to fit a canoe in here!" , commented Anderson; "as the season continuesj I have to strongly recommend yachts to make reservations.n All 21 rooms and two restaurant/bar facilities have reopened.

The same recovery has characterised several of the resort facilities on Harbour Island. The Ramora Bay Club, Dunmore Beach Club, the Harbour Lounge, and all of the local 'watering holes' have put themselves back together during the autumn months, which are usually spent in restoration anyway. In order to peedily rebuild the Dunmore Beach Club, along the island's Pink Sands Beach's owner had to charter air cargo service to bring in needed items.

Dunmore Beach has also extended its deck over the beach, which had over 50eet eroded during the hurricane. Dr. Steve Leatherm n, a marine scientist specialising in disaster-struck coasts, noted that Pink Sands Beach is recovering daily. "Recovery bars of sand are coming back. There is new berm, and it is shallow offshore. It's still one of the nicest beaches in the world, and I've seen many," Leatherman said.

In an interview at the Ocean View Club, owned by Pippa Simmons and partmanaged by Clayton Johnson, Johnson asserted that returning tourists have been pleased; "there is a general feeling that tourists are happy. We don't want travel agents and others to paint a black us, or draw black arrows through North Eleuthera indicating 'keep out'". This was reportedly done. Noting that Christmas crowds were about a third of what they had been, Johnson feels that

't bad media has probably hurt the island more than it deserved."

The general goals of the Harbour Island Hurricane Relief Committee, which is headed by eight members and meets once or more weekly, is to restore ihe island's tourism product and then the infrastructure which thrives off of that product. With this in mind, resorts received priority attention, followed by public facilities and private homes. Restoration has been underway on primary buildings since the hurricane. As a result much of the power and water is running, but many churches and the Commissioher's office are still undergoing repairs. After months of intermittent repairs, most of the the schoolrooms of the island's Primary School are back in operation.

The Committee has worked with relief forces from the British Navy, the Royal Bahamas Defence Force, and the United States Sea Bees engineers. They have received aid in the forms of water, clothes, volunteers, and plants. A recent shipment of flowers arrived from the American Women ᶠs Club, and Johnson expects a new wave of volunteers, many of them Methodists, to arrive in mid January.

Supplies trickle in and the structural face-lift nears completion, one element of the disaster's legacy remains painfully visible. Hurricane Andrew miraculously killed no Brilanders. But it seems to have killed or damaged about every living plant. Some said the island stripped of foliage made it seem denuded, others like winter skyscape.

As Howard J. Seigel, an expatriate landowner and instigator of the Harbour Island Hurricane Relief Fund, writes in a fund-raising letter of Sept. 4, 1992, "The truly horrible damage was what happened to the Island vegetation ...there are few tourists who are going to want to spend their hard earned money to look at a scene that will remind them of Dresden during World War II". With this in mind, natural Seigel beauty. and One-landowner others hN2Bde iéportedly a determined insured his bid coconut to restore trees, Briland and to has itshad his entire grove underwritten and replanted. Others were not so fortunate.

The villas in the historical town have beern stripped of protective buffers of vegetation which had offered cloistered privacy and muffled sounds. The carefully manicured gardens, bountiful fruit trees, and palm groves which had once characterised Dunmore Town have been mangled or uprooted. Most of the stalwart old trees, timeless meeting places, have remained standing, if more barren.

There is hope, however, as Siegel expressed in his letter; "there is absolutely no doubt that rain will help to green the island. The beach is still there, the air is still clean and the color of the ocean can still make you smile." Clayton Johnson pointed out that the beach is now substantially wider, and that nitrogen deposits left by hurricanes encourage growth. "Herman", longtime Briland local fisherman, was not so fazed by the storm, taking it in fisherman's stride and continuing with his work, Many, however, were left homeless by Hurricane Andrew, if only temporarily.

The hurricane has kept most Harbour Islanders, or 'Brilanders', busy. "There has been no job shortage," asserted Johnson. Many Brilanders have hardly been able to leave the island since the disaster, but have concentrated upon Dunmore Town in its hour of need. "Elvis", a Brilander educated in Nassau who runs his own trucking and dumping business, has never been busier. He asserted that since the hurricane he has been working "dawn to dusk" gathering debris and trucking it to the town dump, north west of town.

Elvis's brother, nicknamed "Hitler", is the proprietor of Vickhum's Bar, an all day, all-night gathering spot. AS expressed genuine optimism about Harbour Island emerging from the hurricane, noting that two wealthy investors had just purchased large plots of land on the island's northern end. He anticipates greater unity and even prosperity in the future. "We sure aren't dead!" he said, from across the bar. No, far from it.

23-Year-Old Nassuvian Skippers 70' Sailing Yacht Across the Pacific

Stornoway's voyage westwards — essentially from one boatyard (in the U.S.) to another (in New Zealand)—was often impeded and at times almost abandoned. The Christmas and New Year's season of 1994 found *Stornoway* laying disconsolately in the Galapagos Islands, off South America, with only the owners and Wiberg aboard. The options facing them were few and stark.

They had no captain. The hull was showing signs of leakage, and the dreaded cyclone season bore down on them daily. A lightning bolt had scrambled valuable electrical gear, including automatic steering. They would need hands, and more than three pairs of them. Their insurance was revoked. And they had a South American navy breathing down their backs.

In a desperate bid to wrest his prized yacht from seizure by the local port. captain, the owner, appointed Wiberg as acting captain, responsible for recruiting and training needed crew, navigating, sailing, and delegating watch-system and emergency duties.

With 7,000 more miles of open ocean between they and the repairs awaiting *Stornoway* m New Zealand, Wiberg assumed his first command.

What follows is Eric's account of how *Stornoway* and her meager crew ended up in their Galapagos predicament, and, more importantly, how they sailed their way out of it.

Smoke and soul wafted around my older brother and I as we sat in Mr. Nesbitt's bar in Delaport, on the fringe of Cable Beach. The ice in our drinks was melting fast, but we weren't bothered. It was the last night of November 1993, and I was about to ship out to sea once more, for the longest in my 23 years.

We were in earnest conversation. I lay my concerns out on the table like pieces of tangled driftwood: "I mean, it's a big ocean out there. A long time. A lot can happen, they may *ask me to become Captain.*"

The solace of Otis and Aretha from the jukebox, the comfort of familiar faces, the buzz of conversation, all seemed to recede before that word: Captain. Virtually unutterable among young sailing crew except as a term of address — or of conspired mutiny.

John and I talked about *Stornoway*, that stately sheer of dark blue and stained wood, the majestic outline of her masts, forming the yacht which we had both gone to admire in Nassau harbor. We'd both been sailing awhile, but the very size of *Stornoway,* and the scope of her voyage, was beyond what either of us had faced.

"Don't do it, Eric," he said, "...it's too much, *too soon. Don't let 'em even ask you...*" Though I had to agree, I also felt a restless excitement: it would be a fine way to cap off a steady progression: six summers' worth of working my way from bilge-boy to watch-captain. I had the sailing bug that fall. I'd had it bad since graduating from college in May, and even another Bermuda Race and a yacht delivery (through the

Sargasso Sea from New England to the Bahamas) that summer hadn't satiated me.

I first spotted *Stornoway* on my flight home from a decade of schooling in New England and England. As our plane swooped down Nassau harbor towards Paradise Island, her proud figure briefly filled my portal. I would fulfill my burning again. The following day I was by the yacht's side at the Nassau Harbor Club for a closer look and to learn as much as I could of her.

Stornoway was hand crafted out of Burma teak in her port of registry, Greenock, Scotland, more than thirty years ago. Her owner of fifteen years, Chris, is near twice as old as *Stornoway.* He and the ship's chef, an Italian-Australian woman named Pina, had just spent four years, in Florida preparing for the voyage.

They were bound for Chris' birthplace of New Zealand; two large islands, which lie, nudged between Antarctica and Australia. Theirs promised to be a rare undertaking: sometimes tip-toeing, at others barreling, across an expanse of ocean twenty million square miles in breadth: the Pacific, the largest and among the least populated, watery regions of the world.

In October my brother and I saw *Stornoway* off as she made for; Panama via Jamaica. Already her crew, selected at the last minute, was causing concern aboard. I gave Chris arid Pina my sailing resume, and my brother and I walked away.

Late that November, a fax machine on Cable Beach hummed with a tantalizing offer. The letterhead read S/Y *Stornoway*, Greenock. the sending station was Balboa, Panama. The message, marked URGENT, was brief:

Eric - We've studied your sailing file again, and would like you to join us as First Mate of *Stornoway*, effective on acceptance.

Weekly wage, flight down to Panama, return airfare from New Zealand. Yon will have your own cabin, 'head' (toilet area), and crew to administer. Original mate to be sent home. Plan to push off within the week.

Ports-of-call: Panama, the Galapagos Islands, the Marquesas, Bora-Bora, and Papeete, Tahiti, in French Polynesia. Then the Southern Cook Islands, Kingdom of Tonga, Fiji, and the Bay of Islands, finishing in Auckland, New Zealand, hopefully before the cyclones!

For the "voyage of a lifetime", please respond ASAP. Yours, Chris, Panama.

Tahiti? Galapagos? Marquesas? Islands to an island boy, they sounded so exotic – the offer almost too good to be true. As a student and a dreaming sailor, I had long conspired to hit the highways and sea-ways of the world...

I packed my gear, backed out of a power-yacht job in Palm Beach, Fla., and trundled off to Central America. On the first of December, I landed in the rainy season in Panama City, a capital of coups, and signed aboard.

Right away, as we lay moored under (the Bridge of the Americas, at the Pacific

entrance of the Panama Canal, the power structure aboard was thoroughly shaken. I clung on tenaciously as first the mate, then the crew, and finally *Stornoway's* second skipper packed it in and flew home.

They were told that the voyage was off, that the yacht would be mothballed. But no sooner had they left, in the first of December, than a new captain— veteran sailor Keith—whisked aboard in a flurry and readied us to get underway.

After an overnight 'shakedown' sail to the Taboga Cays, and several weeks spent tinkering with the gear and partying with Canal 'Zonies,' yachties, and Panamanians, the four of us slipped out of the Balboa yacht under cover of bound 800 miles westwards, for the Galapagos Islands, astride the Equator.

The morning of Christmas Eve broke full and clear over us six days later, as *Stornoway* made her approach to our first Pacific landfall. Tradition called for Equator-crossing celebrations, and, as the youngest, I was selected to be the 'Equatorial Virgin', crossing the seams of the earth by sea for the first time.

Dressed as 'the Jailor' in stuffed stockings, Chris roused me from my off watch slumber in the forward most cabin, handcuffed me, and led me aft, to the transom, where I was tried and condemned as the 'virgin' by a costumed 'King Neptune' (Keith), and forced to pay homage to an all-but topless Queen Nefertiti: Pina!

After dousings of food and a feast of fresh-caught fish, we sluiced our way around the island of Santa Cruz and sailed up into Academy Bay, home of the Charles Darwin

Research Station. Nestled among passenger ships and yachts, we dropped two 'hooks', or anchors, folded our wings, and settled down for a week of Yuletide festivities.

We spent the followings days languishing aboard, among nearby islands, or along Tortuga Beach. We swam with playful sea-lions, dared a dip among the sharks, plodded with the tortoises, mimicked the penguins, and dove from the ravines. We celebrated Christmas, Pina's Birthday, and New Year's aboard a decked-out and Christmas lit *Stornoway*, harnessing Pina's cat and letting him roam the decks.

The drums of Junkanoo were replaced by the palpitations of Latin music in the sultry heat, and I ushered in the dawn of the New Year not on Bay Street or Harbour Island, but in a sunbaked Galapagos cafe after partying the morning away at the British Consul's home and the local discos.

Despite all the excitement, though, all did not bode well aboard Our 'magic carpet' ride and the security of yacht and team would soon be whisked from beneath us

The first days of the New Year found us aground in Wreck Bay, our trusty captain stuffing his bags and jumping ship in a flurry of angry recriminations and sexual jealousies, leaving Chris, Pina, and I, in the hands of a militant South American Navy, stranded on the equator, without a certified captain or the means to fly one in.

The Ecuadorian Navy were I threatening to have us to wed to Guayaquil, 1,000 miles

to the East Beneath us reefs, around us insidious water seeped in. To the West lay some 4,000 miles of open-ocean to the Marquesas—the most remote islands in the world.

Chris needed someone who could, and was willing to, navigate across that blue eternity, the mysterious, barren eastern Pacific about which we knew so little. Though not licensed, I had the most sailing experience. I offered my services as navigator and, if needed, as captain.

Chris accepted, and on that first week of January, when cleared in (by the insurers) and called forward from the consolation of the back bench to the trials of the 'hot seat M responded duly. Bucking eager outwardly, somberly scared within, I stepped up to assume my first command.

"*I wanted a mission,*" muses Captain Willard in the opening scenes of Coppola's film APOCALYPSE NOW, "*and for my sins, they gave me one. And when it was over,*" he continues, "*I knew I never wanted another.*"

Nassuvian Skippers Sailing Yacht, Part II

In the last issue of "What's On" (Jan. '95) I left off the narrative in suspense, as I stepped up from the comfort of my position as mate to assume my first command, as captain of the 70-foot classic sailing ketch *Stornoway* bound across the Pacific to New Zealand. Ahead of us (the owner, Chris, the chef, Pina, a cat, and myself) lay our longest passage: some 3,000+ miles to the Marquesas Islands.

The first week of my command found me frazzled and exasperated in Wreck Bay, on San Cristobal, capital of the

Galapagos Islands. New Year's 1994 and a skipper had come and gone. The Ecuadorian Navy was threatening to impound and confiscate *Stornoway* if we lingered, but we needed crew to continue.

While sitting in my favorite cafe, studying a file of crew resumes faxed to me from the Caribbean, I grew frustrated by the paperwork. Looking up, I finally just called over to a nearby table, which was filled with travelers: *"Anyone want to sail to New Zealand?"* A young man blurted back: *"Sure. I'll go!"* but the girl sitting beside him grabbed his arm with a firm *"You will not!"*

He couldn't, but he introduced me to another traveler who might. In khaki and a beard, Trevor made a fine impression. He is my age, and also a recent college graduate. We sped out to *Stornoway* in the dingy. He came aboard with me and met Pina, topless on deck, and, Chris, who he also liked.

I exercised my full authority to recruit him aboard as our needed fourth crewman, to man the wheel and satisfy the insurers. Though slated to return to his travels and family in Vancouver, Trevor joined us. On the spot. A brave man. We'd found our fourth: Chris is an amiable gentleman who with Pina and their cat, Davie, made a triumvirate. Now I had a comrade too.

We spent two more weeks tinkering in the Galapagos. I taught Trevor as much as he'd need to know while I 'crammed' studying *Stornoway's* complex systems and navigational gear. Then we fumigated the hold of roaches and readied to set off on our longest passage - to the Marquesas, in French Polynesia.

On the 23rd of January we pulled *Stornoway's* anchors and headed out to sea. Right away there was trouble down below. We were taking on alarming levels of water through the seams of *Stornoway's* 30-year-old teakwood hull. For weeks, even months, there would be no land.

On Chris' suggestion I agreed to sail us to the nearest anchorage, on Santa Maria Island. It was hairy. After a nighttime approach on an unfamiliar, barely charted shore, we anchored in the historic whaling depot of Post Office Bay, where sailors can still leave letters in an old barrel to be carried on for free. In the morning we saw just how close we'd come to foundering in the reef-strewn bay. I alone discovered, a smudge of our paint on one of them. So close to disaster. I kept quiet.

We bribed a local official with cigarettes and hunkered down to repairs. Two nights at anchor, with flamingos, turtles, fish and lobster everywhere. I practiced the mysterious, ancient art of celestial navigation, tutored by a Chilean Navy officer. We had a universe of constellations to 'shoot' sights of with a sextant. Having tightened the bolts attaching keel to our hull, we were ready.

Our first offshore passage together, and Trevor's first ever, was massive. After eight days and a few flare-ups between Chris and I (shifting the power-structure: his boat, my command, and thus my 'ass on the line'...), we hove-to, coming to an eerie halt. I called for a mid-passage swim, a skipper's and crews' tradition meant to boost morale. It would prove a dangerous exercise.

We were clocking a smart 200 miles daily and crossed our third time zone since Panama. 1500 miles from the Galapagos, we stopped in about the most remote spot in the world. The fabled Marquesas Islands are farther from a continent than any others. Halfway to the ends of the earth can be a lonely place.

To keep your cool when you know you're in the middle of friggin' nowhere and that you're accountable for the lives of four people and your employer's property, insured in the 7-digit range, takes effort. That passage in particular is known for its dangers - freight containers floating just beneath the surface, whales striking the hull in unexplained aggression... silent killers for which there is no warning, little recourse for help, very little time, and a long way to drift if you are sunk. I was one scared puppy, but I kept it to myself. We all did.

We made the Marquesas Islands in an almost record 17 days, swinging into glorious Taiohae Bay, Nuku Hiva to proudly drop our hooks in French Polynesia. In that very bay the young sailor Herman Melville had jumped ship and fled to the Valley of the cannibals - *Typee*. Artist Paul Gauguin, writers Jack London, R L Stevenson, and others have sailed, lived, even died there.

I brought our ship's papers (called 'Zarpe') from the Galapagos to the French Gendarmerie and cleared in yacht and crew. The officials administer a colonial society, sending out police or welfare cheques from behind barbed wire enclosures.

The cyclone season, which we were openly defying, bore on us daily, but we were permitted only a brief stay.

I returned to *Stornoway* and collapsed, exhausted. Though relieved, the navigation and stress were wearing me down. We hiked ashore, rested, and enjoyed a few 'happy hours' and a Valentine's Day' feast before pushing off for Tahiti, where we hoped mail and new faces awaited us. We were fraught with anxiety over threading the Tuamotu, or 'Dangerous' Archipelago of coral lagoons in the passage ahead. Though fringed in palms trees, these atolls, are razored in reefs on which, the KONTIKI raft expedition and others have met grief.

We consumed most of our costly diesel to burst through the Tuamotus ('motu' means atoll) and into a glass-calm, unrippled sea, with 400 miles to go to Tahiti. Drifting for days with neither fuel nor wind, we went slowly mad. Our reflections shone "clearly"; on the unrippled "mirror of the sea" of which Conrad wrote. Trevor and deck in the eerie silence, lapsing into fits of giggling and mad conversations.

During night watches the depth-meter sometimes went from an infinite reading (the seafloor a mile or more beneath us) to flashing a depth of 4-5 feet. This meant, something was passing beneath us at that depth. But what? As always, we continued to flush food, waste, even blood overboard.

Our cabins heavy with sweat and heat, the lure of the pond-like sea around us proved too tempting. Late on the second morning, we swam. Chris had seen a dark shadow beneath us at dawn. All we saw were fish - plenty of them. I swam deep. The others tired and went aboard. The waters were so clear that at 30 feet I could mimic the gestures - smiles and fingers - of the crew from deck.

Then horror. First on the face of Pina. Then Trevor. Then Chris ran to the railing too, and I knew I was in trouble. They pointed behind me. I looked. And there it was. A triangle of teeth framed by a black jaw and two eyes, mounted by one tall fin. Its tail switched from side to side, propelling the shark towards me from directly below.

No time to think. I turned and swam for our ladder, an eon away. It moved in for the kill. Thank god I had no flippers on. only one toehold on our ladder I catapulted onto *Stornoway's* scorching deck. The shark struck. Its teeth closed around our ladder and wrenched half of it away. Silence and panting. Shock and disbelief. The shark had been trailing us - stalking the mother ship - for days, waiting for food. It had come seconds from having me. *Never leave the ship.*

The wind finally picked up. We approached Tahiti, making Venus Point, of Captain Cook fame, in a howling squall. The wind also picked up Chris' "Bahama Papa" hat, and took it. We did pirouettes in the sea to retrieve it. The storm brewed over Papeete, capital city, but we barreled into the harbor jubilantly chanting, "*It's a long way to Pap -ay- ete*" - our own rendition of "Tipperary". The French thought we were mad, which should say something for us! (...pot calling the kettle black...)

We were one month in Papeete, the capital city of Tahiti, waiting for the cyclones to break. Ships and crew rot in port. In the colorful tapestry which is Tahiti, in the rainy

season, in a town of wash-ups, escapists, and even criminals, we languished. Tahiti was what we had come to the Pacific for, I think. In the overall picture, when we conspire our escapes to sea, when we think of the South Seas, perhaps, it is Tahiti that we think of.

On the rock of that expectation our dreams perhaps run aground. In truth, Papeete can be a sad town. A town where dreams are hung up. The 'women' of the night are as likely to be local men dressed in drag. On the waterfront, where the sailors curl up on abandoned wrecks, where wine, bread, and pot are the diets of many, everyone talks of somewhere else.

We had covered more than 4,000 miles in less than a month; like sailing trans- Atlantic, from Nassau to London. Yet we found ourselves not 'across' any ocean, but stuck in the middle of one. It takes days just to *fly* to Tahiti! Chris and I had crossed the Atlantic, but the Pacific seemed just too vast to fathom. We all felt the desperate isolation and struggled with it.

Tahiti was the peak of our outward-bound voyage. Though our morale and stamina were sapped, we each chose to continue. We wouldn't quit, wouldn't fly. At the end of March, we packed up to head out. The weeklong passage to Rarotonga, in the Cook Islands, was mild but steady, with a swell from Antarctica nudging us. It really was 'pacific', or calm - a 'milk run', despite the threats.

We dodged Cyclone Ursula to nip into Avatiu Harbour, Rarotonga for a few days' rest. The only other sailboat there was bound from New Zealand to Nassau - the opposite of our route. On April Fool's Day we motored out of the basin, watched by the 'happy hour' crowd at Trader Jack's. Just as we passed the wreck of the brig YANKEE our engine caught fire, spumed smoke, and cut out.

We had a reef on either side, 100 yards to go back, and 1,000 nautical miles to the next port I said nothing as we slid to a silent halt Just started pulling those trusty sails out, one by one. I am a sailor, specializing in simply moving boats from one port, or one island, to another - not in winning races or repairing engines, perhaps, but in getting there. And if to get to there we would have to sail, then sail we would. And sail we did. Chris understood.

We were all becoming a bit testy. We had been abandoned by our skipper, had fended off attempts to seize *Stornoway*, had sprung leaks, nearly run aground, been attacked by a shark, harassed by a cyclone, and finally lost our engine. We were pissed off, and I proposed we sail directly to New Zealand - that we end the voyage after nearly half a year.

With winter brewing over New Zealand, though, we weren't prepared for the final passage. We needed our engines and provisions. We set sail for the Kingdom of Tonga, weaving our way westwards around coral lagoons and volcanic seamounts (marked 'position doubtful') in our path. A week later, we threaded past a graveyard of wrecks and into the yacht basin on Nuku' Alofa on Tongatapu with only a foot beneath our keel.

We settled in among Tongans, expats, and 'yachties' for a tedious month of repairs, all but broke. I had deep misgivings about that final passage - a 1,200-lunge mile to the south, out of islands like the Bahamas and into cold and rough seas. The days of my unfettered bravado had passed. Chris asked my conditions to continue. "We need more crew", and we found one - Swedish sailor Stefan. On May 4 we set off.

The seas tore off shreds of *Stornoway's* paint. We shared watches, manned and pumped the bilges. Yachts flew by. On May 11 the reassuring beacon of Burgess Island Light pierced the dawn; New Zealand at last! Radios all around the gulf flashed warnings of gale conditions due to set in that night. 'Authoritarian' rule gave way to magical teamwork. At midnight we wove around a disabled tanker and punched through to the mouth of Auckland's sprawling harbor. The wind whipped spray on us in sheets as we ducked behind Queen's Wharf, Auckland, and hoisted the yellow 'Q' (for quarantine) flag victoriously. We had made it.

We lashed *Stornoway* to the pilings, which were her final berth and cracked a bottle of Jamaican rum in a warm toast. We - *Stornoway*, her patron Chris, Pina, Eric, Trevor, Stefan, and a boat-ridden cat - had made it. Made it across the South Pacific in all but the wrong season.

We knew on arrival that we were each free to keep going - around New Zealand - around the *world* in the wrong season if we liked. Only we would have to go it alone. And that, no doubt caused not just obvious relief, but sadness. A soft, painful, unspoken sadness. We huddled around one another for a week or so, and then we each split off, going our own separate ways - homewards.

Epilogue: Seven of the yachts fleeing New Zealand for Tonga that fall were lost in fierce gales. Three persons; a couple and their son, were lost. These words are for those who never make it

Reader's Choice: Feature Book of the Month...

Reading this book, as the most recent biographer of its enigmatic author (Childers was a sailor, Englishman married to a Bostonian, later Irish patriot and "traitor" killed for his cause) points out, is like renewing a friendship - one that lasts you through life and can often be revisited.

It is as relevant to us today as it was in the immediate and controversial context of its publication in 1903, when it served as a real "call to arms" for the British people during the Great Naval Race which preceded the First World War.

The Riddle of the Sands, by Erskine Childers, first published 1903, has been re-published in 1998 by Sheridan House, in a lovely 260-page hardcover edition illustrated by John O'Connor. Price is $14.95. *Erskine Childers, Author of The Riddle of the Sands*, by Tim Ring, is published (and reprinted) in 1996 by John Murray Ltd., London. An enlightening read covering the many facets of Childers' tumultuous life, the book is 332 pages in length and includes 15 pages plus both front and back covers of illustration. Cost' in hard-cover is $42.00.

Man Overboard: A Delivery Skipper Sees His Lifetime in 16 Minutes

On October 8 last year, my delivery crew of two and I were 100 miles south of Block Island, Rhode Island, aboard a 53- foot cruising sloop headed southwest into 20- to 30-knot winds and six- to eight-foot seas. It was our first full day on the second of three consecutive deliveries from New England to Fort Lauderdale, Florida.

While I was off watch and resting below, a loud crack—followed immediately by the sound of flailing lines and sails—woke me and brought me into the cockpit dressed in only a pair of boxer shorts. The mainsheet had parted, and the boom swung wildly across the deck. After heading into the wind, we roller-furled the main. I reefed the genoa for stability, and then began securing the boom, mainsheet, and tackle. In hindsight, this would have been an ideal time to suit up and clip in with a harness.

I grabbed the errant mainsheet with my left hand and a metal Dorade guard with my right. Moments later, the weight of the boom pried my right hand free; I was lifted and swung over the lifelines.

My open-air glide didn't last long. When the boom smashed into the starboard shrouds, my body continued its outward trajectory, and I was flicked into the sea.

Electrified with adrenaline, I came sputtering to the surface. In an effort to save my wristwatch—the band was loose—I noted the time: 2:24 p.m. From that point on, I maintained a steady, very salty, stream of commands to keep the crew active and to regain control.

"Duck!" I yelled. "Don't let the boom hit you! Throw me the Lifesling!"

The mate made it aft of the boom and struggled with our man-overboard equipment. He wasn't successful. The cloth release handle of the white Lifesling disintegrated in his hands, its fibers degraded by sunlight. The portside horseshoe, with 100 feet or more of floating line, was lashed too tightly for him to release quickly. Anyone who carries this equipment must inspect the setup on his or her boat and address these lashings before heading offshore. After what seemed like an eternity, the mate threw the starboard-side horseshoe to me. It had no line, but a strobe light was attached to it.

During my short time in the water, the genoa remained full and pulled the boat farther away. In the cockpit, the seriousness of the situation hit the guys, and precious minutes were lost to panic. All I could do was wait. After 10 minutes, cold and true fear set in. My teeth began to chatter. Finally, my crew managed to jibe the genoa and sail back toward me. With the boat's considerable windage, however, they soon sailed passed me. "Turn on the engine," I pleaded. "Come back!" After frantically pawing at the console, the mate managed to preheat and start the engine—exhaust and steaming water from the waterline conveyed the good news. Instead of risking another jibe, he jammed the engine in reverse. Working against the flailing genoa, they back-paddled the boat toward me to complete the unorthodox rescue.

I reached one arm up toward them, some four feet above me, and was plucked out of the cold October seas. Smiles broke across our tear- and worry-streaked faces, and quick, warm embraces were shared in one big jumble. It was 2:40 p.m.

The entire rescue took about 16 minutes in rough, daylight conditions. I was extremely fortunate, and I owe my life to the actions and dedication of my crew. At 4 p.m. that day, we informed Herb Hilgenberg, via his Southbound II SSB net, that our strobe and horseshoe had been lost.

We found the sheet intact. The entire ordeal had begun when a tooth-sized stainless-steel pin that held the mainsheet block to the deck broke. Had we briefly inspected our equipment before leaving, we might have noticed the worn metal at the base of the block and the frayed lines of our man-overboard module. Our next delivery, I decided, wouldn't be taken so hastily. In a lot of ways, I'm lucky there'll be a next one.

The Cold, Hard Facts, by Robert Crake, M.D.

Here are some things to consider about taking leave of your deck:

- Muscles of the limbs - particularly the arms - become critically weakened while swimming in cold water.
- In a real-world situation, 20 percent of all swimmers will drown in an hour or less in water that is 65 F, and 50 percent will drown in an hour or less in water that is 50 F. Treading water and swimming induce fatigue and lower the body's core temperature.
- Wearing flotation is crucial. Until help arrives, the victim should be as still as the seas allow and assume a position with arms crossed, elbows close to the torso, and legs crossed.

Law Student Sinks Yacht

The law catches up to us in mysterious ways. So I learned this fall when I walked into a 2L Day Division class to find many of my colleagues snickering at me. It turns out that, in the course of research into *Apprendi v. New Jersey* (530 US 466, 2000), my colleague Larry White came across a case, which featured yours truly as the skipper of a yacht, which sank following a fire.

The case is Reliance National Insurance Company (Europe) Ltd. v. Alain Hanover and Daniel Hanover, which was heard in the US District Court for Massachusetts on July 22, 2002 (2002 U.S. Dist. LEXIS 13287). Larry handed me a copy of the case in class. I would like to comment on the case in the DOCKET and provide further insight to our colleagues at RWU Law.

The case stems from events, which happened in late 1999 and resulted in the sinking of a classic, historic yacht off of the island of Trinidad, in the Lesser Antilles (Caribbean), on 23 February 2000. The issue is whether the yacht's owners are entitled to a jury trial against the insurers, and whether the insurers are entitled to cancel the policy because the owners allegedly

116

misrepresented the purchase price (they added $20,000 to the sale price of $130,000 in order to account for expenditures on the yacht). Both parties allege bad faith, with owners Hanover alleging 'unjust enrichment' by the insurers as well. Judge Richard G. Stearns denied both party's cross-motions for summary judgment, and the case is meant to go to trial within a year (in fact, I understand that I am expected to testify as a witness and give depositions).

For the purpose of this comment, I would like to limit my discussion to the facts of my involvement, and to my perspective, legal or otherwise, on the story of the case. I recommend the reader finds and prints the case - I am mentioned by name six times on page 3).

I first heard of the yacht and its owners in late fall, 1999. A good friend of mine referred me to the Hanovers, with whom he had worked in Boston in the then-booming Internet technology sector. In July of 1999 I had started a small yacht-delivery company Echo Yacht Delivery, and, despite a busy fall seasons (during which I was lost overboard in a snowstorm 100 miles south of Block Island for 16 minutes, and had my index finger stripped almost to the bone by an engine alternator), Christmas holidays had seen me spend my meager savings. By January 2000 I needed work, and Messrs. Hanover offered it.

On February 20, 2000, the Hanovers 'closed' on a deal to buy *Stiarna*, a classic wooden sailing yacht measuring roughly 70 feet on deck, which was built in England (designed by Camper & Nicholson) in 1937. Described as a Twelve Meter', *Stiarna* represents some of the finest in sailing yachts built this century. In 1957 she was fitted with a side-mounted diesel engine. She has one mast. A single owner had owned *Stiarna* for over a decade, and by all accounts her condition had deteriorated during this time. As I understand it, the insurers did not commission their own survey of the vessel, but rather were waiting for the Hanovers and a shipwright, Fred Thomas, to overhaul and improve the boat in Thomas' new shipyard on the island of Grenada, roughly 80 nautical miles north of Trinidad. My participation called on me to 1) fly from Boston to Trinidad to assume command of the yacht, 2) organize and implement the delivery voyage from Trinidad to

Grenada, in coordination with her caretaker, Mr. Thomas, 3) oversee the refit in Grenada for up to a year, and 4) skipper her, in restored condition, from Grenada to the Hanover's base in New England, where she would be proudly sailed in Newport, RI. The projected cost of refit exceeded $500,000. My wages were to be comfortable, and included accommodation and transportation in Grenada, which is a beautiful island.

I arrived in Trinidad by air roughly one week before the Hanovers, and immediately set about getting the boat ready for an offshore voyage. This included rewinding the starter motor, changing the oil, bleeding the engine of air locks to make it easier to start, and tightening the fan belts. It also included a check of mast and rigging, available sail inventory, and the seaworthiness (integrity) of the hull. I lived on board, and paid careful attention to the level of bilge water, which led me to seal off several valves, which were fitted 'through the hull'. I liked Trinidad and found a young man, Ashley, who had refit and sailed his own boat, alone, from England to Trinidad, to help me. The island was gearing up for the Carnival, and after long workdays we would unwind in one of two local pubs. The work was hard, the yacht was not too comfortably fitted out, and nights were spent fending off mosquitoes. Work during the day was often filthy, with heavy rains making it more challenging. A snowstorm in Boston delayed the owners for a few precious days, giving me more time to get the boat ready.

On about 21 February I met the owners, Mr. Alain Hanover, and his son Daniel, at Trinidad's international airport. During the drive to the marina at Chaguaramas, they asked me my opinion of the boat. I told them that found the boat to be seaworthy, but recommended that they accept the offer of a local tug boat captain to accompany us for the voyage, with the option of taking *Stiarna* under tow, should the need arise. Mr. Hanover approved this measure, despite a charter cost of several thousand dollars. His attitude was 'if you hire an expert, don't then go and ignore his advice', which I found encouragingly pragmatic.

The owners put us up in a local hotel; we took the yacht for a spin on the engine only, pulled up to the fuel jetty, refueled, and remained there for the night of Feb 22 - 23. The tug CALYPSO II stood by on an adjacent berth, and we agreed to wake at about 4:30 AM for a departure before sunrise, which would enable us to accomplish the voyage mostly in daylight. At about 6 AM *Stiarna* and CALYPSO II left Chaguaramas, Trinidad, bound in convoy to Grenada. Aboard *Stiarna*, of which I was in command, were five men: myself, Ashley the mate, Mr. Hanover and his son Daniel, and a gentleman named Coelho, of indeterminate age (I estimate around 70 years), who, like Ashley, was a shipwright employed by Fred Thomas. Aside from white exhaust smoke emanating from the engine space (a pre-existing condition) the voyage proceeded uneventfully as far as the 'Bocas' - a series of islands and channels called, in English, the Mouth of the Dragon' - through which all shipping into northwest Trinidad must pass.

At roughly 7 AM we cleared the Bocas and made a course pretty much due north. The sun rose on a glass-calm sea with very little wind, and just an ocean swell and an easterly-setting current. During several crucial minutes, however, our situation deteriorated rapidly, leading ultimately to all of us abandoning *Stiarna* to her fate. I was pushing the engine to accomplish two things; catch up with CALYPSO II and stay clear of a sailboat to windward of us, when we started to lose power in the engines. By this time the white smoke had turned black, making it very difficult for me to see ahead, except by standing on the deck behind the wheel. I asked Coelho to advise on the oil pressure of the engine, and was told that the pressure had dropped to nil. I immediately shut off the engine, which both stopped the boat and also made it easier to hear.

Ashley and Daniel were at the mast, where they had raised one small sail (Ashley's orange storm trysail), and were preparing to connect a warp around the base of the mast to a tow line from CALYPSO II, which was returning to assist.

Shortly after shutting down the engine I investigated the engine space and heard a distinct 'cackling', which indicated a possible fire on board. Needless to say, fire is an extreme hazard on a yacht, partly because you normally have nowhere to escape to except the sea. Because the engine is covered by two large doors, which open up on the floor of the yacht's navigation station, it would have been dangerous to open them and ventilate the fire.

So, I opted to check under a small footstep leading from the cockpit. What I saw dismayed me. Orange flames were already at work in the engine space. We had a fire on board, and visibility was extremely poor in the resulting smoke. I had to act quickly. I tried one small fire extinguisher on the fire, but this did not extinguish it. I reached for the VHF short-range radio and informed CALYPSO II that we had a fire on board, asking her captain to stand by alongside to either fight the fire with pumps or rescue us.

CALYPSO II stood by. Next, I ordered the younger crew - Ashley and Daniel - to gather other extinguishers and fight the fire from within the yacht. They went down below using an entrance amidships and I could hear them using extinguishers there. Meanwhile I threw our gasoline container (for the dinghy engine), into the sea and placed several life vests where they could be easily grabbed. I went forward to investigate the fire and found that all extinguishers had been used, but that the fire persisted. At that point I went to the forward most cabin and collected the passports and the boat's petty cash. Daniel and I also hoisted some of the Hanover's personal baggage onto the deck. The situation looked pretty grim, and we were only about three minutes into the emergency. I knew that not only did we have about fifty gallons of diesel on board, but that virtually the entire boat was made of wood, and that the wood in the bilge was oil-soaked.

I turned off the fuel valve leading to the engine and ordered all crew to assemble on the after (rear) end of the boat. My experience running a fleet of tanker ships (30,000-ton cargo capacity) in Singapore for three years had taught me not to let firefighters become injured at their task, since often other crew will risk their lives to save the injured. This could create a 'domino' effect, whereby, say, Mr. Hanover hears the cries of his injured son, races to the rescue, becomes injured, causing more crew to race to the rescue, and so on until a number of men are incapacitated. I did not want this to happen.

On assembling (with the Hanover's gear) on the aft deck, I called CALYPSO II and informed them that we were sending Coelho into the water to swim to CALYPSO II to set up a fire-fighting pump if possible. Another reason was to save the life of our oldest crew. He assured me he could swim, and did successfully make it to CALYPSO II. By this time, we were in danger of losing our VHF communication, as the fire was by now spreading up through the navigation station, only feet from where we stood. I informed the CALYPSO II of my intention to abandon ship, and requested that he stand by to receive us, including placing a ladder over the side. When they complied with my request by stopping their engines a mere 40 feet or so upwind of us, I ordered my remaining crew to don their life vests and abandon ship. They responded with calm efficiency.

Mr. Hanover went first, asking me to bring one of his bags with me. I assigned Ashley to go next and look after Mr. Hanover. Third to go was Daniel, with one of his bags, and I, as captain, was the last to leave the ship. I did not bring either the bags or my shoes. In my mouth I held the crew's passports, and the cash was stuffed in my pocket, from which several bills floated out (this created a funny scenario, where the CALYPSO II's captain directed me to swim and save a number of bills, and I finally gave up on the cash in order to save myself!). Within a few minutes, and by around 10 minutes after 7 AM, all five of us and about two bags were safely aboard the CALYPSO II, a sizeable ocean-going commercial vessel. The captain and I contacted the Trinidadian Coast Guard, and they immediately dispatched a RIB (Rigid Inflatable Boat) to the scene - we were roughly four miles north of the coast guard station. They also sent out a larger (former US Coast Guard) cutter to our assistance.

At that point I felt that my primary duty - to save my crew from injury or death - had been accomplished, but we called for any vessels with sufficient firefighting capability to come to the scene and a photographer to document the vessel's demise. Neither items were available in such short notice, and for an hour we watched as *Stiarna* burned to the water line in the clear dawn sunlight. The Trinidadian RIB was extremely helpful, took statements from me, the CALYPSO II captain, and Mr. Hanover, and even shuttled Mr. and Daniel Hanover to *Stiarna*, enabling them to retrieve their belongings from the after deck. At about 8 AM, her mast fallen, the fire having eaten its way through both sides of the deck around the engine, exploded the diesel and water tanks, and run the length of the boat, *Stiarna* succumbed to the sea and sank in a single, anti-climactic sigh. She left only a few burnt items of clothing and a charred life ring on the surface of the sea, one hundred and thirty-four feet above where she finally came to rest.

Shortly after the sinking, the cutter arrived and all five *Stiarna* crew were transferred by RIB to the cutter and taken in to the Coast Guard base in Chaguaramas. We were given a kind of hero's welcome, treated to blankets and coffee, and offered medical attention, which fortunately was not extinguishers and fight the fire from within the yacht. They went down below using an entrance amidships and I could hear them using extinguishers there. Meanwhile I threw our gasoline container (for the dinghy engine), into the sea and placed several life vests where they could be easily grabbed. I went forward to investigate the fire and found that all extinguishers

had been used, but that the fire persisted. At that point I went to the forward most cabin and collected the passports and the boat's petty cash. Daniel and I also hoisted some of the Hanovers' personal baggage onto the deck. The situation looked pretty grim, and we were only about three minutes into the emergency. I knew that not only did we have about fifty gallons of diesel on board, but that virtually the entire boat was made of wood, and that the wood in the bilge was oil-soaked.

I turned off the fuel valve leading to the engine and ordered all crew to assemble on the after (rear) end of the boat. My experience running a fleet of tanker ships (30,000-ton cargo capacity) in Singapore for three years had taught me not to let firefighters become injured at their task, since often other crew will risk their lives to save the injured. This could create a 'domino' effect, whereby, say, Mr. Hanover hears the cries of his injured son, races to the rescue, becomes injured, causing more crew to race to the rescue, and so on until a number of men are incapacitated. I did not want this to happen.

On assembling (with the Hanover's gear) on the aft deck, I called CALYPSO II and informed them that we were sending Coelho into the water to swim to CALYPSO II to set up a fire-fighting pump if possible. Another reason was to save the life of our oldest crew. He assured me he could swim, and did successfully make it to CALYPSO II. By this time, we were in danger of losing our VHF communication, as the fire was by now spreading up through the navigation station, only feet from where we stood. I informed the CALYPSO II of my intention to abandon ship, and requested that he stand by to receive us, including placing a ladder over the side. When they complied with my request by stopping their engines a mere 40 feet or so upwind of us, I ordered my remaining crew to don their life vests and abandon ship. They responded with calm efficiency.

Mr. Hanover went first, asking me to bring one of his bags with me. I assigned Ashley to go next and look after Mr. Hanover. Third to go was Daniel, with one of his bags, and I, as captain, was the last to leave the ship. I did not bring either the bags or my shoes. In my mouth I held the crew's passports, and the cash was stuffed in my pocket, from which several bills floated out (this created a funny scenario, where the CALYPSO II's captain directed me to swim and save a number of bills, and I finally gave up on the cash in order to save myself!). Within a few minutes, and by around 10 minutes after 7 AM, all five of us and about two bags were safely aboard the CALYPSO II, a sizeable ocean-going commercial vessel. The captain and I contacted the Trinidadian Coast Guard, and they immediately dispatched a RIB (Rigid Inflatable Boat) to the scene - we were roughly four miles north of the coast guard station. They also sent out a larger (former US Coast Guard) cutter to our assistance.

At that point I felt that my primary duty - to save my crew from injury or death - had been accomplished, but we called for any vessels with sufficient firefighting capability to come to the scene and a photographer to document the vessel's demise. Neither items were available in such short notice, and for an hour we watched as *Stiarna* burned to the water line in the clear dawn sunlight. The Trinidadian RIB was extremely helpful, took statements from me, the CALYPSO II captain, and Mr. Hanover, and even shuttled Mr. and Daniel Hanover to *Stiarna*, enabling them to retrieve their belongings from the after deck. At about 8 AM, her mast fallen, the fire having eaten its way through both sides of the deck around the engine, exploded the diesel and water tanks, and run the length of the boat, *Stiarna* succumbed to the sea and sank in a single, anti-climactic sigh. She left only a few burnt items of clothing and a charred life ring on the surface of the sea, one hundred and thirty-four feet above where she finally came to rest.

Shortly after the sinking, the cutter arrived and all five *Stiarna* crew were transferred by RIB to the cutter and taken in to the Coast Guard base in Chaguaramas. We were given a kind of hero's welcome, treated to blankets and coffee, and offered medical attention, which fortunately was not required.

After a cold hour in a warehouse room on the base, we were permitted to take a taxi back to the marina, where we discussed the yacht's sad demise with fellow sailors and with a devastated, shocked Fred Thomas, who was to have overseen a complete refit of the boat in Grenada. The owners were extremely understanding of the crew's position. Since only the Hanovers had been able to retrieve personal gear, and they reimbursed each of us for our lost items and provided for us in the form of new clothes, accommodation, etc. This was very generous of them. After giving a number of statements to authorities at the Port of Spain, I flew back to Boston via Grenada the next day, and am now awaiting the opportunity to testify in trial.

In conclusion, I would like to say that I have no regrets regarding the sinking of *Stiarna* - she was a beautiful boat, but could have been the deathbed of my crew and 1.1 acted decisively, and unlike the captain in Petition of Den Norske Amerikalinje A/S owner of M/ S Topdalsfjord, 276 F. Supp. 163, 1967 U.S. Dis. LEXIS 9070, did not hesitate to order my crew to abandon ship. Once I issued that order, crew was released from their duties to *Stiarna*, and responsibility for abandoning ship lay exclusively with me, as master. It was the right decision. Flames were already consuming the boom by the time we left. My attitude then was that human life and safety was more important than property, and that claims could be settled for the value of the vessel in a safer forum at a later date. Unfortunately, this claim is not yet settled.

Although the Hanovers applied for, and Reliance issued, an insurance policy covering the yacht and crew for that specific voyage, payment of the claim has not been made by end October 2002, nearly three years after the accident. Mr. Hanover has gone to considerable expense to follow up on the claim and settle up with the crew and other parties. I am glad that the parties will soon 'their day in court' and can update you if and when that day comes and I am a participant. Meanwhile, I am proud of my own actions, and of the professional reaction of my crew to a highly difficult and dangerous situation. I am grateful that everyone is safe, and that the litigation involves only loss of property, and not loss of life or limb, as it easily might have been. I will be pleased to discuss this case with fellow students and faculty; after all, *Stiarna*'s loss and the subsequent litigation have played a part in inspiring me to pursue the study of maritime law.

Law Student Sinks Yacht Part II: The Trial (District Court, Boston)

This brief article is part two in a three-part series documenting 1) the demise of the sailing yacht *Stiarna*, of which I was the master, on 23 Feb. 2000, 2) the trial, and 3) the District Court Judge's decision (due later in 2003). The first installment (four pages, illustrated) appeared in the last issue of Roger Williams' Law's DOCKET, Vol. 10, Issue 2. In this installment I would like simply to make several brief observations from my experiences as an 'expert witness' in a bench trial in U.S. District Court. The case in question stems from Reliance National Insurance Company (Europe) Ltd. v. Alain and Daniel Hanover (2002 U.S. Dist. LEXIS 13287).

The trial took place between Monday 3rd to Wednesday, 5th of February, 2003. Goldman represented plaintiff Reliance with two witnesses and Defendants Hanover were represented by Wolfe, with three witnesses, only two of whom were called. The District Judge presiding was Richard G. Stearns, and the hearings were held in the 21st courtroom, 7th floor of the new and impressive Moakley Federal Court Building in downtown Boston, which boasts splendid views of Boston's skyline, harbor, and working waterways.

I learned and observed several things from my first participation in a real trial, much of which will seem obvious to those with experience. First of all, Evidence is actually very, very important. Professor Ritchie had a point! Second, a lawyer who is too aggressive might hurt his or her client's case more than help it. Third, the night before giving testimony can be terrifying, but after a lot of coaching and a good night's sleep the truisms proved true: "relax, answer the question, and above all, be honest".

To recite briefly, Plaintiffs called the yacht's owner, Mr. Alain Hanover, first, and the attorney was very aggressive towards my former employer. So much so that Judge Stearns had to interject several times with "not so argumentative", and "tone it down". After 2 hours or so, Mr. Hanover's attorney spent an hour or so on damage control — Mr. Hanover had also given sworn depositions, and then we were all released for the day, with four witnesses yet to be called. The next day the Plaintiff s witnesses - the man who placed the insurance on the yacht before it sank (he had flown from England) and the man whose job it was to assess/adjust/investigate the claim (he flew from Florida) gave their testimony. I found it interesting (and intimidating) that Defendant's attorney (our party's man) opened his questioning by establishing that neither man had gained formal education beyond high school - a rough way to begin testimony, I thought!

On Wednesday it was my turn to speak, and since Daniel Hanover was not called, I had the floor to myself. Both opposing witnesses had left after the previous days' testimony. Only the Judge, the court Reporter, the stenographer, two attorneys, two Hanovers and I were left in the room. Only one person 'sat in' uninvited on the proceedings, though anyone was welcome to have. I was very fortunate that Mr. Wolfe was a friendly interrogator —while I stood on the threshold of the witness box, he and Mr. Goldman argued over whether I was an 'expert' witness (and thus could give my opinion) and also whether Mr. Goldman could have me first. So, I was pleased that Mr. Wolfe won and allowed me to spend five minutes after swearing in introducing myself, education, and maritime career (watch out for letting sailors talk about die sea!)

The first half hour or so went along smoothly, but with events three years in the past, and conflicting testimony having been given by Mr. Hanover, I had to step carefully in recalling the condition of the boat, on which I had spent a week. Much hinged on my testimony, since I was the only 'professional' at court who had gone over the boat before it sank. By clarifying on the side of the court (a few 'I don't knows'), I was able to proceed without too many hitches, though I suspect that Mr. Wolfe wanted more favorable details from me.

Mr. Goldman wasn't as intimidating as I'd feared he would be, but still he managed to get me against the wall over one issue—intense questioning with only the option of 'yes' or 'no' before you have time to digest the question. Overall, however, I came out alright and stood up to him, asking for clarification when necessary. I was told not to weave tales, just understand and answer the question. Because there were a number of evidentiary objections (fewer than if it had been a jury trial, counsel conceded), there were pauses of several minutes between fines of questions, and clarifications for the stenographer. Both attorneys used my last round of cross-examination and I was released, the judge calling me 'Captain, soon-to-be-attorney' as I left the stand, which was nice.

Readers hopefully had a chance to learn the details of *Stiarna*'s sinking in the last DOCKET, which is still available on fine at the DOCKET homepage. I was a bit disappointed that as a witness I could not 'control the content' of what I said, but was rather limited to answering what was asked of me—often no more. I was never able to describe in court the yacht's actual sinking, because those facts were stipulated, and to say how proud I was of my crew's performance, or how rotten I think it is that insurance still hasn't paid my employer three years afterwards...

My final thoughts on the experience are that evidence is extremely, extremely important whether by deposition, testimony, photographs, old survey reports, insurance documents, correspondence between insurance personnel and also dozens of emails between Messrs. Hanover and myself, some of which was written (by me and us) with no thought given to whether it would appear in trial years later. Objections were made not as often as I thought they could be, but most of them were overruled. One objection that was granted spared me an uncomfortable bit of interrogation.

In his closing argument, Mr. Wolfe harkened to the U.S.S. CONSTITUTION, which like *Stiarna* was, is a seaworthy old wooden boat which has an escort vessel standing by it when they take it out for a sail. Given that the CONSTITUTION was within sight of die courthouse, his closing argument was very poignancy. The judge was helpful to counsel and all of us,

Pointing out each day what he found informative and what he wished to learn the following day. Indeed, Justice Stearns is someone that I would gladly clerk for if given the opportunity. He ran a good court. He gave counsel three weeks to draft final legal arguments, and will rule either in the spring or summer of this year. I look forward to his opinion/decision. None of us could really tell which way he was leaning certainly couldn't—but Mr. Wolfe did say that I helped the Hanover's case, and we shall have to see. I will keep you updated in the next DOCKET!

Law Student Sinks Yacht, Loses District Court Case...

I wish to add some insight into the judge's ruling in Reliance National Insurance Company (Europe) Ltd. v. Alain J. Hanover and Daniel A. Hanover (2003 U.S. Dist. LEXIS 2907). I have previously chronicled this case (2002 U.S. Dist. LEXIS 13287) in the RWU Law DOCKET, Volume 10, Issues 2 & 3.

On March 3rd 2003 Judge Richard G. Steams of the District Court in Boston published his opinion, in which he essentially found the 60-foot wooden yacht *Stiarna* (of which I was in command when she sank off Trinidad on 23 Feb. 2000), to have been unseaworthy both at the time of inception of the relevant insurance policy and also at the inception of the voyage (which, to use the legal term of art, the time that she "broke ground").

Needless to say, my Employers, Messrs. Alain and Daniel Hanover of Boston (who owned *Stiarna* for all of about 2 weeks), and I are disappointed with the judge's ruling, which followed roughly two years of legal sparring between the parties, two court appearances (July 22 and Aug. 14 2002), depositions and three days of a bench trial (3-5 Feb. 2003), in which I testified as an expert witness.

Certainly, this holding does not help my reputation. It is bad enough that a vessel under my command sank. Although I continue to be proud of how my crew and I responded to the fire, and that no one was injured or killed in the efforts to extinguish it, abandon *Stiarna*, and reach the rescue vessel CALYPSO II on that fateful dawn more than 3 years ago; to have a judge find that, in the law's view, I left the dock in command of a vessel deemed unseaworthy adds insult to injury.

As a law student I am learning to be more circumspect in my analysis and judgment; to follow Justice Holmes' admonition not to think too often with my heart as an aspiring member of the legal profession. So, I am willing to say that Judge Steams' decision on whether *Stiarna* was seaworthy or not must have been about as difficult to make as mine was at the time - at 05:00 in the morning, with a new employer chomping at the bit for me to take her off across blue water to another country, while goaded on by the captain and a crew of an escort vessel standing by to assist us, and blinded by the white phosphorous smoke of a faulty exhaust system.

Judge Steams, somewhat poetically, depicts the moment of our 'breaking ground' thus: "There is no question but the loss of the *Stiarna* was an accident. ...Wiberg, who recognized the seriousness of *Stiarna*'s shortcomings, was nonetheless hesitant to disappoint prospective long time employer. Each of the actors, despite his better instincts, had a personal motive for putting caution aside. This perfect storm of bad judgment precipitated the sinking of the *Stiarna*." (2003 U.S. Dist. LEXIS 2907 at 7).

Fortunately, the judge, (who, from his demeanor, insightful questions, and post-hearing summaries I respect greatly), was not all damning about the owners and I - in his 22 or so references to me he notes, "Despite his relative youth, Wiberg was an experienced captain..." (Id. at 6). He adds that "Wiberg's overall impression was that the *Stiarna* was a "tired" vessel" (Id.), and in this observation of a wooden boat built 63 years before she sank, patchily maintained for a decade, and powered with a diesel engine 48 years old and by a mast which was rendered partly unusable by spots of rot, neither of us were entirely wrong.

Like me, Judge Steams had to make a decision on the seaworthiness of the boat that morning based on all the information available to him, and knowing that either way he decided, he would be subjecting himself to possible criticism from his peers. What for me were restless employers are to him the

Appeals court looming over his shoulder. He knew that he was making a decision that could be challenged and over ruled, just as my analysis of the vessel's seaworthiness has been by him.

In doing the matter of law whether *Stiarna* was fit for its intended purpose at the inception of the voyage, the judge relied in part on compromising testimony given by my employer and the yacht's owner in which he claimed that the yacht was 'rotten' from stem to stem, and that the mast was also 'rotten' (Id. at 3, 4). While I take issue with the treatment of the engine as being in the same condition at the outset as when the owners first inspected it (I and others had put considerable time, effort, and money into improving the engine, though not perfectly), I can understand the court's thought process much better from this conclusion (Id. at 9):

"While the aging engine was the immediate cause of the destructive fire, had the *Stiarna* been able to make the passage under sail as was originally intended, it would not have been necessary to place the stress on the engine that in all likelihood caused it to fail".

Despite my assertions that sailing yacht deliveries are often undertaken and executed with reliance on the engines more than sails, sometimes to the tune of 90-100% (many boats make it to Bermuda, for example, after 600-1,000 miles with mere drops of diesel remaining), I do see and appreciate the judge's logic here.

He drives the stake in the heart of our/defendants arguments with the following missive: "A yacht that cannot safely raise its sails or rely on its engine is by definition unfit for its intended purpose" (Id. at 9). Here the judge is on safe ground - indeed virtually unassailable in maritime- think. The defendants/our task would be to assert and prove that the facts (i.e. actual condition of engine on departing) warrant a finding of seaworthiness.

At the end of the day, my testimony, that after close inspection that I only found limited, specific patch of rot, about 6 inches by 3 inches by 1 inch deep, in the mast, and that we thus decided not to use full sails, failed to dissuade Judge Steams. While this is the safer holding, I believe that an element of syllogistic argument was in play, i.e.: "The vessel sank after less than an hour of operation. If the vessel had been seaworthy when it left the dock, it would not have caught fire and sank. Ergo, the yacht was not seaworthy when it left the dock". I think that this reasoning, while perfectly human and understandable, clouded and prejudiced our claim.

What is frustrating is that had the yacht NOT sank, as I envisioned it wouldn't, then there would be no issue; no insurance company revoking their coverage, refunding the premium, and suing my employers in court. That was exactly why the Hanovers sought, applied for, paid for and put in place an insurance policy - in case things went wrong. Well, they did. Five men could quite easily have burned, drowned, or been badly maimed. *Stiarna*, an authentic part of yachting history remains 134 deep north of 'The Bocas', and we have no judgment money to raise her. When the owners went for compensation from Reliance Insurance (whose American subsidiary went out of business that week), they came up with naught. And now the District Court Judge sitting 100 miles or so north of us agrees with the insurers.

The Hanovers are considering appealing to the Court of Appeals in Boston, and I may be asked to testify again to try and assert the seaworthiness of, say, *Stiarna's* engine if not the mast. On the advice of friends and mentors, and believing that it is unlikely that First Circuit will overrule the District Court's opinion, I am inclined to decline the offer and sit this one out. I'm not keen to further hold out my reputation as a master. However, if there are changes in this status and the case proceeds further, I will be sure to let you loyal readers of the *Docket* know!

Thanks for bearing with us. The sinking of *Stiarna* still weighs heavily with me, but now that I have an opinion from a legal expert I feel some sense of closure. I am pleased to have at least had our 'day in court', even after three years. It has been an exciting, interesting and stimulating process, from the deck of a stout, 70-year-old sailing craft in the Caribbean to the docket of an esteemed judge in an old New England sailing port. Thank you for coming along for the ride.

Eleuthera Island Shores Property Owners Association Newsletter

I am a relative newcomer to the mainland of Eleuthera, having first purchased land in EIS in 2001. My family has been based in Nassau as real estate developers and hoteliers since the early 1960's and my extended family go back to developing Hog Island for Axel Wenner Gren, the Swedish founder of Electrolux, in the 1940's. As a family we own land on three islands but I have derived the most satisfaction from EIS because of the size of the island, the ease and availability of both beaches and Harbor Island, and the comparative friendliness of the Eleutherans. I have scouted every major island in the group to buy cheap land. By contrast, I was chased off Rum Cay by a drunken angry mob and the locals of Acklins were so desperate for investment that they literally begged me with tear-filled eyes to stay.

Developments on Eleuthera:

Unlike other islands which may have grown too quickly and caused social upheaval, I find that Eleuthera, in the early 2000's, was depressed and very encouraging of development. Wealthy young investors and transplants have started a community in Governor's Harbor in recent years and Tarpum Bay is likely to be the next high-growth area, as is Palmetto Point. Of course, Lenny Kravitz owns roughly 30 acres near EIS north of Gregory Town and another large oceanfront lot further north, and the glass sculptor Simon Pearce has a home near Rock Sound. Notable pockets of wealth exist on Windermere Island (seasonal mostly, though Carry Rich is developing the northern end for a marina et al, and Mariah Carey recently bought there as well) and Cotton Bay, which is an enclave essentially cut off by the wealthy Columbian who reigns there.

There are interesting efforts in Bannerman Town (cruise ships) and Davis and Cape Eleuthera marinas. One site with immense potential is the former US Navy Base near the Governor's Harbor airport, where they built a facility for small ships on the ocean side and tracked and retrieved NASA assets returning from space. Spanish Wells has attracted a steady and growing stream of hardy investors. I have heard of minor thefts of property in Eleuthera, mostly on sites deemed abandoned, and some break-ins on Harbour Island (normally in rented homes on the first night of a visit) but not heard of crimes against the person ever, which is a relief. Lighthouse Point, on the extreme South of Eleuthera is well worth a long drive and I agree that it is about the most picturesque setting in all the Bahamas.

Infrastructure, Shipping:

In terms of port, road, and airport infrastructure, there have been huge improvements in last decade, including daily high-speed ferry and Ro/Ro connections with Nassau to Harbour Island and Current Cut, lengthening and lighting North Eleuthera airport (ELH) and expanded shipping services to Governor's Harbour and other ports. There is a recent container facility in Governor's Harbour and I never cease to be impressed with Roll-on-Roll-off and other commercial vessels which call at Rock Sound, Governor's, Hatchet Bay (not sure of the schedule), the Bluff, Current, Spanish Welles, Harbour Island, North Eleuthera (the dock called Three Islands there), etc.

Increased maritime service in an archipelago will surely facilitate importation of supplies for building in EIS, and the ferry service has already improved race relations on mostly-white Spanish Wells. See G&G Shipping (Governor's Harbour), Pioneer, Crowley, Cavalier, Eleuthera Express Shipping, United Shipping, Tropical, BahMar Carriers, Betty K Agencies, Ocean Air Bahamas, Seaboard Marine, St. John's Shipping, Bahamas Ferries, SeaRoad, the government mail boats, the MailBoat, and others, including Michael Oakes' fleet of landing craft on Arawak Cay, Nassau.

Infrastructure, Air:

Airline information is available online. The best link I've found is at thecoveeleuthera.com, which has all air information that you will need to fly direct to Eleuthera. They list Continental, Twin Air, Yellow Air Taxi, Lynx, and US Airways Express. For a brief time, Delta ran/runs a direct service from Atlanta to ELH. My favorite is Southern Air Charters - they have never let me down for last minute bookings. Three flights daily cost about $70 to/from Nassau to Governor's or ELH/North Eleuthera. BahamasAir is good for intra-island flights. Rose Kennedy in North Eleuthera is a local pilot who is rumored to fly barefoot and can take you anywhere, anytime, for a price.

Books / Art / Music:

There are several books which I consider must-reads, including Bahamas Handbook and Businessman's Manual by Etienne Dupuch Publications, the Lonely Planet guide, Histories by Albury and Craton, The Elusive Beaches of Eleuthera - 2007 Edition by Geoff Wells and Vicky Wells (Perfect Paperback) and books by Kjeld Helweg-Larsen, who built Buccaneer Hill in Governor's Harbour and dwelled there for decades. Arawaks and Astronauts: Twenty Years on Eleuthera is a start. The best overall history is Eleuthera, the Island Called Freedom, by Everild Young, Regency Press, 1966, last printed 1996. I have not read Cape Eleuthera, Bahamas by Whitney Aldrich, SPA Books (2007), or How to Buy and Sell Real Estate in the Bahamas: Insider's Guide by Matthew Simon (2008) which looks interesting and relevant. Another noteworthy history is Brave Sailors All, by J. Revell Carr, about British merchant seamen who washed up at James' Cistern near EIS after being sunk by a Nazi raider and drifting for over 100 days. It includes photos of the area and rescuers, who are still living. You would be remiss not to buy a print of Eddie Minnis' vibrant and accurate oil painting "Gregory Town" or his highly entertaining calypso music, available in town. Eddie is now a realtor on Harbor Island and a cultural institution in the Bahamas for many decades.

Renting A Car Vs. Taxi:

My worst experiences in Eleuthera have been being over-charged by taxi drivers. It started on my first visit when I stayed at the Pineapple Cove hotel and was recommended to a driver there. While he did provide wonderful narratives and introduced me to useful people, the driver was in the habit of charging very high rates - as much as $90 for a ride by several people to/from the airport. It got to the point where we were paying $75 a ride, sometime $120 a day, and he was making money in the interim. When I got an 'urgent' call to meet me on the road in front of a hotel only to have him fleece my guests and I for $100 in cash, I realized 'never again'. This was after several years of enduring a sort of patron arrangement. No amount of local guiding and conch salad was worth that much. The best day of my local travels was when I finally rented a car. It is a very colorful black-market system that is based entirely on trust:

- Identify someone with a car or van, or jeep
- They tell you where the vehicle is
- Find the key, normally above the windshield visor
- Use the car as long as you want at an agreed rate (usually about $70/day cash)
- Replace the fuel you used, so the fuel gauge/dial is roughly where you found it
- Return the car in the same place with the key and the cash above the visor - Viola!

I have taken all manner of cars - normally a 5–10-year-old US made gasoline car with high fuel consumption, automatic transmission, passable but basic air conditioning, and automatic windows. I must admit that by using EIS roads and many back roads to get to remote beaches, I have caused considerable wear and tear to a number of vehicles, but never been scolded by owners when I return them. If I blow a tire, I pay the replacement value. I always wipe down and empty out the car before returning it as a matter of courtesy. The sea grape trees by Surfer's Beach cause green streaks down white cars, which can be easily removed.

I tell the owner beforehand that I intend to go off road, so they have an opportunity to rent a more durable vehicle. The best sites are generally off Queen's Highway. With a car you have total independence and freedom of movement. On an island over 120 miles long, you can spend days touring and in fact find yourself driving literally for hours from end to end which is unique in the Bahamas. Since the Eleuthera is rarely more than a mile or so wide, there are myriad lovely beaches to visit in close proximity, whether the wind is from the Atlantic or Caribbean/leeward side.

You can rent a car from Hilton Johnson in Gregory Town at 242 335 6241 / Cell 242 359 7585 - he lives at James Cistern, email hjohnson@batelnet.bs. In Gregory Town Austen Thompson (Sr.) will rent you a variety of cars - call 242 335 5028/5128. Their garage is on the hill, overlooking the harbor. If you need to take a taxi just obtain one from the airport or ferry terminal, call one on

VHF 16 or on their cell phone, or borrow someone's VHF radio. It can take an hour or more for someone to meet you in EIS from North Eleuthera Airport (though it is only 18 miles) or Governor's Harbour, so plan ahead.

In summary, the most convenience and fun I have had renting a car is simply to declare, at whatever airport you touch down on, that you want to rent one. Within minutes you will be pointed to a waiting vehicle and can drive away - at least that has been my very satisfying experience to date. It truly is hassle-free. But try to get the owner's number in case you have to ditch the car somewhere different than planned.

Boat Rentals/Excursions To EIS:

Capt. Austen Thompson (Jr.) in Gregory Town can take you on his Boston Whaler for guided snorkeling and sightseeing tours on arrangement. If you own waterfront land, he can show you your lot too. But it is good for you to map its location beforehand since the coast looks quite uniform. Taking a boat on the Atlantic side will require a lot more time and is not always possible - I would suggest leaving from Harbour Island in that case, and exercising extreme caution both transiting the reef to Surfer's Beach and of course anchoring. I would not think you would want to leave a boat unattended on that side. You should have a weather window of 12 hours to avoid being trapped.

The windward side is called that for a reason, and the ocean is open as far as Europe and Africa to the East. Austen Thompson, call 242 335 2198 or ask for him at the hilltop garage in picturesque Gregory Town. On Harbour Island I recommend Michael's Cycles, Tel. 242 333 4433 or VHF Channel 16. Valentine's or other marinas can probably arrange to rent you boat/s or take you on a tour of your land on the East coast. It doesn't make sense to go by boat from Briland to Gregory Town via the Cut as it is too long a trip.

Surveys:

For surveys I am not going to name any individual. I used the "only thing going" and paid $1,100 up front. I think he did a fair job, but it took me half a year and the threat of an imminent visit to get the survey done. He had trouble finding a reliable starting point, so EIS had to provide diagrams. I am told one of the best things is for owners like us to find other owners who are surveyors by trade and ask them to do it for an agreed cash price. I would not pay locally until you have seen the result. Since surveying in EIS often requires cutting significant swathes of bush, I think it is a difficult task and should be monitored. Also take note of what your neighbors are doing because you may find that they, or you, are seriously off the mark! I hear a lot of talk from owners who fear that 'squatters' will take their land. There are two kinds of scams. First, locals may dig up paperwork, often illegitimate, and try to scare you off the land. I am told that showing them your paperwork will get rid of them - it is a form of blackmail or extortion. The only real threat as I see it is a legitimate squatter, but this is very difficult to achieve.

In law school they taught us the simple rule of thumb for adverse possession, easily memorized with the acronym OCEANS. Squatting must meet ALL of the following criteria to be legal: **O**pen (clearly visible), **C**ontinuous for the statutory time period (I think between 7 and 15 years), **E**xclusive (meaning the land must be fenced or sealed off), **A**dverse (meaning if the owner approves it is null and void) and **N**otorious. Basically, for squatters' rights to succeed the owner must have abandoned the land and not visited once during at least seven years, and the squatter must have farmed or somehow exclusively and continuously used it - if they take so much as a vacation the clock would have to start again. With those high standards, I think it is very easy to defeat a squatter's claim. If, on the other hand, you don't visit land you own for a decade, and someone else has made a living from it, well, the law says they deserve it more than you as a matter of public policy. I think you will agree it is hard to argue with the rationale behind the law, which most countries have.

Clearing The Land/Local Labor: My favorite kind of survey is the 'do it yourself' variety. You will need only about $50 worth of equipment from a Wal-Mart type store in the US, and another $50 or so locally. I recommend, at a minimum:

- 200' surveyors measuring tape on a roller that can be rewound
- 600' of clothesline or other durable, perhaps plastic-encased twine

- A boiler-suit or clothes which cover you from ankles to wrists
- Gloves, hat and durable boots - the purpose is to avoid extremely potent poison wood, which has five dark leaves on a yellow stem and black sap which is terribly painful (it is worse in the rain)
- A pair of strong gardening clippers with 2-3-foot wooden handles for mid-size branches
- A locally bought machete with a sharpening file or whetstone
- Lots of beverages, ideally water and some sodas
- Regular tent spikes which you can write on and drive into the corners or street junctures
- A felt tip pen with a plastic surface (i.e. a washing tub or gallon jug) on which to mark or stake out the corners

Labor: I have used both Bahamian and Haitian labor and though both do the same job equally well, I ultimately found that local Haitian labor in Hatchet Bay the most reliable, particularly a man named Leclas, or Nicholas. I have gone to the main square in Gregory Town to inquire after labor from the men playing dominoes there. Often, I have not received much help, and when I did, the fellow/s who did the work reminded me months later that they still expected to be paid more. Since my intent was to spread the money in the local community and engender goodwill, being solicited unjustly for money I had already paid indicates that my plan backfired, as neither of us was happy.

Once you identify worker/s, their schedule will normally be around not working at the hottest time of day, since clearing brush is tough physical labor. I arrange to meet worker/s who hitch, bike, or walk, at the Surfer's Manor hotel, at about 7AM, when it is still cool. I feed them breakfast of eggs and toast for about $5 each and give each cold drink.

I work with them on the site, either clearing sides of a lot or clearing inside of the lines that I have already strung up, using my surveyor's tape measure. One disadvantage of using string of value is that crab hunters who come at night are known to take down and use the clothesline. You need to be very clear about which trees you wish to save (those that give shade, palms, non-

138

poison wood, etc.), otherwise the entire lot will be cleared. Sometimes on their own initiative they will gather all the cuttings into central piles and light them afire after weeks of drying, but this should be monitored as you can upset neighbors if the fire spreads. This led to an eccentric sign painted on a piece of plywood on a charred lot a few years ago. It read: "Joe and Lisa - How could you burn this? Very uncool. Call us - Tony and Jen" or similar. I don't know how long the sign was up! Also note that bush grows back quite strongly within a few rainy seasons.

Over the years travelers have left abandoned VW vans and the like, scattered with empty tins, and there are several abandoned huts on EIS, but the worst has to have been after one of the storms which collected a number of dumps of soaked personal items like books, appliances, and other garbage. If you see such offenses, please speak up so we can stop them together. I have locals find and plant coconut nuts along the edges of the land once it has been cleared and pay them a simple $10 per coconut and $5 bonus if it is still growing in a year. I use the coconuts to mark the corners of the land as well.

I have found the local labor extremely efficient at clearing, and obviating the need for heavy equipment. A team of just two men and I have managed to clear an entire 120' X 80' lot in just two workdays.

Rather than stop for a long lunch, we eat a snack a re-hydrate for about an hour on-site, and I let them go at about 2PM, after which it is simply too hot to continue. The cost in 2005 for this work was $45 cash per day, so including sodas and soft drinks it comes to about $60. I think it a good idea to tip them after a good job, and of course the coconut and burning strategy keeps them active on the land.

Since remitting from overseas is difficult, I pay them in advance and have not been disappointed. I recommend you find a loyal worker first, test them, work with them, and appoint a clear leader who recruits and manages and pays their own team. Based on $60 per person, and a team of 3, that works out to $120/day if you work with them, and $180 a day if you don't. Using this price range, I estimate that you can entirely clear your land for less than $400 in labor, and less than $500 including supplies. Prices may have gone up since, labor must always be negotiated individually, and of course the Bahamas government conducts periodic sweeps of Haitians. If you can't find labor through Floyd Walkes or the other hoteliers who each have gardeners, try Hatchet Bay - one of the bars or cafes - or simply drive through Rainbow Bay in the morning until you spot a laborer. Ask them and hire them on the spot for work the following day.

One of the best values of local labor is simply clearing paths or roads to/from your land. If you point the right direction this can be done quite quickly and efficiently enough that most vehicles should be able to traverse the land. The limestone surface is sometimes so rough and indented so deeply as to make this too difficult, though. In general trees are not more than five or so inches in circumference and the flesh is quite soft with minimal bark, so a machete can make quick work of most of it. The larger trees such as palms you probably want to keep anyway. The soil I found is not very deep and is quite sandy, but trees can grow in soil-filled banana holes. These indentations are also useful for sinking a plastic cesspool system into so that it seeps into the permeable limestone. EIS is blessed with better elevations - of 100' and above - than any other islands I know except Cat Island, which boasts the highest elevations, at a mere 200' above sea level, in the Bahamas. I have cleared paths to both coasts from remote spots for under $100 that was still walk-able years later.

Hotels and Restaurants: In the immediate vicinity of EIS the three main choices are Surfer's Manor and Surfer's Inn actually on EIS, and the Cove Eleuthera Hotel just North of Gregory Town (see website above). I have not stayed at the Inn but hear it is very welcoming and laid back and is particularly popular with surfers. While working I stay at Surfer's Manor because of proximity to the land (no car required) and the full-service restaurant and bar provided by Floyd Walkes, who has immense local knowledge and is a generous host. He has kept a communal library for me there as well and has allowed me to store equipment with him. If hosting guests with bigger budgets, the Cove is a highly memorable stay, particularly for the fine meals and ambiance and to forget about clearing land for a while and have a swim! They have a nice small gift shop as does Gregory Town, which also boasts an ice cream shop. A favorite dining and hotel spot near Governor's Harbour Airport is Cocodima. But, I am told that it was closed in 2007 because the young Italian couple running it embezzled.

There are guest houses in Gregory Town and I think Hatchet Bay, the yacht club at Hatchet has long since burned down, but the Rainbow Bay club house with restaurant is meant to be very nice and the food and camaraderie to be very good. By far my favorite, romantic spot on all of Eleuthera is Rose Gibson's North Side Inn, just east of Rock Sound and past the well-marked Blue Hole, up the hill to the left. See eleuthera.com/rose.html and northsideinneleuthera.com, Tel. (242) 334-2573, email northside@batelnet.bs. This has been my best find along with the very charming Tarpum Bay. The food is local and hand cooked and very good, the views are spectacular, and the welcome is memorable.

Rose Gibson also has several lovely dwellings on the top of the berm, which are amazingly affordable - in the $150/night range - which she mostly rents out to visiting religious and student groups. A great place to cap off a long drive and a day of swimming. A piece of the space shuttle is under her deck. There are numerous wonderful homes and cottages for rent in EIS and beyond - I don't know the central website for such efforts, but renting these obviously supports your neighbors and provides more privacy and freedom.

There is a similar beach side bar called Tippy's, behind Governor's Harbour, and a new development with a bar and restaurant by Palmetto Point which looks promising. For quaintness and genuine charm anywhere along Cupid's Bay, Governor's Harbour is likely to cast a spell on you. I am particularly taken by the public library there which is a kind of expatriate community center, with art classes, internet access, great books, community and family-oriented events, etc. For simple bar life each town has a variety of local establishments, which have always been welcoming to me. Along your travels you will see several places to pull over for a bite or drink. Be warned, though, that gas stations can be 40 miles or more apart.

Conclusion / Websites:

I encourage fellow owners to keep in touch with each other, as there are many ways we can help each other carrying supplies and information to and from the land. I found that doing simple favors, like bringing spare batteries or printer ribbons for my hosts or hoteliers, or donating a VHF radio or GPS set, or books, creates good will, which comes back in spades. The cost of commodities on the island - from fuel to $1 for a tomato - are very high, and so haggling over prices may not be very productive in the long run. After travelling four times around the world and to over 60 countries I have rarely been treated so kindly and with such a genuine welcome as by the people of Eleuthera. I look forward to learning from other owners about tips and advice.

For resources about Harbour Island and Eleuthera in general, see briland.com and myharbourisland.com, Bahamas.com, and Eleuthera.com. Briland, as it is called, has a world of entertainment, restaurants, clinics, an ATM (there is one near the airport and in Governor's Harbor) and other resources and is worth a visit. EIS is unique in that it is one of the last zoned and approved developments with affordable lots and easily transferable clean title, free of the generational land and protected by belts of commonage land. Let's make the most of it!

U-Boats in the Bahamas

If anyone looking from the ridge behind Nassau Harbor or Forts Fincastle, Charlotte, or Montague, had strained their eyes seaward in the last week of February, 1942, they could have seen two German U-Boats, U-128 under Ulrich Heyse, and U-504 under Hans-Georg Friedrich ('Fritz'), steaming past, looking for more prey. Luminaries living in such posh locales included the Governor of the British colony, HRH the Duke of Windsor, his aide-de-camp Lord Brownlow, gold magnate Sir Harry Oakes, his son-in-law Count Alfred de Marigny of Mauritius, real estate developer Sir Harold Christie, Sir Frederick Sigrist (co-founder of Sopwith Aviation), and the Swede Axel Wenner Gren, founder of Electrolux. The channels north of Nassau, the colony's capital, would see nearly a dozen U-Boats in transit, including U-67, U-159, LI-506, U-558, U-753, U-103, U-51S and U-134, *en route* to sink the only United States Navy Airship to be attacked by enemy forces. For three months they were able to dally like tourists lingering over their favorite sites - by the end they were rushed and harried unable to come up for air or see much of anything.

These U-Boats, (the name derives from "Unterseeboat" for 'under sea boat') were the vanguard of 64 axis submarines which would attack or sink over 130 ships representing nearly 600,000 tons of allied shipping (605.000 by the authors' count) in the Bahamas and waters surrounding them, mostly in the winter and spring of 1942. Over 400 survivors from 15 merchant and navy ships would be landed in the islands. If the adage "Britannia rules the waves' still held true, then it could also be said that Germany's flotillas of submarines and their Italian counterparts ruled beneath the seas. For half a year, they struck unchecked terror in merchant seamen sailing through or around the Bahamas, leaving land folk dismayed and littering shorelines with the detritus and human flotsam of war.

Since geographic parameters vary in axis and allied records, the author includes incidents according to whether they occurred anywhere in the 20's latitude or 70's longitude or inside the 'Bermuda Triangle' (Key West/Bermuda/San Juan) or if they are nearer to the Bahamas than, say, Cuba or Florida. Other criteria are if there is a physical nexus with the Bahamas, in that a faraway attack leads to survivors being landed in the Bahamas or owners of Bahamas-registered ships being affected commercially.

While the Bahamas were not the operational centre of any singular campaign during the time- period covered, the archipelago was in the centre of - and straddled - a number of major choke points for merchant shipping traffic, which became flash points. The Bahamas form a sieve through which merchant shipping as well as U-Boats needed to pass in order to reach the US Gulf, the Caribbean, and the Halifax convoys to Europe from Venezuela's oil-producing Maracaibo basin. If the Bahamas were deep (the very name derives from baja mas, or too shallow) then U-Boats would have had to chase ships across ten thousand square miles. Because of the islands the Old Bahama Channel is a mere 20-30 miles across in places, and the Straits of Florida only about 50 miles in width. The islands thus place merchant ships - and their attackers - between a rock and a bard place on two of three sides.

In order to enter the Caribbean, U-Boat crews of 50 to 60 men sacrificed their water tanks to add fuel and range, and gave up bunk space to accommodate the extra provisions required to sail a month back and forth to the new hunting grounds. They were highly motivated and celebrated as elite heroes back home. Germany began picking off defenceless ships near die US and Caribbean coasts shortly after declaring war on the US in two waves of attack named *Paukenshlag* (Drumroll) and *Neuland* (New Land) in January and August 1942. *Neuland* alone, which was directed specifically at the Caribbean, accounted for over one third of all allied tonnage sunk in 1942 - 36%, in fact; an astounding figure. In contrast to those being bombed from the air, Bahamians were to prove that a people could be surrounded by an enemy and hardly even know it.

Tin's short paper concentrates on 22 merchants, as well as three U-Boats sunk in the theatre. This is a snapshot of the axis war on merchant shipping, from a maritime perspective. The equally moving story of RAF and US Navy counter measures and those that tended the survivors ashore is beyond the scope of this research. 'Fritz' Poske in U-504 had more important things on his mind as he steamed past Nassau in February 1942 than the feeble defences of the Bahamas. He had just sunk two tankers off Florida and was in transit to sink the MAMURA, a Dutch tanker of 8,245 tons fully loaded with gasoline, 165 nautical miles northeast of Great Abaco's Elbow Cay Light at sunset on the 26th. The explosion and fire from the attack was so severe that the submarine, firing two torpedoes from 400 meters away, was forced to submerge to avoid the burning fuel, which coated the sea surface. Capt. Peter Dobbenga and 48 others, including 35 Chinese crew, were burned to death or drowned. U-504 had opened up the killing season in the Bahamas.

Ulrich Heyse, in command of U-128 had enjoyed success off the Florida coast then cruised eastward through the Bahamas and sent a torpedo racing into the hull of the O. A. KNUDSEN, a Norwegian tanker carrying 11,007 tons of vaporizing oil, at 3 PM on May 5th 1942. The ship and her crew refused to die, however, and for twelve hours, well into the next morning, the submarine and the merchantmen played a deadly game of cat and mouse. The U-Boat would attack, the seamen would re-board the ship and send Mayday signals (SSS with a call-sign by Morse code), the sub would attack, the crew would board again, repair the engines and steam for land, or extract petrol for the motorized life boat and so on. Though the merchant ship *Nueva Andalusia* reported a ship afire to the US Navy, yet no vessels or aircraft were sent to aid the ship or its crew (this became the subject of an allied inquiry). Just before 3 am on the 6th, Heyse attacked with gunfire, setting the *Knudsen* alight. It finally burned and sank. The allied military and airmen stood by impotent and inactive in the face of many hours of distress calls. They were off balance.

The ships' master, Knut O. Bringedal and 38 crew set off for land, 65 miles away. They reached the coast of Great Abaco, just north of Hole in the Wall, the following day. They were towed ashore by a schooner and landed in the vicinity a lumber mill at Cornwall. One of the men, Able Seaman Olaus Johannesen, was unfit for further travel and when the survivors set off for the hospital in Nassau on the 8"' of March, he was left behind. Two days later he died in the care of the lumbermen, and, when the weather and poor infrastructure prevented their moving his corpse, he was buried on

site. He had been a miner in Svalbard, Norway until he left his hometown at the German occupation. Within a few years the lumber around Cornwall had been harvested and the lumbermen moved on, vacating their temporary community and leaving Johannesen's bones alone in the bush. There no longer is a community called Cornwall, Abaco.

One of his Johannesen's crew mates. Able Seaman/ Gunner Waldemar Lund was blinded in one eye by U-128's gunnery attack. He and the crew were met on arrival in Nassau by the Duke of Windsor who "personally provided them all with new clothes." After he lost his eye, medical authorities tried to list him as unfit for further service, but he vigorously objected, pointing out "that one eye was quite adequate for looking down a barrel and taking aim." He later sailed for many years as a gunner.

Commander Carlo Fecia di Cossato of the Italian submarine (R.Smg.) *Enrico Tazzoli*, acting in coordination with overall U-Boat command in France in a joint venture called Betasom, opened its Caribbean account. *Enrico Tazzoli* prowled to the north of the Bahamas, on the 13th, sinking the 6,434-ton British freighter *Daytonian* 115 miles east of Elbow Cay, Abaco, in 4,500 meters of water. The captain, V. J. Egerton, described a cheerful conversation with Di Cossato, after which he "asked if we wanted anything and then waved goodbye." "The sub captain was a pretty decent chap," the wireless operator said. "He fired only one torpedo and then waited for us to leave the ship before finishing her off with shells from a deck gun." One crewmember was killed, and the 58 survivors drifted in boats for 42 hours before being picked up by a Dutch ship and taken first to Nassau and then Miami.

Two days later the violent reality of the U-Boat war would again be brought directly to the shores of the islands, when the TAZZOLI sent a torpedo tearing into the side of the 8,780-ton British tanker ATHELQUEEN on the 15th of March a mere 50 miles east of Elbow Cay Light, Hope Town, Abaco. It was to be a messy killing of the 1928-built Furness tanker, leading to highly unusual damage: the submarine itself stove in its forward torpedo tubes in a collision with its victim. The ATHELQUEEN was en route from Hull, England to Port Everglades {Fort Lauderdale) Florida in ballast, meaning she was not carrying a volatile petroleum cargo. Captain C. J. R. Roberts led the 49 officers and crew towards nearby Abaco, a voyage, which took them two days, until the 17th. Sadly, three of the men were drowned coming through the surf: greaser David W. Firth, age 52, Senior Third Engineer William Proctor, age 30, husband of Nellie from Cadishead, Lancashire, and Abie Seaman Harold Jones, 21, son of William and Mary Jones of Conway, Caernarvonshire." The remainder of the men were "looked after by local people," before being sent to Nassau and thence repatriated to the UK, no doubt to continue as merchant seamen in that country's hour of need. Jones, Proctor, and Firth were buried in unmarked graves in the berm above the beach, A plaque erected by the Wyannie Malone Historical Museum in Hope Town commemorates the stranding and mentions Captain Roberts' report on 30 June 1942.

On the 10"' of March Di Cossato sank the CYGNET" by a terrifying combination of torpedo and deck gun. A Greek freighter of 3,268 Ions, she sank close to Dixon's Point, San Salvador, that the victims could sec land as 30 of them set out from the wreck. All of them survived, which indicates that they must have received aid from the islanders, however the historical record is silent as to their exact fate. Probably the ship sank at the 'drop off,' where water slides from shallow to 3,000 then 5,000 meters precipitously. If they sought shelter from U-Boats as they cleared Columbus' first landfall in the new world and the Crooked Island Passage, en route from Demerara (British Guyana) to Boston with bauxite, they didn't find it, though U-Boats would not venture into the shallow, clear waters for fear of being seen and bombed from the air.

U-506 under Erich Wurdemann opened up a new killing zone on May 3nl, 1942, utilizing the three channels, which form the boundaries of the large Cay Sal Bank. He sank the Nicaraguan motor ship SAMA, of 567 tons, a mere 30 miles west of Orange Cay, which itself an isolated island south of the Bimini chain and northwest of Andros. The SAMA was owned by the Bahama Shipping Co. Ltd. and registered to Bluefields Nicaragua. She was sailing from Baracoa, Cuba to Jacksonville with a cargo of bananas. All 14 of her crew survived, presumably being taken to Florida.

On 16 May 1942 U-751, skippered by Gerhard Bigalk hit the NJCARAO 95 miles east of Palmetto Point, Eleuthera with a single torpedo. The 1,445 ton US-flag and lightly armed ship was en route from Jamaica to Jacksonville with a cargo of 500 tons of fruit, bananas, cocoanuts and charcoal. In the scramble to escape the ship an officer and six seamen were drowned; the balance being rescued by the ESSO AUGUSTA on the 17lh of May. Reinhard 'Teddy', who entitled his autobiography humbly Ace of Aces describes his entry into the Florida and Bahamas region in command of U-564 that May with characteristic breeziness thus: "...I covered the whole length of the Florida Straits from North to South, sometimes off the Bahamas, sometimes off the American coast. This passage speaks more than anything to the thousands of miles patrolled in and around the Bahamas which have gone largely unnoticed by history.

The U-Boats' grim work would not have been known to Bahama islanders, and indeed the passing of their victims would go unnoticed for weeks, until the ship was overdue in port, survivors landed on a distant shore, or the sub commanders themselves broadcast their attacks and the allies were able to decipher them. A poignant example of a low-technology trading vessel sunk with all hands was the *Albert F. Paul*, a four-masted schooner. U-332 under Johannes Liebe encountered 185 miles northeast of San Salvador and dispatched with a torpedo after deck guns failed to sink the ship in heavy seas. She was carrying salt from Turks Island to her owners in Baltimore and all eight crew were killed, including Captain Southard and presumably his wife Ruby.

At the same time Heyse was attacking the *O.A. Knudsen* the 3,110-ton US freighter *Mariana*, carrying sugar from Guanica, Puerto Rico to Boston, was struck by a torpedo from U-126 under Ernst Bauer. The attack occurred only 30 miles north of Cape Comete, East Caicos Island, and 45 miles east of Mayaguana. All 36 men on board, including Captain Ivan Elroy Hurlstone, were killed when the ship plummeted to the sea floor on a steep ridge, which dropped off from to 5,000 meters. *Mariana's* eight officers and 28 men probably didn't know what hit them - the only groups keeping track of all these attacks were US and Royal Navy personnel who not only didn't warn merchantmen about the U-Boat menace, but intentionally kept the information from the general public. It stands to reason that a few survivors would have made it away from the *Mariana*, since the torpedo hit just aft of the main mast and she was carrying a non-flammable cargo. If they did, they were never heard from again,

On April 20th U-154 under Walter Kolle, sank the region's only Canadian victim, *Vineland* 41 miles north-northeast of Mayaguana. The 5,587-ton, Hog Island-built steamship was en route between Portland Maine and the Virgin Islands when a torpedo struck it aft. A minute later a surface-running torpedo barely missed, but a coup de grace at 9:20 pm tore off the stem section. Still the ship floated, and it took the sub's crew firing five rounds from the deck gun to sink her. Kolle questioned Capt. Robert A. Williams and the 34 survivors (one crewman was killed). They landed on Grand Turk.

On 6 May U-108 under Klaus Scholtz attacked the Latvian steamer *Abgara*, of 4,422 tons carrying sugar from Jamaica to Canada. She went down only 17 miles southeast of Great Inagua Light in 1,500 meters of water, fortunately sparing her crew of 34. They presumably rowed, sailed or motored to Matthew Town, Inagua for assistance. On 17 May U-558 under Gunther Krech, sank the *Fauna* only 25 miles from Mayaguana, and midway into the Caicos Passage, in 5,000 meters of water. The little 1,254-ton Dutch ship had been carrying a general cargo from New York to Turks Island, and the 27 survivors of a crew of 29 made it to Providenciales later that day.

In June 1942 the submarines penetrated deeper into the region, spreading as far as the US Gulf, the Panama Canal Zone, Aruba, Trinidad and beyond to the coast of South America. The Cay Sal Bank would prove a killing ground for both allies and axis seamen. By mid-July Horst Uphoff in U-84 could not penetrate the defences. He "sank two ships and damaged another before hastily retiring to the Bahamas." U-129 under Witte "decided against attempting the Straits," and went around Cuba instead. A mere 21 miles from Cay Lobos in the southern Bahamas, U-157 under Wolf

Henne sank the 6,401-ton US tanker *Hagan* on the 11lh of June, 1942, killing four officers and four crew. The remaining 38, some of them injured, reached Cuba. To the West, U-129 under Hans-Ludwig Witt hit the 3,274-ton US bulk ship *Millinocket*, killing 11 of 35 aboard. It is the closest wreck to Cay Sal Bank, roughly halfway to Cuba.

On the 27, U-153 under Wilfried Reichmann sank the US steamship *Potlatch* 980 miles east of Grand Turk Island. The Bahamas was to be the crew's salvation after nearly a month at sea, Reichmann stayed in the debris field long enough to retrieve a number of tires and inner tubes from the 7,500-ton cargo of army supplies, including trucks and tanks on deck. On arrival in France, he insisted on stringing the inner tubes along the sub's rigging and ringing deck posts with tires as Trophies for rubber-strapped Germany. The U-Boat skipper passed on cigarettes and advice to *Potlatch*'s master, John Joseph Lapoint.

Lapoint earned the US Merchant Marine Distinguished Service Medal for navigating 48 survivors across a vast swathe of nearly 1,000 miles of ocean to the uninhabited south-eastern shore of Inagua. Arriving around 22 July minus two crewmen (one died of a shark bite and another of exposure in the raft, and six were killed in the attack), they were forced to follow wild donkeys to fresh water. The exhausted officers and crew then set out again, making Little Inagua but finding little sustenance. Finally, they sailed to Acklins, and after the 29th of July were tended to by locals. The British, who requisitioned the private power yacht *Vergemere IV* to take the 47 survivors to Nassau, where they arrived on the 1st of August." *Vergemere IV* was owned by one of the Bahamas' true characters, Betty 'Joe' Carstairs, a cross- dressing, lesbian heiress who owned and ran Whale Cay in the Berry Islands as her own personal fiefdom, hosting stardom there and prompting a book entitled The Queen of Whale Cay. A serious powerboat and race-car driver, she funded world record setting speed attempts.

On June 29 Reichman in U-153 struck again, leaving the shattered hull of the US flagged steam ship *Ruth* squarely in Bahamian waters. At dawn U-153 sent one torpedo into the fleeing *Ruth*, of 4,833 tons and carrying 5,000 tons of manganese ore from Rio de Janeiro to Baltimore via Trinidad. The result was an extremely violent explosion, yet the following description of her demise was not untypical:

The explosion ignited the magazine and the whole stern was blown off. She developed a list to port and sank by the stern within two minutes. She sank so rapidly that the seven officers, 27 crewmen and four armed guards had no time to launch boats or to leave the vessel otherwise. Three crewmen managed to swim to a raft that floated free, and another crewman was picked up by the U-boat and placed aboard the raft after being questioned. The survivors were picked up on 4 July by USS *Corry* and landed at Trinidad. *Ruth* came to rest midway between Great Inagua and Acklins Islands, only one third of the distance between Hogsty Reef (an ominous navigational hazard and later the setting of James Frew's U-Boat mystery novel Bahama Passage) and Castle Island Light. This places her in roughly 2,000 meters of water between the aptly named Mira Por Vos ("Look out for us") and Mayaguana Passages, on the edge of Crooked Island Passage.

Helmut Mohlmann in U-571 opened the July ledger by sinking the *J. A. Moffett, JR.* some 52 miles north of Elbow Cay on the Cay Sal Bank on the 8th. The ship was salvaged, as were all 43 of the crew and gun crew who had put up a fight against the subs' shelling and tried to beach the ship. The master, Patrick Sarsfield Mahoney, presumably the last to leave the ship, caught his arm in the life boat's falls - it was amputated. He bled to death watching his ship steamed in slow circles. Merit, Chapman and Scott towed her to Key West that October. On 23 July Uphoff in U-S4 struck the *Andrew Jackson*, a President Line tanker in the same area, but the ship was rescued and put back in service. On the same day Witt in U-129 sank the ONONDAGA, the US freighter carrying 2,309 tons of magnesium ore, killing 20, including a passenger, the master of the *Thomas McKean*, sunk to the east on 29 June by U-505 under Loewe.

The sinking of the four-masted schooner *Wawaloam* on 6 August 1942 by Walter Schug in U-86 has a direct nexus to one of the Bahamas' most colorful expatriate schooner captains. When Captain Louis "Lou" Kenedy requested that his crew of two officers, four crew, one passenger and a dog be fed and towed to shore, Schug's colleagues muttered that he must have brass balls.

As it was, the survivors successfully navigated their way in an open boat towards Canada and were rescued by the merchant ship *Irish Rose*.

On the 12th of August 1942 U-553 under Thurmann transited the Old Bahama Channel after a convoy, in league with U-163 and U-658, but aggressive escorts and their accompanying aircraft deterred them. On the 18th, Staats brought U-508 into the Straits of Florida after transiting the Windward Passage. On the U-131 Gottfried Holtorf proved that a single good day could make an entire patrol and positively influence a career when he cornered three sizeable British ships in convoy TAW-12J up against Cay Santo Domingo and the southern Ragged Islands. In a series of deft shots he managed to sink the 2,300-ton British freighter MICHAEL JEBSON with four torpedoes just before noon. After missing the tanker STANDELLA he fixated on bringing down the convoy commodore's 7,000-ton flagship, the EMPIRE CORPORAL. Thirty-nine of the commodore's crew was taken to Guantanamo, but six were lost including one gunner.

Altogether U-598 left two large hulls in a cornet- only 17 miles west-northwest of Cay Santo Domingo. It was as though he shepherded the ships into a cult-de- sac, like forcing a school of fish onto a shallow flat on a falling tide. He was able to fire into them at will until he obtained the desired results. U-598 boldly remained surfaced during the entire day-time attack.

U-176 under Reiner Dierksen patrolled from 6 April 1943 to when it was hunted down and sunk on 15 May. In that time Dierksen managed to sink two ships in the Old Bahama Channel. The crew of the *Mambi* and *Nickeliner* were rescued by a Cuban Submarine Chaser CS-13, which sank the sub 21 miles south-southeast of Cay Sal, in 450 meters of water. It is considerably closer than the U-I57, which was sunk by the USS THETIS off Key West, and U-159 sunk off Haiti in the Windward Passage. Though divers in Bahamas claim that there are damaged U-Boats in both the Bimini and Berry Islands, and an unverified claim was published in the "Nassau Tribune", that U-342 left parts off Abaco, none of these reports have been substantiated. The author's deduction is that these were post-war wrecks, of whatever provenance. Not all subs are U-Boats, after all. Revered U-Boat historian Axel Niestle in 2002 corrected the record by placing the sinking of Horst Uphoff's U-84 only 408 miles equidistant from San Salvador, Samana Cay, Mayaguana, North and Grand Caicos, bearing northeast to north-northeast respectively, in 4,687m of water.

The Bahamas played unwitting host to U-Boat chronicler Herbert A. Werner in U-230 between 3 and 5 August 1943. In his seminal work *Iron Coffins* Werner wrote "we received orders to continue south through the Caribbean, ...[and] continued our march to the South with caution..." On April 6, 1943 Maus in U-185 scored the last confirmed kill in the islands by picking off the lead ship in Convoy GTMO-83, the US Liberty ship *John Sevier*. She was only 25 miles west-southwest from Great Inagua Light when she went down with 9,060 tons of bauxite ore, her full complement of 57 were rescued by the USS *Bennett* and landed at Guantanamo that very day.

The US Navy had begun organizing convoys along the eastern seaboard of the US, dedicating destroyers in the Straits backed by hunter-killer groups, blacked out the coast, included RAF patrols from the Bahamas and Civil Air Patrols from the US, and signed a cooperative agreement with Cuba and other nations to tighten the noose on U-Boats in the region. As a result, Admiral Donitz re-deployed U-89, U-132, U-402, U-458 and U- 754 away from the area. 1944 in the region was a year primarily of allied activity and axis secrecy. In late December of 1943 U-129 under Von Harpe tried repeatedly to attack convoys entering the Old Bahama Channel and Straits of Florida, but could never penetrate satisfactorily. As a result, he spent much of his 115-day patrol fretting to the north, east and south of the Bahamas. The tables had turned since the easy days of *Paukenshlag*, when Poske, Cremer, and Bauer came south from the American capes to obtain a few easy on their voyage home.

Nassau began World War U by receiving an influx of injured survivors and later developed die capacity to export vengeance on U-Boats in the form of hundreds of aviators in naval patrol craft. The Bahamas also supported aimed merchantmen and even destroyers. Landings by dismayed and disfigured survivors surprised and placed strains on local communities who were literally kept in the dark about the U-Boat presence until debris and people littered their beaches. Hospitals in Nassau tended to stranded survivors, and 'survivor camps' were set up throughout the Caribbean islands along with airstrips. Only one museum, in Elbow Cay Abaco, has memorialized U-Boat victims in the island. Bushranger landed thirty-eight survivors from the *Kollskegg* in Nassau on 11 April 1942 after drifting in the Atlantic for two days and meeting with other survivors from the sunken freighter *Koll*.

The deposit of *Kollskegg*'s hapless survivors and the evident chaos involved in trying to account for persons from disparate ships, origins, nationalities and destinations must have placed an extraordinary strain on and been an inordinate distraction to administrators in bases like Nassau, which were otherwise not directly touched by enemy action. Craton observes, "New Providence acquired an unfamiliar importance, as a school of operational training by the Royal Air Force... and as a base for ocean patrol and air-sea rescue work during the anti-submarine campaign in the Caribbean and West Atlantic." In fact, the U-Boat menace strained local trade and communication amongst the islands and delayed the transport of Bahamian laborers to American fields where a labor shortage threatened the harvest. Yet most ordinary Bahamians were spared any direct inconvenience by U-Boat attacks - amazingly, just about all of the attacks covered herein occurred out of sight of land, in deep water. This, along with wartime censorship, would explain why the battle raging around them has largely been passed over by students of Bahamian history.

There were over 400 survivors landed in the Bahamas, not including the nine men naval aviators rescued by the US Navy off Elbow Cay, Cay Sal Bank, and the crew of the Submarine Chaser SC-1059, which was listed as aground but then salvaged. Likewise, the 73 souls plucked from the Warrington are presumed to have landed in the US. It is hoped that the above survivor and rescuer narratives can provide the basis of a book-length treatment of the subject, since they represent the most truly Bahamian aspect of these attacks.

From the U-Boat perspective, 1942, punctuated by a steady flurry of sinkings and successes and comparatively few failures, ended with a whimper. Sporadic success dragged into mid-1943, becoming more like pulling teeth than knocking them out by the handful, as they had earlier managed to do. The submarines lost the flanking action, which the Italian submarines of Betasom provided when they were pulled closer to the Mediterranean and ultimately were ceded when the Italians switched sides. In July of 1942, Donitz started pulling U-Boats back to more profitable waters, sending boats off Freetown. West Africa and closer to Europe and North Africa (where U-155. U-103, U-510, U-173, and U-515 were sent) to stall allied build-ups there. In the Caribbean they had begun first to lose, and then to cede ground. Deaths by elite and well-trained U-Boat-men rose from a manageable hundred in the region into the thousands as submarines lost their resupply lines in as refuelling subs positioned mid-Atlantic succumbed to fluid, mobile and deadly aircraft-carrier hunter killer groups.

As the war progressed sinkings in the Bahama region became those of, rather than by, U-Boats, and allied losses were attributable as much to self- destruction and weather as any other factor. The Bahamas were as difficult to navigate for the allies, who lost three US naval vessels there. Ill-equipped naval gunners shot at anything that moved, including fellow merchantmen, allied aircraft, and even whales, which were depth-charged in pods during the war. The U-Boats were only able to maintain their dominance in the area for so long before the industrial might and resources available to their enemies, combined with technological developments such as radar, aircraft carriers, and code breaking overwhelmed them. When their attacks in the Caribbean were no longer profitable, they pulled back.

The Bahamas, Turks and Caicos and Nassau were spared the ignominy experienced by ports in St. Lucia, Aruba, Chesapeake Bay, New York, Charleston, the Mississippi River, Sydney, Kingston, and Trinidad and Tobago that were penetrated or mined by U-Boats. Just north of the Bahama region U-584, under Joachim Deecke deposited four German saboteurs on the beach at Ponte Vedra, near Jacksonville Florida, and similar operations was carried out on Long Island, New York, Maine, and Canada.36 U-Boats dealt Bermuda a wrenching blow when a ship carrying essential foodstuffs to the island was sunk. So many horses starved to death that "made it easier to introduce motorization after the war." One could argue that the sinking of the CYGNET off its shores prompted the US to open one of several Bahamian air bases in San Salvador. Mayaguana and Inagua, however, along with the concomitant benefits.

Perhaps the lack of a major single event affecting the majority of inhabitants of the Bahamas accounts for the general but near complete lack of knowledge about U-Boats operating there. The author posits that it is the very absence of a unifying U-Boat event in the Bahamas, such as the sinking of the Yarmouth Castle in 1965w or Hurricane Andrew in 1992. has led to this topic being largely overlooked in histories of the region. This paper sets out to debunk rumors and assert that the truth about U-Boat operations is much more serious and significant than the perception has been to date. With the cooperation of readers and witnesses to the survivors landed and ships sunk, the author hopes that this chapter of Bahamian history will be re-opened and expanded upon. As Michael Craton noted, during the U-Boat invasion of our waters, "For perhaps the last time, the Bahamas occupied a position of strategic importance in time of war."

Wartime Stories of Derring-Do 2011

It was kept quiet at the time, and is still not well known today, that waters adjacent to The Bahamas were an important theatre of war for a few months during the Second World War. Between March and August of 1942, German and Italian subs sought to destroy cargo ships carrying vital war materials, especially oil from Texas and Venezuela, to embattled Great Britain. These ships were easy prey as they transited the narrow shipping lanes running through, around or near the Bahamian archipelago. These attacks and sinkings were not reported at the time because of wartime censorship. Later, they continued to be hushed up, possibly to allay false rumours that Bahamians were aiding enemy U-boats.

In all, some 20,000 vessels were involved in supplying England through The Bahamas and some 75 U-boats attacked at least 110 of them. They sank or badly damaged 12 of them directly in Bahamian waters, leaving 362 survivors to struggle ashore on various islands.

This is a story that has remained largely untold, one that speaks not only of wartime derring-do, but also of the compassion and resourcefulness of Bahamian people from all walks of life; fishermen, lumbermen, well-to-do families and impoverished villagers who rescued and tended to the survivors. In some cases, the survivors were welcomed by no less than the Duke and Duchess of Windsor, the first royals in memory to hold civilian jobs - he as governor of The Bahamas and she as head of the Red Cross.

It is also a story that speaks of the extraordinary courage and resilience of the seamen involved, one that takes place in an area more significant to the war effort than most historians realize. The Bahamas was as important to the Germans as a hunting ground as it was to the Allies for its location as an international transit hub.

England would have lost the war without the precious cargo transported through a few narrow and dangerous channels: the Old Bahama Channel, a mere 20-30 miles across in places; Northeast and Northwest Providence Channels; the 50-mile-wide Straits of Florida; and various channels leading to and from the crucial Windward Passage. This is where most action occurred as the U-boats waited for ships to emerge from the various choke points.

O. A. Knudsen Goes Down: In February 1942 German *Kapitanleutnant* Ulrich Heyse, Iron Cross 2nd Class, in command of U-128, had already sunk two American tankers off Cape Canaveral, Florida, when he decided to round the north coasts of Grand Bahama and Abaco to hunt for bigger prey in the Northeast Providence Channel. After passing only 17 miles from Hope Town, Abaco, he sighted the 11,000-ton tanker *O. A. Knudsen*. It was Thursday, March 5, 1942, and this would be the first hostile sinking of an Allied ship in Bahamian waters.

Capt Knut Bringedal of the *Knudsen* had left Port Arthur, Texas, bound for Liverpool via Halifax carrying vaporizing oil. Most of his crew were fellow Norwegians who had managed to escape the Nazi invasion and occupation of their country roughly a year before. That morning, Heyse fired a torpedo that left the Knudsen dead in the water. However, Bringedal managed to restart his engines and began limping towards Abaco, roughly 80 miles away. He sent a Mayday that was received by other ships at sea, and also by the U-boat.

A second torpedo missed but a third slammed into the Knudsen, killing British deckhand George Smith. The Norwegian skipper loaded 24 of his men into a sailing lifeboat and sent them off for Abaco. He and the remaining crew transferred to a motorized lifeboat and, when they thought it safe, re-boarded the ship to send Mayday signals, repair the engines and again try to steam for land.

That evening, Heyse began shelling the tanker. He fired some 20 rounds into the ship, killing another crewmember. By nightfall the Nueva Andalusia, among other ships, reported a ship ablaze at the Knudsen's position, yet no Allied aircraft or vessels deployed to assist the ship, something that infuriated Bringedal and later became the subject of an inquiry. Bringedal put his men back into the motorboat and headed west, while the L7-/28 headed east, flying a victory pennant after destroying the largest Norwegian tanker then afloat. The Knudsen finally burned and sank on March 6, although neither skipper witnessed it.

Bringedal caught up with the sailing lifeboat the following evening and took it under tow. They made landfall north of the Hole - in-the- Wall lighthouse late at night, on the southern extreme of Great Abaco, near a lumber mill. This could have been Millville, Cornwall or Alexandria, lumber towns that no longer exist today.

One of the survivors, gunner Waldemar Lund, described the settlement as "... a negro island with only three white families." He wrote: "We were quartered in a chapel and given first aid and bandages by a negro nurse." Lund, who had been blinded in one eye during the attack, later met the Duke of Windsor in Nassau, who personally provided the crew with new clothes. Medical authorities tried to list Lund as unfit for further service, but he argued that "one eye is quite adequate for looking down a barrel and taking aim." He continued to sail for many years as a gunner.

Meanwhile, alerted by radio, the authorities in Nassau dispatched a hospital ship-likely the inter-island yacht, Content S- to pick up the castaways. The Nassau

Guardian and The Tribune reported that the captain and his surviving crew were met in Nassau by the Duke and Duchess and other officials. The papers continued to update readers on the survivors, detailing their departure for Miami, then New York and printing a letter of thanks from Capt Bringedal.

Able Seaman Olaus Johansen Gamst, 57, unfit to travel, was left behind in Hope Town to be tended by a medical officer, a nurse, and a handful of lumbermen.

He died and was buried there.

Italian Ace Sinks Two: A few days after the Knudsen went down, the Dutch-built freighter Cygnet, with a Greek crew aboard, was torpedoed after it exited Crooked Island Passage, en route from Demerara, British Guyana, to Boston with a cargo of bauxite and rubber.

The charismatic Italian submarine ace that sank her, Count Carlo Fecia di Cossato of the U-boat Enrico *Tazzoli*, was one of the most effective of the Italian commanders, di Cossato sank six ships east of The Bahamas within a 10-day period in 1942. Tragically, di Cossato went on to take his own life after Italy signed an armistice with the Allies in 1943, and the surrender of the Regia Marina, the Italian navy. For his wartime exploits, he received the Gold Medal of Military Valor, Italy's highest military honour, among other medals for bravery. Today, there's an Italian submarine named in his honour.

On March 10, the *Tazzoli* arrived within sight of San Salvador, ready for action. One of the crew, Antonio Maronari, mused in his diary, 'after a month of sea and sky ... here lies the first land discovered by Christopher Columbus, that if he had never existed, we might have found today ourselves! Too bad!"

Maronari claimed that just before midnight, following the first attack on the Cygnet, the Greek victims cheered them on from their lifeboat. "Apparently, perhaps because they are just five miles from land, they did not mind and instead, they show a great sporting spirit: it seems that they are commenting on the accuracy and the effects of our shooting," wrote Maronari.

An enigmatic character described in survivor statements as "a one-legged American by the name of A B Name," rowed out through the reef with two locals to guide the survivors ashore. According to reports, an unnamed 10-year-old boy said he heard an explosion and thought the men had come ashore in two rowboats. The men were taken to Nassau on the regular mail boat, the Monarch of Nassau.

In Nassau Mrs Ypapanti Alexiou remembers visiting 10 of the survivors in hospital and the Greek Orthodox priest, Father Theodore Spirtos, hosting those well enough to take meals at the Alexiou family's Gleneagles restaurant. The church also provided an apartment on Frederick St not far from the present site of the Central Bank. The Greek Consul, Christopher Esfakis, also aided the survivors, along with members of other Greek families such as Datnianos, Maillis, Esfakis, Psilinakis, and Mosko, who are still prominent in The Bahamas today.

After sinking the Cygnet, *Tazzoli* travelled north towards Abaco and its next victim, the 6,434-ton British steamship Daytonian. The diarist Maronari wrote: "After the night has swallowed all the latest tendrils of gold, the air cools and suddenly a light breeze ruffles the surface of the sea which has become gray. A pulsating light shines on the north coast of the island. The lighthouse of San Salvador works even in time of war? Is this an American's joke?" Coming from war-torn Europe it was difficult to believe the lax or non-existent security measures in The Bahamas and US East Coast. This entire flank was left exposed essentially from January to May of 1942.

The Daytonian had cleared the Northeast Providence Channel on its way from Mobile, Alabama, to Halifax and Europe with general cargo. On March 13, di Cossato

fired a torpedo and shells into the ship, sending it to the bottom some 100 miles east of Hole-in-the-Wall. Again, di Cossato was considerate. Capt V J Egerton of the Daytonian reported that the submarine surfaced after the crew had taken to the lifeboats and "the sub commander hollered to us and asked if everything was all right. He also asked if we wanted anything. Then he waved good-bye."

Only one man was lost, dying of a heart attack shortly after the ship was struck. Senior wireless operator Anthony William Coy, 27, of London, said the sinking marked the sixth time his ship had been blown from under him. "The sub captain was a pretty decent chap," he said. "He fired only one torpedo. And then waited for us to leave the ship before finishing her off with shells from a deck gun."

Egerton and 50 crew members drifted in six lifeboats for 42 hours before being picked up by a Dutch vessel and taken first to Nassau then to Miami on the steamer Eda K.

Enrico Tazzoli Strikes Again: Steaming in from Europe for the Northeast Providence Channel, Capt. C. J. R. Roberts on the tanker *Athelqueen* was concerned after hearing about the sinking of the *Daytonian* on his assigned course through the same waters. His concern was not allayed by the sudden appearance of a US military aircraft, which directed him to rescue the ship's survivors by flashing "SOS follow me." After diverting for a full 24 hours in a fruitless search, the *Athelqueen* resumed its course for Hole-in-the-Wall.

On March 15, a torpedo penetrated the engine room on the port side, 20 feet from the stern, closely followed by a second. When the *Tazzoli* surfaced less than a mile away, the ship's marine gun-layer opened fire. This forced the submarine into a rapid dive, but it did not sink deeply enough and rammed into the side of the *Athelqueen*, disabling the torpedo tubes.

The crew of the *Athelqueen* set off in lifeboats, but by late afternoon it seemed the tanker was levelling and might survive. Capt. Roberts was preparing to re-board her when di Cossato opened fire with some 60 rounds of shells, sinking the ship in about 15 minutes.

Roberts ordered all three lifeboats to stay together for a 65-mile voyage to Abaco, but they got separated and his boat arrived at the reel line three or four days after the other two. Roberts and his men got caught in the surf before finally breaking through to make a sale landfall. Not so fortunate were the crew in a boat that hit the reel, violently throwing the third officer overboard. The crew, thinking the boat had been holed and that the third officer had jumped for it, got panicky and five of them jumped overboard and started swimming for the shore.

The third officer managed to climb back into the boat but was unable to find the five swimming men. He caught up with the chief officer's boat and landed safely on the beach at daylight. Two of the men who had jumped managed to reach the island but the other three were either drowned or killed by sharks. They were greaser David Firth, 52; senior third engineer William Proctor, 30, from Cadishead, Lancashire, and able seaman Harold Jones, 21, of Caernarvonshire.

It is a matter of speculation whether their bodies remain north of Hope Town, on Elbow Cay, where historian Anthony Bennett has photographs of cairns of stones resembling three graves. A graceful limestone monument to the sinking overlooks the beach.

In his official report, Roberts wrote: "I looked round the island and saw some small boys looking at us so I spoke to them and asked if there were many people on the island, at which time they ran away and brought along the commissioner and the padre. The commissioner took us up to the village and billeted us in the various houses and sent for a yacht from Nassau.

"On the following day, March 18, the yacht arrived and took us to Nassau, where we stayed for eight days, afterwards going across to Florida. The gunners saved one Lewis gun together with a quantity of ammunition and this was left with a military officer at Nassau, who had it mounted in an official motor-boat."

Sailor Alan Heald told the *Bahamas Handbook* from his home in Preston, England, that a kind woman of Abaco wove him a straw hat, and that in Nassau he was adopted by the Farrington family. Fie also fondly remembers dancing to a gramophone on a balcony with one of the Farrington daughters.

On June 27, 1942, Capt. Wilfred Reichmann of UU53 sank the US steamship *Potlatch* 980 miles east of Grand Turk island. The survivors spent nearly a month at sea on a raft before being rescued. The 6,085-ton freighter was a major kill for Reichmann, who stayed in the debris field long enough to retrieve a number of tires and inner tubes from the 7,500-ton cargo of army supplies.

Potlatch Capt John Joseph Lapoint later earned the US Merchant Marine Distinguished Service Medal for navigating 48 survivors to the uninhabited south-eastern shore of Inagua, where they arrived around July 22 minus two crewmen. One, Ernest Miller, died after being bitten by a shark they had captured. The other died of exposure. US Navy gunner Estil Dempsey Ruggles told the *Handbook*, "When I got out of the lifeboat I fell flat on my face in the sand." He described how his shipmates foraged for mussels, molluscs, anything they could eat. They were too weak to kill the wild donkeys they found but followed them to fresh water.

The exhausted officers and crew then set out again, finally reaching Acklins in the southern Bahamas. After July 29 the British, who requisitioned the private power yacht *Vergemere IV* to take them to Nassau, tended the 46 survivors. The *Vergemere IV* was owned by one of The Bahamas' most flamboyant characters, Betty "Joe" Carstairs, a British heiress and powerboat racer who lived on Whale Cay in the Berry Islands.

Debunking a Myth: As the war progressed, the U-boats were able to maintain their dominance only for so long before the resources of the Allies and technological developments such as radar, aircraft carriers, and code- breaking overwhelmed them. When their attacks in the Caribbean were no longer profitable, they pulled back to the open Atlantic. The compelling story of U-boats in The Bahamas lies not only in the human interactions, which, for survivors, still resonate some 70 years later, but also in debunking myths.

By risking their own safety and surrendering meagre comforts to the war effort, Bahamians contradicted the unfounded rumours that they aided and supplied the German submarines. They did not, as the record bears out. There is not one shred of documentary or witness evidence that a U-boat exchanged so much as a signal or pack of cigarettes with anyone land-based in The Bahamas, though they sometimes pilfered from doomed ships or seamen. Instead, the people of The Bahamas stuck their necks out to help seamen in need. More records are becoming available all the time, but the last of the participants in the "Battle of The

Bahamas" are dying. To date, no book focusing on the war and The Bahamas has been written. This is a story that needs to be told.

U-Boats Attack Three Ships off Abaco.

It is fair to say that Abaco was the busiest area of German and Italian submarine activity during World War II - particularly the spring of 1942. Eighty percent (4 out of 5) of the Allied merchant seamen buried in the Bahamas are still located on Abaco. Out of 111 patrols to the area, over 20 scoured the coast of Abaco; a dozen rounded Hole in the Wall Light, and ten others rounded the island to the north. Countless others passed between Abaco and Bermuda. Twelve ships were sunk near or east of Abaco, including the *Mamura, Clan Skene, Tonsbergsfjord, Montevideo, Raphael Semmes, Everalda, Fairport*, and *Yorkmoor*.

Out of 344 survivors landed in the Bahamas, 89, or 25%, came ashore in either Hope Town or Cross Harbour to the south. One sub, U-128, came within 17 miles of Elbow Cay Light. Many others used Hole in the Wall as a navigational aid after Atlantic crossings, mostly from France. The three attacks on Allied merchant ships which were closest to Abaco were the *O. A. Knudsen*, sunk 65 miles from Abaco by U-128 on 5 March 1942, the *Daytonian*, sunk 115 miles away by the Italian submarine *Enrico Tazzoli* on 13 March, and the *Athelqueen*, also sunk by the *Enrico Tazzoli*, two days later and 80 miles away. As a result, 26,000 tons of precious shipping was lost off Abaco's shores in just a ten-day period. At 11,007 tons, the Norwegian tanker *O. A. Knudsen* was the largest tanker sunk in the entire million-square-mile region during the war. It was also the first ship sunk in the Bahamas area.

The *Daytonian* survivors were rescued by a Dutch ship – the *Rotterdam* – a few days after it was sunk. Since the survivors were not taken to nearby Abaco but to Nassau, this article will focus on the landing of survivors from the *O. A. Knudsen* and the *Athelqueen*. The *O. A. Knudsen* was German-built and took an entire day to sink. During that time Capt. Knut Bringedal and his men shuttled back and forth to the ship getting fuel for their motor lifeboat and sending SOS messages (which the Americans received but did not respond to). Just after midnight on the 7th of March the 32 survivors in two boats (a dead British crewman was left on board) made it to the base of Hole in the Wall Light but wisely refused to cross the reefs at night.

Fortunately for them, at 2 am a schooner came out of the dark and hailed them. This was possibly the Arena, over 50 feet and skippered by Capt. Sherwin Archer and his son Bobby. The schooner towed them all of that morning to the rail-head at Cross Harbour, which led to the logging community of Cornwall. The settlement was described, in language acceptable at the time, as "a Negro island with only three white families... [they] were quartered in a chapel and given first aid and bandages by a Negro nurse." Mr. J. W. Roberts of the Abaco Lumber Company – also a Member of Parliament – helped to accommodate the men and arrange for transport to Nassau aboard the *Content S.* the following day. Sadly, one of the crew, 57-year-old widower and former miner Olaus Johansen of Tromso, Norway, was left behind and died amongst the lumbermen. They buried him "on the spot" and the grave was only recently re-discovered.

The 32 other Norwegians went on to Nassau where they were met by Wallis Simpson, the Duchess of Windsor, who was head of the Bahamas Red Cross in support of her husband, formerly King Edward VIII and the Governor of the colony. Some of them were hospitalized and all but one Canadian were taken to Florida and thence to New York where they shipped out again. Several of the crew were sunk on other vessels, and a number of them were killed in the war.

The *Athelqueen* was a 8,790-ton British molasses tanker *en route* from the Liverpool area to Port Everglades Florida in ballast to load a cargo for England. Though she was convoy for most of the round trip, as she approached Abaco the ship was unescorted and alone. On the 10th of March she diverted to find survivors of the ship *Charles Racine*, sunk by the Italian submarine *Finzi* north of Puerto Rico. On the 13th she learned of the destruction of the *Daytonian* by another Italian sub, the *Tazzoli*, east of Abaco, and on its track. Then, on the 15th of March Captain Robert's ship took a direct hit from a torpedo and rapidly began to sink.

When the submarine, under Count Carlo Fecia di Cossato, surfaced, British gunner V. Coleman was waiting. He managed to fire some erratic shots from the ship's 4.7-inch gun. This was enough to force the submarine into a crash dive. The momentum of the attacker was such that it could not submerge enough before passing beneath the ship. As a result, the bow of the submarine was badly damaged and the torpedo tubes bent. The sub was crippled for the balance of the patrol. The men abandoned the sinking *Athelqueen*. Then the sub surfaced again near the bow, where the guns could not reach it, and shelled the ship 128 times until the ship sank.

All 49 of the men assembled in three boats and made for Elbow Cay, Abaco, which was roughly 80 miles to the west. One man, the Second Engineer, had a broken arm from the torpedo explosion. The boats arrived off Hope Town on the night of 16 and 17 March at different times. Captain Robert's boat arrived first and tried to go round the island to the lee, but was caught in the reef surge. After trying to row away, the exhausted men gave up and aimed for shore, trying to bump their way to safety. It worked, and the men landed on the beach, where they rested in the dark.

The other two boats were not so fortunate. The Third Officer's boat was overturned in the surf and 5 men were tossed into the waves and refused to get back on board. The Third Officer regained control of the boat and made it back outside the surf line, while the 5 swimmers stuck out for shore. Three of them drowned, and their bodies were not immediately recovered, however two survived. The Third Officer's boat met up with the Chief Mate's boat and they waited till sunrise. At that time, Radio Operator Alan Heald writes, "...two fishermen came to tow us in – one navigating and the second steering through the reefs."

At sunrise, Captain Roberts wrote that he "...looked round the island and saw some small boys looking at us, so I spoke to them and asked if there were many people on the island, at which time they ran away and brought along the [district] commissioner and the Padre. The commissioner took us up to the village [Hope Town] and billeted us in the various houses and sent for a yacht from Nassau." Alan Heald wrote that on the beach he was "...met by islanders and taken to houses where we were given food and found a place to rest. The Methodist minister's home was swamped by the addition of 20-odd crew members...".

166

Heald continues: "...The islanders couldn't have been kinder to us.... The Roman Catholic priest visited us and offered to let our families know we were safe... One

islander took me to his 'estate' to show me his crop of sugar cane and his palm trees. He generously cuts some cane and a coconut for me to eat... A woman islander wove me a hat from some kind of vegetation. The one thing that surprised me was seeing a small girl wheeling a pram which contained a recently born baby. ...I was told that this 14-year-old was a married woman and that the baby was hers."

A few days later the men were taken to Nassau on the government launch *Content S.*, the same vessel that had rescued the *O. A. Knudsen* men less than ten days before. The British sailors gave their 3 large lifeboats to the islanders, who towed them to the ship while singing a hymn with the line "God be with you till we meet again." In Nassau the men were billeted at the Lucerne and Rozelda hotels, where the Duke of Windsor bought them a beer.

After some recuperation time the *Athelqueen* sailors were repatriated to England via Montreal, Canada in various convoys. Alan Heald was sunk two more times within two months and afterwards moved to a shore job. The three dead men, Harold Jones, aged 21, William Proctor, 30, and David W. Firth, 52, are buried behind the berm under cairns of local stones. A monument in their memory was recently erected.

U-128's attack on O. A. Knudsen

The inter-island schooner Arena under Captain Sherwin Archer left Marsh Harbor Abaco bound for Nassau on the afternoon of Friday the 6th of March, 1942. Though the motorized mail boats *Stede Bonnett* and *Prescilla* had been plying the trade to Nassau and Abaco even had air service in the form of a 21-seat Catalina amphibious plane, Captain Archer and his son Bobby, the relief captain, used their 50+-foot converted sponge fishing sailing schooner to supplement the service. His sloop was to ply its traditional trade for a decade from 1940 to 1950, when even though it upgraded to an engine the Arena was supplanted by the motor vessel Tropical Trader, ending the days of sailing merchants between Abaco and the capital of the colony.

The night of 6th and 7th of March was fairly calm, with a light south-easterly wind but a persistent swell which crashed against the base of the cliffs at the Hole-in-the-Wall Light at the very southern tip of Great Abaco Island. Hole-in-the-Wall Light illuminates the deep-water northern edge of the forty-mile wide Northeast Providence Channel. Built in 1836 and completed in 1838, it was the first lighthouse built in the Bahamas by the Imperial Lighthouse Service. The light stands at 168 feet height and its single white flash illuminates the sea for 23 miles, or since the *Arena* passed the mostly white settlement of Cherokee Sound to starboard that evening.

Arena was navigating past Schooner Bay and towards the re-assuring beacon and approaching Conch Sound Point and Lanthorn Head after the midnight change of watch. Suddenly, at 2:00 am, the eerie arc of white light from the lighthouse illuminated something incongruous and startling – could it be? There was a raft of two small lifeboats bobbing in the water outside the breakers. The men were calling in heavily Germanic accents – and signaling with little lights. Could they be Germans attacking the Bahamas? Who were they?

Arena eased off the main sail and bore down on the boats – not too close to the reefs – to hear their story. The Captain, Knut Bringedal, called over that they were shipwrecked Allied seaman from Norway. Their ship, the *O. A. Knudsen*, had been sunk two days before during a day-long battle some 75 miles to the east (by the German submarine under *Kapitänleutnant* Ulrich Heyse, aged 35). They had half a dozen injured men on board, one of them, Seaman Olaus Johansen critically. They didn't know the coast line and didn't want to attempt a landing without local guidance. Was there any way that Captain Archer could divert his course and take the men under tow?

Faced with an unexpected humanitarian mission, in a remote British colony which had not been touched by the war, Captain Archer and his passengers and crew responded in the finest traditions of the sea. They invited the injured and crowded men on board from the two lifeboats and accommodated them as best they could. But then they faced a quagmire – the *Arena* was just a sailing boat and there wasn't much wind to propel it. On top of that, with two heavy life boats in tow and 39 men on board it would go a lot slower.

Since the *O. A. Knudsen*'s boat had a motor in it, and they had salvaged 25 gallons of gasoline from their sinking mother ship, it was decided that the rescued boat would

take the rescuing schooner in tow. This they did, tying the *Arena* behind the motorboat, and the lifeboat behind the *Arena*. With a local on board the motorized lifeboat they motored at about two or three knots three miles around Southwest Point and into the lee of the wind where it was calmer.

By sunrise about 5:30 am they were passing the abandoned settlement of Alexandria and by 6:30 am had rounded Cross Harbour Point, seven miles up the coast. The nearest settlement was a lumber camp named Cornwall, whether the third of fourth such migratory camp remains uncertain. In it were three white families and several black Bahamians, a small church, and even a nurse.

The motley group approached the community by their export pier, which was the terminus of a small temporary railroad. The *Arena*'s men steered the rag-tag convoy for this shallow point. Then the schooner anchored and the two life-boats were tied up along the jetty. The men were shuttled ashore and the word passed quickly to the managers and workers at the mill – they had three dozen shipwreck survivors to tend to – work would have to be put on hold for the day. Soon the owner of the mill, and the local Member of Parliament for Abaco, Mr. J. W. Roberts, of the Abaco Lumber Company, was alerted.

From that point on, whatever was needed was put at the disposal of the survivors, including a radio to contact Nassau. From there the motor boat, Content S was dispatched, along with doctor, Dr. Lyon, sent by the Chief Medical Officer for the colony, Dr. Cruikshank. Transportation was summoned in the form of the yacht *Content S* – as well as the nurse, a motor truck to move the men from the rail head to the community, and whatever else was required. The lumber mill was essentially cut off without reliable road access to Marsh Harbour, the main community on the island. They and their new charges would have to fend for themselves.

The following day the survivors from the O. A. Knudsen left Cross Harbor for Nassau, where they were met by the Duchess of Windsor, American Wallis Simpson, whose husband had resigned his role as King Edward VII and been sent to govern the Bahamas during the war. Also, members of the Red Cross, which the Duchess was President of, and the local press and populace thronged around Prince George Wharf in Nassau to see the new arrivals, the first survivors of a German submarine to be landed in the Bahamas ever.

Sadly, the next day Seaman Olaus Johansen, aged 57 and the widowed father of five children who fled a mining job in Svalbard the year before, died in remote Cornwall and was buried "on the spot". His grave lay overgrown and undisturbed for 70 years until amateur archaeologists from Marsh Harbor discovered and photographed it in 2011.

There is no memorial to the incidents and men of *O. A. Knudsen* in the Bahamas – or to the timber harvesters who tended to and rescued them – only mile after mile of Abaco pine covering the spot where the drama played out two generations ago....

U-Boats in Bahamas in WWII: A Local Witness

The morning of Saturday 7th August 1943 began clear and calm, with good visibility from the bluff on which the town of Clarence Town, Long Island, Bahamas is perched. During the summer when school was not in session young Ancil Rudolph Pratt was able to take his father's horses out to pasture in the morning. He and his friends Wellington Smith, Kipling Simms, Jeffrey Strachan and Isaac Taylor liked to take the horses to the coast southeast of Clarence Town and enjoy playing on the seashore while the horses ate fresh grass.

Pratt remembers that it was a clear sunny day and the boys had made it to the bluffs around midday when they all saw something so unusual that they remembered it to their dying days, and confirmed it by looking at photos later. They were several miles southeast of town on the bluffs. A boat of some sort emerged from the water about two miles out to sea. They could clearly see the "sail" or conning tower, but not any people on deck or on board. The craft was moving slowly and leaving a wake behind it. The boys could clearly see machinery on deck.

Judging from the comparative distance between telephone poles strung along the coast, which are spaced roughly 200 feet apart, the judged the length of the vessel to be about 200 feet. After ten to fifteen minutes the submarine submerged, though a kind of radio mast was still visible. The sun was over their heads at midday, the submarine headed from left to right away from land, towards the southeast. The boy's backs were to the high bushes and trees. They watched the mast cutting through the water and heading away.

Asked whether he had witnessed a submarine in Bahamian waters during World War II, Mr. Pratt, a former insurance salesman in Nassau for 25 years who runs a shop in Clarence Town and is a well-respected member of the community, he replied "it couldn't be nothing else." It also could not have been any other day – Sunday the boys would have been in Church and in weekdays engaged in either school or church. "This is not no story," he says, "I'm telling you I saw it with my own eyes."

The channel off Long Island was used by eight German and Italian submarines in World War II: the Italian submarine *Finzi* and the German U-boats U-84, U-108, U-129, U-185, U-508, U-732, and U-751. U-84 had transited the Crooked Island Channel east of Long Island on 10th July 1942, and the British Admiralty reported a submarine spotted on the 22nd of July, which might also have been U-129 under Hans-Ludwig Witt, however the sub was described heading southeast (same direction as U-84) and Witt was heading back to Europe.

Neither can be verified with certainty, though possibly the sighting of U-84 was made on an earlier date by fisherman and reported on the 22nd when they returned. The source of the sighting was "Hardbargain South Side Long Island, course South East." Hard Bargain was a largely abandoned salt harvesting community, also just south of Clarence Town Long Island.

Given the certainty of it being a Saturday in early August 1943, it was much easier to verify the sighting by young Pratt and his friends.

On Saturday the 7th of August 1942 *Oberleutnant zur See* Claus-Peter Carlsen, aged 23, was conning his submarine, U-732 back to Brest, France. He was on the 58th day of an 83-day patrol during which he attacked Allied ships three times and was counter-attacked more often, first by two US Kingfisher reconnaissance airplanes, and another time driven away from a convoy by two American destroyers. On the afternoon of Friday the 6th of July U-732 put the north coast of Cuba astern and passed west of Great Inagua in the southern Bahamas. At 10 pm local time on the 6th Carlsen noted his intention in the sub's log book, or KTB, that he intended to take a winding course through Crooked Island Passage as part of his return voyage.

By 2 am on Saturday U-732 was able to take a visual bearing on Castle Island Light at the southern tip or Acklins Island. He noted that the light was "shining peacefully and is very good for position-fixing." At 5:30 am the submarine submerged, having ventilated and charged its batteries on the surface. By submerging it made itself less vulnerable to detection and attack by enemy aircraft and ships, however their transit of the winding passage was only about halfway completed. They would need to verify their position before they were through. At 10 am they were southeast of the coast of Long Island, and by early afternoon were only seven or eight miles from land. If the submarine was on the surface it would have been visible from an elevation ashore with 12-mile visibility on a clear day.

During the hours between 2 pm (it might have been noon depending on the time difference between Germany and the Bahamas), and 4 pm, when the sub was next reported east of Clarence Town, Carlsen did not record anything, whether he surfaced or not was not noted. Certainly, if it was surfaced the sub could achieve four times its submerged speed of about three knots, allowing it to cover substantially more ground. It is also possible that before crossing the wide Atlantic Carlsen wanted to visually verify his position, particularly to line up a safe passage between Samana Cay to the south and Rum Cay and San Salvador to the north. In particular there are two large, Spanish-colonial-style churches on the bluffs east of Clarence Town which would have served as reliable beacons enabling a captain to confirm his exact position.

Whether Carlsen took the calculated risk of surfacing southeast of and out of sight of Clarence Town proper will not be known with certitude. He demonstrated in writing a propensity to approach landmarks and verify his position as recently as passing Castle Island Light some twelve hours before. The evidence suggests that five pairs of eyes witnessed the submarine indeed surfacing for a short time before heading east to break free of the shallow Bahamas and head back for Europe, where U-732 arrived on the last day of the same month. If so, it would be the only verifiable incidence of a living witness having seen a German submarine patrolling in the region – one Saturday morning out of some 1,500 other patrol days where the enemy prowled the watery region around the islands over the course of more than two and a half years.

Sir A. J. Adderley and His Ship *Emma Tuttle*.

Part I: Introduction

Sir Augustus John Adderley, KCMG, descended from Loyalist settlers to the Bahamas and rose to own a fleet of eleven sailing vessels and paddle steamers. A member of the Legislative Council in the Bahamas and Commissioner to the West Indies, he owned the Hermitage in Nassau and Salt Cay.

One of his vessels, the schooner Emma Tuttle had a storied 65-year history which included quelling an insurrection on a guano island and being captured by the United States Navy running the blockade to southern states. Amazingly the original captain managed to wrest control of his ship back and sail it from off the Delaware Capes to Rum Cay Bahamas during the Civil War.

Part II: Sir Augustus John Adderley

Augustus John Adderley was born in the Bahamas on 19 May, 1835. His great grandfather was Abraham Adderley, an American Loyalist who emigrated to the Bahamas by 1773 and between 1778 and 1783 was granted 720 acres in Long Island. His grandfather was Nehemiah Thomas Adderley, a planter born in Nassau 11 September 1773, died 2 January 1845 in Heron Bay, Long Island. Nehemiah's wife was Harriet Walker, his mother Frances nee Lewis. Augustus' father was the Honorable Henry Adderley (born Long Island 1803, died London 1875) a "merchant and politician in the Bahamas." His mother was Mary Ann (nee Perpall, 1806-1882) from a "Minorcan family, which had relocated to Nassau."

His parents had a dozen children, from whom his sister Eliza Margaret stand outs. Born in 1833, in 1854 she married Sir George David Harris, a London merchant who exported leather-ware polishes and pastes from the UK to the Bahamas. Augustus married Letitia Anne Hall. Annie's father William Henry Hall owned the Hermitage, a historic retreat in eastern Nassau which still stands. Later in their marriage they lived in Douro Place, Kensington, London with their daughter and her husband, Frederick Beaumont, who kept a studio in the Adderley home.

In the 1850s and 60's Augustus was active in the purchase of mostly ocean-going schooners of American and Bahamian construction. These included, in alphabetical order, the schooner *Agnes* of 8 tons (built in Abaco in 1860), the 5-ton schooner the schooner *Emma Tuttle*, the *Eugenie*, built 1859, the paddle steamer *Fanny and Jenny*, 207 tons and 450 horsepower, the sloop *G. Garibaldi*, of 4 tons, the schooner *Ida* of 26 tons, built 1850, schooner *Julia Marshall* of 47 tons, built 1849, schooner, the schooner *Laura* of 50 tons built 1847, schooner *Sue*, 78 tons, *Volant*, 96 tons built 1847, *W. Y. Leitch* of 35 tons built 1853.

It would appear that Adderley was involved in business with his brother-in-laws family, the Harrises. S&H Harris was a firm selling "household requisites" including waterproof blacking used for leather. In 1861 the Harrises wrote to Foreign secretary (later Prime Minister) Earl Russell as follows: "It has been our practice ever since the

establishment of mail steam—ship communication between New York and Nassau, Bahamas, to ship general merchandize from London to New York for re-shipment to Nassau."

They go on to complain that the US government was confiscating items deemed intended via blockade running for the rebellious south. Adderley's part in the equation was to provide cargo service between New York and Nassau on his larger ships, the *Emma Tuttle* and the *Fanny and Jenny*. In 1868 Augustus and his father Henry "invested in the London and Westminster Bank, using the Harris address as their London contact." In 1884 he purchased the Hermitage in Nassau from his father-in-law William Henry Hall and in 1886 he bought Salt Cay, northeast of Nassau from Charles King Harmon - he sold it in 1872 for a ten-pound profit.

As Adderley's businesses prospered so did his civic responsibilities. He became in turn a Member of the Legislative Council of the Bahama Islands, a Royal Commissioner for the Bahamas and Executive Commissioner for the West Indian Islands. In 1883 he authored a 56-page pamphlet for the International Fisheries Exhibition in London entitled "The Fisheries of the Bahamas." In 1886 he was the Executive Commissioner for Jamaica at the Colonial and Indian Exhibition, London. The same year he was awarded the K.C.M.G. in London

Part III: The *Emma Tuttle* Early History

The schooner *Emma Tuttle* was built in East Haven, Connecticut in 1849. The exact origins of her name are not known, however a little Emma Louise Tuttle from New Haven died at aged 9 – her parents were Lucius & Hanna and she died September 8, 1845, less than four years after the Emma Tuttle was launched in the same town.

The two-masted sailing ship was built of wood. Her dimensions were 74 feet in length, 23 feet 7 inches wide, and 6 feet 8 inches deep. She had a bullet-shaped bow, a square stern, no figurehead and a single deck. Although the tonnage rose from 100 tons to 117 tons over her career after she was flagged to Nassau Bahamas in 1861, the vessel had a remarkably constant career, lasting until at least 1915 – over 65 years – under the same name.

For the first twelve years of her life Emma Tuttle was registered to New Haven, Connecticut and traded coastwise and from the West Indies to the US under the United States flag. Her captains during this period included George M. Bunnell, James H. Woodhouse, George W. Jarvis, Daniel Cornell, J. B. Carver, and Oliver W. Miller, who, along with Adderley seems to have been the vessel's final owner. In 1859 Miller was the skipper and Cornell the owner. By 1880 she had been given an official number (46044) and was flagged to Nassau, Bahamas, and was owned by Adderley. The ship seems to have had a busy career well beyond her original coastwise trade. On May 10 1858 she was reported due in from Matanzas, Mexico with a cargo of Pineapples under Captain Oliver Miller. In 1859 she was carrying mail between San Juan Puerto Rico and New York.

On 24th July 1860 Captain Bunell was involved in helping to Burnell put down a "negro" insurrection on the Sombrero Guano Island guano mining port near Venezuela. The island was a base to some 200 workers of African descent and 12 white traders. According to the *New York Times* an American overseer named Mr. Snow was temporarily put in charge of British and Danish subjects of African descent. The freemen resented the Americans for that country's continuance of slavery, and specifically they detested Snow, who had been a mate aboard ships and was accustomed to meting out strict discipline and harsh punishment. Four of the black men resolved to murder Snow, and with support of accomplices managed to smash his skull with a guano rock.

Captain Burr of the ship *Warren* imprisoned the lead insurrectionists but the situation remained very tense. Captain Bunell of the *Emma Tuttle* raced Petersburg, Virginia, where the ship arrived August 10th 1860. His report led to the drafting of a posse of 50 Irish "hands" from Richmond, armed with at least as many revolvers, who were dispatched to quell the insurrection and liberate the 12 white overseers. How the situation was ultimately resolved is not known, but the *Emma Tuttle* contributed a key role in communicating the events to the mainland.

The *New York Times* of July 1861 shows her having left Saint Kitts in the West Indies for the Bahamas on the 19th of that month. The schooner appears to have had a steady career, and was listed in the 1880, 1890, 1900, 1910, and 1915 Mercantile Navy Lists. By 1915 her tonnage was listed as 108 and year of build 1859 – and Adderley was still listed as the owners, though he had been dead by then for 10 years – Adderley must have had assignees. Her final demise is not known.

Part IV: *Emma Tuttle* evades US Navy capture

Adderley and his business partners appear to have placed the *Emma Tuttle* in the potentially very lucrative yet highly risky trade of blockade running – sneaking much-needed supplies and war materiel into Confederate ports and hoping that the alert US Navy didn't intercept the ship. By early December 1862 it looked as though the game was up. William A. Parker, Commander of USS Cambridge had this to report to his superior, Acting Rear-Admiral S. P. Lee, head of all Union blockading operations, in Hampton Roads, Virginia. The date was 3 December 1863 and the port that Parker reported from was Wilmington, North Carolina:

At dawn "....the schooner *Emma Tuttle* was observed lying under Smith's Island, less than a mile from shore. On spying us she slipped chain and stood to the S.E., coasting along Cape Fear Shoal. We overhauled her after a chase of 10 miles. The captain of said schooner acknowledges his intention of running the blockade. No other vessels in signal distance. ...The captured schooner *Emma Tuttle* was from Nassau with an assorted cargo. I have sent her to New York under charge of Acting master's mate W. F. Durgin, with the papers and necessary orders. She had a contraband cargo."

On December 7, 1862 the northern papers crowed that the *Emma Tuttle* was captured by the US blockade off Wilmington, North Carolina. "At about 8 o'clock AM the *Cambridge* returned with the schooner *Emma Tuttle* of Nassau, also trying to run the blockade. At noon the schooner *Brilliant* of Nassau was chased by the United States steamers *Daylight* and *Mount Vernon*, thus making three vessels lost to the rebels in one day."

Dawsons *Daily Times and Union* January 6, 1863 reported that "The schooner *Emma Tuttle*, captured by a Yankee cruiser and put in charge of a prize crew, has been

recaptured by the original officers and crew who were confined on board. She has been taken back to Nassau with prize crew as prisoners." The *New York Times* of Sunday the 25th of January 1863 places the date of her return to Nassau at Monday the 19th of January: "The schooner *Emma Tuttle*, J. B. Carver, Master, was captured on the coast of North Carolina, early this month, by the Federal gunboat *Cambridge*, and a prize crew put on board. The weather becoming boisterous, and the Prize-master being an inexperienced navigator, he requested Capt. Carver to resume his command of the vessel, and take her to the nearest port. This he refused to do, unless the vessel was restored to him. Upon the Prize-master's acquiescence, Capt. Carver again took charge, and steered the *Emma Tuttle* to Rum Cay. The Prize-Master and his crew arrived at Nassau on Monday last."

This was followed shortly by a report entitled "Interesting from Nassau - recapture of the schooner *Emma Tuttle*, Charleston: "A Nassau letter, of the 22d [December, 1863], received here, reports the recaptured and arrival at Rum Cay, of the schooner *Emma Tuttle* taken by the Yankee blockaders off Wilmington. It appears that a terrific gale sprung up, and the Federal Captain and prize crew becoming alarmed, released and sought the assistance of the Captain of the captured vessel. The latter, with the mate and cook, succeeded in getting possession of all the arms on board, recaptured her and took her to Nassau. The Yankee officer and crew were landed at Nassau."

Months later the Union Navy appear to have been none the wiser as to the fate of W. F. Durgin and his prize crew. Commander S. P. Lee of the US Flagship USS *Minnesota* reported to the Honorable Gideon Welles, Secretary of the Navy in Washington that he had "….no information regarding the Acting Master's Mate W. F. Durgin." He wrote on 20 February 1863 that "I knew nothing more of the *Emma Tuttle*, the prize in his charge, than that she had arrived at Nassau, in charge of her original crew, as I had learned from paragraph in the public prints."

Part V: The *Fanny and Jenny* and General Robert E. Lee's Golden Sword

As mentioned, the *Fanny and Jenny* was a sizeable vessel at 297 tons, propelled by two side-wheel paddle wheels of 450 horsepower. This was altogether a larger beast than the comparatively small 108-ton *Emma Tuttle*. The *Fanny and Jenny* was built of iron and was 202 feet long, 28 feet wide and 13 feet deep. The vessel began its career as the *Scotia* built by Wigram and Company of Blackwell, England in 1847. As well as her engines the ship had sails to propel it. Harrison and Forwood of Liverpool purchased the *Scotia* to run the blockade and had two successful

178

voyages before the ship was captured by USS *Restless* in Charleston on October 24th, 1862.

Augustus Adderley was able to purchase the *Scotia* at a northern prize court auction and re-christened the ship *Fanny and Jenny*. The profits of running the blockade were highly alluring. By late 1863 the only port still reasonably passable to blockade runners was Wilmington, North Carolina. It is said that General Robert E. Lee of the Confederacy stated "If Wilmington fails, I cannot maintain my army." The *Fanny and Jenny* succumbed to weather, not the northern blockade. On the night of February 9th, 1864, she grounded near the recent wrecks of the *Dee* and *Emily of London* near Masonboro Inlet on Wrightsville Beach.

According to historian Dr. Chris E. Fonvielle Jr., "strong circumstantial evidence suggests that... [*Fanny and Jenny*] carried a gold sword destined for General Robert E. Lee." Commander Pierce Crosby of the USS *Florida* captured 25 of *Fanny and Jenny's* crew. "The *Fanny and Jenny's* cargo reportedly comprised only a few small articles of merchandise and a good deal of coal, but one of her engineers informed Commander Crosby that there was a handsome sword, gold mounted, for General Robert E. Lee on board. It was destroyed with the vessel; it was a presentation sword."

The sword was allegedly sent by an English nobleman and was valued at the equivalent of $42,000 in today's currency. Though the location of the wreck of the *Fanny and Jenny* is generally known in the Carolinas, the sword has never been found. The USS *Florida* assisted by the USS *Cambridge* tried to salvage the *Fanny and Jenny* however southern sharp shooters kept the sailors at bay, and locals managed to burn the three stranded ships to the waterline. The sword has since become "the Holy Grail of blockade running at Wilmington during the Civil War."

Part VI: Epitaph

It would appear that Adderley and his colleagues wasted no time after the Emma Tuttle's arrival at Rum Cay on the first week of January, 1863. Within two weeks her freedom must have been obtained by the authorities in Nassau and W. F. Durgin and his men deposited there, because by the 27th of January the Emma Tuttle was back off the coast of the Carolinas, trying to run the blockade again. On that day the USS *Hope*, under Captain Florence, managed to intercept her off Charleston, a port known to be well blockaded by the Union, suggesting the desperation the owners must have felt.

On February 14th 1863 the *New Albany Ledger*, in Indiana, reported in that the *Emma Tuttle* was in sorry state, apprehended off Charleston on accusation of possible blockade running: "The schooner *Emma Tuttle*, flying the English flag, on the 17th of January last, off Charleston. She purported to be from Nassau, bound for Baltimore, though at the time she was steering southeastward. The vessel has been pronounced unseaworthy, but her cargo, consisting of a number of bags of salt-peter [used in gunpowder], with the greater portion of her crew, has been sent to Philadelphia. The schooner has been taken once before, but her crew succeeded in recapturing her."

The vessel did not reward the Yankees as quickly as they had hoped, as at her first auction she was not sold. According to the New York Times of March 3, 1863, "All the prize vessels and cargoes captured by the Blockading Squadron and other war vessels that have been brought to this port have been converted into money, with the following exceptions, viz.: Steamer Bermuda and schooner *Emma Tuttle*." Since she reverted to Adderley's ownership for several more decades, it can only be assumed that he managed to buy her through agents in New York the second time around, just as he had with the *Scotia* in New York earlier, converting her to *Fanny and Jenny*.

Historia del Sumergible U153 (in Spanish, u-historia.com)

Alumni Reflection on Lyford Cay School

I first attended Lyford Cay School, as it was then known, in the fall of 1974. I was four years old and one of four children from Cable Beach who attended the school. I'll never forget that on my first day there was a boy who refused to leave his car and kept yelling, "I'm not going!" His mother and the headmistress at the time, Mrs. Millar, managed to carry him out of the car. I promised myself not to behave like that.

I was to spend five school years at Lyford Cay School, from kindergarten to fourth grade. Some of my happiest memories consisted of the game days when we could compete at fun sports like the three-legged run with my friend Chris Dinnick, the sack race, and, perhaps most fun of all, the dog show where we brought our dogs Honey (a golden lab) and Chippy (a black potcake) to compete. Of course, I have other memories: guilt over stamping on the tail of a lizard and seeing it fall off (I was hugely relieved to learn that their tails grow back), and wariness of the occasional corporal punishment meted out. I also remember the thrill and nervousness at being entrusted by some of the faculty to leave the gates with cash in order to buy them goods at the City Market! However, of all these experiences, the school's proximity to the sea was to have the most profound effect on me.

The Canal and Ocean:

Apart from the lessons, the homework, uniforms, the various crushes that develop at that age, the spirited softball games, the competition over who got the best lunch, the car pools, and seeing our first film on a large reel at a birthday party (Treasure Island at the Wilkinsons), the nearby ocean made the biggest impression on my young mind.

At that time in the club's history there were no buildings, walls, or working roads between the school playground and the edge of the canal. This meant that a curious loner like me could wander across the field during recess and sit enchanted at the lip of the canal, staring at the beckoning sea. From the edge of the concrete canal I could see lovely fish darting out from under the boat: jellyfish, larger fish in the deeper water, and all manner of little sea creatures. I was enraptured.

There was an authentic, working fishing smack kept moored along the sea wall. I will never forget its orange painted, chipped and dry deck, the white hull with a pretty blue stripe at the water line, the tiller, the fish-well, and the scales of past victims scattered across the cockpit. And, of course, the mast, the sails tucked away, and the outboard engine. It was all very tantalizing for a boy of about six.

By far the most vivid sentiments that I remember from these peaceful, thoughtful sessions on the water were that I wanted more than anything to venture out to sea, beyond the canal entrance, and to experience adventures on the world's open waters. Also, I dreamed that one day I would build a house along the east side of the canal where there were no houses – and still aren't any. The first dream I managed to fulfil over the next 25 years, though admittedly I have not reached the stage in my career yet where I can fulfil the second!

Sailing Away

In summer camp in North Carolina and in the waters of Cable Beach I learned how to sail a Sunfish. At 17, I sailed offshore – out of sight of land – with an uncle in Sweden. At 18, I was paid to race from New England to Bermuda – 660 miles away – and sail back. I was hooked. I went to boarding school in Newport, Rhode Island, and the school had its own yacht, which I sailed in The Bahamas.

At Boston College

I joined the sailing team. Over the next four summers I managed to cross the Atlantic Ocean and race yachts to, or deliver them back from, Bermuda numerous times. I even once sailed into Nassau from Bermuda after spending two weeks at sea in a failed attempt to cross the Atlantic. Since I had no way of informing my parents, they were surprised when I arrived home!

At age 23, I was chosen to command a 68-foot wooden sailing yacht from the Galapagos Islands to New Zealand; the voyage across the Pacific took five months. By age 25, I earned a license to skipper 100-ton vessels. After three years in Singapore operating big tanker ships, I moved back to Newport and started my own company transporting yachts globally, but mostly from New England to the Caribbean and back. Between 1987 and 2007, I sailed to or from Bermuda over 30 times, mostly as captain.

To be sure, there were lots of adventures and stories. I made numerous voyages between ports in Canada and Maine, and as far south as Florida. I was knocked overboard in a snowstorm at dusk in my underwear and was rescued after 16 minutes in the water. Off Trinidad, a large yacht caught fire, burned and sank under us. We were enveloped in lightning storms, deprived of food (two weeks on a bowl of pasta and a slice of bread daily), and I once tried to deliver the wrong yacht. When I was running tankers, four men died and two ships were lost.

Swallowing the Anchor

After all this, I realized that the life of an itinerant yacht captain was not the most secure future for me, and I hung up my sea boots at the age of 36, some 20 years after I started and with no regrets. I obtained two graduate degrees; married, secured full-time work in the New York area, and my wife and I had a child. I also devoted time to writing and publishing books – five so far. I still stay in touch – via online tools that we could only dream about in the 1970s – with my schoolmates from Lyford Cay International School. I was even invited back to campus to speak about a book I wrote about The Bahamas during the World War II era.

Throughout all of life's voyages, I fondly remember when I first got the bug for global adventure, an impressionable little boy in a school uniform dangling his legs over the edge of a canal, looking out to sea and dreaming of crossing oceans.

My voyage isn't over, but it's been a great ride so far, and I hope it will be for generations of Lyford Cay International School students going forward. My life motto was originated by sailor-historian Samuel Eliot Morison: "Dream dreams, then write them. Aye, but live them first." What dreams will you live out?

U-Boats in the Bahamas

Starting shortly after the United States' entry into the war against Germany during World War Two in December 1941 there were 170 enemy patrols by German and Italian submarines into the waters around the Bahamas and Bermuda, both British colonies at the time. These submarines patrolled for a total of 1,505 days in the area and sank 181 ships worth an aggregate of over 1 million tons (1,013,315 Gross Registered Tons) during a three-year period up to the end of 1944.

The geographical area covered consists of roughly 1.2 million square miles of ocean, and has not been comprehensively treated in any one historical text to date. In contract the regions around Cape Hatteras, the US Gulf, and the Caribbean have each been treated by Michael Gannon, Homer Hickham and Gary Gentile (Hatteras and Operation Drumbeat), Gaylord Kelshall (Caribbean) and Melanie Wiggins (US Gulf). The rule of thumb has been simply:

did the casualty occur closer to the shores of the Bahamas and Bermuda than to any other land mass.

There is overlap with the coasts of Florida, Cuba and the Greater Antilles, as the area stretches east of Florida to east of a line connecting Bermuda and Anegada in the Caribbean. Around Bermuda an arbitrary square is drawn, 800 nautical miles on each side, or 400 miles in radius around the island. The area including the Bahamas east to Bermuda (Havana – Savannah – Bermuda – Anegada) is roughly 1 million square nautical miles, and the area north, west, and east of Bermuda is roughly 200,000 square nautical miles for a combination of 1.2 million.

Most of those ships (70) were US-flagged steam ships or motor tankers, and most of them had sailed from or were destined to the port of New York. This is their story, and that of the survivors. Overall, the aggregate tonnage of the US-flagged ships attacked in the region amounted to nearly half a million GRT (406,105 tons). The average tonnage per ship was 5,800 GRT – a considerable size at the time.

The 70 US-flagged vessels were manned by 3,343 persons, including passengers, some of them military personnel and their families. Of these nearly 1,000 (939) lost their lives, and 2,869 survived and either landed on their own volition or were rescued by other merchant ships, naval vessels (predominantly from the US Navy) or aircraft (again, predominantly from the US Navy based in Bermuda).

Four hundred and ninety-one survivors were landed in either the Bahamas or Bermuda. Since only the 47 men from the SS *Potlatch* were landed in the Bahamas from US ships, the balance, or 444 persons, were landed in Bermuda.

Background / Allied Defenses:

The best way to summarize the 181 attacks is chronologically. There were basically two waves of German submarine attacks: Operation Drumbeat focused on New York and Cape Hatteras, which lasted from January to March 1942 and Operation *Neuland* (literally new land), focusing on the Caribbean and US Gulf, which began in late Spring 1942 and continued into the summer, peaking in July. After that attacks were intermittent, with a small revival in the latter half of 1944, however as these patrols resulted more often in Axis rather than Allied losses, they had less impact on accounts of merchant marine survivors.

At first the US lacked the adequate equipment and materiel to protect their southeastern flank, and what vessels they had were being deployed to Japan and the Pacific Theater (post-Pearl Harbor) in disproportionate numbers. As a result, only a few destroyers and coastal patrol craft manned by untested crews were deployed to protect thousands of ships along thousands of miles of coastline against hardened veterans in lethally effective U-boats. The results were predictably deplorable: in the winter and spring of 1942 the Allied lost, for a time, a crucial tanker every ten hours - most of them in transit from Venezuela and the Dutch Antilles or the Houston area to Halifax then the UK.

For a time, losses in the US Eastern Sea Frontier accounted for a full third of all Allied losses to U-boats globally, which is considerable given that the Germans patrolled as far afield as the Arabian Gulf, New Zealand, South Africa, Argentina, West Africa, the Arctic and the Mediterranean. At first the US commanders allowed tourist venues along their coasts to maintain lighthouses, hotel lights, and traffic and automobile lights, which proved excellent backdrops for submarines to silhouette their victims with – that lasted until May of 1942, for up to four crucial months.

The best proven defense for merchant ships - convoys - were not implemented and command regions not adequately decentralized, until the spring of 1942, allowing the Germans and a flotilla of four Italian submarines named Betasom for "Bordeaux *Sommergibili*, or Submarines from Bordeaux France, to take full advantage of the weakened defenses to wreak terrible, deadly havoc.

Eventually, by the summer of 1942 some semblance of control was overlaid on the region by the Allies in the form of convoys only sailing in daytime, with air and naval escort, regular air patrols from the US east coast, Bahamas, Caribbean, and Bermuda, breaking of the Enigma code's fifth rotor wheel, and coordinated attacks by carrier-based hunter-killer groups based permanently in mid-Atlantic which attacked not only front line U-boats but the supply tankers (called "milk cows") which enabled the subs to carry out sustained patrols to the US Gulf and Caribbean and Brazil lasting up to three months.

U-Boat Patrols:

The first Axis submarine to penetrate the area around Bermuda and Bahamas was the lead boat of Operation *Paukenschlag*, or Drumbeat, the famous one-two-three sub U-123 (U simply stood for *untersee* or under sea boat), under Reinhard Hardegen. He arrived on the 20th of January, 1942, roughly six weeks after Hitler declared war on the US in accordance with his promise to Japan. The last submarine to leave the theater was U-518 under Offerman, in September 1944, two years and nine months later.

On average U-boats spend two weeks motoring from Germany or France to arrive in the region, and two weeks returning, leaving Type IX and Type VII subs only about a fortnight to patrol along the American and Caribbean coasts, unless of course they

refueled en route, which they often did by mid-1942. Boats passing Bermuda generally attacked the US from Hatteras to the Virginia and Delaware Capes up to New York and New England, sometimes including the Canadian Maritimes and Straits of Florida. On average they spent a week in the Bermuda area, generally transiting for 3-4 days each way, east and west bound.

The attacks on the Bahamas were by virtue of the complex geography, longer and the targets more diverse – including the US Gulf, Central America, Panama, the north coast of South America and even Trinidad and the Guyanese ore routes. It took the submarines on average a week just to transit from Bermuda to the Windward Passage or the Mona Passage, Old Bahama Channel, and Straits of Florida. So, the average patrol in the Bahamas area was double that of Bermuda at fourteen days. Most of those boats (they were called boats because they were primarily on the surface and submerged to evade attack, to attack undetected, and avoid bad weather) were refueled between the Azores and Bermuda, though sometimes further west.

In January of 1942 five Drumbeat boats arrived off Bermuda, followed by four or five more waves to both Bermuda and the Bahamas: 13 attacked the following month, 16 in March, and a record 30 in April. As part of Operation Neuland 18 boats penetrated the region in May, 20 in June, 15 in July and 15 in August. At its peak there were a dozen Axis submarines in the region on the first of July 1942. The Italians were a rear-guard action operating north of the Caribbean and east of the Bahamas, spending long successful patrols on slower less maneuverable boats which were less suited to wolf-pack style coordinated attacks.

The peak having been reached, patrols tapered off. In September 1942 there were but three patrols initiated, none in October, and one in November, with none the following month. In January 1942 one sub entered, in February four did, with none in March and two in April. There were some small spikes in patrols going forward, with five in May 1943, one in June, and seven in July. Then one each the following three months. November 1943 was another blip with four patrols initiated, most of them fruitless and resulting only in Allied attacks on the U-boats. By then the short spring offensive by the Italians was long over. In 1944 there were token patrols to keep the Allied defenses tied up and off balance: two in February, one each in March and April, and a final rally with two in June and the last patrol in August 1944, beset by a hurricane.

U-Boat Attacks:

The 170 Axis submarine patrols resulted in attacks on 181 merchant ships in the area, or an average of more than one attack per sub per patrol. Admiral Karl Doenitz, overall commander of German U-boats expected more from his men and pulled them back to other areas if their hit ratio was not high enough to stem the massive tide of US ship building by 1943. Of those 181 ships, 70 were US-flagged and thus relevant to this study. There were roughly a dozen Panamanian-flagged tankers which were almost invariably owned, operated and crewed by US personnel; however, they were not US flagged.

In terms of the ports those 70 ships sailed from or to, New York appears more often than any other (nine sailings, or roughly 15%), followed by an array of ports in the US Gulf, Caribbean, Middle East and Africa, as far afield as Australia (via the Panama Canal). The leading destination port was also New York, with 11 (about 20%), followed by Baltimore, Jacksonville, Boston and Philadelphia.

Most of the ships – roughly 50 - were steam-driven dry-cargo ships, but several were motor ship and 20 were the most valuable target of all: tankers, lynchpin to the supply chain allowing Great Britain to carry on the fight against Fascism in Europe. These larger, more modern ships were highly prized by the Germans, and the Esso fleet alone lost half a dozen such vessels in this theater alone.

The cargoes carried were as various as the ports: bananas, jute, coconuts and fish intermingled with barrels of diesel for remote bases, airplanes assembled and not, ammunition, food, bauxite for aluminum to build planes, paint, burlap, rubber, linseed, sugar, molasses, Navy fuel oil, onions, and general cargo fitting every description from dry-goods, including passengers.

It is not possible to detail the attacker and circumstances of all 70 merchant ships in the space provided, however a breakdown by month gives an idea of peak attack periods. In February the Pan Massachusetts, Cities Services Empire, Republic, Oregon and W. D. Anderson were all attacked, mostly off the east coast of Florida and surrounding waters by U-128 under Heyse and U-504 under Poske. The list of ships hit in March is longer: *Mariana, Barbara, Cardonia, Hanseat, Olga, Texan, Colabee, Oakmar, Muskogee* and USS *Atik* were mostly sunk in the Old Bahama Channel off Cuba by U-126 under Bauer. The Atik was a US Navy decoy or Q-ship lost with all hands to U-123 and the same sub sank the *Muskogee* with the same sad result.

April 1942 saw the loss of the *Gulfstate*, an attack on the *Comol Rico, Catahoula, Esso Baton Rouge, Esparta, GulfAmerica, Esso Boston, Leslie, Robin Hood, Alcoa Guide, Steel Maker, San Jacinto, Mobiloil, Federal*, and Pipestone County. In general, the first part of the month was waged off the Florida coast, the latter further north, west of Bermuda. May was another deadly month, witnessing the loss of the Afoundria, Delisle, Santa Catalina, Halsey, Java Arrow, Ohioan, Nicarao, Lammot du Pont, and Alcoa Shipper, most of them off Atlantic Florida.

June saw fifteen attacks with the following ships succumbing: West Notus, Domino (attacked while drifting, escaped), Illinois,

City of alma, Delfina, USS Gannett (abandoned by her British escort off Bermuda), Esso Gettysburg, Hagan, Millinocket, Cheerio (a schooner sunk off Puerto Rico), and the *Potlatch*, whose survivors reached the Bahamas after nearly a month adrift in a single boat and rafts. This was followed by the loss of five ships in two days: Raphael Semmes, Sam Houston, Sea Thrush, Onondaga, and Thomas McKean. It was a bloody month for Allies.

July of 1942 was certainly the peak of Axis success in the region, with 11 ships struck, including the City of Birmingham (372 survivors landed in Bermuda), Bloody Marsh, Norlandia, Umtata (being towed after being struck in Castries St. Lucia by Albrecht Achilles in U-161), James A. Moffett, Oneida, Fairport, Gertrude (a diminutive swordfish boat carrying 20 tons of onions), William Cullen Bryan, Andrew Jackson (one of the "President" ships), and the Ruth – reported sunk in the Bahamas but actually east of the Caribbean by U-153 under Reichmann, which was itself sunk weeks later of Panama).

The final throes of German attacks on the area resulted in the loss of two ships (James Sprunt, obliterated when its cargo of ammunition detonated, and Virginia Sinclair), and in May the John Sevier and Nickeliner. The final sinking of a US-flagged ship off Bahamas and Bermuda took place in July 1943 with the attack on Cherry Valley by U-66 under Markworth, though the US-manned and US-escorted Panamanian-flagged tanker Pillory was dispatched off Puerto Rico in late 1944.

The Survivors:

Among the US-flagged ship the overwhelming majority of survivors were landed in Bermuda, which had highly effective 365-degree air patrols around the island starting as early as 1941 based on lend-lease agreements between President Roosevelt and Prime Minister Churchill. The Naval Air Station and Naval Operating Base in Bermuda contributed largely to the total of 444 merchant seamen and passengers landed on that island.

The rescued merchant seamen were supplemented by the 62 men rescued from the USS Gannett, a small patrol boat sunk 7 June 1942 (the rescue pilot disobeyed his standing orders by landing on the sea to pluck the injured to safety and was commended for doing so).

By far the majority of survivors were landed from the City of Birmingham – 372. That ship was being escorted to Bermuda and was the island's commercial and logistical lifeline when lost. The escort, USS Stansbury succeeded in both attacking U-202 under Linder and rescuing most of the survivors several hours later, however two passengers and a stewardess drowned and a crew later died on board. In May of that year the City of Birmingham, whose skipper survived a U-boat sinking in WWI, had rescued 25 men from the British Ship Empire Dryden and landed them in Bermuda.

The other US ships which landed men on Bermuda were the Oakmar, with 30, the Robin Hood, with 24 and West Notus with 18. Oakmar was hit by U-71 under Flachsenberg while proceeding from Calcutta to Boston. Two men drowned abandoning ship and the captain an officer and two other crewmen's lifeboat was never found and they perished. The other 30 men were picked up by the ship Stavros and landed in Bermuda four days after their ordeal began.

The *Robin Hood* was sunk en route from Cape Town to Boston by U-575 under Heydemann on the 16th of April 1942. Out of a complement of 38 men 14 were killed. The balance of 24 survivors were picked up a week later by USS *Greer* and deposited in Hamilton Bermuda. West Notus was proceeding from Argentina to New York carrying flax seed when a torpedo from U-404 under von Bülow stopped her on the First of June 1942 between Hatteras and Bermuda. Four men were killed and half the survivors in one lifeboat were found on the high seas and taken to New York. The other 18 were found by the Greek steamer Constantinos H. and taken to Bermuda, where they reached safety on the Fifth of June, five days after the attack.

Perhaps the most colorful survivor saga in the region was that of the Weyerhaeuser-owned SS *Potlatch*, on charter to the US government to bring supplies to Montgomery and Patton via Suez. The ship was lost east-southeast of Anegada and the men were given wrong direction by the German officers of U-153 under Wilfried Reichmann. Of 55 men, six were killed in the attack and the balance were cast adrift on four rafts and a single 26-foot lifeboat. Forty-nine men set out without a good compass or sextant, but Captain John Joseph "Jack" Lapoint held them together for nearly a month.

Though one man (John Miller) succumbed to a shark bite and delirium and died at sea, 48 men missed the Caribbean proper and drifted for 27 days to land on Great and Little Inagua islands, Bahamas. Finding water by following jackasses, but little food, they struggled to Acklins Island, where under the glow of a welcoming lighthouse the elderly African-American second cook David Parson died in the arms of his skipper.

The 47 survivors landed in Pinefield, buried Parson in Anderson Settlement, and were rescued by a lesbian Standard Oil heiress Marion "Betty" Carstairs in her speedboat *Vergemere IV* and whisked to Nassau. There they were met by the Duchess of Windsor, Wallis Simpson, and her husband, the former King Edward VII before being repatriated to Miami and New York to continue the supply war and the Battle of the Atlantic, the longest known continuous battle.

Conclusion:

The story of these 70 US ships and their 500 or so survivors is a compelling one which had largely been untold. With the extraordinary amalgamation of information available from recently declassified documents, published resources from the likes of Jurgen Rohwer, and websites like uboat.net, the facts of each individual case become more easily accessible.

The National Archives and Records Administration (NARA) in the United States as well as US Coast Guard and US Navy archives, and The National Archives in Kew Gardens, United Kingdom, as well as the national archives of Bermuda and Bahamas, contain a trove of information on these topics.

Regrettably but inevitably the first-hand participants in these human-interest dramas are largely dead or dying, so the opportunity to provide rich narrative material on these episodes has never been more compelling. One of the reasons the story has not been told is that at the outset at least, the Allied suffered ignominious defeat at the hand of the German and Italian marauders. Britannia may have "ruled the waves" as the saying goes, but the Axis powers controlled the beneath the seas, keeping the defenders under siege and off kilter, never sure where the next attacks would materialize.

Another is that the islands and bodies of ocean where the attacks occurred were sparsely populated or rarely sailed, and diffuse at best. After all, the subject matter was literally fluid: it was not uncommon for a ship flagged in distant lands to be

struck far from home near Bermuda or Bahamas, her crew cast into the waves to be discovered quite by chance by friend or foe. There again, rescue was happenstance, as depending on where the rescuing ship was bound, survivors might be deposited anywhere from West Africa to Canada, the US, or the islands.

The fact is that despite a death rate of some 60 percent amongst U-boat officers and crews, roughly fifteen of the submarine commanders – nearly ten percent – are still alive, as are Navy Gunners and a handful of merchant crews from participating ships. Their children and grandchildren are the custodians, sometimes unwittingly, of a trove of images and accounts of these experiences, as are collections such as that of the Steamship Historical Society of America.

War in Paradise

During World War II 170 German and Italian submarines, or U-boats, sank or damaged 193 Allied merchant and naval vessels around the islands of the Bahamas and Bermuda, which were both British colonies at the time. This accounted for over one million tons of shipping lost to Axis raiders. Lasting most intensely from February to July 1942, they accounted for 20% of Axis submarine successes globally in February, 33% in March, 38% in April, then 23% in May, 21% in June and 12% in July, 1942.

Yet the story is little known, mostly because the subs were on missions to Cape Hatteras and New York, the Straits of Florida and the US Gulf, and the Windward Passage and the Caribbean, not Bahamas and Bermuda *per-se*. However once ships started avoiding Cape Hatteras the U-boats also withdrew from the mainland towards Bermuda, to follow their prey. The main Axis thrust was to sever the waterborne supply of oil from the US Gulf and the islands of Aruba and Curacao flowing to the UK via Halifax and New York in Britain's greatest time of need. And in that they almost succeeded, for a brief but treacherous time sinking a tanker every 10 hours of the coast of the Americas.

Who sank all these ships? A cadre of mostly German but four Italian submarines which aggressively attacked the exposed US and Caribbean coastlines in operations Drumbeat (off Cape Hatteras) and *Neuland* (to the south and Caribbean). These patrols included Italian incursions, refueling missions as well as to land saboteurs off Florida and Long Island, New York and mine ports like Charleston, Norfolk, Jacksonville, and Puerto Rico. Altogether these incursions amounted to over 1,500 individual patrol days, keeping the Allies on edge.

To avenge all these attacks only four submarines were sunk in the region: two near the Florida Keys and two near Bermuda. Two were the result of the U-boat giving away its position via radio or a pattern of kills, the others were discovered by chance by aircraft. Eventually the Allies instituted coastal convoys and extensive air coverage, forcing the U-boats into the Caribbean and the coasts of Latin America. Remarkably over 12 of the U-boat skippers involved in these patrols are still alive.

Of those vessels sunk, 70 were flagged to the US and 51 to the UK. From these 506 American survivors landed in Bermuda and 48 in the Bahamas, one of whom died and was buried in remote Acklins Island. There were 1,276 Allied survivors landed in Bermuda and 324 in the Bahamas and Turks & Caicos. Of those landed in Bermuda, 595 were British or Canadian and 506 from US-flagged ships. They came from large ships like the passenger ship *Lady Drake* (256 survivors, including women and children) and the small schooner *Helen Forsey*, whose men – hardy Nova Scotia fishing stock – rowed and sailed for 12 days on their own, to be met by surprised Bermudian fishermen on arrival.

The first British landed in Bermuda came from the *Uskbridge*, sunk in October 1940 west of Scotland – 21 of her men were taken to Bermuda. Likewise, 34 survivors out of 176 officers and men from the Canadian destroyer HMCS *Margaree* were landed in Bermuda in October 1940 after their ship was sunk in a collision. In January 1942 four dead and dying engine room staff, some of whom had survived a boiler explosion on merchant ship whose name was censored, detoured to Bermuda to bury them at St. Paul's church in Paget.

The American survivors of the navy patrol craft USS *Gannet* were, like some of the men from the *Derryheen*, *Melbourne Star* and *San Arcadio*, rescued by daring seaplane pilots who landed on the ocean at great peril to themselves and their craft. There were two hardy Norwegian skippers who, when offered rescue, initially refused it: Captain Finn Rusti of the sunken *Grenanger* preferred his lifeboats over the safety of the rescue ship *Almenara*, saying there weren't enough lifeboats and food for his men. Captain Knut O. Bringedal of the *O. A. Knudsen* initially told Captain Foster of the schooner *E. P. Theriault* that he preferred to make his own way in lifeboats to Miami, but then relented because of the severely injured men in his boat. One of them, Olaus Johansen, was buried two days later on Abaco Island.

The American steam ship *Potlatch* was sunk east of the Caribbean and 49 men spent a month sailing and drifting in a 26-foot boat and four rafts until they landed on Great Inagua, Bahamas. One man died of a shark bite then another, within sight of a community and salvation, in the arms of the captain, John "Jack" Lapoint, who listed his relationship to the deceased African-American steward as a "friend." Two days later they were rescued by a dashing tom-boy heiress named Marion "Joe" Carstairs, a tax exile from the UK who helped set speed boat records and owned her own Bahama island, Whale Cay, whose small defense force she ruled. The men were taken to Nassau on Carstairs' yacht *Vergemere IV* and met on arrival by the Duchess of Windsor, head of the Red Cross, whose husband the erstwhile King Edward VIII was Governor of the colony, which was deemed an innocuous enough backwater for him to rule during the war.

The Duchess, whose predecessor Lady Dundas had been sent to Kampala, Uganda for the balance of the war to make room for them, served as the welcoming committee for all 255 Allied survivors landed in Nassau during the war. Several of the victims' ships – the *Cygnet* of Panama, *Athelqueen* and *Daytonian* of the UK – had been sent to the bottom by the Italian corsair Carlo Fecia di Cossato in the submarine *Enrico Tazzoli*, which sank a ship a day for over a week before colliding with the *Athelqueen* in March 1942 and limping home to Bordeaux.

The first Allied survivors landed in the Caribbean were Robert Tapscott and Wilbert 'Roy' Widdicombe whose ship the *Anglo-Saxon* was sunk by the German raider *Widder* on 21 August 1940. The two survived for 70 days over 2,800 miles to land on Eleuthera, Bahamas. Widdicombe accrued funds from speaking fees but was drowned when the ship he was on (the *Siamese Prince*) was sunk near the UK. Tapscott killed himself. Overall, there were 9,448 men thrown into the sea by Axis submarines in the region in World War II. Of these, 24% or 2,247 were killed outright or drifting, un-rescued or overturned in boats and rafts. Another 7,211 or 76% managed to be rescued by Allied craft or to sail and drift their way to friendly shores. Only 16% of them, or 1,552 made it to the Bahamas, Turks & Caicos or Bermuda, where for the most part they were quickly patched up, repatriated and sent back to the front in the Battle of the Atlantic.

One reason this author believes the story has been untold is because the ocean so vastly overstretches the small land masses across over 1.4 million square miles of ocean covered. Another theory is that the British colonial authorities were embarrassed by the loss of prestige evoked when locals discovered emaciated, oil-covered and naked Allied sailors washing up on their shores. Surely the war could not be going well for their overlords? Strict censorship at the time allowed these far-flung incidents to be brushed under the carpet of officialdom, quite as HRH the Duke of Windsor was banished to the Bahamas via Bermuda during the war. Though Britannia may have ruled the waves, as the saying went, for a time the enemy ruled beneath them.

U-Boats off Bermuda, Part I: Introduction, Axis Activities

There were 143 Axis submarine patrols to the area roughly 450 nautical miles around Bermuda during World War II. These patrols resulted on attacks on 80 Allied vessels, including one naval ship (USS *Gannet*). The most intense period of attacks was between January and August 1942, and the German offensives during this period were named Operation Drumbeat

(*Paukenschlag*) and Operation New Land (*Neuland*). One of the submarines was Italian and sailed for the Betasom Flotilla, a joint venture between the Germans and Italians based in Bordeaux, France. U-505 was not on a patrol when it came to Bermuda in June 1944 – it had been captured and was taken to the island in secrecy for analysis.

Operation *Paukenshlag* (literally translated as timpani beat, or drumbeat), was ordered by Adolf Hitler shortly after Germany declared war on the United States on 11 December 1941, in the immediate aftermath of the attacks on Pearl Harbor by Japan. The relevance of Operation Drumbeat is that in order to reach the US coast off New England, New York, the Virginia Capes and Cape Hatteras, the most direct route took the submarines through the Bermuda region. This applied to their return voyages to bases mostly in France as well.

En route to and from the US the subs of course continued to sink lone shipping targets. Overall, these attacks were devastating on the largely undefended US coastline: 609 ships of 3.1 million tons – roughly 25% off all Allied merchant ship losses in the war – were sunk at a cost of 22 Axis U-boat losses. In the Bermuda region 80 ships were lost at a cost of two enemy submarines (U-158 and U-84).

The first wave of Drumbeat boats - the larger Type IXs – departed France on the 18th of December 1941 and arrived off Bermuda starting on the 20th of January 1942. During a few weeks Hardegen in U-123 sank seven ships, Kals in U-130 took six, Zapp in U-66 five, Bleichrodt in U-109 four and Folkers in U-125 sank a single ship. There were five waves of Operation Drumbeat. Operation *Neuland*, which followed, was aimed more to the south and the Caribbean but the U-boats still skirted Bermuda. These included the smaller, more manoeuvrable Type VII submarines. Looking at a composite chart of all Axis submarine patrols around Bermuda, it is clear that most of them were heading to or from Cape Hatteras or to and from the Straits of Florida, the Windward Passage, the Bahamas and Caribbean.

August 1944, with 11 months in that time period during which no patrols were begun. The first patrol to the Bermuda region began on 20 January 1942 and the last patrol began 24 August

1944. There was only one day – 2 March 1942 – where four submarines entered the region on the same day. There were five on 8 February 1942, 21 March 1942, 11 April 1942, 17 April, 1942, and 9 July 1942, when three subs entered on one day. Subs entered the region in pairs on 19 occasions. The busiest single month for patrol commencement was April, 1942, with 25 patrols begun that month, or almost one a day. The most active single day was the 28th of April 1942, during which there were no fewer than 14 Axis submarines patrolling the waters around Bermuda.

In 1942 there were five patrols begun in January 11 in February 13 in March 25 in April 19 in May 14 in June 15 in July 14 in August, three in September, and none again until 1943. Then there was 1 in February 3 in April 5 in May 4 in July 1 in August 2 in October, and 4 in November. In 1944 there was 1 each in March, April, June, July and August. The months with zero patrols were October, November, and December 1942, and January, March, June, September and December 1943, and January February, and May, 1944.

The longest patrol in the area around Bermuda was by Hans-Ludwig Witt in U-129 and lasted 24 days. There were three patrols – by U-84, U-509, and U-156 - which were merely dips into the region for a day or so. There were six patrols which lasted over 20 days, 23 that lasted from 11 to 19 days, and nine which lasted ten days. A dozen patrols spent nine and eight days in the area, six spent seven days, 14 spent six days, 14 spent five days, 23 spent four days, 14 spent three days, six spent two days and three spent a single day there.

There were only two U-boat commanders who patrolled the Bermuda region three times; Horst Uphoff in U-84, who was sunk by Allied aircraft south of Bermuda on the 7th of August 1943, and Reinhard Suhren (known as "Teddy" to his colleagues), in U-564. Aside from those two, there were 29 skippers who made two patrols to the Bermuda region, amongst whom Erwin Rostin in U-158 and his crew, who were lost west of Bermuda on the 30th of June 1942, also to Allied aircraft based in Bermuda. There were 78 commanders who made one patrol to Bermuda, plus U-505 which was under the command of the US Navy when it arrived in Bermuda in June 1944. Overall, there were 108 individual U-boat commanders who led 143 patrols. That indicates that 35 submarines came back for multiple patrols.

The ranks used to categorize U-boat commanders were those they attained at the end of their careers. There were 71 commanders with the rank of *Kapitänleutnant* and 48 who were ranked *Korvettenkapitän*. Eleven attained the rank of *Oberleutnant zur See* and one of *Oberleutnant zur See* (R). Nine were *Fregattenkapitän* and only one (Heinz-Ehler Beucke) was *Kapitän zur See*. Di Cossato, the only Italian commander, was ranked *Capitano di Corvetta*.

Erich Topp in (among others) U-552 sank the most ships during his overall career; 35 ships for 197,460 tons, followed by Heinrich Lehmann-Willenbrock in U-96 who sank 27 ships of 194,989 tons. Georg Lassen of U-160 sank 26 of 156,082, followed by Heinrich Bleichrodt of U-109 who sank 24 ships of 151,260 tons. At the other end of the spectrum Rupprecht Stock in U-214 sank only a single ship of 200 tons, and 12 other skippers didn't sink any ships at all over the course of their careers.

Certain commanders achieved multiple attacks in the Bermuda region in 1942 – 1944. Di Cossato of the *Enrico Tazzoli*, Scholtz of U-108, Hardegen of U-123, and Schnee of U-201 all attacked five ships. Bleichrodt in U-109 and Rostin of U-158 attacked four each in the region, and the following each attacked three ships: Von Bülow of U-404, Witt in U-129, Rasch in U-106, Feiler in U-653, Forster in U-654, and Flachsenberg in U-71. These skipper each initiated attacks on two ships: Schuch in U-105, Linder in U-202, Würdemann in U-506, Suhren in U-564, Hirsacker in U-572, and Markworth in U-66.

The most decorated commander to have patrolled Bermuda was Reinhard Suhren, with the Knights Cross with Oak Leaves and Crossed Swords with the War Merit Cross 2nd Class with Swords added in 1944 and the U-Boat War Badge with Diamonds in March, 1942. Erich Topp of U-552 also earned the Knights Cross with Oak Leaves and Crossed Swords the U-Boat War Badge with Diamonds. Otto von Bülow of U-404 also received the Knights Cross with Oak Leaves, as well as the U-Boat War Badge with Diamonds and the War Merit Cross 2nd Class with Swords, very similar to Suhren's but without the Crossed Swords to the Knights

Cross. On the Italian side Carlo Fecia di Cossato of the *Enrico Tazzoli* was awarded their armed service's highest decoration: a Gold Medal of Military Valor as well as two silver medals for bravery (he killed himself after Italy switched sides). He also had a submarine named after him in 1980. Kurt Diggins, German commander of U-458 was awarded the Italian medal in Bronze for Military Valor.

Overall, 61 out of the skippers of 143 patrols were awarded Knights Cross in some iteration, and 40 received no decorations over their career. The balance received a variety of awards and additions to the Knights Cross, including Wounded Badge in Silver with U-Boat Front Clasp, Iron Cross First Class, U-Boat War Badge 1939, Iron Cross 2nd Class, and German Cross in Gold.

Overwhelmingly, most of the boats – 68 out of 143 – were Type VIIC, followed by the Type IXC, of which there were 42. There were 13 IXB and 8 IXC/40, and six VIIB and three VIID types. There were three milk cow-type tanker subs of the XIV type and one Italian of the *Calvi* Class. Overall, there were eight classifications of sub, however three were iterations of the VII type (77 overall) and three types of the IX class (63 overall). There were four U-boats which returned for three patrols to the Bermuda area: U-84, U-98, U-129, and U-564. It is noteworthy that the submarines did not necessarily have the same commanders for each patrol. There were 63 U-boats which returned to the region twice and 69 for whom there were only single patrols to the area.

There were a total of nine different flotillas represented by the submarines which attacked the region. However, membership in a flotilla did not necessarily determine which ports the subs sailed to or from, as they moved from base to base, flotilla to flotilla, and repositioned. Members of the 10th Flotilla, for example, sailed from Saint Nazaire, Lorient, Kiel, Helgoland, Kristiansand, Lorient, and La Pallice. There were 41 submarines in the 2nd Flotilla, 25 in the 1st, 23 in the 10th and 20 in the 7th. The 3rd Flotilla was represented by 18 U-boats, the 6th Flotilla by 7, the 9th by five and the 12th by two – the tanker boats. The lone Italian submarine in the region sailed for the Betasom Flotilla based in Bordeaux,

France ("Beta" is for Bordeaux and "Som" for *Sommergibili*, the Italian word for submarine).

Most of the Axis submarines that patrolled Bermuda - 52 out of 143 - left from Lorient. Thirty-one departed from St. Nazaire, also in France, and 29 from Brest. A further 13 left from La Pallice (near La Rochelle) and two departed from Bordeaux. A dozen departed from Kiel in Germany, two from the island base of Helgoland (Heligoland in Danish), and two left from Kristiansand in Norway, using their patrol to the Americas to re-position from the Baltic to French ports.

Lorient was also the lead port for the U-boats to return to after their patrols, with 54 submarines going there, followed by 30 to St. Nazaire, and 23 to Brest. There were 19 U-boats sunk or captured. La Pallice had 13 U-boats return there following Bermuda patrols, Flensburg two, Bordeaux two, and El Ferrol (in neutral Spain) one. Three subs were sunk in the Bay of Biscay en route to France, three off Cape Hatteras, and one each off Panama, Virginia, Key West, New Orleans, the Azores, Cuba, Haiti, and Halifax.

The age ranges of the commanders of submarine patrols around Bermuda were between 23 (Offermann and Carlsen) and 47 (Wolfbauer, who had fought in the First World War). There were 63 commanders killed in the line of duty or otherwise; one committed suicide rather than face execution, another dove from the conning tower and struck a saddle tank. This study does not account for whether commanders became Prisoners of War during or after the conflict, only whether they survived the war.

The commanders were mostly (83 of them) in their 30's. Seventy-nine were in their 20s and two were in their 40's. Perhaps the most striking statistic is that there are estimated to be, at the time of writing in July, 2015, 11 commanders who are still alive. They are: Carlsen, Petersen, Lauterbach-Emden, Stock, Markworth, Wissmann, Wintermeyer, Hardegen, Siegmann, Geissler, Schulze, Schutze, and Borchert. In their twilight years their wizened commanders can reflect on the day that their war machines penetrated the vulnerable flank of North America and patrolled the azure Gulf Stream waters around Bermuda with devastating effect 70-plus years ago.

This article is dedicated to the memory of Capt. Warren A. Brown, Sr., who immeasurably helped the author's sailing career.

U-Boats off Bermuda, Part II: The Allies

During World War II there were 1,224 survivors landed in Bermuda from 24 ships (one US Navy, one Royal Canadian Navy), between 17 Oct. 1940 and 27 February 1943. Most of them were passengers on liner ships, followed by merchant sailors and then naval officers and men. The largest number of survivors were from the *City of Birmingham* (372 landed 1 July 1942, nine fatalities), and the *Lady Drake* (256 landed 6 May 1942, 12 fatalities). The fewest were the schooner *Helen Forsey* and *Melbourne Star* with four each.

Some men from the following ships were landed by air: *Derryheen*, USS *Gannet*, *San Arcadio*, and *Melbourne Star*. Only the following succeeded in rowing and sailing their way to Bermuda on their own: *Helen Forsey* (four Canadians) and *James E. Newsom* (nine Canadians). While most survivors were picked up by other merchant ships, a number were rescued by naval vessels: *Jagersfontein*, *City of Birmingham*, *Lady Drake*, HMCS *Margaree*, *British Resource*, and USS *Gannet*.

Of those landed in Bermuda, most (12 ships / 243 men) came from British ships, five ships from USA accounted for 506 survivors, and three Canadian vessels for 299 persons. Other ships whose men landed in Bermuda were flagged to Uruguay, Sweden, Norway, and Netherlands (one ship each). The longest survival voyages on open boats or rafts were experienced by six ships:

- *Melbourne Star*: 38 days
- *Empire Dryden*: 19 days
- *Fred W. Green*: 18 days
- *San Arcadio*: 15 days
- *Helen Forsey:* 12 days
- *Stanbank*: 10 days.

All the other 18 ships experienced voyages of nine days or less, with five ships' crews on the water for one day or less. There were several weeks of particularly intense activity on shore, when several ships' survivors arrived in Bermuda:

- End October 1940: *Uskbridge* 28 Oct and HMCS *Margaree* on 1 Nov 1940.
- Mid-March 1942: *British Resource* on 16 March and *Oakmar* on 24 March 1942.
- End April 1942: *Agra* and *Derryheen* on 22 April, *Robin Hood* 25 April, and *Modesta* 26 April, 1942.
- Early May 1942: *Lady Drake* 6 May, *Empire Dryden* 8 May, *James E. Newsom*, 10 May, and *Stanbank* 15 May.
- Mid-June 1942: *West Notus* 5 June, USS *Gannet* 7 June, *Melbourne Star* 10 June, *L. A. Christiansen* 12 June, and *Fred W. Green* 17 June 1942.
- Early July 1942: *Jagersfontein* 28 June, and *City of Birmingham* 3 July 1942.

Some, like the *Derryheen*, *Maldonado*, *Uskbridge* and *West Notus*, only had a portion of their crew landed in Bermuda, the others were rescued by ship or air and taken to different ports. Excluding the passenger ships, the average number of men per ship with survivors landed in Bermuda was 27 men.

Including all ships attacked around Bermuda (but excluding the *Uskbridge* and HMCS *Margeree*, which happened before Operation Drumbeat, which targeted the Hatteras/Bermuda area in January 1942), the attacks began on the 24th of January 1942 with U-106 under Rasch's attack on the *Empire Wildebeeste* and ended on the 27th of February, 1943 with the attack by U-66 under Markworth on the *Saint Margaret* some 1,140 nautical miles from Bermuda.

Inside the 450-miles-from-Bermuda circle, the last attack occurred on the schooner *Helen Forsey* on the 6th of September 1942, by U-514 under Auffermann. That would mean that attacks inside the basic circle lasted 18 months, though of course the patrols lasted longer – into 1944 (see Axis attacks section). The busiest month of attacks was April, 1942 with 20, followed by May 1942 with 15 and March 1942 with 14.

The only months during which there were more than one attacks were January to July 1942, so it can be generalized that the sustained attacks lasted for the first seven months of 1942, though many patrols transited the area and occasional attacks were made (as in one a month) after that period.

- January 1942: 4
- February 1942: 9
- March 1942: 14
- April 1942: 20
- May 1942: 15
- June 1942: 11
- July 1942: 3
- August 1942: 1
- September 1942: 1
- February 1943: 1

Several dates stand out for having more than one attack (because of the use of German times to record attacks, and since German time is some six hours ahead of local, Bermudian time, and even more ahead of US East Coast time, attacks which occurred on the night of, say January 1st, might be recorded as having occurred on the 2nd of January, German time).

- 20 April 1942: 4: *Agra, Empire Dryden, Steel Maker,* and *Harpagon*
- 5 May 1942: 4: *Lady Drake, Stanbank, Santa Catalina, Freden*
- 16 February 1942: 2
- 6 March 1942: 2
- 20 March 1942: 2
- 1 April 1942: 2
- 6 April 1942: 2
- 22 April 1942: 2
- 20 May 1942: 2
- 1 June 1942: 2

There were 3,942 persons aboard 80 ships attacked by U-boats between 24 Jan 1942 and 27 February 1943 (13 months – excluding the *Uskbridge*, sunk off Iceland). 957 were killed, or a mortality rate of roughly 25%. 2,985 survived. Of the survivors, 1,224 landed in Bermuda, which is roughly 41% of the survivors and 31% of the overall number of people attacked.

Out of 80 ships the majority, or 44, were steam ships laid out to carry general, or dry bulk cargo, as opposed to tankers or other types. There were eight motor ships which carried dry or general cargo, meaning 52 out of 80, or 65% were dry cargo ships. There were 21 tankers, of which 18 were the more modern motor tankers and three were steam tankers. Thus 26% of the ships carried liquid cargoes, and most of them were motorized, whereas most of the dry ships were propelled by steam-driven machinery.

Additionally, there was a US Navy minesweeper (USS *Gannet*), two schooners (*Helen Forsey* and *James E. Newsom*, both Canadian), and four passenger ships, of which three (*Lady Drake, San Jacinto* and *City of Birmingham*), were steam and one (*Jagersfontein*) was motorized. Some other ships, including the *Fairport* and *Santa Catalina*, carried passengers as well as freight.

Gross registered tonnage is different from deadweight tons: the GRT refers to the estimated weight of the ship in the water, with crew and equipment. Deadweight tons (DWT) refers to the amount of deadweight cargo that one can safely carry aboard the vessel. Though readers might find it confusing, the deadweight capacity often exceeds the GRT, just as a mule may be able to carry more than its own weight. For example, the *British Resource* weighed 7,209 GRT but carried 10,000 tons of benzene and white spirit.

There were only five ships (*Frank B. Baird, Leif, Astrea, Anna,* and *Freden*) between 1,191 and 1,748 tons, and two – both schooners – less than 1,000 tons: *James E. Newsom* at 671 tons and *Helen Forsey* at 167 tons. In the 9,000-ton range there were five ships, in the 8,000 range seven, and in the 7,000 range 11 vessels. In the 6,000-ton range there were 10, the 5,000-ton range 14, and the 4,000-ton range only six. Between 3,000 and 4,000 tons were six ships and from 2,000 to 3,000 tons there were also six.

The total gross registered tonnage (GRT) of all 80 ships was 473,420 tons, so the GRT of the average ship would be 5,918 tons. The largest ships were *San Gerardo* (12,915), *Victolite* (11,410) and *Montrolite* (11,309). There were four ships between 10,000 and 10,389 tons: *Narragansett, Opawa, Jagersfontein*, and *Koll*. Generally, the motor tankers were larger than their dry-bulk cousins: of the top 25 ships by tonnage, all except *Lady Drake, Westmoreland* and *Hardwick Grange* were either tankers or motor ships.

Out of 80 ships, 12 of them, or 15% were proceeding in ballast, in other words their cargo holds or tanks were empty except for water or sand, carried to keep them at a safe trim for ocean passages. The *Halcyon*, for example, was 3,531 tons and carried 1,500 tons of ballast to keep the ship steady in rough seas.

On the dry cargo side, the cargoes were the most varied. They included coal, motor boats, military stores, beer, nitrates, motor trucks, chrome ore, cement, bauxite ore, phosphate, aircraft, locomotives, timber, manganese ore, mahogany, anthracite coal, refrigerated cargo (i.e. meats, butter), gas storage tanks, metal piping, flour, automobiles, wine, cereal, canned meat, wool, eggs, leather, fertilizer, explosives, bags of mail. The variation continues, with ships carrying wheat, tungsten, nitrate, fuel in drums, steel, tires, small arms, fats, flax seed, tobacco, licorice, rugs, "war supplies," construction equipment, cigarettes, tanks, lead, asbestos, chrome ore, concentrates, copper, resins, cotton, zinc concentrates, asphalt, burlap, rubber, linseed and tea.

On the tanker side, cargoes varied from petrol and paraffin to linseed oil, crude oil, fuel oil, aviation spirit, high grade diesel oil, gas oil, lubricating oil, gasoline, heavy crude oil, benzene and white spirit, kerosene, furnace oil, and petroleum products. The *Helen Forsey* was not a tanker, but rather a schooner, nevertheless she carried molasses and rum – presumably in barrels, not in bulk.

Ships attacked in the Bermuda area flew the flags of 11 countries: Britain (UK) (34 ships), USA (15), Norway (12), Canada (5), Sweden (4), Netherlands (3), Panama (2), Uruguay (2), Argentina (1), Latvia (1) and Yugoslavia (1). Great Britain/UK accounted for 43% of ships lost in the region, the US 18% and Norway 15%, the others trailing significantly. Nine out of the 34 British ships, or 25% of them, were tankers. In contrast only two out of 15 US-flagged ships, or 13%, were tankers. On the Norwegian side, five out of 12, or 42% were tankers.

Eleven ships left from New York, followed by 10 from various ports in the UK and 10 from Trinidad the three lead destination ports. Eight left Bermuda, seven left Curacao in the Dutch West Indies (invariably tankers loaded with petroleum or distillates), five from the US Gulf, and two from British Guyana. Five ships had

205

made stops in Cape Town on their way from Middle Eastern and Indian ports. Four ships sailed from Halifax.

A number of ships – 10 - had last called at Port-of-Spain, Trinidad, to receive bunkers, or fuel, on long voyages from South America or South Africa. One sailed from Buenos Aires, four from Norfolk or Hampton Roads, Virginia. Three sailed from Panama (having left New Zealand or Australia), and four left Philadelphia. One left from Savannah, another three from Saint Thomas in the US Virgin Islands. One ship left Portuguese East Africa (present-day Mozambique) and another from Recife, Brazil. Yet another sailed from Montevideo, Uruguay. Small ports like Turks & Caicos and Barbados were hailed by the schooners.

Ship destinations are somewhat clouded by the reality that if the ship is included in this study it was attacked by an Axis submarine and most likely never made it to port. Twelve were going to Halifax but 16 were going to Canada: two to St. John, as well as Sydney Nova Scotia and Montreal. Sixteen as well were going to New York. Six were destined for Bermuda, one for Aruba, one for Baltimore, one for Iran, 11 to Cape Town and thence the Middle East or India.

Two were destined for Venezuela, one for *Cuidad Trujillo*, Dominican Republic, three for Curacao Dutch West Indies to load petroleum products, one to Freetown Sierra Leone, one for Georgetown, British Guyana. One was bound for Iceland, two for Norfolk or Hampton Roads Virginia, two for Philadelphia, one for Pernambuco, another for San Juan and yet another for Rio de Janeiro. One ship was bound for Texas City and another for Trinidad, and yet another for Pointe-a-Pitre, Guadeloupe.

The overall goal of this study was to include ships attacked within a roughly 450-mile circle around Bermuda, and the majority – 68 out of 80 – of the attacks occurred within that circle. There is a fine line between attacks which occurred off the US coasts of, say New England and Cape Hatteras, and Bermuda, and some ships were included whereas other, like USS *Atik*, were not.

For the most part, exceptions to the 450-mile-radius rule were made because the attacks occurred to the east and south of Bermuda, where they might not receive book-length treatment otherwise, and because Bermuda was the nearest land to the site where the ships were attacked, and was thus naturally an island to which the men may have set out to find salvation. In other cases, the ships were included simply because, even though they were sunk far away (*Uskbridge* and *Saint Margaret*) the men were ultimately landed in Bermuda – or at least some of the survivors were. Since this study is about Bermuda under attack by U-boats and the men and women who landed there in World War II, then the story of the relevant attacks and rescues are included.

The average distance from Bermuda (excluding the *Uskbridge*), was 350 nautical miles (a nautical mile being 1.18 statute, or land miles). The *Modesta*, sunk on 25 April 1942, was the closest to Bermuda at 121 miles, or ten hour's steaming at 12 knots. Next came the *Harpagon* the same week (20 April 1942) at only 164 miles distant, followed by the *Raphael Semmes* and *Westmoreland*, both 175 miles away and both sunk in June 1942. The *Tonsbergsfjord* was sunk 176 miles from Bermuda by the Italian submarine *Enrico Tazzoli* in March 1942. *Astrea* was sunk the same week by the same sub 194 miles from the island, and the *Ramapo* and *Fred W. Green* roughly 185 miles away.

There were 22 ships struck between 200 and 300 nautical miles from Bermuda and 33 between 300 and 400 miles away. Eight Allied merchant ships were attacked between 400 and 500 miles from Bermuda and four between 500 and 600 miles away (there may have been more if Cape Hatteras was included in this study – it was not). These ships would have been sunk to the east and south of Bermuda, as the US mainland is only about 700 miles from Bermuda to the north and west.

Five ships were sunk more than 600 miles from the island but were included in this study because their survivors were landed on Bermuda: *Uskbridge* and *Saint Margaret*. The other three ships were the *Pan Norway* (743 miles away, sunk 27 January 1942), the *Triglav* (919 miles, sunk 9 July 1942) and the *Athelknight*, sunk 1,000 miles away on the 27th of May, 1942.

The average or composite ship, based on the above analysis, would have been British-flagged, 5,918 tons, had 49 men and/or passengers on board and been carrying a general, or dry cargo. The most likely departure port would have been New York with destination ports in Canada and New York and the most likely time to have been sunk would have been April in 1942. Typically, the ship would be sunk by a German submarine 350 miles from Bermuda and 12 men would be killed in the attack. Of the balance, 15 of them would be landed in Bermuda and the others – 22 – would be landed elsewhere. Most of them would be rescued by other merchant ships or Allied naval ships, with a small percentage gaining salvation from sea airplanes.

Ultimately history is told not so much in statistics as through the eyes of the participants. Behind every number in this analysis were the tales of men and women caught unawares and pitched into the merciless North Atlantic. That the majority of them survived and a good number made landfall in Bermuda is a testament not only to the tenacity of their rescuers, who came across the seas and from the clouds, but also to the survivor's good fortune.

For many the ordeal was not over, as they had to ship out on other vessels and brave the same seas again to reach North America or Europe. As illustrated in these pages, the people of Bermuda, civilian and those in uniform, did the very best they could under the circumstances to welcome, accommodate, and resuscitate the survivors so that they could sally forth and adjust back into their individual roles in an all-consuming, global war which continued for a further three years.

U-Boats off Bermuda, Part III: The Aviators

During World War II there were thousands of reconnaissance and other flights flown out of Naval Operating Base (NOB) and Naval Air Station (NAS) Bermuda – mostly from Kindley Field. Many of them were amphibious flying boats and almost all were flown by the US Navy. The war diary for Patrol Bombing Squadron VP 105 notes that "Operating conditions in the area were extremely favorable and permitted all crews excellent opportunity for training in their new type aircraft. The morale of all personnel was high and living conditions were good."

"Manifold recreational facilities were available to all, including golf, tennis, sailing, swimming, and fishing, plus the additional luxury of an ideal climate. Operations during the squadrons' stay at Bermuda consisted of offensive anti-submarine sweeps and long-range patrols covering up to 2,400 miles per trip." Though it would be impossible to list all activities of the various squadrons based in Bermuda during the war, certain individuals can be highlighted for their attacks on U-boats and rescue of Allied survivors from the seas.

On the 7th of March 1942 150 miles south of Bermuda German submarine U-128 under Ulrich Heyse dived when two PBM Mariner flying boats (USN VP-74) appeared from low cloud. The first aircraft released two depth charges set for 50 feet just as the U-boat's stern disappeared, but they were duds. A second pair of depth charges was then dropped, followed by two more from the other aircraft. U-128 escaped undamaged and remained submerged until dusk. (Source: Uboat.net and Office of Naval Intelligence, or ONI).

On the 7th of April 1942 U-571 under Helmut Möhlmann had just sunk the Norwegian tanker M/T *Koll* when it was surprised on the surface and attacked unsuccessfully over a period of hours by three US Navy aircraft. One was piloted by Lieutenant (Lt.) Commander John W. Gannon, another by Lt. William W. Soverell, and a third by Lt. A. E. Carlson.

Lt. George Koch attacked an unknown submarine on the 15th of April. On the 8th of July 1942 Lt. John Hitchcock attacked U-134 under Hans-Günther Brosin, and though neither aircraft nor sub was mortally damaged, the airplane limped back to Bermuda with bullet holes in its propeller and fuselage. When the Halcyon was sunk by U-109 under Heinrich Bleichrodt north of Bermuda on 6th February 1942 the PBM Mariner aircraft P-12 of squadron VP 74 flew to the rescue and vectored the merchant ship *British Prestige* to pick up survivors.

On 3rd July 1942 Lt. Junior Grade George W. Brown attacked a U-boat twice unsuccessfully – possibly U-134 under Brosin. Two days later Lt. (j.g.) John R. Steetle of the US Naval Reserve sighted what may have been U-159 under Helmut Freidrich Witte south of Bermuda and north of Puerto Rico and attacked. On his way back to base Steetle encountered U-527 under Herbert Uhlig but, since he had spent his bombs on the first attack, had nothing with which to damage the submarine.

The two successful attacks on submarines resulted in the sinking of U-158 under Erwin Rostin and U-84 under Horst Uphoff. Lt. Richard E. Schreder was led to the location of U-158 on the 30th of June 1942 by signals intelligence, which was impressively accurate. Rostin on U-158 was in the habit of punctually informing headquarters of his impressive tally of ships sunk. Right on schedule he began transmitting northwest of Bermuda and Schreder dove in from behind the clouds for a kill.

At first it seemed the depth charges did no damage, however one of them lodged in the casing, or deck of the U-boat, so that when the boat crash-dived, the pressure ignited the bomb at the designated depth and the detonation destroyed it. The below illustration shows the officers "sunbathing" on the conning tower – this might have included the neutral Spanish skipper of the ship *Everalda* which Rostin had sunk days before.

Whilst Schreder was awarded the Naval Air Medal and his fellow officers Ensign Jack "Jocko" Gierisch and Radioman Wrencie Vickers were also so honored, the next pilot to sink a sub in the region received no accolades for it. He was Lt. Thomas Rudolph Evert and on the 7th August 1943 he and his crewmates attacked a German submarine south of Bermuda, however they were denied credit and Evert perished in a training exercise in the Bay of Biscay months later. Here is a detailed account of the attack by renowned U-boat historian Dr. Axel Niestlé:

"A Liberator B-4 of VB-105 USN, operating from Bermuda, sighted a surfaced U-boat steering a course of 90° true, identified as a probable 500 tons Type VII boat, at 1045 in position 27°55n/68°30w. The aircraft attacked it in the face of heavy anti-aircraft fire with a stick of four Mk47 depth charges, reporting a straddle with at least two charges exploding on the starboard side and one on the port side.

The fourth charge probably became a dud due to technical failure of the arming wire. The U-boat attacked continued in a tight turn to the left for the next 16 minutes, exchanging gun-fire with the circling aircraft. Then the boat started to dive, whereupon the aircraft dropped a Mk 24 Mine 100 feet forward of the swirl just as the top of the conning tower went under.

Due to reduced visibility owing to a rainsquall no direct results were observed but about twenty minutes later a narrow oil slick extending crosswind for about ¾ of a mile was observed close to the diving position. Several other similar streaks appeared within the next three hours while the aircraft circled the location of attack. The attack was later classified as "U-boat present and probably damaged"." The victim was U-84 under Horst Uphoff, responsible for sinking or damaging 7 Allied ships of over 37,000 tons. This author has met with Lt. Evert's son, US Representative Tom Petri, and will begin a long effort to bring proper credit to his father.

U-Boats off Bermuda, Part IV, The Survivors & Bermudians

On the 3rd of July 1942 the *City of Birmingham*'s rescuers deposited 372 survivors in Bermuda, a week earlier, on 28th June the *Jagersfontein*'s rescuers dropped off 99 more, and 62 arrived in two airplanes and a ship from USS *Gannet* on 8 June 1942. Those landed in St. George's had the privilege of riding on the railway from that end of Bermuda to Hamilton – in one instance the railway was started "after hours" at night for such a journey. The landing of 256 survivors from the Canadian passenger ship *Lady Drake* illustrates the kind of reception which even war-beleaguered Bermuda could lay on for strangers to their shores:

There was a grand reception for the USS *Owl* and her survivors when they arrived at Shed #6 in Hamilton at around 10:30 am that morning – May 6th 1942. The Mayor of Hamilton, S. P. Eve was on hand, along with the Governor of the colony and the Commandant of the US Naval Operating Base. According to the *Royal Gazette and Colonist Daily*, "On the dock as the rescue ship warped in were officers of the various British and American Services in Bermuda. Along Front Street were lined ambulances from the U.S. Mobile Base Hospital. The Director of Health, Dr. Henry Wilkinson, and civilian, army and navy doctors were there."

The article continues; "The grim event was not without its light touch. Among the survivors was a Greek prisoner who was in the brig of the torpedoed ship. He is now comfortable in Hamilton Gaol." The reporter also picked up on the exchange between a passenger named Miss Canfield and her rescuers: "As she came ashore, her lifebelt still in her hands, Miss Canfield turned towards the rescue ship where crewmen of the torpedoed vessel were lined up on deck. "Keep your chins up boys," she called out. "Are you alright?" "You bet," came the response from the grinning seamen, "You've got what it takes, lady!"" Since Miss Canfield had been a guest of Police Constable and Mrs. Gooch of Pembroke Parish, it is presumed that she returned to stay with them.

By 10:45 all the survivors were disembarked, and at 11:30 Admiral Jules James, the Commandant of NOB Bermuda was aboard, followed three minutes later by His Excellency Viscount Knollys, Governor of Bermuda, who "came aboard and thanked the ship for the assistance rendered. A "Well Done" was received from the Admiral."

While it is possible to list most of the several places the men were put up in Bermuda, it is only partially possible to list the many individuals who helped the survivors of the *Lady Drake*. Fortunately for the eight hospital cases, "None of these is believed to be seriously injured. There were also a few exposure and shock cases of a minor nature." There was a single US citizen aboard and he was met by Mr. Alonzo B. Cornell, Field Director of the US Red Cross, which used the United Services Organization's Club in The Flatts.

Others of the men were accommodated at the United Services Club at the Hamilton Hotel. L. N. "Dickie" Tucker made what room he could at the Bermuda Sailor's Home, "cramming his premises with survivors." The Naval Recreation Rooms were made available as were local hotels. Other hostelries made available were the A.M.E. Lyceum on Court Street, at the A.M.E. Church (Rev. D. M. Owens, D.D. providing the welcome). There the men were provided with sandwiches, soup and coffee, clothing and cigarettes.

Lady Knollys, wife of the Governor visited the men at the Lyceum to provide "ditty bags" and chat with the survivors. This was a distribution point for gifts from citizens and merchants. Gift boxes included soap, handkerchiefs, shaving kits, and cigarettes. A subscription was begun to raise funds for the survivors and by the first afternoon it had reached 30 British Pounds. Survivors also went to the Canadian Hotel and the Church of God on Angle Street, Hamilton. The proprietor of the Canadian Hotel, James Richards, "spent a considerable sum for clothing for the survivors."

For the officers Mrs. A. B. Smith provided the use of her home, Inverness, in Warwick Parish. The officers who stayed there are reported on 20th of May 1942 to "have expressed their keen joy of the place. It is like home to them. The cottage has been supplied with a cook and inhabitants of the district are doing all they can to make the stay of the survivors a pleasant one. Each day vegetables are brought to the cottage by neighbors and the environment for the officers is a particularly satisfactory one. Moreover, the cottage is conveniently located near the ferry."

On Wednesday 13th of May the *Royal Gazette and Colonist Daily* ran a column entitled "U.S.O. club News" in which they attempt to thank some of the families and individuals "who contributed so much to the comfort of the survivors." The list reads like a "who's who" of Bermudian society: Mrs. J. J. Outerbridge, and "Mesdames Earl Outerbridge, Manuel Nunes, Leonard Gibbons, Ernest Larry, Stalker, Richard Rutherford, B. C. C. Outerbridge, Lauchlin MacDougall, Randolph Tucker, Sheila West, Dorothy Ann Outerbridge and Jessie Fleming. Miss Thomas and Miss Vogan, District Welfare Society Nurses,.... Mrs. Powell Chrichton and the

American Emergency Relief Fund for 6 dozen sheets and pillow cases," and the Bermuda Women's Auxiliary Force (B.W.A.F.) "who gave pajamas and slippers for all the men." Others mentioned were Mrs. George Rubick, Mrs. Kent, Mrs. Ethel Tucker, Mrs. Horace Pearman, Miss Zadiee Penniston and G.S.O. girls the Misses Nadya Gardner and Winnie Haskell."

There is even a letter cited from survivors "on the point of departure" that may (or may not) have been from survivors of *Lady Drake*. It reads: "It was not only what you did for us, the innumerable kindnesses which we shall all remember, but the spirit of friendly anticipation of our wants which made our visit to Bermuda so delightful. ....If this is an example of Allied co-operation such a team is bound to win."

Captain Warren Brown Sr. wrote the following letter to the author in May 2014: "Survivors were looked after by The Bermuda Sailor`s Home. Their address is now 22 Richmond Road, Hamilton. Many survivors were put up at Westmeath guest house. I met many of them as the building belonged to Stanley Conyers and his son was one of my best friends. As a consequence, I was often over there.

Look up the Ladies Hospitality Organization in Bermuda. Although not mentioned, my mother and father and a Mrs. Bridges were the ones that carried out most of the work in looking after the sailors. I spent many an evening there helping my parents. We also always had at least two sailors staying at our house. They usually did not say a great deal about their role as everything was always hush, hush."

Conclusion:

Although Bermudians were already hard-pressed due to population spikes, and though in the cases of the *Freden, Anna, Lady Drake* and *City of Birmingham* the loss of the ships represented a significant disruption of the supply chain to the island, the islanders put on a brave face and got right down to the work of accommodating survivors, passengers, servicemen and merchant sailors alike. It was no easy task, but the sailors were on the front lines of the Battle of the Atlantic and needed to be returned to vessels to carry the war and its materiel to Europe.

Survivors, though often dazed, sunburned, and dehydrated, spoke glowingly of their time on the island and their treatment by its people. Though comparatively a side show to the larger war, Bermuda was at one point in 1942 virtually encircled by U-boats, which used Gibbs Hill Light as a navigational fix. Because of censorship the extent of this siege may have been little known at the time except for the arrival of 1,224 survivors, however now is as good a time as any for the facts to become known, particularly as the survivors are embarking on final voyages of their own.

Yacht Pleiades Wreck Bahamas WWII YP-453

The site where the motor yacht *Pleiades* was built in 1928 at the Consolidated Shipbuilding was situated in the Morris Heights, the Bronx, across the river from Manhattan's Harlem River Drive at 193rd Street. Rudder magazine of November 1929 (page 64) described Pleiades as a "Cruising House Yacht," its authors writing that she and her sisters *Kegonsa, Zinganee, Ardea, Lone Star, Nashira*, and *Vitesse* are "...a fleet of distinguished-looking fast, roomy cruisers – all familiar to yachtsmen in New York waters and the Sound. The interior arrangements of this yacht have been especially well planned, and her appointments reflect good taste throughout." Motor Boating magazine added that the seven boats in the series share an "...exceptionally large deck house together with the ample after deck and very high speed. ...Owner's quarters are found in the deck house and after portion of the boat and comprise the large living and dining room in the deck house together with two double staterooms and baths below deck. In the forward portion of the boat are the quarters for the crew, captain's stateroom and galley" (December 1929 pages 26-28).

The after deck alone is described as 21 feet by 12 feet. The yacht was further fitted with "ice machines, electric windlasses, running water to all fixtures and baths, [and] electric lighting systems." 3 M/V Pleiades under way. Note the fairly high mast and the bunting flying. Rudder magazine, November 1929, page 64. Photo by M. Rosenfeld. Courtesy of Mystic Seaport Museum of America and the Sea, Mystic, CT. Consolidated Shipbuilding "was a builder of luxury yachts, the result of the merger of Charles L.

Seabury Co., originally established at Nyack [New York] in 1885, and Gas Engine & Power Co. ....the companies operated jointly for many years: their activities were consolidated under the Consolidated Shipbuilding name during World War One. The yard was located on Matthewson Road, in the Bronx, in what is now Roberto Clemente State Park. After WWII, Consolidated bought the Robert Jacob shipyard on City Island and closed the Morris Heights yard. It ceased to be an active shipbuilder in 1958, but continues as a yacht repair center" (Tim Colton, shipbuilding history.com/history/shipyards/6yachtsmall/consolidated).

The name Pleiades originates in Greek and also Hindu mythology. The name refers to the seven daughters of Atlas whose names were *Maia, Electra, Celaeno, Taygeta, Merope, Alcyone*, and *Sterope* (thefreedictionary.com). Pleiades refers to a cluster of stars in the constellation Taurus. Though there are several hundred in the cluster, six of them can be seen by the naked eye. Fittingly the yacht was last of seven in the series to be delivered. The yacht Pleiades' dimensions were 78 feet, nine inches (by almost all other accounts 82 feet overall), with a beam of 14 feet four (or six) inches and a draft of six feet nine inches aft and three feet 11 inches forward. Her tonnage is listed in the 1933 Lloyd's Register of American Yachts as being 51 tons net and 75 tons gross (fully loaded with fuel, water, passengers, etc.).

In another list of Consolidated yachts, her displacement is listed as 39.99 tons. Her official number was 227205, and Consolidated both designed and built her as their hull number 2898. 4 Pleiades' propulsion consisted of twin gasoline engines of four cycles and six cylinders. In the list of Consolidated-built vessels her propulsion was "2-6 cyl. 7 X 8.5 R," also described as "7 X 8.5 Speedway". It appears that she was originally powered by gasoline engines.

In 1937 the Fogal Boat Yard in Miami reported to Motor Boating magazine that they re-powered Pleiades with twin Budda diesels (Motor Boating, December 1937, page 106). The engines are listed as developing 300 horsepower, or 150 horsepower each. The hull was fabricated of wood. Her speed was originally given by Consolidated as 23.27 knots, and years later as half that: 12 knots when propelled by the new, less volatile diesel engines.

Pleiades was commissioned, built, bought and owned by only one private individual: Joseph Lester Parsons, Sr. of 88 High Street Montclair, New Jersey, 110 William Street, New York City, and Via Vizcaya, Palm Beach, Florida. Born in September 1871, he was educated in public schools in Montclair. In 1886, at the age of 15 he started work as an office boy at the United States Fire Insurance Company, over which he would later become president. He married Lucille Frances Myers in Brooklyn in 1903, and they had a son and two daughters. Parsons was, in the words of a law case in 1931, "a man of wide experience, who had been in the fire insurance business for over twenty-five years, and was then the President of two fire insurance companies" (Lucille F. Parsons and J. Lester Parsons v. Federal Realty Corporation, 12/15/31).

He was vice-president and from 1903 a co-owner of Crum and Forster, parent of US Fire and Insurance Co. In 1919 Parsons was vice president of the North River Insurance Company, and he served as a director of the Williamsburg City Fire Insurance Company and the New Brunswick Insurance Company, among several others. He was active at the New York Historical Society, the Sons of the American Revolution, and the Essex County Country Club (The American 5 Broker and Business Man Blue Book, 1921). From March 26, 1925 he was a member of the prestigious New York Yacht Club. Both his namesake son and grandson attended Princeton. Pleiades' main deck salon looking forward. Note the radio on right, which was later ripped out by the US Navy. From Motor Boating magazine, December 1929, page 27. Photograph by M. Rosenfeld. Courtesy of the Mystic Seaport: Museum of America and the Sea, Mystic, CT.

In September 1937 Parsons' wife Lucille died. His daughter Lulu married George W. Vanderbilt. In January 1938 Parsons married Helen Boynton Wells of St. Louis Missouri in New York (The New York Post, January 26, 1938). The newlyweds took "a honeymoon cruise in the bridegroom's yacht, the Pleiades, in which he usually passes several months in Southern waters. They will return to New York in the spring (Ibid.). On January 12th 1941 the Palm Beach Post reported that Parsons entertained a "men's luncheon followed by cards" aboard Pleiades the 6 previous day. On February 6th 1941 the Parsons and guests took the Pleiades on a weekend cruise of the Florida Keys (Ibid.). In 1954 Mr. and Mrs. Parsons cruised the South Pacific and Japan on the RMS Caronia under Captain Williams. His son J. Lester Parsons Jr. (Jay) was a cofounder in 1965 of the prestigious maritime law firm of Burke & Parsons in New York, which is still extant.

His descendants continue to be benefactors of a variety of causes, among them the Henry L. Ferguson Museum of Fishers Island, New York, where his son and daughter lived until 2013. After more than 13 years of service to the Parsons family and extensive cruising from the Florida Keys to New England, the Pleiades lasted just over 10 months in the US Navy before a trained crew wrecked her in the Bahamas. During her civilian life the crew required to man the yacht consisted of a captain, engineer, and small crew to serve guests. In all likelihood Parsons conned the wheel for some of the time. Within six months of Germany declaring war on the United States Parsons gave Pleiades to the US Navy. For his patriotism he was remunerated the princely sum of one dollar on the 8th of June 1942, when the yacht lay in Miami (she was "accepted as a gift"). Two days later, on the 10th of June, the Chief of Naval Operations directed she be delivered to a US Navy conversion yard and placed in service post-haste. The earliest record which the US Navy kept on the yacht was dated the 9th of May 1942, at which point they were performing due diligence prior to assuming ownership. A "conversion progress record" is dated the 18th of May 1942, though actual conversion had not yet begun. Once the handover was complete work proceeded rapidly.

Since the navy was under siege by German U-boats ravaging the east coast of Florida and Bahamas at the time, they were under tremendous pressure to do something about the menace, but had inadequate numbers of 7 destroyers and submarine chasers available from other theaters, such as the Pacific, which was being treated as a priority at the time. From these various circumstances emerged collection of amateur yachts which were either manned or donated by civilian personnel in a patriotic effort to help protect the home front from foreign invasion (two sets of saboteurs were nevertheless landed in mid-1942 in Amagansett Long Island, and Punta Vedra, near Jacksonville). The US Coast

Guard called this group of volunteers and their sail and motor vessels the Coastal Picket Patrol. More romantically they were known as the Corsair Fleet, and pejoratively as the Hooligan Navy. Others, like Parsons, opted to donate their vessels outright not to the US Coast Guard, but to the US Navy. Those donated to the navy tended to be larger in size. The tradition of donating or loaning large yachts to the US Navy dates at least to the First World War, and tales of the deplorable state the yachts were returned in make for colorful reading. Pleiades was delivered to the US Navy at the Merrill-Stevens yard on June 9, 1942.

The Merrill-Stevens Dry Dock Company, located at 1270 Northwest 11th Street on the Miami River, was founded in 1885 in Jacksonville. It moved to Miami in 1923 and was foreclosed on in 2011. Until that time the firm claimed to be the oldest continually operating business in Florida, having survived 126 years. According to naval records, conversion on the Pleiades began the very day she was delivered and continued for roughly five weeks, until the 22rd of July, 1942. H. M. Wright oversaw the conversion. Two barbettes, fixed armored housings at the base of gun turrets, were manufactured for the vessel. Twin 50-caliber machine gun mounts were installed, along with a lead counterbalance weighing roughly 150 pounds on the after end of the forward gun. The instructions read "Government to furnish guns and assist in installation of two guns." A life raft was installed on the cabin top, starboard side.

At least 150 8 gallons of fuel were supplied, along with fresh water to fill all the water tanks. A ladder was constructed from the weather deck to the cabin deck on the starboard side symmetrical to the existing one to port. The companionway and seat to starboard of the pilot house were removed to enable another ladder to be fit connecting it to the pantry. The plush interior of Pleiades before its conversion by the US Navy. Rudder magazine, November 1929, page 65. Photo by M. Rosenfeld. Courtesy of Mystic Seaport Museum of America and the Sea, Mystic, CT. Chocks strong enough to accommodate a navy-furnished launch were installed on deck, as were pipe stanchions in the cabin. The engine room blowers were relocated and improved, as were suction ducts. A locker in the salon was converted to gas tanks, and tanks in the pilot house were removed. A mess table to accommodate a dozen men was installed, along with benches made of cypress. Pipe berths were rigged in the aft staterooms. An escape hatch was cut out 9 above the engine room. Air tanks were installed and connected to the engine room, and a 30- gallon drum on the main deck was fitted with pelican hooks for quick dumping. A gas tank was converted for lube-oil use and pipes run from the pilot house to the engine room.

The bearings were re-packed, struts and propellers were ground, and zincs fitted. Engineers pulled pistons numbers five and six on both engines, and calibrated them and the liners. Connecting rod bearings were supplied, along with gaskets and valves. The four heat exchangers were found to be leaking and fitted with new gaskets. An escape ladder was installed on the door to the head, or bathroom, in the forward crew quarters. Another ladder connected the galley and the pantry. The shutters in the cabin were converted to the sliding type. Additional ventilators were installed throughout. The bilge vent was extended to exhaust outside and two buckets filled with sand were provided, along with a gasoline generator. On deck ports were blanked with wood, the radio and cabinets were removed, as were dressing tables, awnings, and windshields. The salon windows were removed and blanked, the after cockpit was decked over, life rails were erected, and depth charge racks were fitted. Two small boats and their davits were removed. Hand pumps were fitted, as were ready-service boxes for ammunition for the .50-caliber anti-aircraft guns. Navigation, recognition, and signal lights were installed – to achieve this a pulsator switch was fitted to the mast, and blinker lights were mounted on the yard arm. A remote-control cable from the bridge to the radio was fitted, as was an antenna on the mast.

The electrical systems were completely overhauled, as were a number of pumps, a compressor, blowers, searchlight, and the batteries. The Frigidaire was recharged and repaired. Two coats of camouflage painting were applied – the hull in Navy Blue 5-N and the above the deck Ocean Gray 5-O. There were splotches of paint applied above to confuse the 10 enemy. Masts were colored Haze Gray 5-H. Canvas coverings were dyed in Deck Blue 20-B. All marks and identifying names and numbers were carefully painted over. A designation number however was painted white on the bow. A pilot and engineer were procured for sea trials. Overall the cost of conversion was $9,851.09, compared to an estimate of $12,481.00, meaning the yard was $2,629.91 under budget. Some of the work was shared with the Miami Shipbuilding Corporation. Pleiades sailed from the Merrill-Stevens yard at 3:30 pm on the afternoon of July 22nd 1942. Soon she was to be renamed USS YP-453, the YP standing for yard patrol craft. According to Tim Colton "the Navy created its initial fleet of YPs from about sixty Coast Guard boats no longer needed after the end of prohibition.

This fleet grew to about 650 for WWII, mostly by the acquisition and conversion of private yachts and fishing vessels. After the war, all these boats were sold off and the YP became a training craft, primarily at the U.S. Naval Academy" (Shipbuildinghistory.com). 11 Another image of Pleiades before the US Navy conversion. Rudder magazine, November 1929, page 65. Photo by M. Rosenfeld. Courtesy of Mystic Seaport Museum of America and the Sea, Mystic, CT. Pleiades was formally accepted into service as USS YP-453 by the Seventh Naval District in Miami on Wednesday the 29th of July 1942 – this can be considered her commissioning date. Another source (Com. 7), states that Pleiades was "placed in service July 29 1942 at section base Port Everglades Florida," and that Lieutenant Junior Grade (JG) George Callies, US Naval Reserve (USNR) was the officer in charge, however the telex was dated August 2, 1942 and may be referring to the vessel's position at that later date.

The Seventh Naval District extends from Jacksonville in the north to Miami in the south, along most of Florida's eastern seaboard. This would have been a natural choice to deploy the vessel, as it was already located in the region and the need for defensive weaponry on that coast at that time was acute. The decision to keep the former yacht close-by may have also reflected an opinion by the navy assessors that the boat was not fit for a long voyage to other destinations such as New York or New Orleans, or the Caribbean, though this would not be consistent with the navy outfitting the boat for service and manning it. If they didn't think they yacht was seaworthy they would have never commissioned her in the first place. The Daily Admiralty Bulletin of the 5th of September 1942 noted that YP 453 was transferred to maintenance on the 28th of August 1942, indicating that there were at least some teething problems with the vessel, and perhaps some serious structural or propulsion-related issues which needed working out. YP-453's active career in the US Navy lasted between the 29th of July 1942 and the 5th of April 1943 - formally the 28th of July, 1943, when she was struck from the Navy Register, or 12 rosters, exactly one day shy of a year since her commissioning. YP-453 patrolled the east coast of Florida from Miami to Jacksonville, including Cape Canaveral, where the majority of submarine attacks in the region took place.

Her complement was vigilantly on the lookout for enemy submarines, coordinating with other all manner of vessels, from naval to merchant marine and coast guard. According to David Wright of Navsource.org, 30 July 1942 found the YP-453 busy with anti-submarine warfare (ASW) duties in the sea lanes between Palm Beach and Jupiter Inlet. A week later, on the 6th of August she performed escort duties for convoy KN 127 (Key West North) along with the US Navy tug Sampson. The following week she was escorting a freighter named SS Florida from Miami to join another convoy. By 26 August 1942 YP-453 was on standby duty in her home port of Port Everglades with YP-248 and the Koasa.

By the 4th of September she took up special duty off the torpedoed and largely abandoned freighter SS La Paz, which was carrying cases of whisky from Virginia to Chile and was beached off Fort Pierce, Florida. On 21 October the men were en-route to Fort Pierce, and the 5th of November found them bound back to Port Everglades. On the 9th of December 1942 YP 453's new commanding officer, G. S. Kilner, like his predecessor a Lieutenant junior grade in the US Naval Reserve, assumed command of the former Pleiades. A day later he was joined by C. H. Lindenberg, Lt. (j.g.), USNR, who served as executive officer, and five days later by R. J. Nesbit, also Lt. (j.g.) USNR and two ensigns in the USNR, E. S. Powell and D. J. O'Connell. Together with 14 other sailors of various ranks, there were 19 souls on board, at the most, since various personnel rotated off the vessel. 13 YP-248 ex-Benmar, a 57-foot Chris Craft converted for navy duty in WWII. She worked in tandem with YP-453 on at least two occasions in 1942 and 1943. From WWII Archives, wwiiarchives.net/servlet/photo /2638/760.

The New Year found Lt. Kilner in command and the ex-Pleiades in Miami by 17 January 1943. By 3 February they were patrolling between Port Everglades and Fowey Rocks, southeast of Miami. On the 12th of March they had moved north to patrol between Palm Beach and Port Everglades. On the 17th they were on guard duty at Port Everglades (David Wright email, November 19, 2015). At the end of March, 1943, YP 453 was stationed at the Port Everglades Section Base, still in the Seventh Naval District, still patrolling up and down the tempestuous Gulf Stream. They were also escorting merchant vessels between Florida and the Bahamas, which required regular sailings for mail, supplies, and personnel, civilian and military. Even the Duke of Windsor, wartime governor of the colony, and his wife Wallis Simpson, required occasional escort on their yacht Gemini and other craft between the islands and the mainland (Edward du Moulin, My Life, Herreshoff Museum Press, Bristol RI 2008) The first sign of trouble that spring appears in the War Diary of the Commander, Gulf Sea Frontier, on Monday, April 5, 1943. Entitled "YP-453 Aground at Entrance to South 14 Bimini," it reads: "The YP-453, escorting three small merchant vessels from Miami to Nassau, ran aground at the entrance to South Bimini and requested assistance.

The CGR-7007 was ordered to proceed to the scene, weather permitting. The three merchant vessels proceeded independently to their destination." (letter from Nathaniel Patch, RDTR2, National Archives and Records Administration (NARA), College Park, MD, to author of April 2, 2013). The following day (Tuesday), it was reported that "The CG-7007 departed Port Everglades at 0650 EWT today to assist the YP-453. ...The time of her arrival was estimated at 0830 EWT. The YT-338 escorted by the YP-248 departed Miami today at 0900 EWT for the same purpose. They were expected to arrive at 1400 EWT." The YT-338 was a US Navy tug built in Chicago in 1942 and delivered in November of that year. She was later designated YT-338 Nesutan (Hans van der Ster, Marcol Archief Production, www.towingline.com). YP-248 was built as the Benmar in Algonic, Michigan in 1940. She was a

57-foot Chris Craft converted power yacht (shipbuildinghistory. com/history/smallships/yp).

By Wednesday, April 7th the situation showed glimmers of hope. Two other naval vessels were dispatched to assist: YP-612 and YHB-14, which left Miami that day at 8 am. But even the rescuers required rescue: by 10:45 am YP-612, built in 1926 as the yacht Maroc of 93 feet, was limping ahead on a single engine while trying to repair the other one. By 11:15 am they informed the Seventh Naval District that they were unable to make running repairs, so YP-534 was dispatched from Port Everglades to render assistance. Both vessels returned to Port Everglades by 5:50 pm that evening. Meanwhile YP-453 had four compatriot vessels standing by off South Bimini: CG-7007, YT-338, YP-248 and YHB-14, which had arrived earlier that day. Though the former Pleiades was still aground, the war diarist noted that "operations are proceeding satisfactorily and it is expected to be refloated with the next high tide." 15 Indeed on Thursday April 8th the tug YT-338 was able to advise headquarters that at 12:24 pm YP-453 was refloated. Although "the hull was full of water ...the vessel still had sufficient buoyancy to float. The tug was attempting to tow her to a protected anchorage in the area." There were at that time 10 men aboard YP-453 and they transferred to YHB-14, which then left South Bimini at 12:55 pm bound for Miami. It would be the end of Lt. Kilner's and his men's working relationship with their charge.

For the better part of four days, from Monday the 5 th to Thursday the 8th, the men of YP-453 struggled to salvage their vessel. It must have been a sleepless period, wet, cold, exposed to the elements, fighting around the clock against the incoming water. What is not known is whether the boat was an anchor when it dragged ashore, whether it lost propulsion, was flooded, or simply drifted there. No official reason is given for why the patrol craft left its convoy duties in the first place, and why they didn't enter the harbor in Bimini right away. As for the YP-453, her deep draft in such a semi-submerged state prevented her from being towed into the harbor at Alice Town, Bimini for repairs. Instead, the small convoy (four vessels including the YP-453) headed south for the comparatively scant shelter provided by small cays south of Bimini. At 5:10 pm the Seventh Naval District's Salvage Officer instructed CG-7007 to take over YP-453 at Barnett Harbour, on the Great Bahama Bank. The Coast Guard vessel's instructions were to stand by the abandoned patrol craft. 16 A satellite image showing Barnett Harbour, between South Bimini and Gun Cay, Bahamas (to right) and Miami's Biscayne Bay to the left.

The term "harbor" to describe Barnett is a misnomer, as it is really just a part of the lip of the shallow Great Bahama Bank. The two are separated by roughly 50 miles of turbulent Gulf Stream ocean (http://mapcarta.com/19824870/Map). Barnett Harbour is little more than a cluster of rocks barely above sea level, but constitutes a destination or waypoint for vessels coming across the Gulf Stream from Florida and accessing the shallower and comparatively sheltered waters of the Great Bahama Bank. Barnett Harbour is located in position 25°38'15"N by 79°19'00"W. It is three miles north of Gun Cay, which itself lies just north of North Cat Cay, and 3.25 miles south of Port Royal, South Bimini Island, which lies just south of Alice Town and Bailey Town on North Bimini, the capital of the Bimini District of the Bahamas. The region is known above all as a deep-sea fishing destination 17 due to its direct and easy proximity to Florida and the Gulf Stream. It is one of the first landfalls in the Bahamas, being only 44 nautical miles east of the cut outside Miami's Biscayne Bay. By Friday the 8th of April YP-453 was intentionally beached. The navy and coast guard personnel continued to try to save her for a week or so, since there is a further entry regarding YP-453 on Thursday April 15th.

That entry indicates that the former Pleiades was "aground on Bahama Bank and damaged beyond repair." Then the little ship's death knell was struck: "Authority was requested to strike it from the Navy list and destroy the hull after salvaging the engines and other removable material" (Com. 7, R-152105). A postscript relates that "all possible machinery and material [was] removed and stored; hulk has broken up." Indeed, on the 28th of July 1943 USS YP-453 was formally stricken from the United States Navy Register and given up for good. There is no telling exactly how the engines and other machinery (winches, generator) were disposed of, or whether or not they were auctioned off to locals in nearby Bimini rather than transported back to Florida. In a navy press release dated October 2nd 1943 the patrol craft was reported "destroyed by grounding in the Bahamas 15 April 1943."

A subsequent Naval Intelligence Report of Losses dated May 2, 1946 simply states that they vessel was "Destroyed by Grounding." Since World War II, and particularly the advent and popularization of SCUBA diving from the 1970s onward there have been persistent rumors of a German submarine in the Bimini Islands. Aside from a discounted report of a piece from U-432 in the Abaco Islands (the submarine never came to the Bahamas – in fact it never left northern Europe), the most emphatic claims of sub sightings point to Bimini. Diving entrepreneur Stuart Cove reports that a submarine was reported off Bimini and that divers blew apart the hull in the 1980s to get better 18 access. As a result, the hull has broken up and disintegrated.

Others report clearly seeing a submarine off Bimini from the air. While it might be possible that the US Navy, which conducts extensive and secret submarine tests on nearby Andros (at their AUTEC, or Atlantic Undersea Testing and Evaluation Center), left the carcass of a submarine there, it is highly unlikely that the only German submarine known to have been sunk within hundreds of miles (U-157 sunk off Key West), could have drifted north in the Gulf Stream to Bimini. Sunken subs simply don't float north – they don't float at all. Could it be possible that the World War II submarine which divers and enthusiasts have been reporting off Bimini was in fact the remains of Pleiades, or YP-453? Queries to a number of diving operators in Bimini are inconclusive. None of the present-day operators, including Stuart Cove and salvage expert Marcus Mitchell have actually dived on or witnessed the alleged submarine.

The mystery – and whether the loss of YP-453 had anything to do with it – remains unsolved. Most likely, with her fittings and machinery gone the YP-453's wooden hull and beams would have disintegrated quickly, and there would be almost nothing left of the vessel and its hull except stringers, fasteners and odds and ends from her construction in the Bronx in 1929. Even these would be likely buried deep in the sand or covered with coral in the intervening 73 years.

Mailboats: A Personal Introduction

Why write about mailboats? It is a question I have often been asked, most recently by a group of yachtsmen visiting from the States. When I describe my passion for these slow-plodding beasts of burden to the folks on the docks at Potters Cay or to friends and family members, they seem to understand, but not everyone does. And not every reader will. So here, after telling the tales of over 100 of these varied craft and the dozens of islands they serve, in the afore-gone features, goes.

In the early 1980s, when I was not yet a teenager, my parents – both expatriates who had lived several decades in the islands and honeymooned in Treasure Cay – took my three siblings and me on a mailboat voyage to Abaco. The voyage left quite an impression on us – being able to bring as many belongings as we wanted, to roam freely over the vessel, and to enjoy the fresh sea breeze the entire way was a thrill unmatched by air travel. It was also an unusual way for an expatriate family to travel at the time, though by no means unique, it was perhaps bohemian of us, or at least we thought so.

Once my brothers and sister and I figured out that we could get from Nassau to Harbour Island each way for about the cost of entry into Club Waterloo, we were hooked. From the late 1980s onwards Captain Moss of the Bahamas Daybreak III came to know us – the family that preferred to ride the mailboat. I was once challenged, by a resort owner on Briland, as to why I would possibly take the mailboat? I hadn't really thought of the reasons – for some reason the idea of going to the airport and paying what I believed would be a lot more money seemed preposterous to me; something that rich people did. Ironically the prospect of flying seemed to me to cheapen the experience, as though stopping for a few minutes at Spanish Wells and then navigating the Devil's Backbone with its hairpin turns, skimming the wreck of a sunken locomotive and brushing along the beach was a way of somehow earning the way to decadence on the island. Then again, we stayed mostly at the modest Royal Palm rather than Pink Sands!

Somehow over the years Potter's Cay dock worked its way into the family lore. Like the time our mother waved us off on the Daybreak at the crack of dawn, only to realize that we had taken the keys to her car, leaving her in a nightgown, downtown (thank goodness for understanding cab drivers!). Or the time that a girlfriend and I arrived there on the fishing vessel Sea Star, also at dawn, to wait for a ride as the sun rose over Nassau Harbour. Or the time that a group of friends joined us for bon voyage drinks at Big Daddy's. At 11:30 pm I went over to the mailboat which was to carry us and informed the captain that we would return by midnight. However, he misunderstood me, thought we were aboard, and cast off just as we ran up the dock to do a pier-head leap, just in time! Or the time when we turned back to the dock late at night because the captain's nephew, who was serving as crew, forgot his radio – it was handed to us by outstretched arms, in those days before iPhones, from another mailboat by understanding sailors.

Have I taken more mailboat trips than other Bahamians? Not by a long shot. Half a dozen voyages to and from Harbour Island, a few more perhaps on the modern Bo Hengy and Bo Hengy II. A longer cruise on the United Star to Acklins Island, on which we shared the voyage with the new doctor-in-residence from the Philippines. I asked him his specialty – he replied that he was a veterinarian! There was a voyage from Nassau to Black Point Exuma, San Salvador and Rum Cay which didn't end so well when the boat ran aground off Port Nelson and I received a cold reception when I was rowed ashore, as I was (correctly) taken for a real estate speculator.

Perhaps the happiest mailboat trip was the one that ended in Potter's Cay at dawn. The aforementioned girlfriend and I boarded about midnight the day after Christmas Junkanoo and voyaged to Bullock's Harbour, Berry Islands. From there we set off for Moore's Island's only settlement – Hard Bargain. But halfway there we were startled to wake to commotion and see a sheer wall of white steel looming out of our porthole. In all the excitement of loading and unloading the cargo our otherwise earnest skipper had forgotten to deliver the mail to the Berry Islands, and was having a cruise ship divert to complete the errand for him. We spent a night in Hard Bargain, alongside a vessel named "Jesus Savior Pilot Me," listening to the tales of old timers, on an island where strains of Yoruba were recorded as recently as the 1970s. From there we voyaged to nearby Sandy Point and the mailboat lay over for a few days. But we were eager to get back to Nassau and accepted a graciously offered ride aboard the Sea Star, arriving in time to celebrate New Year's Junkanoo in the capital. A memorable trip indeed.

Nowadays one has the added convenience of bringing a vehicle, as we have done to Abaco and North Eleuthera. And I once brought a bicycle to Mastic Point, Andros. But as many readers will know, renting a vehicle in the family islands can be as simple as asking around, finding the car, and leaving the agreed daily rate in cash, along with the keys, behind the visor. My brother and I once went camping in Eleuthera to be met with the same kind of queries: why not stay in a hotel? For the same reasons one takes the mailboat – to get that little bit closer to nature, or at least to think you are. To get that little bit closer to the people who populate these wonderful islands, to hear and feel the breeze, not see it through an airplane portal at 3,000 feet.

Why take a mailboat? If I had to be entirely honest, the motivations were mostly selfish. In my teens and twenties when I was single it was to get away from Nassau and all those married people after the crescendo of Christmas and New Year's during Christmas holidays home from school and college. Later it was to look at land to invest in by being able to see several islands on one trip, always moving forward, rather than fly to one island, return to Nassau, fly to another island, go back to Nassau, and so on. Partly I was escaping work at the family business – playing hooky as it were. Partly there were romantic aspirations – find a companion and head off together into the unknown for a few days, by picking the first mailboat to leave, wherever it would take you.

Pack a cooler full of sodas, beer, and sandwiches and you never know what daybreak, or the next wave, will bring you. Perhaps to an island that wasn't even on the itinerary, but where the captain needs to visit his sweetheart du jour. It's happened more than once. Besides, when the crew catches or buys fresh conch or fish, they are just as likely to share it, perhaps in exchange for a cold beer, a fair trade. That line trailing behind the ship may produce a fearsome barracuda, or it might just be trailing a pair of trousers being naturally washed by the wake. On a mailboat, you just never know for sure, and I guess that is the mystique – along with necessity, transport, trade, friends and family and a host of other rational reasons – that drives people like me back to mailboats. And I hope – as my parents did – that my son catches the bug as well. He is after all named after one of the communities dear to our hearts and accessed by the Bahamas Daybreak III those decades ago – Dunmore Town.

History of Mailboats in the Bahamas, 1804 – 2016

Vessels have been carrying people and goods between the islands of the Bahamas since the time of the Lucayans over 1,000 years ago. Indeed, the Bahamian archipelago – like those of Greece, the Philippines and Indonesia – is reliant on work-horses like its mailboats to ply between the islands carrying everything from people to pin-cushions, tractors to pickaxes. Pinning down which years such trade has been government subsidized proves a challenge, but not an insurmountable one. The quest is as relevant as ever, as presently there are 18 mail boats based at Potter's Cay in Nassau serving over 45 communities on 14 of the family islands, Bimini to Inagua.

Though what we know as mailboats will carry everything from church pews to livestock, sodas and beer, passengers, nails, mattresses, vehicles and pretty much everything in between, the focus of early inter-island service was concerned primarily with the mails, as upon that cargo the subsidies relied. Initially the offices of the Bahamas Gazette served as the post office, then in 1761 came the "earliest known record of a letter being sent from the Bahamas." In 1788 "an act for the establishment and regulation of a post office was passed." In 1858 British postage stamps were introduced but only a year later "the Bahamian post office became independent of London, and issued its own stamps."

As for the origins of the service, one detailed source is the book Bahamas Early Mail Service and Postal Markings, by Morris Hoadley Ludington (Alpha Philatelic Printing & Publishing Co., Washington DC, 1982). He cites the Bahamas Gazette from 1784, the Bahamas Royal Gazette from 1804, and numerous other sources which he read from the originals in the public library which used to be the goal. He notes that "a vessel called the Nassau Packet sailed a number of times during 1799 between Nassau and Charleston," but this was not inter-island mail service. In 1802 Henry Moss of Crooked Island was made Acting Postmaster (p.8), followed by a Mr. Leitch in Nassau. According to Ludington "...the first mention found in the Bahamas newspapers of Crooked Island and of a Mail Boat being sent from Nassau to meet the Packet there," was of the Mary and Susan, Captain Fisher, dated Friday 21 September, 1804. The vessel is described as an "armed Government schooner," as during the Napoleonic Wars "many privateers were active throughout the West Indies." (p.9). Soon other vessels – like the John Bull, Captain Fulford, a Government felucca, and the schooner Nassau, Captain Gibson, appear, along with the Packet Lord Spencer, on the route to and from Jamaica and England. By 1821 the schooners Dash and Paragon are described as plying the same route, connecting islands within the Bahamas with mail coming from outside the colony.

In a description of mail boat services dated 5 June 1832 Smyth relates to Goodrich that mail packets came "from England and America through the Bahama Islands using Crooked Island as the chief mailing station." This was extended to Kingston, Jamaica. This was referred to as intra-island mail service. Truly inter-island mail service is believed to have begun with the 35-foot-long schooner Dart, which was enlarged at its mid-ships twice over its career. Built about 1867 in Harbour Island, it was owned by John Saunders Harris of that island. One of its captains was William James Harris, born 1848. The boat served Harbour Island and Spanish Wells Eleuthera from Nassau for over 50 years until about 1922 when it was lost in a

hurricane. Accommodation aboard was segregated. Michael Craton and Dr. Gail Saunders, in their seminal work Islanders in the Stream, Volume II, write about Abaco that "....sailboats had been replaced by government-subsidized motor mail boat services to most other islands by 1929."

Ludington lists 25 mail vessels plying the inter-island routes of the Bahamas between 1849 and 1885. Chronologically, these were the Palestine, Experiment, Union, President, Electric, Eugene, Georgina, Amelia Ann, Brothers, Mary Jane, Jane, Arabella, Quick, Jimmie, Admired, Dart, Cicero, Charlton, Rebecca, Osborne, Argosy, and Attic. By 1849 the following Bahamian ports were being served by mail on a regular basis: East end of Eleuthera, Port Howe, San Salvador, Little Exuma Harbor, North end of Long Island, Port Nelson, Rum Cay, Sandy Point, Watling's Island, Great Harbour, Long Island, Long Cay, Crooked Island, and Inagua.

In March 1865 the government sought to "provide for more frequent Communication between certain islands of the Bahamas and the Seat of the Government." This may have been an indirect response to the recommendations of Thomas C. Harvey to the Colonial Secretary, C. R. Nesbitt, in 1858 in which he reported "The great variety of productions in the Bahamas would .....if there existed an inter-insular steam communication, become available to all, and the cultivation of the land and development of many valuable resources, would speedily follow the power of obtaining a sure market. At present some cays are, at times, absolutely destitute." The resultant act ("Inter-Insular Communication, 28 Vic. C. 18") found that the previous act for a single vessel was inadequate. Therefor, the new act empowered the Governor, on the advice of the Executive Council, to "....hire by the year, or otherwise, for the service.... a good and sufficient vessel and pay therefor the sum of money as the same can, by public tender, be procured for not exceeding in the whole sum of five hundred pounds per annum." The act was good for five years.

In May 1867 (30 Vic. C.18) the government specifically enabled subsidized mail service between Nassau and "the Inhabitants of the districts of Eleuthera, Harbour Island and Abaco." The government was authorized to procure "...fast-sailing vessels of not less than 20-tons burthen, each to be employed in the conveyance of fortnightly mails." The act authorized the procurement of three different vessels. Interestingly this act confirms the existence of service to Inagua, instructing the post master in Nassau to "make up mails... as he now makes up and dispatches mails by the mail vessel running between Nassau and Inagua." The act sets out a tariff for the carriage of freight and passengers – capping the amounts by law. It even governs luggage. The receipts were to go into the public treasury. There were nine port covered under this act: Gregory Town, Governor's Harbour, Tarpum Bay, Rock Sound, Spanish Wells, Dunmore Town (Harbour Island), Cherokee Sound, Great Harbour and Green Turtle Cay Abaco.

Within a few decades there were acts passed to fill in the gaps between Inagua to the far south and Abaco to the north. For example, "Act (No. 7 of 1907) establish[ed] an Inter-Insular Mail Service in the Bahamas. It empower[ed] the Governor in Council to establish a Mail Service between Nassau and the Out Islands, and to cause contracts to be made for this purpose." This 1907 act was further amended and expanded by "An Act to Establish an Improved Inter-Insular Mail Service" passed in August 1948.

Through it, the "Governor establish[ed] mail service between Nassau and the Out Islands." Its geographic scope is broad, as it covers trade "....between one Out Island and another Out Island and between settlements in any Out Island district." It also states that the service may be performed by vessels propelled by sail, steam, or "other mechanical power" such as motors.

The act is granular in its coverage, making allowance for the "sufficient supply of life-saving apparatus and boats, the employment of a competent master and crew, over-crowding, cabin accommodation" and so on. It also calls for the periodic examination of mail vessels and their life-saving equipment. The lists of islands groups covered is extensive, from Inagua and Crooked Island to the Biminis. There are over 50 communities listed – 10 in Andros alone. The proscribed tonnage of the vessels range from 20 to 150 – the largest for the longest routes and only 20 tons for the comparatively short passages from Nassau to the Current in Eleuthera. The act includes specific costs to carry items ranging from "half firkins and kegs, jars and demi-johns" to "tierces, hogsheads, and other vessels not exceeding thirty gallons." It includes "Madeira, horseflesh wood, yellow wood and other timber.... Potatoes, yams and other roots... mares, mules, and cattle, lignum vitae and braziletto [wood]....".

The next overhaul of the Mailboat Act, as it is known less formally, came in 1966, and again the rules were tweaked in 1974 and 1987. Interestingly, mailboat owners with dual roles in government such as Sir Roland Symonette and Sir George Roberts had hands in shaping legislation. Then in 1995 and 1996 the "Rates for Carriage of Freight" rules were amended again, basically updated and modernized to keep the investors, entrepreneurs and mailboat owners in their livelihood. The latest version on the Official Website of the Government of the Bahamas is from October 1966 – an amended version of the 1948 act. On the site is the agreement, which mailboat owners can enter into with the government. This requires the service provider to subject their official logs twice yearly for inspection, and to keep up the ship's Registration Certificate, Business License, and Inter Insular Mail Shipping Rates. If the vessel and its officers and crew and the service provided are deemed not up to government standard, then the government can revoke the license and with it the agreement.

In 2008 it was reported in March that the government had signed a three-year contract with mailboat owners and operators, "in response to complaints by mail boat owners and operators that the tariff does not take into account that the cost of doing business has escalated and the cost of fuel has also increased exponentially." The tariff they amended was drafted in 1996. In a contemporary article from The Eleutheran, the Honorable Sidney Collie wrote that "My Ministry is aware and very concerned about the price of diesel fuel and the impact that it is having on the mail boat industry and the economy as a whole." The article continued, observing that "...the Family Island residents depend heavily on the mail boat for transportation of goods and other essential services." In short, the Mailboat Act and its amendments remain a vibrant, to some degree flexible documents, enabling mailboat operators to continue to serve remote communities with affordable, reliable access to the capital across the decades and centuries.

It is noteworthy that government subsidy of the mails has enabled at least one mariner and entrepreneur, Captain Ernest Dean of Sandy Point Abaco, to make his career, motivated at first by the need to obtain regular supplies of milk for he and his wife's infant children. Starting in 1949 when he constructed the mailboat Captain Dean in Sandy Point by hand, without electricity (it took over two years to build), he went on to commission and ply six vessels under the same name and numerous others owned and operated by his family before his recent death. His life, boats and career is chronicled in the book Island Captain.

In March 2015 the Minister of Transport and Aviation announced that the government had allocated $3.1 million towards wreck removal, refurbishment, the expansion of warehousing, the repair of the causeway and installation of bathrooms at Potter's Cay. Despite attrition like the sinking of the Andros mailboat Lady D. in July 2014, whose wreck still clutters otherwise useable dock frontage, it would appear that the inter-island freight and mail service can, with help, remain as vibrant a part of the Bahamian islands' fabric as it has been for at least 200 years.

Mailboats of and to Abaco Islands

Mailboat service to Abaco and the Abaco cays began as early as 1894 with the remnants of a salvaged vessel and continue to this day. Though the primary port is Marsh Harbour, mailboats have, over the years, also served Sandy Point, Cherokee Sound, Hope Town, Man-O-War Cay, Green Turtle Cay and other settlements. As an illustration of how adaptive Abaconians are, there is even a daily high-speed passenger boat connecting eastern Grand Bahama with Little Abaco Island instituted this century. There are also numerous freighters which serve Abaco directly from eastern Florida and Nassau, however in this article we will focus on those vessels that carried mail – as well as passengers and cargo – between the islands of the Bahamas (principally Nassau) and Abaco and its islands.

Though perhaps more illustrative than exhaustive, twelve vessels have spanned the past 120-plus years to connect Abaco with the capital, its markets, services and people. Until the 1950s these boats were often the only connection to the largest city in what was then still a colony. Writing in 1983, Steve Dodge, in his book Abaco, The History of an Out Island and its Cays, observed that "Despite the advent of airplane service to Abaco during the past thirty-five years, Marsh Harbour as well as other Abaco communities are still dependent on the mailboat for freight service, as anyone viewing the empty supermarket shelves on a Tuesday or a Wednesday can testify – 'no milk until the mailboat comes in' is a common refrain." Although this author doubts that a delayed mailboat would cause such shortages today, still, the importance of these vessels to the survival of businesses, communities and even individuals in days of yore would be too easily overlooked. Captain Ernest Dean of Sandy Point for example, was inspired to spend 2.5 years building his first mailboat because he and his wife Eula would run out of milk waiting for the mailboat to come in from Nassau.

The dozen vessels, in chronological order were the sailing vessels Albertine Adoue and Arena, the motor vessels Priscilla, Content S., Stede Bonnet, Richard Campbell, Beluga, Almeta Queen, Arena, Tropical Trader, Deborah K. II, Captain Gurth Dean and Legacy. These range in size from the aforementioned Albertine Adoue which was made from the scraps of a larger vessel into a 60-foot schooner to a 160-foot steel freighter, the Legacy, with a salvaged lifeboat, the Beluga, ferrying cargo between Cherokee Sound and Crossing Rocks. The Content S. was a converted yacht which at one point was registered to Lake Champlain in Vermont, and was tended to by "The Queen," the lifeboat from the British tanker *Athelqueen* which was sunk by an Italian submarine off Hope Town in 1942 – the boat was a gift from her grateful officers and crew and was featured in a painting by renown Abaco artist Alton Lowe, whose Albert Lowe Museum is a fine repository of mailboat ephemera.

The original Albertine Adoue was built by Kelley and Spear in Bath, Maine in 1890. She was 171 feet long and 36 feet wide and although a three-masted schooner was equipped with an auxiliary engine. The vessel was named for the wife of prominent businessman Bertrand Adoue of Galveston, Texas. He and his partner Jean Jacques Mistrot invested in blockade running in the American Civil War – apparently profitably. While bound from Philadelphia to Galveston with a cargo of coal, the ship foundered near Spanish Cay off Little Abaco on the 29th of March, 1894. Enterprising locals built a schooner from the timbers, with the resulting craft being 60 feet on deck with two masts. She was to serve the Bahamas as a mailboat from Nassau for 29 years under the same name. Her owners in 1926 were R. J. Farrington and William Augustus Roberts. Among her Bahamian captains were Hartley Roberts, Osbourne Roberts, Roland Roberts - all sons of William Augustus Roberts, her owner. In 1923 the Albertine Adoue was replaced by the motor vessel Priscilla. On Christmas Day 1930 the Albertine Adoue suffered the same fate as her namesake, and went aground in North Carolina laden with liquor during the Prohibition and was lost.

The Albertine Adoue was not popular with the government Commissioner in Hope Town, who wrote "It is impossible in these progressive days [1922] to expect a mail service to be satisfactorily performed by a sailing vessel. Apart from speed there is no comfort or privacy to be obtained for passengers." He further hoped that a motor vessel would "....take the place of this wind jammer." The vessel nominated to take the schooner's place was the Priscilla, a steel-hulled 100-footer propelled by a 115-horsepower Fairbanks Morse diesel engine. Rumored to have been a racing sail yacht, her contribution to mail service "significantly reduced the degree of Abaco's isolation and made commerce more feasible."

With the implementation of wireless service to Nassau the same year, Dodge notes that what would have taken a fortnight before 1925 took just minutes in terms of transmission of information. According to Evan Loew the cook on board was his relative Osgood Loew, the mate was Howard Loew, and the Captain Hartley Roberts (same as with the Albertine Adoue). Although the Priscilla could never be as fast as a telegram, and was "no panacea," her contribution to trade was considerable if imperfect. Among the other settlements she called, Green Turtle Cay was included. In August 1932 the vessel was "blown ashore and destroyed" during a hurricane. Another account, in Wayne

Neely's book "The Great Bahamian Hurricanes of 1899 and 1932," more modestly states that "M/V Priscilla reported some damage to the structure of the boat."

The Content S. was launched as the yacht Percianna II, having been built for Percy Hance by J. M. Densmore in Quincy, Massachusetts in 1920. In 1934, Hance sold it to Howard E. Spaulding of Shelburne Vermont and Palm Beach Florida. It lay unused in Florida for a number of years before being re-flagged to the Bahamas and re-purposed to inter-island trade, for which it was not ideally suited. In 1940 Nassau merchant Richard Wilson Sawyer purchased her with the name Content and added the "S" presumably for "Sawyer." Her Captain was Stanley Weatherford of Great Guana Cay, whose relatives confirm that he commanded her. According to "Pappa" Floyd Lowe, born 1920 and the erstwhile patriarch of Green Turtle Cay Abaco, the yacht was the "wrong ship" and "not a boat for mail service" on the Abaco-Nassau run, being narrow and deep draft and fitted out as a yacht, without the large cargo holds which would make such a ship profitable. Sawyer seems to have recognized this, as Content S. was only dedicated to Abaco service for about a year. It was better suited for its other purpose – carrying passengers in comfort. He chartered her out to the Duke and Duchess of Windsor for a tour of the islands early in their tenure in the colony.

In March 1942 she was shaken out of layup by the Duke to rescue survivors of two ships the O. A. Knudsen and *Athelqueen* from Abaco. The first batch of 38 men were picked up at Cross Harbour, the second group of 46 at Hope Town. Survivors mostly slept on deck – one of them later said she looked like the royal yacht in her finery. The Content S. was lost in a collision with the Foundation Aranmore off Cuba in 1946. The Queen was the affectionate term for the *Athelqueen*'s lifeboat which was given to Hope Town citizens as a gift from survivors (three of whom drowned trying to make it to shore). According to Vernon Malone The Queen was burned after its useful life shuttling people, mail and cargo to and from mailboats was expended.

The Stede Bonnet was launched at Symonette Shipyards in Nassau and Hog Island (Paradise Island) on 4 June, 1942. She was 119 feet long, 225 tons and her single diesel engine propelled her at 12 knots. Her captain was Lloyd Talmadge Albury of Man-O-War Cay. The boat's original name was Royal Navy-issue: MM 194. According to Sir Etienne Dupuch ("A Salute to Friend and Foe"), "British Admiralty contracted for two trawlers to be built in Nassau. They were launched in a ceremony by the Duke of Windsor. Intended for service in Singapore, which fell to the Japanese before they were commissioned and therefore never brought into action." One became the Stede Bonnet, named after a famous pirate, the other the Church Bay, which later burned in downtown Nassau. An online commentator added this colorful rendition of the coconut telegraph: "That Omni present Short-Wave Radio played its part in announcing the arrival of the Mail Boat. The Captain would simply key his mike on the ship's radio and announce, "Stede Bonnet reporting; just left East Side Marsh Harbour on the way to Hopetown. Someone please tell Mr. Robley Russell to bring the Tender out by Parrot Cay for freight and passengers. Stede Bonnet out.""

The mailboat Richard Campbell was built in 1937 by the enterprising Sir George William Kelly Roberts of Harbour Island, and named after his first son. The vessel was 85.6' long, 16.3 feet wide, 8 feet deep and weighed 89 tons. She was a wooden sailing sloop (single mast) with an auxiliary motor. Her captain was named Russell – In the book "Islanders in the Stream" he and the mate were described as "a "Conchy Joe captain and mate and all-black crew." The authors Saunders and Craton continue: "Cherokee Sounds was only the first of the six Abaco settlements at which the Richard Campbell called, following a routine that, though tedious, greatly raised Jack Ford's admiration for the seamanship, efficiency and toughness of Captain Russell and his crew." On the topic of Cherokee Sound, which was shallow and required shuttling of small vessels to carry cargo and people ashore, Captain Granville Bethel devised an ingenious way to supply the similarly isolated community of Crossing Rocks to the south – he salvaged a lifeboat from a torpedoed Allied freighter which had washed up there. According to his son Patrick, the small craft was renamed Beluga and plied its route from 1945 or so into the 1950s fitted with a small engine.

The Almeta Queen was built for War Supply in Toronto in 1942 and converted to sail in 1946. Captain Ernest Dean speaks of utilizing her services to tow one of his new-built vessels (the Captain Dean II) from Marsh Harbour to Nassau around 1965. At that time her captain was Sherwin Archer. Her owners were the Abaco Trading Company Ltd. of Nassau and she appears to have largely carried crawfish between Abaco, Florida and Nassau, so her progeny as a mailboat may be in doubt. In August 2007 was sighted in aerial photographs rotting on the River Platte of Argentina. Another vessel which was not exclusively a mailboat but which carried parcels and passengers was the sloop Arena, also skippered by owner Sherwin Archer, who became a senator for Abaco in 1964. His mate was his son Bobby. The Arena, which appears in the lovely book "Out Island Portraits" by Ruth Rodriguez, was supplanted in 1950 by the Tropical Trader, about which little is known. There was a Tropical Trader built in the Turks & Caicos in 1950 but it is listed as a sailing vessel and Dodge writes that the Abaco Tropical Trader was a motor vessel.

By 1970 a large steel diesel vessel had taken over the route from Nassau to Abaco carrying mail – the Deborah K II. Not believed to have replaced a similarly named ship in the Bahamas, this vessel was 348 tons, could carry 474 tons, was built in 1965, Bahamian flagged, and is believed to be still in service. This large vessel which has the lines of a European-built coaster, was for many years the primary link between Marsh Harbour at least and Nassau. In modern times Southern Abaco is served by the sizeable motor vessel Captain Gurth Dean. Owned by Captain Ernest Alexander Dean (Jr.) of Sandy Point and Nassau, the ship weighs 500 tons and can carry 600 tons of cargo. Built by Rodriguez Coden in Alabama she was launched on October 13th 1999. Her route takes her to Sandy Point, Moore's Island, and Bullocks Harbour in the Berry Islands. Her captain is John Dean. Note that the dozen or so vessels built and skippered by the Dean family patriarch Captain Ernest Dean Sr. of Sandy Point are covered in a separate article.

The motor vessel Legacy, built by the same yard as Captain Gurth Dean in Alabama, is a roll on / roll off type ship (Ro/Ro) which is 160 feet long, 36 feet wide and 485 gross tons – also capable of carrying 600 tons of cargo. Thoroughly modern and shallow draft, it was built in 2002 and still calls at Marsh Harbour, Guana Cay, Green Turtle Cay and Nassau on a weekly basis. Commissioned by her owners, Dean's Shipping Limited of Nassau for the specific Bahamas trade, this vessel represents a new generation of service to the islands – continuing a long line of entreprenurialship in shipbuilding and investing and calculated risk-taking that has covered a dozen decades, as many vessels, and everything from yachts to lifeboats to converted schooners and spongers to modern landing craft. It is worth noting that with the possible exception of the Deborah K. II, Abaco has avoided the trend of some other regions to purchase older ships from Europe and trade them until they become either dive sites or fodder for South American operators.

Mailboat Service to Eleuthera Islands

Although the Dart is given credit as the first mailboat to serve North Eleuthera from Nassau, it would appear that her predecessor the Mary Jane has earned that distinction. The Mary Jane was a 41-ton schooner built of wood in 1853. Rather than a government-subsidized mail route, however, the Mary Jane was financed by a joint stock company, with half the funds raised in Nassau and the other half in Harbour Island. According to Anne and Jim Lawlor's "The Harbour Island Story," in 1868 such a "company was set up and the Harbour Island packet schooner Mary Jane carried the mail and passengers from Dunmore Town and Spanish Wells to Nassau." She held the mail, cargo and passenger route to Harbour Island, with stops in Spanish Wells, until 1870 when the Dart replaced her. Owned by a Harbour Islander named John Cleare and named after his daughter, she would have an active career of 47 years until broken up in Nassau in 1900.

The sailing schooner Dart was built around 1867 and was 35 feet long on deck, though enlarged twice during her career, which lasted until she was lost in a hurricane before 1930. Her owner was John Saunders Harris of Harbour Island. According to a placard hanging in the lobby of The Mail Boat Company in

241

Nassau, "The Dart was the first scheduled mail boat from Nassau to Harbour Island. Originally a pilot boat of about 35 feet in length, she should sail from Harbour Island to Nassau in the record time of eight hours. She lived up to her name and won many regattas in Nassau, until she disappeared during a Bahama hurricane. Twice she was lengthened by adding to her amidships."

The Lawlors go on to say that ""Captain, William G. Harris, a veteran sailor, had captained both previous Harbor Island mailboats, the Dart and the Endion." This suggests that the Dart was the first Harbour Island mailboat. Another of the boat's skippers was William James Harris, born 1848 in Harbour Island. It appears to have been a family endeavor. The Dart was said to have been able to accomplish the voyage to Harbour Island in eight hours, an impressive time for sailing vessel. In "The Land of the Pink Pearl" by L. D. Powles in 1888, the author points out that the cabin was for "whites only." By 1922 the Dart was replaced by the Endion, having served for roughly 50 years.

The Endion was 90.8 feet long, 14.1 feet wide, and 8.6 feet deep. Weighing 61 gross tons, she was propelled by a Fairbanks Morse crude-burning engine, and could accommodate 17 passengers in two staterooms (the passages after all were quite short). Originally built in Boston in 1898 as a private yacht of that name and in May 1917 was purchased by the US Navy as a section patrol boat during World War I. She served as USS Endion (SP-707) until stricken from the Navy List in October 1919 and sold. Her Bahamas owners were the Harbour Island Steamship Company Limited which purchased her at public auction. The Lawlors write that "In October, 1921 the sailing ship Endion was bought in New York, refitted and converted and converted to a power vessel, in Harbour Island, to accommodate passengers." From the same source we learn that Captain Albert Sweeting took delivery of her and was the vessel's master for the next 17 years. Her first voyage with the mail contract was on 17 January 1922. According to an advertisement in the Nassau Guardian, ""In October, 1921 the sailing ship Endion was bought in New York, refitted and converted and converted to a power vessel, in Harbour Island, to accommodate passengers." Endion plied the route until 1939 until replaced by the Lady Dundas – her final fate is unknown.

Built in the spring of 1939, the Lady Dundas was designed by Harbour Island resident and American ship designer Lawrence Huntington and built by Messrs. Berlin T. and Harry Albury of wood in Harbour Island. Lady Dundas was 92 feet long, 19.5 feet wide and 9.3 feet deep. Rigged as a schooner, she was also propelled by a Fairbanks Morse 150 horsepower engine which pushed all 115 tons at 10 knots. Her cargo capacity was 80 tons. She was owned by the same Harbour Island Steamship Company which owned the Endion before her. Two of the vessel's captains were William G. Harris and Roy William Smith, Esq.. According to the Lawlors, her launching was a special event: "Just a few months before the somber days of the Second World War, flags flew and the Harbour Island town band played as Lady Dundas, the Governor's wife, broke a bottle of champagne over the bow of the Lady Dundas. This was the first of the inter-insular mail-boats that gained Harbour Island new fame." Within a year the Dundas' were pushed out to make room for the Duke and Duchess of Windsor – their new assignment? Kampala, Uganda. The vessel's end was more ignoble – in 1974 she was arrested in Port-au-Prince Haiti and seized on suspicion of smuggling drugs.

The motor vessel Noel Roberts was built in 1943 by Sir George W. K. Roberts, who was to own eight mailboats in the Bahamas before passing away in the mid-1960's. The vessel was 115 feet long, 23.3 feet wide and 11.3 feet deep, and weighed 180 gross tons. Her engine was 180 horsepower and she was built of wood. She served North Eleuthera until at least 1957, though carried freight as far afield as Jamaica. All vessels owned by Sir George Roberts, who named this one after his son, a Member of Parliament in his own right, were covered under the "Roberts Dynasty" column of this feature. The same applies to the Air Swift, a former US Navy craft built of wood in 1943 by Thomas Knutson Shipbuilding of Halesite, New York. Sir George Roberts purchased her around 1948, and she served North Eleuthera right up until the Bahamas Daybreak replaced her on the Harbour Island run in the 1970's. According to Jeff Albury her remains lie in shallow water off Six Shilling Channel, between Rose Island and The Current.

The motor vessel Current Queen was purchased in 1965 by brothers Gurney Elon Pinder and Stephen Pinder to serve Spanish Wells. Built of wood, she was 64 feet long and her original name was Spanish Rose. In 1977 the brothers sold the vessel, which had been running to and from Spanish Wells for 12 years, to interests in The Current settlement in Eleuthera, who renamed her the Current Queen and diverted her to their new home port. Her final fate is unknown. The second Spanish Rose was 75 feet long, also built of wood and a motor vessel. Her owners were also the Pinder brothers Gurney and Stephen. The boat was equipped with refrigeration, enabling them to haul frozen crawfish – an essential commodity – from Spanish Wells to market in Nassau. In 1997, whilst en route between Nassau and Spanish Wells in daytime the vessel sank – the captain and his family members and crew were all rescued. Jerry Hulse, the travel editor for the LA Times wrote in 1985 that "If you're in no hurry it's a bargain--only $18 for the five-hour ride, which includes a soft drink and a sandwich and a world of untroubled waters."

The first Eleuthera Express was built as the Spiekeroog in Wihelmshaven Germany in 1962. Her other names were Wischhafen and *Treasure Trader* until 1979 when Captain Junior Pinder purchased her for the run to Rock Sound, Governor's Harbour, Spanish Wells, and Harbour Island. She was a large motor ship of 250 gross tons and 400 ton cargo capacity. Her tenure was short-lived as in the early 1980s she was sold to "a group in Miami who renamed the vessel" according to a conversation with Captain Pinder. She sank between Haiti and Cuba in the late 1980s. It is possible that as the Treasure Trader (1978-1979) she traded in the Bahamas as well.

The justifiably named Current Pride was built of wood probably in the 1970s and continued to serve Upper and Lower Bogue, The Bluff, Current Island, North Eleuthera, and Gregory Town, James Cistern and Hatchet Bay / Alice Town in South Eleuthera. The vessel weighs 88 gross tons and her master is Captain Patrick Neilly. Richard M. Langworth, bicycled Eleuthera and utilized the Current Pride to get there from Nassau. In 2009 he wrote: "The Current Pride is a microcosm of the old Bahamas, laden with produce (this really is a "banana boat") and Eleutherans heading for the big city. You can't pay for the entertainment you get free. One gent spent the entire voyage singing and shucking peas; another trolled part of the way and hooked a giant barracuda which flopped around on the deck and scared some of us passengers. The sturdy, wood-hulled Current Pride shook off high seas and covered 52 miles in four hours—and cost only $30, including coffee, sandwiches and soft drinks."

The Bahamas Daybreak III has gone by several names, including simply Bahama Daybreak. She is 110 feet long, and can carry 24 passengers in enclosed cabins – more on deck. At latest check the vessel serves South Eleuthera (Governors Harbour, Hatchet Bay) leaving Mondays at 5pm, then North Eleuthera (Bluff, Spanish Wells, Harbour Island) leaving Nassau Wednesdays at 5pm. Her captains include Captain Quincy Sawyer and Captain Ashok – a previous master, Captain Moss, now serves with Bahamas Ferries. According to the Tribune in 2006 her owner is Captain Theophilus Stuart of North Eleuthera. Details of this vessel's dimensions and pedigree are Spartan, but she is believed to have been serving these routes since around 1985, meaning Bahama Daybreak III has been in service roughly 30 years.

The mailboat Harley & Charley is 91 tons and roughly 100 feet long. Originally proposed for service to Andros, in the late 1980s she was serving Governor's Harbour and Hatchet Bay. By around 2000 this vessel no longer showed up on ship lists and databases – fate unknown. Another vessel about which very little is known is Captain Fox, which served as a mailboat from Nassau to Governors Harbour and Hatchet Bay in the late 1990s, leaving 1pm on Thursdays, taking six hours and costing $30 each way. By the 2000's this vessel was also not listed as active, and like the Harley & Charley her final fate is unknown.

The second Eleuthera Express is a modern vessel purpose-built for the Bahama trades in Louisiana in 1996/1997. She is 250 gross tons and capable of carrying 400 tons of cargo. Fitted with a large crane on her foredeck, with wide hatched and a squat, broad wheelhouse, and a square stern, this light green ship has become a fixture in Eleuthera in the intervening decades. Her captain is

Junior Pinder, believed to be at least a co-owner. Her route includes Harbour Island, Spanish Wells, Rock Sound, and Governors Harbour.

Although not strictly mail boats – they carry freight and passengers mostly – the Bo Hengy and Bo Hengy II have revolutionized sea travel – nay travel in general – between Nassau and North Eleuthera, providing a fast, efficient and affordable alternative to both conventional mailboats and aircraft. Built as Hull # 5 by Pequot River Ship Works in New London, Connecticut the original Bo Hengy was named "after a Harbour Island shipwright Henry Sawyer, known as "Bro Henry" which then became Bo Hengy, who on top of wooden vessels made fish traps and tools for fishermen and spongers in the 1920s. In 1922, authors Anne and Jim Lawlor write in their book "Harbour Island Story," "...built the first 5-horsepower motor boat in Harbour Island." Her impressive specifications include that she is 115 feet long, 27.5' beam, draft said to be 5', catamaran hull, 209 gross tons, capable of 177 passengers. Powered by MTU engines, 4,726 horsepower and flagged to the Bahamas (increasingly inter-island boats are flagged to Panama or other countries). Her owners are Bahamas Ferries Limited conveniently situated at Potter's Cay Docks.

In May 2009 after ten years of service was sold to the Red Funnel Group of Southampton UK for service to Cowes, Isle of Wight, UK. This reverses the usual trend whereby many vessels were acquired second-hand from Europe and sold on to Latin America. The Bo Hengy II was built in 2008 to replace her predecessor. She is 135 feet long, capable of 400 passengers (or harbor cruise, no luggage), and 394 passengers' inter-island. Powered by Cummins engines, the vessel is capable of 25 knots. It features cold and dry storage, interior seating for passengers, weatherproof luggage stowage. She is 540 gross tons and capacity for 53 tons of cargo. Leaving by 8am the vessel makes the trip to Harbour Island in a few hours and permits visitors to take a day-trip to picturesque Dunmore Town – something unthinkable in the days of the Mary Jane, Endion and Dart.

Mailboats to Northern Islands

In other articles in this feature, we have covered three mailboat-owning dynasties and the histories of mailboats to northern and southern Abaco as well as Eleuthera. Now we focus on the other islands of the northern Bahamas, namely Freeport, the Berry Islands, Bimini, Andros, the Exumas and Long Island.

FREEPORT: Perhaps because of Grand Bahama's proximity to Florida as well as its thriving commercial free port, as well as its recent growth (since the 1960s), Freeport has less of a history and variety of mailboats than some of its sister islands. It is nevertheless a rich tale. The Church Bay was launched as a Royal Navy minesweeper, HMS MMS 194, at Symonette Shipyards in Nassau and Hog Island on 12 November 1942. Craig Symonette confirms the vessel was built in the third slip or "ways" and that Jenkins Roberts was the overseer. Having never entered military service it was instead put to commercial use serving Freeport as well as Cat Island. By 1952 she was owned by the Three Bays Corporation and when she burned at the dockside in 1973 was rumored to have been owned by Oscar Johnson, MP for Cat Island, who denied ownership. The tug Mako II rammed and sank the burning hulk in Nassau Harbour.

The Lady Eula, owned by Captain Ernest Dean of Sandy Point Abaco and named for his wife, served Freeport, Andros and North Cat between 1978 and 1981. The Marcella (I) was owned by the Taylor Corporation and family, and served Freeport from roughly 1985 to 2007. Her replacement Marcella II was said to be on the same run between 1986 and 1988, and the Marcella III between 2007 and 2009. Then a more modern era was ushered in with the 450-passenger, Chinese-built Fiesta Mail, which was built in 2002 and serves Freeport as well as Fort Lauderdale. All five vessels are covered in greater detail in other articles. Sweeting's Cay at the far east of Grand Bahama benefited from Captain Dean's addition of this cay to the runs made by his vessels Captain Dean I to V and Champion II. It is worth adding that there is now a high-speed passenger service, Pinder's Ferry Service, between McLean's Town Grand Bahama and Crown Haven, Abaco.

BIMINI: Like Freeport, Bimini benefits from its close proximity and relatively easy access to Florida and the commercial opportunities to be had. It is closer to Miami than to Nassau. Nevertheless, the islands have a proud history of freighter and mail service – for example the vessel Bailey Town was built there in 1946, was 46.5 feet long and owned by Theodore R. Saunders, and the F. A. Marie of 57.7 feet, though built in the Cayman Islands in 1928 was owned by William D. Weech Jr. in Bimini in the 1950s, who also owned the 58.5-foot Peloris – none are known to have carried mail however. The Bimini Mack, just shy of 100 feet long and built in St. Augustine, Florida in 1981, she traded into the 2000s and in 2005 the owners were listed as the "Bimini Businessman's Association, Alice Town," suggesting a kind of cooperative. The 126-foot motor vessel Sherice M. has been serving Bimini since roughly 1995 and continues to operate today. Her captain is Shawn Munro and co-captain is Emmett Munroe. In fact, the Munroe family is believed to be the owners of the blue ship, which is kept in fine condition.

BERRY ISLANDS: Bullocks Harbour has been served by the Dean family of Sandy Point Abaco since the 1950s, and people come from the other Berry Islands to Bullocks to collect mail etc. The Deans and their vessels Captain Dean to Captain Dean V as well as the Champion II are covered in another article in this feature.

ANDROS: The Gary Roberts, owned by Sir George Roberts, plied between Nassau and Andros, including Lowe Sound, between 1942 and 1978. She was 66 feet long and built in Harbour Island, with two masts for auxiliary sailing. The Taylor-family-owned Cape Hatteras served North Andros between 1962 and 1968. About 56 feet long and motorized, she was skippered by Captain Nathaniel Bruce Taylor. Then the Marcella took over the route, also serving Mayaguana, until 1987. In roughly 1970 the Delmar L., 82 feet long, made of steel at St. Augustine Shipbuilding, took over the route until the early 1980s. She served Kemp's Bay, Bluff, Long Bay Cay, Driggs Hill, and Congo Town as well as Nassau and sometimes Florida. Goldfinger was a 104-foot-long former lighthouse tender which in the 1970s was, according to Jim Kerr in an article in the Abaconian, "sold for service as a mailboat [and] sank in a storm on a run to Andros." Another boat about which we have scanty information was the Miss Beverly which according to a telegram from the Bahamian to the US government (leaked by WikiLeaks) in 1975, was serving Andros as a mailboat. The Dean family vessel Lady Eula briefly served Andros as well as Cat Island between 1978 and 1980. The 91-ton wooden vessel Harley & Charley was proposed for service to South Andros in 1989, though at the time it was serving Eleuthera. It is not known whether it served Andros.

The Mangrove Cay Express II served Andros between roughly 1988 and 1995. She was 72 feet long and served Mangrove Cay and Lisbon Creek Andros under the ownership of the Reverend Herbert King. The 94-ton vessel Gloria was listed as serving Mangrove Cay Andros in 1989, as was the Central Andros Express (62 tons) and the Big Yard Express (102 tons), according to a study done for the government by Trevor Hamilton & Associates of Kingston Jamaica. The Lady D. was built in 1992 with the appearance of a tug or supply vessel and skippered by Captain Prince Munroe. She served Fresh Creek, Staniard Creek, Stafford Creek, Behring, Blanket Sound, and Browne Sound, Central Andros until her unfortunate demise at Potter's Cay Dock Nassau, when she took on water and has remained there since, taking up valuable commercial space.

The 127-ton Lady Margo II was built in 1971 at Bayou La Batre, Alabama. She was listed in a travel guide as serving Andros in the mid-1990s. The Lisa J., 123.4 feet long and built in Marstal Denmark in 1960, has a fascinating history. Capable of rolling on vehicles as well as accommodating passengers, she was named Ellen Soby until 1973, then the Runden until 1999 when she was intended for sale to Italy but sold to the Bahamas instead. When her career carrying freight and passengers to Mastic Point, Morgans Bluff and Nicholl's Town ended around 2007, she was sold to Honduran interests. In the Bahamas she was said to have been owned by the North Andros Shipping Company Limited. The Lisa J. II is no less interesting, having sailed in Europe as the Schokland from the time of construction in 1952 in the Netherlands until 1985, when she was sold to interests in the Bahamas. Her captains were said to include Captain Bowleg and

Captain Adderley. The ship is 143.5 feet long, 24.5 feet wide and draws 10 feet, with a speed of 8.5 knots and weighs 298 gross tons. She plies the same route as her predecessor.

Mal Jack was built in 1983 and weighed 172 tons. She is believed to have served Andros in the late 1990s and was grounded in Andros in April 2001. It was sold to owners in Honduras and towed from Freeport to Roatan in 2006. Captain Moxey is a fine, well-maintained modern vessel built in 1998. She weighs 370 tons and serves Kemps Bay, The Bluff, Long Bay Cays in Andros generally on Mondays. Her captains are Boycel Moxey, Jr. and Kevin Moxey, and the owners are Moxey Shipping. It is believed that there was a predecessor serving Andros under the same name, as a Captain Moxey is listed in the Trevor Hamilton study in 1989. Both vessels were named after Captain Hezron Lenox Moxey, a renown boat builder and sloop racer, who as a youth "sailed the waters between Haiti, Cuba and The Bahamas, trading fruits, cows, rum, cigars and other goods" from his native Duncan Town, Ragged Island. A number of his seven children became captains in their own right. He was inducted into the Bahamian Sailing Hall of Fame in 1990 and awarded the British Empire Medal in 1997.

The Lady Kathreina, built in 2005 and 122.75 feet long, fitted with a bow ramp for rolling cargo, served Mangrove Cay and Fresh Creek, in South Andros. She was built of steel in Chauvin Louisiana and is skippered by Captain King and is still in operation. Lady Rosalind, built in 1967 in Mississippi has been serving North Andros since roughly 1990 and continues to do so as part of the Taylor Corporation fleet. She is 391 gross tons. Lady Rosalind II was built in 2006, also in Chauvin and serves North Andros under the captaincies of Gifford Johnson, Eddins Taylor and V. H. Black. She is owned by Pirates Well Investments and managed by E. B. Taylor and was featured in the docu-drama "Murder in Paradise" in 2013.

EXUMA: It is believed that the Exumas have a much richer history with mailboats than this author is able to divine, however an early vessel serving those islands was The Brontes, built in 1921. Forty-two tons and capable of carrying 30 passengers, she served San Salvador and Rum Cay under the commands of W. P.

Syles and a Captain Burrows. She was lost in a hurricane in July 1926 near Highbourne Cay. We then jump ahead to the little-known Staniel Cay Express which is presumed to have served its namesake in the Exumas from the early 1970s to 1975. The Miranda 1977 – 1992, Taylor Corp. She was 76 feet long, designed as a fishing vessel, and was skippered by Rolly Gray. She was lost off Hope Town on April 6th, 1975.

The mailboat Captain C. is believed to have served Black Point and other Exuma communities from the 1980s to the present, though the present vessel was clearly built in the last decade or so. She was recently skippered by Etienne Maycock, Sr. The modern vessel is of steel and over 125 feet long and is still trading. The 214-ton Grand Master was built in 1983 by San Sebastian Marine in St. Augustine Florida and is skippered by Lenny H. and Lance Brozogzog, a father-son team, as well as Captain Rolly Gray. They serve Georgetown Great Exuma, leaving Tuesdays and taking 12 hours at a cost per passenger of $40.

The 97-ton Lady Blanche is said to have served the Exuma Cays between at least 1988 and 1994. The 154-ton Lady Frances was built in 1989 in Houma, Louisiana and serves Black Point Exuma, Rum Cay and San Salvador. The 443-ton Island Link was built in 2004 in Caboolture, Australia and presently serves Georgetown Exuma as well as Long Island. Her owners are listed as Munson Shipping of Bank Lane and managers as Bahamas Searoad of Potter's Cay West. Her captain is Jed Munroe and she is a roll-on, roll-off (Ro/Ro) vessel which leaves Nassau on Tuesdays. The 485-ton Ro/Pax (roll-on, passenger) vessel Seawind is said by her owners Bahamas Ferries to serve Exuma since her construction in 2003.

LONG ISLAND: Long Island has been an important destination for more decades than this author is able to trace, however we can start in the 1960s, when the Taylor family served Long Island as well as Mayaguana with their 90-foot-long wooden vessel Marcella, built by St. Augustine Florida shipwrights. Her captain was owner Nathaniel Bruce Taylor as well as his son Eddins Bruce Taylor. She burned to the water line at Salt Pond, Long Island in 1986. The 430-ton Abilin was built in Duisburg, Germany in 1962 and was photographed in 1998 serving Long Island by consultant

Captain Calum Legett. She is believed to have begun her Bahamas career in the late 1980s, and she is believed to have been sunk in 2007. The Dean family of Sandy Point own the 91-ton Nay Dean, which has served northern Long Island since 1985. She is 91 tons, built of wood, and owned and skippered at least part of the time by Captain Ernest Alexander Dean.

The Sherice M. is 126 feet and is said to serve Salt Pond, Deadmans Cay and Seymours Long Island, departing Nassau on Mondays. She is a trim, smart light-blue motor freighter owned by the Munroe family and skippered by captains Shawn Munroe and Captain Emmett Munroe. She also serves Alice Town and Cat Cay Bimini. Another Dean family vessel, the Mia Dean has been serving southern Long Island, including Clarence Town since about 1990. She is still operating, with distinctive blue, black, red and white striping, and is believed to be 146 tons. Other vessels thought to be serving Long Island from Nassau include the Island Link (since 2004), the Bahamas Ferries East Wind (since 2007, serving Simms and owned by Bahamas Ferries), Sea Spirit (former United Spirit, since 2008, owned by Captain Thomas Hanna), and a vessel named Captain Emmett serving Salt Pond, Deadmans Cay and Seymours since 2010.

Mailboats to Southern Islands

SAN SALVADOR AND RUM CAY: These two islands are linked by many of the same mailboats, since Port Nelson Rum Cay is essentially along the way to and from Nassau and Cockburn Town San Salvador. The Brontes served both isles between 1921 and her loss in 1926. The British motor vessel Monarch of Nassau was built in Cheshire, England in 1930 and delivered from there in 19 days. Originally named the Sir Charles Orr after a governor of the colony, she was purchased by the Monarch Line, owned by Sir George Roberts. In 1942 she was serving San Salvador when she rescued 30 officers and men from the Greek ship Cygnet, which had been torpedoed by the Italian submarine Enrico *Tazzoli* within sight of Dixon Hill Light. Sold in 1951 to Carl Sawyer, she traded bananas and fruit among the West Indies, her 16 passenger cabins presumably broken up.

Sir George Robert's former US Navy patrol craft the Drake traded to San Salvador as well, between 1956 and 1964. The San Salvador Express, 111 feet long and built in Mississippi in 1953 served under Captain Roy Oral Lockhart from roughly 1972 to 1975, when she was named the Johnette or Jeanette Walker and was under suspicion of collusion in the drug trade. She was sold to Panama as the Pack One, where she still trades. In 1976 the substitute mailboat to Rum Cay was named in one study as the Lady Moore, an 80-foot supply boat sunk off Nichols Town, Andros as an artificial reef.

The Willaurie was built in the Netherlands in 1966 as the Willmary and traded extensively in the UK early in her career. Between 1980 and 1988 she serviced San Salvador and Cat Island, as well as Rum Cay. Her owners were listed as W. B. Hart of Nassau. Her loss was nearly as exciting as her career. In August 1980 her passengers were rescued by the Royal Bahamas Defense Force and she was laid up and foundered in 1988. She was raised and while being towed washed ashore near Clifton Pier. The day after Christmas 1988 Stuart Cove and colleagues towed her to near Goldings Cay and scuttled the ship, and she is now a dive attraction.

The 32-ton Treasure Lady was built in 1981 as the Tar Heel in Morgan City, Louisiana and between 1997 and 2012 served San Salvador and Rum Cay as a mailboat. After that point she was sold out of the Bahamas presumably to Honduras. The 464-ton stern-ramp vessel Lady Emerald was built in Chauvin Louisiana in 2003. Her skipper is Bill Williams and her owners G. M. Patton of Nassau. She presently serves Rum Cay, San Salvador and Cat Island. The aforementioned Lady Frances serves Rum Cay and Salvador as well as Black Point Exuma.

CAT ISLAND: The settlements on the leeward side of Cat Island have been served with mailboats for a century or more, however the first known schooner servicing the island was the Mountain King from the 1920s until she was lost in a hurricane in 1926. She was built by the Reverend James Smith of Port Howe, Cat Island. She was lost off Little San Salvador whilst under Napoleon Rolle and Elliston Bain, who disagreed over seeking shelter from the storm. All except Rolle were lost. The Monarch of Nassau served

Cat Island in the 1930s and 40s, and is credited with taking Father Jerome Hawes, the Hermit of Cat Island to his new home. The Church Bay, seen earlier serving Freeport, provided mail and passenger service to the island between 1932 and her loss by fire in 1973.

A vessel named the New Day (ex-Sea Salvor) applied for a license to serve Cat Island from 1973, under ownership of the Freedom Shipping Company of Nassau. The Lady Eula was purchased from Captain Ernest Dean in around 1980 by Cat Island interests, however by 1981 it had been grounded off San Salvador and was a total loss.

The Willaurie served Cat Island as well as San Salvador between 1980 and 1988. The purpose-built North Cat Island Special, roughly 80 feet long and grey-hulled, plied the route to Bennet's Harbour and other Cat Island ports from the mid-1980s to the 2000s Though her fate is unknown, there is a new vessel named North Cat Island Special II (built 2001) which is believed to have taken over the route.

The 98-foot-long Sea Hauler, owned and operated by Captain Allan Russell, Sr. of Cat Island served the island between 1989 and 2011. Around that time, it was grounded and abandoned off Long Island. She served Smith's Bay, Old Bight and New Bight, in south Cat Island. In 2003 this vessel was involved in a fatal collision with the United Star in an event which resulted in four deaths, an amputation and dozens injured. Twelve years later it is still a sensitive issue for survivors and their families. The Mia Dean catered to the needs of Cat Island in the 1990s, as did the Lady Eddina between 1995 and roughly 2000. Built in 1969 in Mississippi she served Bennett's Harbour, Arthur's Town, Orange Creek and Dumfries. This ship was owned by the Taylor family and operated by Pirates Well Investments. She was named Stonewall Jackson until 1995 and is no longer trading. The Lady Emerald sailed to Cat Island as well as Rum Cay and San Salvador.

The K.C.T. is 165 feet long and has served northern Cat Island since about. She is a stern-loaded ro/ro vessel owned by Captain Thomas Hanna of The Ro-Ro Company. The trip takes some 26 hours and costs $90 each way. Another of Tom Hanna's vessels is the VI Nais – which has served north and south Cat Island since it was built in Chauvin Louisiana about 2007. A brand-new addition to the Bahamian merchant fleet is the New G., completed in 2015 and delivered in February of this year. Her owners are the Consolidated Marine Group of Soldier Road, Nassau. She is 155 feet long and 486 gross tons, capable of going 10.5 knots. She is believed to be trading in the southern Bahamas.

MAYAGUANA: Since the Taylor family hail from Pirates Wells, Mayaguana and their investment vehicle carries that name, most of their aforementioned ships have served Abraham's Bay Mayaguana, namely: the Nonesuch (Capt. Fed. Black, 1933 to 1940), Marcella (1969 to 1987),   Cape Hatteras (1962 to 1968), Lady Rosalind (1987 to present) and the Lady Mathilda (1998 – present). The Lady Mathilda is 135 feet long (extended from 110 feet), and built in Chauvin, Louisiana. In 2010 a Department of Education test question features distances run by the mailboats Captain Moxey, Lady Mathilda and Emmett & Cephas. Her captain is Nigel Davis and she proceeds as far south as Inagua. There is also a little-known vessel listed in 1975 as that Abastasha but possibly the Lady Tasha which is described in a telegram leaked by WikiLeaks as serving Mayaguana, Crooked Island and Acklins Island.

CROOKED ISLAND, LONG CAY/FORTUNE ISLAND, CROOKED & ACKLINS: Long Cay, also known as Fortune Island, to the south of Crooked Island, has perhaps the longest history of handling mail from Europe and North America, as it was a trans-shipment point for mail and stevedores for vessels entering and leaving the Caribbean via the Windward Passage in the days of sail as well as steam. Particularly British mail vessels and German liners would call there until the First World War and beyond. However, we must by necessity jump to the modern era, when the New Day ex Sea Salvor served these islands from roughly 1972 to 1980. In 1975 the Abastasha or Lady Tasha served Crooked and Acklins and in 1989 Jamaican researchers determined that a vessel named the Commonwealth of 96 tons was on the route. By roughly 1995 the Windward Express sailed to the southern Bahamas until about 2000.

Recent service (1996 to 2007) was provided by Captain Hanna's United Star. At 170 feet long and 417 gross tons, she was built in Chauvin, Louisiana and was the other vessel involved in the collision with the Sea Hauler in 2003 which claimed fatalities. She sailed as far south as Inagua and was sold to Honduran interests and named the AJ Transport or the Coimar Transport. The Taylor-owned Lady Mathilda also sails to Crooked and Acklins as well as Inagua and has done so since 1998. Both the Sea Spirit (ex-United Spirit, since 2008) and the Sea Spirit II (since 2010) have sailed to Crooked and Acklins islands. The Hanna-owned K.C.T. covers the islands since 2000 and the VI Nais sometimes does as well, though her primary route is to Cat Island.

RAGGED ISLAND: This sparsely populated island group centered around Duncan Town boasts a long and distinguished boat building heritage and has produced notable captains (Moxey and Lockhart among them). By way of illustration, in 1956 there were 22 sail cargo vessels built or owned in Ragged Island, out of a total of just over twice that number in the Bahamas. In more recent times the Gleaner Express is listed as serving Ragged Island in 1973 as featured in the shipping column of the Nassau Tribune. Since 1988 the Emmett & Cephas has served the island chain – she was owned by the Munson Shipping Company of Nassau and may have sank in 2001. One-time owner of the vessel Emmett Munroe was awarded the British Empire Medal.

Captain Munroe purchased the Emmett & Cephas along with an uncle, and with his sons later acquired the Sherice M. as well, followed by the Island Link. They also own and operate the Wash Bowl on Ida Street, Nassau. In 1989 the Current Queen was said by Trevor Hamilton & Associates to have been trading to Ragged Island. The Captain C. is also believed to have been on the same route since the late 1980s.

INAGUA: Inagua has been served in the 1930s and 40s by the aforementioned Monarch of Nassau, followed in the 1950s by two cargo vessels named the Inagua Trader (158 feet, 350 gross tons) and Inagua Ranger (same rough dimensions), both of which were owned by the West India Transports, Limited of Matthew Town. It is unknown whether they carried the mails or rather just construction equipment and personnel and possibly salt from the salt industry on the island which was run for many years by Morton Salt.

Between 1948 and 1982 mail service was assumed by the Air Pheasant, which was a former US Navy vessel. Her master was Captain Anton Lockhart, born 1906, of Ragged Island. The boat was launched by Luders Marine in Stamford Connecticut as the USS PC (patrol craft) 1015 on 30 August 1942. In 1945, as the Sub Chaser (USN SC) 1015 she participated in the capture of the German submarine U-858 off Cape May, New Jersey (the submarine had surrendered). She was also the US Coast Guard Cutter Air Pheasant (WAVR 449) until 1948 and thereafter owned by the Morton Salt Company to ferry people and supplies to and from their salt works in Inagua. The vessel was featured in a lengthy article in the Bahamas Handbook entitled "A Passage to Inagua," by Michael Mardon, along with detailed photographs. In fact, a number of mailboats have been featured in the American and European press, usually under the themes of escaping from it all, getting off the beaten path, and seeing the islands from sea level, like a local.

Presently and since 1998 the Lady Mathilda, owned by the Taylors, serves Inagua as well as Mayaguana, Crooked Island and Acklins Island. These communities have all come to rely upon the services of these steel and wooden workhorses of the sea, and though the relationship is not always symbiotic, it can expect to continue so long as it remains economical for people and their parcels to traverse the harsh ocean environment to and from their homes and business from the southern Bahamas some 400 nautical miles to the capital and beyond.

Roberts Family Dynasty

Sir George William Kelly Roberts, KT, CBE, lived between July 19, 1906 and June 24, 1964. During that time – particularly in the late 1920s – he transformed and standardized the subsidization of mailboats as well as financed the construction and operation of at least eight vessels. In order of year built they were the Alice Mabel (purchased in 1923, when he was 17), Richard Campbell (1937), Gary Roberts (1940), Air Pheasant (1942), Drake (1942), Noel Roberts (1943), Air Swift (1943), and the Captain Roberts (1945). According to Anne and Jim Lawlor in their book "The

Harbour Island Story," they were owned under the holding company Richard Campbell Limited of Nassau. This is their story.

Sir George was born on Harbour Island, Eleuthera the son of Captain George Campbell and Nellie Maud Roberts, whose ancestors arrived from Bermuda with the Eluetherian Adventurers in 1647. According to the Lawlors, as a young man George "sailed before the mast on the three-masted schooner Bentley under his father before moving to Nassau at the age of 12. As a self-made man he grew to own the City Lumber Yard....". He married Freda Genevieve Sawyer at Trinity Wesleyan Church in Nassau on January 7th, 1929, when he was 23. Together they had three sons: Richard Campbell (in 1929), Gary William Kelly (born 1934), and Noel Sawyer Roberts (in 1938). From the late 1950s the family residence was "Lucky Hill" on Eastern Road, near Dick's Point Road in eastern New Providence.

Sir George was active in politics, and served in the House of Assembly from 1935 (aged 29), to 1955, and as a member of the Executive Council between 1946 and 1954. He led the Government between 1949 and 1954 and was president of the Legislative Council (LegCo) in 1954. He served briefly as the President of the Senate of the Bahamas, from January 1964 until his death on June 24 of that year. On New Years' Day 1958 he was awarded the Commander of the Most Excellent Order of the British Empire (C.B.E.) and knighted. He is buried on the grounds of the library named after him in his hometown of Dunmore Town, Harbour Island.

The sailing vessel Alice Mabel was a 47-ton schooner with more than one mast and an auxiliary motor. She was built in Marsh Harbour, Abaco in 1923. It is not known which islands the vessel served, though it is safe to assume that Eleuthera was among its ports of call. Richard and Susan Roberts say that one of her skippers was Captain John Carey. By 1940 the small ship was no longer listed in mercantile navy lists.

The Richard Campbell was built in Nassau in 1937 of wood. At 89 gross tons, she was 85.6 feet long, 16.3 feet wide and 8 feet deep. The vessel is described as a single-masted sailing sloop with an auxiliary motor. For ten years until roughly 1947 she plied between Abaco, Miami and Nassau. In "Islanders in the Stream,

Volume II" Craton and Saunders quote an account of the vessel in 1947 as a "rickety, cockroach-infested boat (nicknamed "Wretched Campbell"), with its Conchy Joe captain [Russell] and mate and all-black crew." According to author Kevin Griffin the Richard Campbell was employed in "12-day voyages through the Out Islands."

The motor vessel Gary Roberts had two masts but was primarily propelled by a 100 horsepower Cooper-Bessemen diesel motor. She was 66 feet long, 16.5 feet wide and 7.2 feet deep. Weighing 59 gross tons, she was built in 1942 of wood by Earl and Gerald Johnson, family friends of Sir George's, in Harbour Island. She was named after the Roberts' son, Gary William Kelly. The Lawlors, in their history of Harbour Island, have collected a photo of the vessel.

The Air Pheasant, built of wood in 1942, was a sister ship to the Drake in as much as her dimensions were 110.8' long, 17' wide and 6.5' deep. Constructed by Luders Marine in Stamford Connecticut in 1942 she had two General Motors 1,540-horsepower engines, could make 21 knots, and weighed 148 tons. She was known as USS PC 1015 (patrol craft) until 1942, then SC-1015 (sub-chaser), and USCG Air Pheasant (WAVR-449) from 1945 to 1948. Presumably sold to the Bahamas in 1948, she replaced the Monarch of Nassau on the San Salvador mailboat run. Then it appears that Roberts chartered her to the Erickson brothers for their Morton Salt Company to serve Inagua. One of her captains, at least in 1964, was Anton Lockhart of Ragged Island, who was born in 1906. Tragically he lost his young wife, sister and brother-in-law in a collision with the American freighter Robert Luckenbach off Castle Island on the 7th of June 1931. According to published reports, the Air Pheasant also served Fortune Island/Long Cay, Crooked Island and Acklins in the 1950s and San Salvador in the 1970s. The ship was scrapped in 1982, signifying the end of a 44-year career in the islands.

The motor vessel Drake was built by Robinson Marine Construction in Benton Harbor Michigan in 1942 for the US Navy as USS PC 541, a patrol craft. Weighing 136 tons, she was 110.9' long, 17' wide and 6.5' deep. Her twin 1,540 horsepower engines propelled the boat at an impressive 21 knots. After serving in the navy the vessel went to the US Coast Guard between 1945 and 1948 when it went to a New York fishing company until 1954 then the Crosland Fish Company, based in Key West as the Drake. George Roberts purchased her in 1956 and put the vessel to use between Nassau, Rum Cay, and San Salvador in the southeastern Bahamas. She traded through 1964 when she was mentioned in a "Holiday" magazine article. A vessel of similar dimensions but named "Bahamas Drake" is listed as having wrecked and sunk off the Exuma chain on the 29th of December 1968. Probably this was the Drake.

The Noel Roberts was built of wood by Earl and Gerald Johnson in Harbour Island in 1943. She was 115 feet long, 23.3 feet wide, 11.3 feet deep, and weighed 180 gross tons. She was named after George and Freda Roberts' son Noel, who went on to represent Harbour Island in parliament between 1972 and 1977, and then from 1987 to 1997. Immediately upon being launched during considerable fanfare alongside the Government Dock in Dunmore Town, the Symonette-owned former minesweeper BA 2, built for the Royal Navy in WWII, towed her to Nassau to be fitted with an engine. In 1948 she is recorded by the Kingston Gleaner as having carried a load of lumber as far as Kingston Jamaica. In 1957 she was on the British mercantile marine lists, and was recorded as still trading in 1961. The vessel's final disposition is not known.

The Air Swift was built of wood in 1943 by Thomas Knutson Shipbuilding of Halesite, New York. Her dimensions were the same as Air Pheasant and Drake (111' X 17' X 6.5'). Her original name until 1945 was USS SC 1340, then USCGC WAVR 471 Air Swift until 1948. It is assumed that George Roberts purchased her in 1948, as she became an institution in the Bahamas, serving right up until the Bahamas Daybreak replaced her on the Harbour Island run in the 1970's. During the 1960s the vessel served Harbour Island and North Eleuthera. According to Jeff Albury her remains lie in shallow water off Six Shilling Channel, between Rose Island and The Current.

The short life of Sir George's 111-foot motor vessel Captain Roberts, named after his father, is chronicled best by Anne and Jim Lawlor. The boat was commissioned by Roberts and built of wood by Earl and Gerald Johnson in 1945. She was fitted with a

Fairbanks Morse diesel motor. According to the Lawlors, "This was the third boat built for him in four years by Earl and Gerald Johnson..... Unfortunately, in October 1945, freakish winds destroyed a number of small boats on Harbour Island and the Captain Roberts was wrecked on its maiden voyage." According to the website wrecksite.eu, the location of the Captain Roberts' final resting place is near Great Isaac Light north of the Bimini Islands, suggesting she may have been on her way to or from Florida when wrecked.

Sir George Roberts is believed to have been a driving force behind "An Act to Establish an Improved Inter-Insular Mail Service" passed in August 1948. It establishes that the "Governor may establish mail service between Nassau and the Out Islands." Roberts was a member of the Executive Council at that time. The influential "Inter-Insular Mail Shipping Act" of 1966, based on the 1948 act and the basis of legislation since, is largely credited to Roberts' efforts in the legislature. It standardized aspects of the carriage of mail, passengers and cargo within the Bahamas, as well as government subsidization of the fleet of mailboats which carried them. According to the entrepreneur and ship-owner Craig Symonette, son of Sir Roland Symonette, "It was Sir George that designed the first MailBoat Subsidy Act....still in place to this day."

Taylor Family Dynasty

The Taylor family's mailboat dynasty began in 1933 with Captain Fed and Mrs. Mary Jane Black, of Pirates Well, Mayaguana. Pirates Well is a small community nestled in an expansive and beautiful bay on the northwest coast of Mayaguana, which is in the far southeastern Bahamas (present population about 250). The vessel which they purchased was named the Nonesuch, and was 21 tons, and had two masts, making her a schooner. Built of wood in 1880, presumably in Abaco, her first owner was Benjamin W. Roberts of that island. Between 1900 and 1910 he sold her to William Henry Edgecombe of Andros, who then sold her to James R. C. Young of Nassau in about 1920.

According to Captain Fed Black's grandson, Captain Eddins Bruce Taylor, Black used the Nonesuch to carry freight and passengers between Nassau and Abrahams Bay and Pirates Well, Mayaguana. This lasted less than a decade, as from 1940 the vessel no longer appears in the Mercantile Navy register. Since then, the Taylor family have commissioned and/or bought vessels which have been made in Alabama, Louisiana, Florida, Singapore, China, Netherlands and Germany. They have never stopped their entrepreneurial investments in the country's trade.

Captain Nathaniel Bruce Taylor, a nephew of Captain Fed Black, continued the family tradition of providing mail and passenger service to Mayaguana and beyond. He formed a company called Pirates Well Investments and in 1962 purchased a 56-foot-long wooden mail boat named the Cape Hatteras. The boat, which was propelled by a 671 General Motors diesel engine, was built in the US in the 1950s. Under Captain Taylor's command she served Mayaguana from 1962 to 1968, when it was sold to fishermen in Spanish Wells, Eleuthera. She was Bahamian flag from 1962 until her unknown demise.

The next vessel which the patrician Taylor purchased he named the Marcella, or Marcella I. She was a 90-foot wooden cargo boat built in 1969 by shipwrights in Saint Augustine, Florida. Most of her superstructure was to accommodate passengers, though the vessel had a derrick located on the fore deck for cargo. She served both Mayaguana and nearby Andros from Nassau during a long career which lasted nearly 20 years. The captains were Nathaniel Bruce Taylor and his son Eddins Bruce Taylor. Late in 1987 she burned to the waterline in Salt Pond, Long Island and was a constructive total loss.

The Marcella II was built in Germany in 1956 of steel and was purchased by the Taylor family in about 1987. Less than a year later, in 1988, the vessel was severely damaged in a storm and became an artificial reef off Long Island, which still draws divers. According to Captain Eddins Taylor, this vessel was the first steel-hulled mailboat to be owned by black Bahamians.

The Marcella III began her career as the Wilhelmshaven, Germany-built Jade in 1959. The yard itself was named Jadewerft, or jade works, and her hull was kept jade green by the Taylors. In the Bahamas the vessel served Freeport as well as Mayaguana and other island groups as the need arose. He was 364 tons and could carry 480 tons of cargo. Less than 10 feet deep she could steam at 8.5 knots. Her captain was Captain Limas Taylor, who presently commands the Fiesta Mail.

The Taylors purchased Jade in 1981 and traded it under the Bahamas flag under that name before naming her Marcella III. The Taylors sold her to Haiti early in the 21st century, and she became Miss Eva I then Michelda, and is presently trading under the Bolivia flag in South America, some 55 years after her launch. With her low freeboard and extensive length, she was a familiar site to many along the Bahamian waterfront in the 80s and 90s.

Next the Taylors purchased the Miranda, which was built in Delfzijl, Netherlands in 1966 as the Geulborg. The Taylor Corporation purchased her from Wagenborg Shipping in 1977 and put the ship to work trading between Miami and the Turks & Caicos, serving Long Island, Exumas and Mayaguana with mail services between 1977 and 1993. Her Captain was Robert "Bob" Garroway from St. Vincent. Then the 176-foot-long, 399-ton ship was sold to Haitian buyers around 1993 and renamed the Paradise Express. Under new ownership, Honduran flag, and the name Gilbert Sea, the vessel was impounded by US authorities on the Miami River. Ultimately in 2002 the ship was towed to sea 1.5 miles from Palm Beach Inlet and sunk as an artificial reef.

In 1998 the steel freighter Lady Mathilda was built by the Russell Portier Shipyard in Chauvin, Louisiana, and the Taylors purchased her. She is 135 feet long, having been extended from 110 feet some years ago. Her captain on the mailboat run to Acklins, Crooked Island, Inagua and Mayaguana is Captain Nigel Davis. She has twin engines and can carry as many as 70 passengers. In December 2010 the ship had a minor fire while at Potter's Cay Dock, Nassau, and on October 16, 2012 her crew fished an errant car from the harbor – its occupant was not found.

The roll-on, roll-off (ro/ro) landing craft Trans Cargo II was built at Mickon Shipbuilders in Singapore in 1986. In 1998 the Taylors purchased her from Egyptian owners, and with one of their nephews on board for the passage, had it delivered from the Mediterranean Sea to the Bahamas. The ship is 191 feet long, 46 feet wide, and 1,015 gross registered tons, with cargo capacity of 1,400 tons. She can also carry passengers. Her captain is David Hyde of Honduras. Like the Lady Mathilda the ship had twin engines and twin propellers for redundant reliability. Initially the ship had contracts for the BEC but after they failed it was put to use carrying aggregate and sand from Freeport to Bimini, among other jobs.

The Lady Rosalind was 156' long and built by Bollinger ship yards in Lockport, Louisiana. She was 233 gross tons and made of steel. The Taylors bought her in 1987 and she traded under Capt. Limas Taylor to the southern Bahamas. Then in 1997 the vessel struck a rock and was damaged beyond repair.

Lady Rosalind I was built as the OMS Maverick by Halter Marine in Chickasaw, Alabama in 1987. The Taylors purchased her from sellers in Texas in 2002 and she serves North Andros from Nassau. At 391 gross tons, she is painted gray and has a large cargo deck astern of the wheelhouse. Her captains over the years have included Captain Willie Wilson and Captain V. H. Black. Lady Rosalind II was built by the Portier Shipyard in Louisiana in 2006 and presently serves North Andros from Nassau. She is 198 feet long, 43 feet wide and is 498 gross tons. Her captains have included Captain Eddins Taylor and Captain Gifford Johnson.

The newest and largest of the Taylor Corporation and Pirates Wells Investments' fleet is the Fiesta Mail, which can carry up to 450 passengers between Nassau and the country's second largest city, Freeport. The ship is 228 feet long, 50 feet wide, and draws 11.5 feet. It is 2,485 gross tons, can speed at 12.5 knots, and carry 710 tons of cargo. With a cargo ramp at the stern, it can carry rolling stock. It was built in China by Xinhe Shipbuilding of Tianjin in 2002. The owning entity is The MailBoat Company Ltd. of Nassau, which is run by Captain Elvin Taylor. Not only does the Fiesta Mail carry freight and passengers to and from Freeport, but it calls at Port Everglades Florida as well.

Overall the Taylor family – Captain Fed Black, Captain Nathaniel Bruce Taylor, Captain Limas Taylor, Captain Eddins Bruce Taylor, Captain Elvin Taylor and other family members who help run their companies – have contribute a great deal to inter-island trade amongst particularly the southern Bahamas over the past 80 or so years. As Captain Eddins Taylor says, "We are the biggest mailboat firm in the Bahamas. Period." They certainly have already achieved – and continue to contribute a great deal to interisland trade in the Bahamas.

Tractor Tugs

Although what are now known as tractor tugs have been in fairly wide use in US markets since the early 1980s, their origins can be traced to 1928. In that year a vessel was launched with an innovative propulsion system, named *Torqueo* ("I spin" in Latin) on Germany's Lake Constance. The inventor was Ernst Schneider and the firm was Voith. Together they created the Voith Schneider propeller, or VSP. The novelty was that the 60 horsepower vertical blades in such a way as to act as both a propeller and a rudder. This cycloidal drive enables vessels such as tugs and ferries to be highly maneuverable.

VSPs are often built with thrust plates or propeller guards beneath them. These protect them in case of grounding, and act as a nozzle during slow RPMs. The VSPs offer an additional advantage in reduced cavitation. Ferries in Germany and the UK were fitted with VSPs, and by 1940 80 ships as far afield as Japan had incorporated the propulsion system. Three ferries in Woolwich, England still use 1963-built VSPs fitted ahead and astern. The US Navy built a dozen VSP minehunters in the 1990s. The French Navy has 16 VSP tugboats today.

In 1950 Joseph Becker, founder of Germany's Schottel, invented an azimuth thruster utilizing a Z-drive transmission. Using 90-degree gears, there is no longer a need for rudders, as the pods can be rotated 360 degrees. The two types of azimuth thrusters are mechanical and electrical transmission. The mechanical variant utilizes either L-drive or Z-drive thrusters. The electrical variants are called "pods," and the motor is embedded in the pod, which is connected to the vessels' machinery electrically. The second variant was invented by Friedrich Pleuger and Friedrich Busmann in 1955 and later improved upon by the conglomerate ABB, with the introduction of their Azipod technology in the late 1980s. Used by tugs, navy vessels, cruise ships and other classes, the largest pod thrusters today are fitted in the *Queen Mary 2*.

In the commercial towing market in the US, Clancy Horton at Dravo shipyard designed and built the *Dravo Pioneer* in 1959 in Wilmington, Delaware. This vessel had a Kort nozzle equipped around its single propeller. It was rated at 1,640 horsepower, and weighed 224 gross tons. They later built two more similar prototypes. At least one was sold to Moran Towing who decided after about two years that it underperformed. McAllister Towing purchased the flanking rudder tugs and modified the position of the shaft and the bearings in relation to the rudder. Because these tugs were able to steer and hold position both in forward and reverse, McAllister and other firms built many more in the next decade.

Gaston in *The Tug Book* notes that tractor tugs have proven their worth in close-quarters ship-assist work "requiring intricate maneuvers in difficult tidal conditions." He crows about "their ability to apply thrust in any direction and handle equally well when going astern," as well is reducing the risks of capsizing. He notes forward-mounted azimuth drives have been largely supplanted by stern-drive vessels. "This type of tractor," he notes, "combines the higher bollard pulls possible with the azimuthing unit with the inherent advantages of the tractor concept." Jeffrey Wood's 1969 treatise on tug design (*Caldwell's Screw Tug Design*), makes no mention of tractors.

G. H. Reid, in his 1986 book *Ship handling with Tugs* defines tractor tugs in the empirical sense, as those with propellers located forward of midships. He continues: "The tractor tugs derive their distinctive name from their principal method of employment. They are designed for pulling and are much less likely to capsize than conventional tugs when doing shipwork on a towline. ...they usually work stern first when required to push against a ship." He notes that though very similar, the Schottel drive in a nozzle has advantages over the Voith Schneider Propellers when it comes to bollard pull – an important factor in shipdocking increasingly larger ships, particularly with regard to transverse arrest – the sudden braking of a ship in a channel.

Reid gives tractor-type tugs the following advantages: excellent ahead power, maneuverability forward and aft, no need for a stern line, good power with a Kort nozzle, undiminished backing power, and superiority for towline work – which includes diminished risk of capsize, which he points out is the greatest risk facing most harbor tugs (tripping over their own lines). The disadvantages are the high costs of maintenance, the need for front-propelled tugs to push a ship stern first, and the risk of damaging the propellers when grounding.

Buckley McAllister points out that "While tugs like the *Dravo Pioneer* were technologically significant in that they permitted the tug to steer in reverse, they were not forward mounted, nor did they involve omni-directional trust. According to purists, the term "tractor tug" should only be applied to vessels with bow-mounted propulsion, pulling the vessel along rather than pushing it like a conventional propeller. Today, the term is popularly used to refer to tugs using any omni-directional thrusters, like Voith Schneider units or 90-degree angle propellers or azimuth thrusters known as Z-Drives."

Wilmington Tug, built earlier Z-Drive tugs back in 1977- the TINA, built by Gladding Hearn and *Sally* (1987). The resource tugboatinformation.com adds that TINA was "powered by two Detroit Diesel GM 16V-71N diesel engines, turning two Murray and Tregurtha "Z-drives" outfitted with two Federal propellers for a rated 1,070 horsepower." They continue, adding: "It has been a long standing controversy as to which company actually constructed the first "Z-drive" tractor tug in the United States. Between Wilmington Tug's Tina of New Castle, Delaware and Thames Towboat's *Paul A. Wronowski* of New London, Connecticut.

In 1997 US Naval Reservist Commander John Baucom wrote that "Tractor tugs embody entirely new technology, and they are particularly useful for docking and maneuvering ships. They have capabilities that the conventional tugs of any configuration-flanking rudders, Kort nozzles, twin propellers-do not possess. Their use and performance in the Panama Canal is well known... ...tractor tugs make up Singapore entire docking force. [They] maintain position when backing without having to rely on a stern

267

line or quarter line to stay in shape." He quotes Captain Jim Nolan, another Merchant Marine Naval Reservist, saying that "They are the greatest invention since macadamized roads."

Today, Moran Towing has 36 tractor tugs out of 105 in Q1 2016. As of 2016, the McAllister Towing fleet has only one Voith Schnieder Propeller: the MATTHEW which was acquired from Foss as the ORION (ex-AMERICA), built 1982. Roughly half of the 70 or so tugs in the fleet are Schottel-driven ASD tractor tugs. McAllister currently owns two of the first North American built Z-Drive tugs *Alex McAllister* (1960) and *Brooklyn McAllister* (1986).

In terms of range of power, it is interesting to note that the San Juan Bay Pilots Corporation in Puerto Rico published their tractor tug requirements in February 2006, declaring that tankers over 701 feet would require two tractor tugs and over 751 feet two tractor tugs and one conventional tug. It is worth noting that there are already 18,000-plus TEU ships plying the world's ports, which are over 1,300 feet in length. These can require 5 tractor tugs each.

Horses in the Bahamas

My siblings and I, graduates of LCIS in the 1970s, grew up hearing the crack of start guns indicating that the horses were off below our house on Prospect Ridge. One winter horses broke free and ran across our tennis court, leading us to believe that their hoof-prints were from Santa's reindeer. After the oval closed to racing an eerie quiet settled over the tracks, and we explored the abandoned stables as they were gradually overgrown into the early 2000's.

Over hundreds of years horses in the Bahamas have been used for transportation, racing, competition, and in the tourism trade. Most likely, horses were introduced by accident sometime in the 1600s. Milanne Rehor, head of Arkwild of Abaco explains that "There are at least 13 Columbus-era Spanish ships on the reefs... and Spanish ships of the Conquest always carried horses, so their presence on the island makes sense." There used to be hundreds of wild horses on Abaco, but a rash of shootings, toxic leaks following a hurricane, loss of habitat and other factors lead to the last mare dying in recent months. The breed, known as the Abaco

Barb, a rare strain of the Spanish Barb, may yet rebound through genetics.

On the southern edge of the Bahamas, where herds of jackasses have thrived, there have been numerous shipwrecks, each of which likely introduced animals ashore, including the *Santa Rosa* (1599), the French *Le Count De Paix* in 1713 and the *Infanta* (1788). Now the wild donkeys are in danger of going the way of the Abaco Barb: in March 2014 the Minister of Environment said "people have been shooting them in large numbers," [a team] spent three and a half days [in Inagua] and saw no donkeys during the first two days." A writer for *Boating* magazine in July 1967 observed that on Inagua "wild cattle, pigs, and horses gallop freely." In 1942 wild jackasses led 48 American sailors from the U-boat-sunken ship *Potlatch* to drinkable water on Inagua, saving them after nearly a month in a lifeboat.

There were horse races recorded by Nassau's *Royal Gazette* at least as early as 1805. The only large horse-racing facility in the Bahamas stood from 1934 until 2011. Governor Sir Bede Clifford instituted cricket, polo and horse racing to attract high-end visitors to the colony following prohibition and the Great Depression. It worked. Former bootlegger George Murphy opened Hobby Horse Hall behind Cable Beach in 1934. The horses were not thoroughbreds, but a smaller local breed mostly from Exuma known as quarter horses, for their speed at running a quarter mile. The jockeys were also small: they averaged 90 pounds and 14 years of age. "These horses grazed on jumbey grass, which – unbeknownst to island farmers of the day – contains mimosine, a toxic amino acid that causes weight loss, infertility, goiters, and hair loss." At Hobby Horse they were fed oats, bran and hay. The track was owned in succession by the Bethell brothers, the Earl of Carnarvon and Tim McCaulcy, Alexis Nihon, and Dr. Raymond Sawyer.

A wide cross section of society patronized the track, from international movie stars to local gamblers - men and women across the racial and socio-economic spectrum. "Accomplished women riders, who could not compete in the States, were welcomed." Author Kim Aranha writes that "many of the race horses were abandoned and died after the race course closed. Melissa Maura rescued many of them. My brother Craig

Francis who owned Caribbean Shipping gave Melissa and the rescued horses free overnight passage on the *Mereghan II* to Miami."

Canadian horse breeder Edward Plunkett (EP) Taylor, who developed Lyford Cay Club and LCIS, owned a horse named New Providence, born in 1956, which in 1959 became the first thoroughbred to win the Canadian Triple Crown. Taylor's Windfields Farm outside Toronto was a world-class horse training and breeding facility for decades, and boasted 1964 Kentucky Derby winner Northern Dancer as a stud. His 1954-foaled thoroughbred gelding named Lyford Cay won Canada's top prize, the Queen's Plate in 1957.

There is a long history of horse-drawn surreys, or carriages, carrying visitors, particularly in historic Nassau. During the time when cars were replacing horses Arondale Griffin took passengers on his surreys from Frederick Street as far as forts Charlotte and Montagu, and the Nassau Beach Hotel. Now extensive traffic prohibits such long trips – inhalation of exhaust fumes harms the horses, and the bleating of horns and close proximity to traffic startles them, despite blinders. Griffin's grandson Thomas Harcourt Demeritte owned nine horses and six carriages in 1993. His grandfather used to hand-build the carriages out of wood. Demeritte, known as "Horseman," worked from 4:30 am to 10:30 pm, mostly giving tourists tours from Parliament to Frederick to Church, Nassau, or Shirley Streets. He admitted that "...the tarmac can be very painful for a horse. The horses that are skinny are that way because they fret."

There are at least seven stables offering horse riding opportunities to visitors to the Bahamas. One is at Coral Harbour, another east of Nassau, and yet another near Nassau's airport, three on Grand Bahama, and a seventh recently opened near Governor's Harbour, Eleuthera. Carnival Cruise Lines owns and operates a horseback riding experience with about a dozen animals at the island they operate named Half Moon Cay, formerly Little San Salvador. Equestrian Bahamas is the official National Federation of horse riding in The Bahamas.

The Windsor Equestrian Center, or Happy Trails, is a place where anyone can take miles-long trail rides including along a beach and lake around Coral Harbour since 1977. There has been a stable at Camperdown Riding Club, off Eastern Road, for many decades, educating riders aged six and up in the art of riding as well as competing in hunter/jumper events. A 16-acre private equestrian ranch named Moon Stone Stables is presently being offered for sale in Lyford Cay. The stables outside Governor's Harbour are named Ocean View Farms and Horse Trails. A foal named Maya Moon, has made it into popular culture, with a book about her by Humane Society President Kim Aranha, who writes "Maya Moon was born at the private farm, or more accurately stables, of Mrs. Patricia Vazquez on South Ocean, called Finca Nati. Her mother Jazz had been in a 'petting zoo' of sorts locally."

Mariposa Stables was founded in 2008 by Erika Adderley and her husband, Miguel Coello in Mount Pleasant, near Lyford Cay. Ridership has grown from 14 to nearly 50 since then. There are five horses rescued by the Humane Society on the property, three of them from Eleuthera. That is where twelve LCIS students train as part of the Elite and Developmental Sports Program (EDS) – part of the school's International

Baccalaureate curriculum since 2014. EDS "offers high quality coaching and training opportunities to athletes who have outgrown the regular school mandated PE classes and after-school clubs." The stables offer boarding, lessons, and training on 9.5 acres. Hilda Donahue, ranked #2 worldwide for endurance racing, recently hosted clinics at Mariposa, and highly skilled judges fly in. The school does not pay for the horse's upkeep. The season starts on the local circuit in October. In September EDS students are recognized with an End of Year awards banquet.

Mariposa's Fall Fest Horse Show features the Bahamas Junior Classic, in which unde-17 riders compete for a Hunt Seat Equitation Medal. Other categories of competition include Equitation Champion, Hunter Champions, and a Pony Hunter Division. Riders compete in horse shows throughout the Bahamas, as well as Toronto, and Ocala and Venice, Florida, where they lease horses. Training occurs during electives on Friday and an expanded PE lesson during the week. Students can arrange further single or group training sessions at other times, with some girls riding 4-5 times a week. Frederic Bournas explains that LCIS aims to create a scholastic riding league with other schools on the island for young riders of all levels in the 2016-17 school year.

Dean Family Dynasty

Captain Ernest Dean was born the son of a fishing boat captain in 1915 in Sandy Point, Abaco. His parents were James Alexander Dean (1889-1966) and Leah Hunt Dean (1886-1923) who died when Ernest was a boy of eight years. His father's fishing smack was a two-master named Champion and he had a part ownership interest in the vessel. At the time Sandy Point was not connected with other communities in Abaco except by the sea and the people of the small settlement eked out their existence by fishing and sustenance farming. A year after his mother's death, at age nine Ernest was sent to assist the lighthouse keeper of Cay Sal Light in far southern Bahamas, bordering Cuba. In exchange the boy would learn to read and write, as the keeper, Chatham Albury, had educated Ernest's uncle the same way.

At the age of 14 Ernest served about his father's schooner the Champion and by 17 the young man was in command. He would remain a captain – and very much a community leader – since, and until his death in the early 2000s. Much of the material of this article is drawn from his autobiography entitled "Island Captain," co-written by Gary W. Woodcock and published by White Sound Press in 1997. Ernest first met Eula Clarke of Cherokee Sound when he was 18, in about 1933. She was the daughter of Wilfred and Lillian Clarke. They were married on November 19, 1936, a union that would last until her death almost 60 years later. The wedding had to wait until Ernest had built them a house next to his fathers on West Bay Street, Sandy Point. Together they kept a shop – or rather she kept a shop, as he was mostly at sea – called E. and E. Grocery and Dry Goods, the motto of which was – and is – "all under one roof."

A home wasn't the only thing that Captain Ernest built with his hands – in order to enter the mail freighting business, he spent three years hand crafting, mostly alone, a 35-foot sailing vessel named Captain Dean after his father, himself, and his infant sons. Begun in 1949 and not launched until February 1951, the boat was made from hand-hewn pine from pine fields as far afield as Hole-in-the-Wall Light and madeira and dogwood roots from Gorda Cay. The roots of these hardwoods had to be dug out by hand, and when found unsuitable for the joinery required, were rejected. He hand-cut the keel in the forest then towed it with a small dingy back to Sandy Point from Cross Harbour, sometimes drifting windless for hours, other times tacking against the wind. It was back-breaking work and only someone gifted with true determination would have completed it. With as much help from local craftsmen as they could afford, their income supplemented by Ernest's fishing, the couple achieved it.

Ernest cut and bent the sails and headed to Nassau to convince the Colonial Secretary in charge of mailboats – a Bahamian – that he deserved a mail contract to serve Sandy Point, Moore's Island, and the Berry Islands. At the time there was no mail service to those small communities, and the one person who had tried, Charles Sawyer from Marsh Harbour in his quaintly named vessel Ought to Go, had failed to make a go of it. But Dean persisted, pointing out that the fishermen who carried the mails provided unreliable and intermittent service and young families like his could go weeks without fresh milk from the capital for their children. Eventually the Commissioner relented, and the Captain Dean was put to work with the first mail service to southern Abaco and the Berry Islands. The craft was sloop-rigged, 30 feet at the keel, 40 feet on deck, with a 15-foot beam and a five-foot draft. At first, she had no engines but relied instead on the Trade Winds to propel her.

The Captain Dean plied her trade, eventually adding Sweeting's Cay, Grand Bahama to a busy route. Her owner said that "she was built strong because my life and the lives of my crew depended on her." Carrying people rather than just cargo changed Captain Dean's perspective: "I couldn't think just about the money anymore. I was providing a service at reasonable fees and fares that these people hadn't had before. They were depending on me to keep going. ...Passengers ate what the crew ate, basically fishing boat food." He made room for six to eight passengers as well as four crew to work the cargo and manage the vessel. As he wrote, "the government paid me only to carry the mail and set all the rates for freight and passage. Any passenger fares and freight charges were paid to me." Eventually an engine was added to the vessel. In 1953 Ernest Dean released the Captain Dean to his son James to go crawfishing with and purchased the larger, wooden-built Margaret Rose. She was five feet longer on deck (45 feet). The vessel was also sloop-rigged and had a Perkins diesel engine.

Dean only ran the Margaret Rose for "a few years," before trading up again, this time for the 112-foot motor ship Clermont, which had twin General Motors engines, but was "big, old, wooden, and leaky." By this point Dean was supplementing his income by hauling live crawfish from the various out-ports to Nassau. He also tried carrying live conch, but it didn't pay due to unscrupulous receivers who would take the conch on credit then refuse to pay, claiming the mollusks had died in his absence. The crawfish was packed on ice purchased at Butler's in Nassau. Dean rationalized that if the ice melted the crawfish were in cold water, but if refrigeration – which was more expensive – failed, then the creatures died and rotted. After less than a decade, in 1962 the Clermont sank off Abaco. Fortunately, there were no passengers and the two boats – with mail bags – managed to make it to shore. The Captain Dean then filled in as the mailboat again.

Right away Dean ordered the Captain Dean II, which was built by Johny Albury and Walter Hatcher in Marsh Harbour. She was wooden with a 60-foot keel, a 14-foot beam, and five feet of draft. As well as the main deck where cargo was handled and stored, the passengers and crew quarters fitted out, etc. there was a top deck and pilot house for the officers to steer the ship from. The boat was built entirely of native woods, 4 X 4 inch with two-inch planking. Rather than sails propulsion came solely from two Perkins diesel engines. To have the hull fitted out with housing Captain (later Senator) Sherwin Archer towed the hull behind his vessel the Anita Queen. Six years later, in 1968, the Captain Dean II caught fire and sank between the Berry Islands and Abaco. Two boats with seven people each, including a four-year-old and a two-year-old survived a blustery night and were blown to Whale Cay, Berry Islands using the flat oar blades as sails. To Captain Dean's immense relief everyone survived to be flown to Nassau from Chub Cay.

Meanwhile Dean chartered the mailboat Captain Moxey to fulfill the mail run to Abaco and the Berry Islands – a common but exhausting practice of substituting boats that continues today. True to form Dean commissioned the Captain Dean III from St. Augustine, Florida. The lumber mills were closing and more men were returning to their communities, becoming fishermen or farmers, settling down and providing a growing market for building materials, fuel for their small boats, and obviously groceries. But the boatyards in Abaco were no longer building large vessels, hence the look westwards to the States for newbuilds. The Captain Dean III was 90 feet on the keel, 18 feet wide and had a five-foot draft. She could carry 16 passengers and had a large cargo capacity. She was wooden and had a large Caterpillar engine. Launched in 1969 she barely made it to Freeport because the seams had not properly soaked and sealed, but they made it. Plus sawdust and wood chips from the construction clogged the bilges in the Gulf Stream, with a northern wind. Eventually in 1973 the vessel was sold to interests in Bimini to provide mail service there, and was sunk on the Mackey Shoal Buoy between Bimini and the Berry Islands.

The Captain Dean IV was in the works soon enough, and Dean's son James filled the mail run with his boat the Miss Dean in the interim. This ship was also wood and very similar to her predecessor, only stronger. Ernest Dean handed command of the Captain Dean IV over to his son John and in about 1977 the vessel was lost off Abaco in a storm. Fortunately a Mayday was sent and received by the US Coast Guard, who managed to hoist all 15 men and women aboard their helicopter. The ship was salvaged and towed to Miami where it was learned that several planks had been stove in. After that Captain Dean decided to build his next vessel, the Captain Dean V, of steel, and so he did. It would be "the first steel boat in all of the Bahamas designed and built just for the mail service." At that time there were steel boats operating in the Bahamas, but most of them originated in Europe or the US Gulf. The Captain Dean V ran from 1979 to 1985, first under Ernest Dean then under John Dean. It sank at the Frederick Street dock in

Nassau in a fire that claimed the life of Captain Stanford Curry. Her hulk was sold to Haitian interests.

Captain Ernest supplemented his runs to Abaco and the Berry Islands with calls at Freeport, Andros, and Cat Island when time permitted. On assurances that he would be given the mail contract he constructed the Lady Eula, named after his wife. She was 90 feet on keel and had a single Caterpillar engine: "a very spacious and modern boat." Ernest's son John took over running her to Andros, Freeport and Cat Island. At this time there were political moves by individual island groups to have their "own" mailboat and skipper, as in from that island. Some resented being served by an Abaco skipper and entrepreneur. So, as he had done in Bimini, Captain Dean sold Lady Eula to interests in Cat Island. Due to a navigational error the boat was run aground on San Salvador and pummeled on the coast. Finally, in 1986 Captain Dean modified the scope of his ambition and built a smaller vessel, the Champion II (after his father's fishing smack on which he had experienced his first command. She was 75 feet long – that way she could trade to the US without having to obtain a load line certificate required of longer vessels.

Decades after having built her by the sweat of his brow Captain Dean and his daughter came upon her amongst a crowd of fishing craft at Potter's Cay Dock. It was 1993, 44 years after her keel was hewn in the Abaco pine fields. A main on board protested that the boat wasn't the Captain Dean, to which Ernest retorted "This was the Captain Dean. I should know, I built her. Captain Dean's beloved wife Eula died in 1995. By then Ernest was a revered patriarch in the community of Sandy Point, and his opinion on matters such as the new high speed ferry's terminus in his community was highly valued. His family continue to operate their store was well fishing and passenger vessels such as the Nay Dean and the Mia Dean throughout the Bahamas as well as to the US. In June of 1988 Governor-General Taylor presented Captain Dean with the Queen's Medal along with a Certificate of Honor. In 1995 he was invested with the British Empire Medal, again at Government House in Nassau, this time by Governor General Turnquest. Captain Dean learned of these awards via mailboat. When his wife's body was returned to Sandy Point from Nassau, she was carried home – to the strains of the song Amazing Grace – across the bar to the community by their son's mailboat, the Mia Dean, which is still plying today.

Hanna Family Dynasty

From the early 1800s to 1911 members of the Hanna family owned ten vessels of various sizes in the Bahamas. The patriarch of the Hanna clan in the Bahamas appears to be John Hanna, who was born in Aberdeen Scotland and set sail for the Bahamas with three children, John, George and James, with Edward Tobias being born on the voyage to the colony (his nickname was "Salt Water"). John senior went on to become a Member of the Houses of Parliament in the Bahamas, however most of his descendants appear to have settled in the southern island of Acklins. J. Hanna was listed in the Bahamas Gazette as a slave owner on Crooked Island in 1799. One of his grandsons was named Thomas.

In 1868 William H. Hanna of Long Bay, Crooked Island owned a 19-ton schooner named Augusta Justina. In 1935 Castell Rivas Hanna of Pompey Bay, Acklins owned the sloop Delightful. By 1911 five other Hannas from Acklins owned the locally-built schooners Barbara Ellen, Charm, Excite, Mary, and Sea Bird. Their owners were John James, Philip Hannah, Conrad C., William H., and Thomas Benjamin Hanna. J. E. Hanna, owned the schooner Molly registered to Grand Bahama. So, 100 years ago the family were already a vessel-owning dynasty, however modest some of the craft may have been (all were from 4 to 18 tons). Additionally Alexander Hanna owned the 9-ton schooner Venus in Crooked Island. He was born in 1840 and passed away in Pompey Bay in 1923, five years before Arthur Dion Hanna, later Governor General of the Bahamas, was born there.

While little is known about his exact connection to the Hannas of Acklins 200 years ago, Captain Thomas (Tom) Hanna has been a substantial ship owner in his own right, contributing significantly to inter-island as well as international seaborne trade between the Bahamas as well as Florida in the last quarter century. Capt. Hanna has owned at least five large vessels, most of them with bow-ramps called roll-on, roll-off, or Ro-Ro type which are shallow draft and well suited to cargo work to remote islands with limited infrastructure like Spring Point Acklins.

Over his career some of Hanna's trading firms have gone under but Hanna has managed to rebuild under new names, sometimes with the same vessel. His business has also survived one of the deadliest accidents in recent Bahamian history – the collision of Sea Hauler with the United Star on 3 August 2003, resulting in four deaths, an amputation, and 25 injuries.

On a more positive note, following Hurricane Irene in August 2011 his vessel the KCT was one of the first on-scene to bring relief to Cat Island, and last year the New G., which he designed, commissioned and had built, was introduced as the newest mailboat into the Bahamian fleet. Past vessels have included the United Star (served 1996-2007), Sea Spirit II (ex-United Spirit), VI Nais, KCT, and New G. – all still operating today for Carib-USA Ship Lines Bahamas, Limited, of Nassau, with Hanna as president. Though not all are always strictly mailboats, they fill in for each other and provide essential services to the Bahamas and are Bahamian owned and operated.

The motor vessel United Star was built in 1996 by either Chauvin Shipbuilding or Portier Shipyard in Chauvin, Louisiana. She is 178' long, 36.5' wide, 417 gross tons, 500 deadweight or cargo carrying tons. It is a Ro-Ro cargo vessel with accommodation and bridge aft made of steel. She was owned and operated in the Bahamas by Hanna from launch to 2007. The ship served the Bahamas on long-haul voyages to Mayaguana, Acklins, Crooked Island, Long Cay (Fortune Island), and Inagua. In 2003 her master was Capt. Rodney Miller. In August 3rd 2003 was in a severe collision with the Sea Hauler 14 miles south of Eleuthera. The Prime Minister termed the event a tragedy of national importance.

A committee was formed to investigate the incident. That report, through a government-appointed Wreck Commission, was presented to the Minister of Transport and Aviation on January 4th, 2005, however efforts by this author to unearth it have so far been unsuccessful. The incident led to a number of lawsuits, including at least nine civil actions filed in the Supreme Court against the government. In 2007 United Star was sold the

Compania Internacional Maritima (Coimar Transport) of Roatan, Honduras.

The Sea Spirit II was built as Russell Portier in 1999. In September 2007 she was renamed the United Spirit for one year, or until August 2008, when she Sea Spirit II. She is 498 gross tons, 750 cargo-carrying tons and was built of steel at Russell Portier Shipyard, Chauvin Louisiana. Hanna has been her owners since 2007, under different companies. She serves Acklins, Long Cay and southern Long Island, leaving Nassau Tuesdays afternoon. According to a Tribune article dated February 7, 2011, Hanna was chased by a number of creditors and removed his vessel from the Bahamas Maritime Authority Registry in December 2007, changing ownership from Carib-USA to Ro-Ro Company Ltd. Despite all this the vessel's trading seems to have been uninterrupted.

The boat VI Nais is 487 gross tons, 587 cargo-carrying tons, 190 feet long, powered by two Mitsubishi engines rated 927 hp at 1,400 rpm. The engine manufacturer stated that "provide owners with much better fuel consumption than the older engines that [Hanna] had been operating." They related that the engines are rated Tier 3 with the US Environmental Protection Agency. Portier Shipyard built her in 2007. The vessel serves North and South Cat Island, taking about 24 hours, and costing $60 each way. Over her career it appears she was also chartered to GG Shipping to ply from Florida to the Bahamas. For a time, her owners were MMS Ship-management of Palm Beach. Another owner was the Ro-Ro Company of Nassau. She is flagged to Panama.

Hanna's fourth vessel, the KCT, is 165 feet long, powered by Mitsubishi engines rated 630 hp at 1,600 rpm. She serves Fresh Creek and Central Andros, spending Wednesday to Saturday there and Sunday to Tuesday in Nassau. She has also served Acklins at $90 each way for a 26-hour voyage every ten days. Since she was built in 2012 it has been owned by Hanna under either the Ro-Ro or Carib-USA brands.

In August 2011 the KCT was one of the first ships to arrive in Cat Island with relief supplies from the Bank of the Bahamas following Hurricane Irene. KCT brought "a container packed with love and crammed with proof that people cared. It bore furniture, paper goods, cleaning supplies, food, toiletries, clothing and more. The owners of the M/V KCT, refusing to accept pay for shipping relief supplies." Furniture donated from homes in Lyford Cay were re-purposed for those in need on Cat Island.

The ship New G. is indeed new: it is 178' long, 40' wide, 10' (aft) to 6.6' deep forward. Her speed is 10.5 knots, and holds crew, 486 gross tons, 145 net tons, and 587 cargo tons. New G. is a landing craft type Ro-Ro vessel, flagged to Panama. She was built of steel in 2015 delivered in February. According to a Carib-USA spokesperson, New G. was "designed and engineered by Tom Hanna at a private shipyard." Officially her owners are the Consolidated Marine Group located in the United Building, Soldier Road, Nassau. As well as being a relief ship on other routes, the New G. serves North and South Cat Island, arriving in Nassau Monday, taking freight Tuesday, and leaving Wednesday evenings. We hope this vessel has an illustrious and successful career in the Bahamas.

Overall Captain Thomas Hanna is an exemplar of those owners who adapt to changing market conditions, take immense risks by expending considerable funds for new-built ships in foreign yards (the US is a cabotage shipping market, protected from foreign competition, and thus an expensive place to build vessels), and providing innovative design solutions custom-fit for the Bahamas, as well as forward-looking propulsion technologies which are better for the environment and also more fuel-efficient.

Though Hanna's maritime roots can be traced to remote Pompey Bay Acklins (also the site of the largest Lucayan settlements in the country), and go back hundreds of years, including a dozen or so vessels, this entrepreneur's outlook is thoroughly modern, and practical. He has shown that even in legal and financial adversity he and his colleagues can re-invent themselves and survive, rising from the ashes. Hanna is one of the most private owners that this author has contacted, as in, not even a website. When we finally met the captain was busy cleaning up his company's small working area on western Potter's Cay with a forklift and by hand – in person, working alongside the officers and men from his ships.

Wooden Boats, to the 1960's

There were three basic but distinct types of mailboats serving the Bahamas over 200 years: wooden, European, and modern, meaning purpose-built, steel, twin-screw vessels. For each epoch we will look into the colorful histories of a half-dozen or so vessels. In this feature we will cover wooden boats built between 1867 and 1977, many of them sail, some of the latter ones fitted with engines. Specifically let us take a look at nine summaries of the career histories of the Dart (c.1867), Kate Sturrup (1890), Endion (1898), Arena (c.1910), Content S. (1920), Old Horseye (1930), Selma Rose (1947), Spanish Rose (1977), and Current Pride (c.1980).

Dart was built as a 35-foot harbor pilot boat in c.1867, for speed and agility in crossing the Nassau bar and placing and retrieving pilots aboard visiting ships. Sporting two masts, the schooner was enlarged twice. Believed to have been built in Harbour Island, she served that community and Spanish Wells, setting a record at the time of eight hours for the passage. Owned by John Saunders Harris of Eleuthera, the Dart is credited with providing the first regular inter-island mail and freight service, as opposed to those vessels shuttling mail from steam-ship depots on Fortune Island (Long Cay) and Crooked Island to Nassau.

Dart won a number of racing regattas under the command of various members of the Harris family. According to the Taylors of Mayaguana, there was a "colored deck hand" nicknamed Old Blarney who would fire a small cannon from the foredeck to announce her arrival at the Harris Wharf, at the foot of Pine Street in Dunmore Town. According to historians the cabins were reserved for white passengers. The historic little vessel served for over 55 years and is believed to have been lost in a hurricane in 1922.

The 51-ton schooner Kate Sturrup was likely built in Harbour Island in 1890. Two years later she briefly replaced the Dart on the Nassau – Harbour Island run for just a year. She was owned by Henry William F. Sturrup, and one of her later captains was Arnold Ingraham. The Tribune of May 10, 1916 records that the Kate Sturrup served its civic duty in delivering members of the Third

Bahamas Contingent on the first leg of their long journey to Europe to fight in the First World War.

The Tribune editor, Captain Dillet, followed the contingent as far as Jamaica, writing: "The Police Band discoursed a variety of music in fine style from the deck of the "Colonia" while she was towing the "Zellers" and the "Kate Sturrup," and when a rag time item was on, many people, both on the boats and on the land, swayed themselves to the time thereof in rhythmic fashion. Those who witnessed the scene will not easily forget it, and many who would scorn to weep loudly found a strange choking sensation at the throat as this new body of soldiers left our shore.... ...Those of the contingent who sailed on the "Zellers" were under the care of Capt. Cole, while Capt. Dillet had the control of those who embarked on the "Kate Sturrup."" Forty years later Kate Sturrup left the Bahamas permanently for Jamaica.

The Endion was built in 1898 in Boston as a 103-foot private yacht, with an oil-burning engine and capacity for 18 passengers in two staterooms. After a stint as a US Navy vessel (SP-707) in WWI, she was purchased at auction by the Harbour Island Steamship Company (Albert Sweeting, Director, value set at US$7,000), in 1921 to replace the Dart. After a refit in New York in October of that year, Endion was delivered to the Bahamas by Captain E. B. Sweeting, with crew Gerald Johnson, Roy Sweeting, Percy Bethel, Frank Johnson, Nick Sawyer and Albert Sweeting. Her other captains included Albert Sweeting and William G. Harris. The Guardian noted that "every 10 days, for the price of 8 shillings cabin or 5 shillings steerage, tourists and locals could visit historic and picturesque Dunmore Town - the ideal health resort of the Bahamas."

The diminutive 50-foot sailing sloop Arena began its career as a humble sponger on the Bahama Banks in the late 1800s. With the demise of that industry in the 1920s, she was put to work by the indefatigable Captain Sherwin Archer of Abaco, as the last of the wind-driven mailboats serving that island from Nassau. In her classic photo-essay of the northern Bahamas entitled Out Island Portraits, Ruth Rodriguez described Archer as "Man-O-War's Sears Roebuck. He cheerfully entered each order in his notebook, whether it was a packet of needles or a new engine for a boat. His small miracle: everything delivered in good shape and – weather permitting – on time."

The motorized mail boats Stede Bonnett and Prescilla had been plying the trade from Nassau to Abaco, there was even an air service in the form of a 21-seat Catalina amphibious plane. Captain Archer and his son Bobby, the relief captain supplemented the service. His sloop was to ply the traditional trade for a decade from 1940 to 1950. Then, it was upgraded and an engine was installed. Ultimately Arena was supplanted by the motor vessel Tropical Trader - thus ended the days of sailing merchants between Abaco and the colony's capital. Archer went on to become a senator representing Abaco.

The mailboat Content S. began its career as the 110-foot wooden motor yacht Percianna II in Quincy, Massachusetts in 1920, where a researcher recently discovered the original slipway of the J. M. Densmore boatyard where she was built. For 16 years the yacht served various owners, from a socialite member of the New York Yacht Club named Percy, then a Mr. Spaulding from inland Vermont, then she languished in Miami under the name Content until Carl Sawyer of R. W. Sawyer in Nassau found and purchased her in 1936, adding an "S" to her name, presumably for Sawyer.

Two of her Bahamian captains were Stanley Weatherford of Green Turtle Cay, and Roland Roberts of Eleuthera. Grover Theis – Waterfront Reporter for The Miami News, wrote on March 27, 1940: "now with a converted yacht in the service offering deluxe accommodations, it is not unlikely at all that lots of folks who hesitated about taking the "tramp" trip will slip off on the Content for a little vacation excursion and see for themselves what lies in our front yard." Content S. had accommodation for 12 passengers and she was originally put on the run from the northern Bahamas to Miami. According to "Pappa" Floyd Lowe, patriarch of Green Turtle Cay as well as Patrick J. Bethel, of Cherokee Sound, the vessel was more of a yacht than a cargo carrier and never did particularly well as the latter.

Underutilized in Nassau, the Content S. was chartered by HRH the Duke of Windsor to sail from Nassau first to Cross Harbor Abaco to rescue survivors of the Norwegian tanker O. A. Knudsen on the 8th of March 1942, then about a week later to Hope Town to rescue survivors of the British tanker *Athelqueen*. She dutifully carried these many passengers on deck to Nassau. One of them, Alan Heald, still living in Preston, England, was so impressed that he thought they were rescued by the royal yacht Victoria and Albert. Whilst serving as a banana boat in the West Indies she was rammed, sunk by the tug Foundation Aranmore off Cuba in 1946.

The mixed sail and power 87-footer Old Horseeye began its career as the motor vessel Patricia K. in 1930, in the slipway of Berlin Albury at Dunmore Town, Harbour Island. Almost 100 gross tons, the motor was 165 horsepower. The original owner was Kelly's Lumber Yard, and Allan H. Kelly named it for his daughter Patricia. After 1940 John Percy Sweeting of Harbour Island owned it. While she may not have strictly carried the mail contract, this colorful vessel with an unforgettable name nevertheless added to Bahamian maritime lore.

Author Dave Gale of Island Marine, Parrot Cay Abaco recorded in Ready About: Voyages of Life in the Abaco Cays that "in 1956 she was leading an equally hard life as an inter-island freighter, smelling of old wood, flaky paint, and diesel fuel. Her helmsman turned her wheel in the protection of a pilothouse, perched tugboat style, at her bow. She rolled, but she didn't heel. Her helmsman could not hear her bow wave because of the insistent diesel engine that plunged her headlong into each wave without a care for easing her over it, and its throb was felt as well as heard throughout her hull. The vibrations worked their way up through the helmsman's feet and occasionally set a wheelhouse window to sympathetic rattling. ...As a Bahamian boat, it was easy to assume she'd been named for the Horse Eye Jack. [She] had a charter with a hardware and lumber company to carry freight from Miami to Nassau."

Benjamin Roberts of Marsh Harbour writes that his father built the Selma Rose (also spelt Zelma), in 1947 in Abaco. She was a 30-ton wooden motor vessel under the command of Captain Edison Higgs. Though little is known about her early life, with the help of Mrs. Eldwith J. Roberts and the June 6, 1952 St. Petersburg Times, we know that six persons tragically drowned when at 2:50 am on June 1st 1952, whilst transporting passengers from Nassau

284

to Spanish Wells, she was overwhelmed by 15-foot seas near Fleeming Channel. Among the dead were a 23-year-old nurse, Oona Newbold, her 18-year-old sister Carol, a 61-year-old Sunday school teacher from the UK, crew Welbourn Pinder and Ephram from Andros, and Charles Algreen (44) of Current. The cargo of lumber, furniture and canisters of gasoline shifted in the momentous seas and she capsized quickly. A sloop named Sally managed to rescue 17 survivors clinging to flotsam.

Remarkably an 18-month-old child named Terrance Lightbourn survived. His father Paul managed to find the infant in a submerged cabin and pull him out by a little foot. Nurse Oona Newbold directed the parents in successfully resuscitating the child, then she herself drowned shortly thereafter. The survivors then got by clinging to the wreck and a dinghy until some eight hours later, when the boat sank and rescue arrived. It was rumored that Captain Higgs swam all the way to Current to summon help, however given that it was 10 miles away, and rescue arrived in eight hours, this is unlikely. A folk song recounting the wreck of the Zelma Rose was released around 1954, popularizing awareness of the incident.

The 75-foot Spanish Rose II was built in 1977, most likely by shipwrights in her home port of Spanish Wells. Her owners were the brothers Captains Gurney Elon and Stephen Pinder of that port. Her primary purpose was to replace the first Spanish Rose (from 1965), running frozen crawfish tails to Nassau so that they could be shipped to the US market in Florida. The boat was available to passengers, as evidenced by an article in the LA Times by Jerry Hulse on May 12, 1985, reading in part:

"If you're in no hurry, it's a bargain - only $18 for the five-hour ride, which includes a soft drink and a sandwich and a world of untroubled waters. Don't get me wrong, [Spanish Rose II] isn't the Queen Elizabeth 2. Sometimes an errant chicken will run squawking along the deck in a flurry of feathers, a dog hot on its spurs. But there are compensations. If the seas are smooth, it's a pleasant journey, and occasionally someone will break out a guitar and strum calypso melodies."

In a 2013 article in The Eleutheran, Captain Gurney Elon Pinder relates in the laconic style characteristic of mariners, that sometime in 1997 "....Gil Pinder said to me, I have 26,000 pounds of lobster tails to go to Nassau.... I said no problem and loaded them with my wife and nephew..... We got into Nassau 8:30am – off loaded and left to return between 3:00pm and 3:30pm that afternoon. At 4pm I had to put out a Mayday call – the boat was sinking and rapidly. We were in the ocean, and in the engine room the water was up four feet, but no lives were lost. We launched a lifeboat, paddled off, and we didn't even get wet."

Very little is known about the 88-ton motor mailboat Current Pride, except that she is still operating, and believed to be the last of her tree-derived breed plying the islands of the Bahamas on a commercial basis, carrying the mails as her brethren have for over 200 years. Her master is said to be Captain Patrick Neilly. For a relatively diminutive vessel, she has a busy schedule, connecting Nassau with the entire western and most of the northern coasts of 120-mile-long Eleuthera, from Upper and Lower Bogue, The Bluff, Current Island, and Gregory Town, to James Cistern and Hatchet Bay/Alice Town, a produce-exporting port which was blasted through the coast to provide a lagoon protected 350-degrees around.

For those that wish to ride this historic vessel, they can do so in a few days. She departs Nassau every Thursday at 7am and returns from Hatchet Bay on Tuesdays at 11am. The voyage lasts for five hours and this unforgettable experience costs $30. Call the Potter's Cay Dock Master ahead of time to be sure! Through the Current Pride the tradition of transporting freight and passengers amongst the Bahamas aboard wooden boats enters its third century.

European Boats, to the 1990's

If we divide the Bahamian mailboat fleet into three parts, the wooden, the European, and the modern, this author finds the middle epoch the most colorful. Whereas at first the wooden vessels were drawn locally and often hand-built, their lives for the most part began and ended in the islands, near where they were born, as it were. During phase three, the modern era, most mailboats are built in the US Gulf or Florida, and are for the most part somewhat charmless to look at, with efficient twin-screw propulsion, square steel sterns, and utilitarian, but not graceful, cranes and ramps sticking out of their foreparts.

However, during the 1950s to 1980s there came to the Bahamas a dozen or more graceful European freighters, rescued from their careers plodding along the stormy North Sea coasts and up British and European rivers with coal and other commodities, to serve the balance of their days in the sunshine, carrying or mail and cargo for us. Perhaps I am drawn to them because my father, a Swede, took the same route. Though most of them lay their weary hulks to rest at the bottom of Bahamian waters, some of them have gone on to Central and South America, where they may still be operating. Sadly, to my knowledge, none of them are still active in our islands.

Few vessels in Bahamian history have had the kind of storied past as the humble freighter Bahamian, the remains of which can still be found between Paradise Island and Blue Lagoon Cay. She was built as the racing yacht Candace in Leith England in 1882 apparently for an aristocratic British playboy. At 168 feet long, 24 feet wide and 12 feet deep she was a substantial ship of 269 gross tons with a 500-horsepower engine. From the 1880s to 1930 or so she served the Royal Navy as HMS Firequeen, the flagship of an admiral. Then she was assigned to the Imperial Lighthouse Service in the Bahamas as a lighthouse tender named Firebird. In 1935 the Firebird Captain was W. Moxley, the Second Officer was H. Pinder, F. Pool was the Chief Engineer, and Cleveland Malone was radio officer. For the list of the crew and officers of the Firebird, see The Early Settlers of the Bahamas and Colonists of North America by A. Talbot Bethell.

In 1941 the underwater photographer J. Ernest Williamson shot scenes about the Firebird for Paramount's famous film Bahamas Passage. Later she was the inter-island freighter Bahamian for eight years and Charles Munro of Nassau was her owner and likely the captain. Sometime in the 1950s, she was "reduced to a plain, general cargo ship, her stately masts were chopped off, while peeling paint and rust appeared on the hull. ....the failing derelict had one tune of glory yet to play. Tied to the wharf, waiting to be stripped of her engines and fittings, the dock master received a call that nearly 100 Bahamians were marooned on a small island 20 miles away. They were awaiting rescue from a hurricane with raging winds heading their way, but none of their small boats available to him could hold more than a dozen people."

"The captain of the Bahamian was summoned and quickly assembled a crew, cranked up the engines and headed into rough seas hoping the old vessel would hold up for one more voyage. It was a rocky trip, but the seasoned craft made it safely to the island, loaded everyone aboard and made it safely back to port." Wrecked just west of Blue Lagoon Island (Salt Cay), north of Paradise Island (Hog Island), she is now known as the Mahoney Wreck in 25-45 feet of water.

How many countries can boast that a local entrepreneur re-purposed a World War II life boat into a mail and freight boat on a local route? That is exactly what happened when Captain Granville Bethel of Cherokee Sound, Abaco. His home port was shallow and required shuttling of small vessels to carry cargo and people ashore, so Captain Bethel devised an ingenious way to supply the similarly isolated community of Crossing Rocks to the south. He salvaged a lifeboat from a torpedoed Allied freighter which had washed up there. According to his son Patrick, the small craft was renamed Beluga and plied its route from 1945 or so into the 1950s fitted with a small engine. The boat could have come from the O. A. Knudsen, the *Athelqueen*, or the Daytonian, all sunk off Abaco by German and Italian submarines in March 1942, or from any of the 130 other ships sunk around the Bahamas in WWII.

The Marcella II was built in 1956 at Busumer Schiffswerft in Busum, Germany. Her predecessor was the Bahamian-built Marcella I, built in 1969 of wood, 90', burned in Salt Pond, Long Island in 1986. She had been captained by Eddins and Nathaniel Taylor, sons of the owner, from Pirate's Wells, Mayaguana. Marcella II was 170' long, 298 gross tons and built of steel. She presumably traded coastwise from Germany 1956-1980s when she served Freeport from Nassau in around 1988, she was badly damaged in a storm and became an artificial reef off Long Island. Capt. Eddins Taylor of the Taylor Corporation, owners, said that this Marcella II was the first steel-hulled mail boat owned by black Bahamians.

Marcella III has been trading in Europe, the Bahamas and South America for 57 years under different names, and is believed to be still sailing today – in Bolivia. She was built as the Jade, with green coloring throughout, and delivered in Neue Jadewerft, Wilhelmshaven, Germany on June 2, 1959. Because the yard shares a name with the ship, she was probably built on spec, or without a buyer lined up yet. About 130 feet long, the ship was 364 gross tons, 9.2 feet deep, and could carry 480 tons of cargo.

Purchased by the Taylor family in Germany in 1985, she motored across the Atlantic to her new home under Captains Limas and Eddins Taylor, then served Freeport from Nassau for many years, leaving Wednesdays at 4 pm. Marcella III traded in the Bahamas for some 22 years, still under the original green color scheme, before the Taylors sold her on to Haitian buyers in 2007. Renamed Miss Eva, her new owners then sold her to Bolivian interests around 2009 and she motored south to that country, on the southeast coast of South America, where she is believed to be trading as the Michelda.

The Andros mailboat Lisa J. began its career shuttling school children and others between the islands of Denmark in the 1960s. This unique-looking ship was originally named Ellen Soby from 1960 to 1973, then Runden until1999, then Lisa J. She is 123 feet long, 28 feet wide and only 8.6' deep. Weighing 347 tons, her MaK diesel engine, pushed the ship at 12 knots with as many as 150 passengers and 25 personal cars. She was built by H. C. Christensen's Staalskibvaerft in Marstal, Denmark, where she served the communities of Soby and Faaborg, then Sejero and Havnsoe. From 1999 she was intended for the route from Naples Italy to Procida, in the Adriatic, however she was sold to the North Andros Shipping Co. Ltd. and instead and sailed across the Atlantic in July. Lisa J. was on the route from Nassau to North Andros, namely Nicholl's Town, Mastic Point and Morgan's Bluff, departing Wednesday evenings.

Sometime after 2005 she was sold on to Honduran owners, where she is today. It is interesting to know how history lives on in vessels: in 2009 I was working in Freeport at a mixed-use ship yard when a Danish yacht sailor said he couldn't believe his eyes, but there was the ferry that took him to school as a child! It was the Runden, or Lisa J., with its original name! Scottish maritime consultant Capt. Calum Legett kindly provided rare photos of her at work.

The Ablin was built in 1962 by MAN GHH Dock & Schiffbau, Duisburg, Germany. Her tonnage was 430. Very little else is known about this striking looking coastwise vessel, except that in the 1980s we was purchased by Bahamian owners and voyaged here. Thereafter she served ports of Long Island until around 1998, when she is listed as "detained." It is believed that in 2007 she was sunk either "on" or "as" a reef in the Bahamas.

There have been two vessels of this name, however the older, European version was built as the Spiekeroog in Neue Jadewerft Wilhelmshaven, Germany, the same yard which produced the Marcella III. She has also been named Wischhafen (1974-1978), and Treasure Trader (1978-1979), whilst trading in Europe. The ship is 250 tons, with 400 tons of cargo capacity. She served in the Harbour Island, Spanish Wells, Rock Sound, and Governor's Harbour from 1979 to the late 80s. In the early 1980s she is believed to have been sold to owners in Miami, who renamed her. Capt. Junior Pinder is the master of the present, newer Eleuthera Express. He informed one of the ship's original owners, Capt. Jan Rautawaara of Finland that the original ship sank between Cuba and Haiti in the late 1980s or early 1990s.

The enigmatic Dutch freighter Miss BJ was launched as the Sambre in 1965 at the Apol A., Scheepswerf C.V., shipyard in Wirdum, Netherlands. She was 152' long by 24.9' wide by 8.5' deep, and roughly 330 gross tons. She served European coastal ports and rivers from 1965 - 1973 under the ownership of Kamp's Scheepvaart En Handelsmaatschappij, N.V., of Groningen, Netherlands. Then between 1990 and 1999 she was named Juleta and owned by Trans-Bahama Shipping Ltd., possibly also Mail & Ferry Services MVBS. After lying unclaimed for a time at Prince George Dock, the ship was deliberately scuttled off Nassau on 22 June 1999. According to "What's On Bahamas" this is now a dive site off the coast of Atoll Cay northeast of Nassau.

The mailboat Willaurie was built in 1966 as the Willmary at Hoogezand SW of Hoogezand, Netherlands. She was 138' long by 25' wide, and 199 gross tons. Her single German 290 horsepower engine pushed her along at 8.5 knots. In the 1960s she was sold from Netherlands to a firm named Antler Ltd. of London, UK, and was used for coastal trades to ports like Goole, Charlestown, Hartlepool and Fulham. In 1980 her classification by Lloyds Register was withdrawn and her flag changed from UK to Nassau, where W. B. Hart owned her. While in the Bahamas she served Rum Cay, San Salvador, and Cat Island in the southeastern Bahamas, presumably from 1980 - 1988.

This is another vessel whose demise is at least as interesting as her career, as she continues to attract tourists – divers – to our islands. According to a dive website, whilst carrying passengers and freight among the Bahama Islands on the 2nd of August 1980 Willaurie experienced engine trouble and passengers were taken aboard Royal Bahamas Defense Force vessel/s. Apparently, the ship was berthed at Potter's Cay for years, for in 1988 it was reported foundered, or at least partially sunk, there. Then it was raised and was being towed west when in heavy seas the tow line parted. The towing vessel managed to get the Willaurie to Clifton Pier, southwest New Providence, where it sank. Then local dive operator Stuart Cove patched her enough to be towed several miles west to a point Southeast of Goulding Cay, where he sank her as a diving attraction the day after Christmas, 1988.

The vessel had a very low freeboard, suitable for coastal waters but less so for open ocean passages to places like the southern Bahamas. I recall as a child and teen seeing her at Potter's Cay. To me the vessel epitomized the romantic, tramp-steamer, "rust bucket" image of the mailboat fleet, a grand old lady waiting to die. At the same time her European lineage was clear, giving her an exotic air. In the early 1980s the Ministry of Transport & Aviation has entries for both "Proposed mail boat M/V Will Mary" and "Contract mail service Will Laurie Vol. 2" Today she sits defiantly upright, atop a reef. In the nearly 28 years since she was sunk, the Willaurie has become a premier dive site, and images of her have graced the photo collections of divers in all corners of the globe, a fitting tribute to her international provenance.

The Miranda has been owned not only by the Taylor mailboat dynasty (12 ships) of Mayaguana, but by Dutch, American, and Honduran investors as well. She was built as the Geulborg by Sander Gebroeders in Delfzijl, Netherlands in 1966. Wagenborg Shipping owned here until 1977, when the Taylors purchased it, delivered it to the Bahamas and she traded from Miami to Turks & Caicos and Exumas as well as Long Island. One of her captains in the Bahamas was Captain Robert "Bob" Garroway from St. Vincent. Her dimensions were 176' long, 28.5' wide, 9.2' deep, 399 gross tons, and a 450-horsepower engine propelled her at 9.5 knots.

In 1996 the Taylors sold her to Haitian owners and renamed the Paradise Express until 1999, when a Honduran company purchased her, with the name El Compa. From 1999 she was known as the Gilbert Sea, owned by the Gilbert Shipping Corp. of San Lorenzo, Honduras. However, she seems to have rotted away in the Miami River. The website divespots.com adds that "She was seized by the US Customs Department - 74 pounds of cocaine were found hidden inside the false bottom of a 55-gallon drum - as part of Operation Riverwalk, and is now part of Governor's Riverwalk Reef. The front portion of the wheelhouse was painted with murals [and she] was sunk in 90' of water just 1.5 miles from the Palm Beach Inlet, and is quickly becoming a haven for tropical and game fish."

The Betty K VIII continues a 130-plus-year tradition of European-built vessels supplementing the fleet providing mail and freight services amongst and to and from the Bahama Islands. Though built in 1984 by Lurssen Werft, Bremen, Germany, and connecting Florida and beyond with the Bahamas, she is flagged to the tiny port of Avatiu, Rarotonga, Cook Islands (where, coincidentally, the author has sailed to). The ship is a general cargo ship of 2,191 gross tons, capable of carrying about 1,500 tons of cargo. Since May, 2014 she has been plying the cargo route between Miami, Nassau and Abaco under the ownership of the Betty K. Line of Nassau.

This Bahamian owner, though not strictly a mail carrier, deserves mention. According to their website, they have been serving The Bahamas since 1920 and grown to be full-service shipping company operating between Miami, Nassau, and Abaco. Betty K. was named after the daughter of the founder, the Late Mr. C. Trevor Kelly. A fully-owned Bahamian company was born out of an idea from the owner, who saw the need to purchase a boat to take care of their personal needs. The boat, then nicknamed the "Potato and Onion," would transport lumber for the Kelly families."

The original Betty K. and the smaller Kelly vessel Ena K. provided an indispensable service, connecting the colony to the US during the war, when larger Canadian ships were withdrawn to their homeland. These little ships returned hundreds of Allied sailors to the mainland after their ships had been sunk by German and Italian submarines off the Bahamas in 1942. Canadian historian and author Kevin Griffin adds that "The 164-ton Betty K. was built in 1938. The "motor boats," as the Duchess [of Windsor, Wallis Simpson, wife of the Governor, formerly King Edward VIII] called them, offered sailings every Sunday, Tuesday and Thursday in each direction between Nassau and Miami. Before the war, they had sailed from Miami at Noon and from Nassau at 2 pm but [during World War II in the early 1940s] they moved back and forth as cargo offered. More than eighty years later, Betty K Agencies Ltd of Nassau would introduce the sixth and seventh ships of that name, the 1,457-ton Betty K VI in 2004 and 2,028-ton Betty K VI.

The Grounding and Salvage of *SC-1059*

In early December of 1944, *SC-1059* was assigned to Task Unit (T.U.) 03.1.8 along with four other vessels; *PCS-1425* which was the lead ship and "radio guard", *PC-1564*, *SC-1057*, and *SC-1058*. The composition of the other vessels in the Task Unit varied - on the 11th of December it was composed of *PC-1564*, *SC-1058*, *SC-1059* and *SC-1295*. They were assigned to escort a 14-knot convoy known as YAG-32 between Miami and Nassau.

The pilot of convoy YAG-32 reported a radar contact which was disappearing. This was evaluated as "possible" even though it is now known that the last German submarine left the region in early September 1944, and therefore it could not have been an enemy craft. At 2:44 am T.U. 03.1.8 was told to scramble for an anti-submarine patrol in the Northeast Providence Channel.

The group, led by *PC-1564* was under way by 4:35 am. *PC-1564* was a considerably larger vessel, at 174 feet length, it was manned by 65 men and displaced 450 tons. The weather was fair, with a low pressure expected over Miami around midnight, flying conditions were poor over Jacksonville, and the temperature was between 44 and 47 degrees Fahrenheit in the morning - typical cold front conditions in December.

Lt. (J.G.) Tobin had his crew cast off before sunlight on Monday the 11th of December. By 5:15 am *SC-1059* was abeam the sea buoy off Miami and accelerated eastwards at 12.5 knots, in company with the other four ships in the task unit. Between 7:30 and 08:00 am *SC-1059* was sent to investigate a light, then it rejoined the group. By 9:35 am they were eight miles north of Great Isaac Light at the entrance to the Northwest Providence Channel in the Bahamas, again heading east. The radar unit was on and at 10:20 am Tobin also activated the sound gear under water, allowing the SC to detect enemy submarines beneath the sea.

At 4:00 pm the group headed southeast to clear the southern coast of Great Abaco Island, resuming an eastward course at 7:00 pm. At 10:15 that night the naval convoy had Hole-in-the-Wall Light, Abaco to the northwards, or off the port beam, and Little Egg Light in northern Eleuthera bearing to the southeast, or off the starboard beam. They were right in the middle of the 30-mile-wide Northeast Providence Channel.

At 10:20 the group was ordered to turn to the right and head due south, passing not far west of the islands off North Eleuthera. Their speed was 12 knots. Less than an hour later, at 11:32 pm, the course was changed again to 139 degrees, or southeast. As a precaution, speed was reduced to 5 knots. Since *SC-1059* was not the point vessel, it steered by the "wake light" or stern light, of its sister, *SC-1058*.

Then disaster struck. At twenty minutes before midnight *SC-1059* ran hard aground on Six Shilling Cay, at the entrance to the Fleeming Channel. Emergency soundings revealed that there was 4 feet of water under the bow and 6 feet aft. Since the keel of *SC-*

1059 extended 6.5 feet from the waterline, the sub chaser was hard aground.

Six Shilling Cay is a shallow islet less than a mile long (including off-lying rocks) and 50 feet wide. It marks the northern end of the The Fleeming Channel, which itself is only a mile wide at its narrowest. The Fleeming Channel connects the deep water of the navigable channels with the shallow sand banks in the bight of Eluethera. In daylight shallow-draft vessels can utilize the Fleeming Channel to access Eleuthera, the Exuma Islands, and the southern Bahamas generally. Even then great care in navigation must be taken due to the sand banks which are shoal in places, and numerous coral heads.

Based on the location of the wreck (25° 16' 24.43" N., 76° 54' 27.38" W., though Tobin erroneously placed it at 25° 14' 50" N., 76° 57' W., placing it 23 miles to the southeast on the sand banks west of Eleuthera), it can be inferred that *SC-1059* was on the port, or eastern flank of the Task Unit. It can also safely be assumed that the lights which presently mark the channel were not then in place, or they would have been seen.

Where the commander of *PC-1564* thought he was, or was trying to go, is a matter of conjecture. What is known is that he led his formation into a trap of cays and reefs, and rather than turn west or north away from danger, he turned further east and south. *SC-1059* merely followed its leader right onto the rocks.

Though the grounding must have been both terrifying and sobering, the men on *SC-1059* were not idle. At first the situation seemed salvable. At 15 minutes after midnight on the 12th of December the men moved the heavy ammunition aft, and for a little while the vessel came off the shoal. A quarter hour later she was again aground, and ten minutes after that the port anchor was let go to secure *SC-1059* against being moved by the tide and waves. The engines were shut off at 40 minutes after midnight on Tuesday morning.

By 2:00 am *SC-1059* lost power when the generators were flooded and shut down. The crew of 25 officers and men were mustered and all accounted for. By that time the sub chaser was heeling over 20 degrees to starboard, or on its right side. In the words of Tobin, "water [was] slowly entering ship."The bilge pumps would have been designed to keep a moderate amount of water at bay, but not a deluge.

By 15 minutes after midnight, just 35 minutes after the casualty *PC-1564* radioed the Gulf Sea Frontier to report that *SC-1059* was aground broadside in shallow water and that both the engine and rudder were damaged. They requested a tug be sent from Nassau. They reported that *SC-1059* was not taking on water yet, but that they were standing by, as were the other vessels of the Task Unit. The darkness and shallow water were preventing them from providing aid.

Fifteen minutes later *PC-1564* informed Miami that the situation had deteriorated and that the sub chaser was then pounding badly and taking on water in the engine room. They requested that a shallow-draft tug be sent in order to rescue the crew. Less than three hours later the U.S. Navy tug *ATR-29* was dispatched from Miami and told to make all speed to the scene of *SC-1059's* demise. The Gulf Sea Frontier dispatcher in Miami contacted the Royal Air Force base in Nassau to render assistance in extracting the 25-man crew. They were informed that an RAF crash boat, a high-speed rescue boat similar to a motor torpedo boat (MTB) and used to rescue downed aviators, would be on scene by 8:20 am. The distance from Nassau was some 25 miles, or two hours at 12 knots boat speed.

Hope came after sunrise. The RAF crash boat arrived presumably around 9:00 am and delicately launched a wherry, or small boat, which a member of its crew rowed over to the stricken sub chaser. By 11:40 am the wherry had taken off five American sailors: Suslow, Zarnick, Pascoe, Pikul, and Harris, leaving 20 officers and men aboard. According to the Miami headquarters, these men were shuttled over to *PC-1564*, which apparently lacked the means of retrieving the men itself.

Half an hour later two RAF men returned in the wherry, this time removing sailors Trezza, Brown, Jacobs, and Richards, and leaving 16 men on board *SC-1059*. With the benefit of experience it only took five minutes for the second batch of survivors to reach the nearby *PC-1564*. At 1:46 pm the RAF crash boat reported having removed 11 men from the sub chaser. It returned to base, arriving back at Nassau at 3:30 pm. From all reports, the 11 survivors were taken back to Nassau, and the balance of the men remained with *PC-1564*, though it is not entirely clear.

Rescue of the sailors - but not the officers - continued through the afternoon of the first day of the ordeal. At 1:30 pm Brown and an RAF sailor returned to the grounded ship and took off Coxswain Szoke, Fisher, Tremblay, and Brown. It took them 15 minutes to return to the patrol craft. Only Brown and Tremblay remained on *PC-1564*, leaving a total of 14 men aboard the U.S. craft. These men settled in to an anxious night of cold food, no light, and constant discomfort as their ship ground away on the sharp coral, exposed to the swells from nearby deep water.

Local help arrived again the next day, Wednesday, the 13th of December, in the form of a Bahamian sloop named *BA 79*. The origins of this vessel are unknown, however the Symonette Shipyard in Nassau had constructed two 120-foot wooden minesweepers earlier in the war, and it is possible that this was one of them (the other became the inter-island mail-boat Stede Bonnet, mostly serving Abaco).

The Bahamians in the sloop dropped anchor a mere 200 yards from the stern of *SC-1059*, which supports the impression that the wreck occurred near deep water. They sent over two small boats, and offered assistance. This grand gesture was not taken up, as the boats were cast off by 9:00 am, just ten minutes after tying up alongside. The sloop may have been a local fishing craft doing what they could to offer local knowledge and assistance.

Early in the afternoon of the same day *ATR-29* arrived. *ATR-29* was a rescue tug built by Wheeler Shipbuilding of Brooklyn, NY and delivered only a few months before, in April, 1944. Designed for heavy duty, deep-water work, the vessel displaced 852 tons, was 165 feet overall, 33 feet wide and drew 15.5 feet - not exactly shallow draft. Though it only had one propeller, the ship could develop 1,600 horsepower and motor at 12 knots.

By 4:05pm on the 13th the ATR had completed its 220-mile voyage and launched a power vessel which boarded the *SC-1059* to appraise the damage. When the launch returned to the tug five minutes later it took with it Hearn, Denhardt, Fisher and Kern, leaving ten of the original crew aboard the sub chaser. At 5:10 pm the tug's power launch returned with gasoline and a handy billy, a portable pump used by ships. By 6:15 *ATR-29's* launch and its crew had left the sub chaser for the night. The ship was grinding less and now the men had a tool with which to fight the ingress of water.

The following morning, Thursday December 14th the sea had changed direction to come from the southeast, and hit *SC-1059* on the port bow. At 9:10 am the tug's power launch arrived with a salvage crew. By 10:30 the men were using the handy billy pump as well as a 3-inch pump to discharge water from the sub chaser. By fifteen minutes after noon a lead patch was secured over a hole in the officer's wardroom. By 1:30 the same kind of patch was applied to the hole in the engine room.

By 4:00 pm the launch had returned to the tug, taking with it Kline. This means that there were nine men left on board *SC-1059*. No doubt these men had no means of cooking hot meals, no lights except torches, and no plumbing via which to relieve themselves. The interior of the vessel must have been soaked with sea spray and rather uncomfortable.

That afternoon the commanders at Gulf Sea Frontier ordered the other members of Task Unit 03.1.8 - *PC 1564, SC-1058* and *SC-1295* to return to Miami, as their services would no longer be needed. Presumably the *SC-1059* crew remained on the scene aboard *ATR-29*. The Task Unit wisely decided to wait until daylight and left the following day, Friday 15th December. Based on the rather languid work-days of *ATR-29* and the departure of the escorts, it can be inferred that the *SC-1059* was deemed salvageable, and that they rescuers were settling in for more of a siege than a pitched battle against the elements. In any event, this was to be the case.

On Friday the 15th the Task Unit departed and at 8:45 am *ATR-29's* salvors arrived aboard *SC-1059*. By 11:00 ammunition had been moved from the magazine to the deck. A whale boat from *ATR-29* completed the delicate task of moving eighteen depth charges from the sub chaser to the tug. By 4:00 pm the salvors had left the stricken ship. At 5:07 *ATR-29* took up strain on a hawser connected to the sub chaser in the hopes of moving it off the reef, however the tow line parted. At 8:00 pm the pumps were shut down for the day. Apparently *SC 1059* was not in immediate danger of sinking.

Saturday 16th of December at 6:00 am began with starting two three-inch pumps. For the first time in five days they were able to get the ship on an even keel, in other words, got the water out of the starboard side to the point that the ship was balanced. This happened at 8:20 am. Unfortunately five minutes later the ship heeled five degrees to port. Ammunition was moved from the port side to mid-ships, but then *SC-1059* tilted ten degrees to starboard again - this was still ten degrees less than it had been at the outset.

While the ship leaned to either side the tug was arranging to pull her off the rocks. At 10:50 am a second attempt was made to pull *SC-1059* clear of the coast, however by 11:45 the attempt had failed and the tow line was cast off and brought aboard the tug. At 2:00 pm Hearn, Denhardt, and Kern returned to their ship, meaning there were now a dozen of the original complement aboard. That night a 3-inch pump was operated from 8:00 pm. At five minutes before midnight two whale boats from *ATR-29* managed to haul *SC-1059* over on its port side.

At 8:10 am on the morning of Sunday 17th December the life-rafts were found to be missing from *SC-1059*. They must have been on the port side and poorly lashed, and washed overboard in the darkness. There appears to have been no effort to pull the ship off the rocks on that day, perhaps in observance of the Sabbath.

The following day, Monday the 18th of December was an active one. By 9:45 am a series of confidential technical items were removed from *SC-1059*. This must have been in the event the sub chaser sank after being pulled off the rocks, but it was also to lighten the vessel and increase the chances of being pulled off. Equipment removed included radar receivers and transmitters, switch boxes, and magnetron tubes.

Then good news. At 10:20 am *ATR-29* began its third and final attempt at salvaging *SC-1059*. This took place almost exactly 48 hours after the last attempt. Laying the sub chaser on its port side and removing equipment must have helped, because by 11:10 am *SC-1059* was again afloat, for the first time in a week. By 11:45 the smaller ship was alongside the tug and being prepared for the long voyage back to Miami, across the tempestuous Gulf Stream.

Soon the *SC-1059* would be outside the Bahamas. At 1:45 the voyage commenced at 5.5 knots, with the sub chaser alongside the starboard side of the tug. At 3:20, *ATR-29* stopped to transfer gasoline for the pumps. Twenty minutes later they were moving again. By 5:30 it was decided that *SC-1059* was stout enough to be towed roughly 300 feet behind the tug. By 6:30 pm this was affected. At 10:05 pm, whilst constantly checking the bilges and the hawsers, the duo passed south and west of Hole-in-the-Wall Light, Great Abaco. They were homeward bound.

With both 3-inch pumps running *SC-1059* was towed westward throughout the duration of Tuesday the 19th of December. At 8:15 am the crew came alongside the tug for breakfast, which Lt. Tobin refers to as "chow". It appears the crew on the smaller boat literally pulled themselves along the hawser to reach the mother ship - tiring work, even when both were stopped, given the respective tonnages of each ship.

At 12:25 pm more chow, this time lunch, was passed over by the helpful crew of *ATR-29*. At 3:30 that afternoon the small convoy passed Great Isaac Light to port and began crossing the Gulf Stream for Miami, some 70 miles distant. The sub chaser men appear to have gone without hot dinner that night

By Wednesday the 20th of December *SC-1059* was close to Florida again. By mid-morning they were back at Pier 3, Miami, moored port-side-to at the very dock their voyage had begun eight days earlier. Shortly afterwards the crew were transferred from ATR-29 back to SC-1059 and muster was held. If any of the men had indeed voyaged to Nassau on the RAF crash boat, then they must have returned to Miami by air or ship in the interim, as Tobin proudly states "all present or accounted for."

Special mention is made that "morning colors" were flown, indicating that the ship was back in shape and able to fly the national ensign. It must have been a great relief for some degree of normalcy to have been restored and for the crew to have reunited in home waters. Just before noon *SC-1059* cast off for the cross-harbor voyage to Merrill Stevens dry dock, which was at the time doing booming business converting and repairing civilian and military vessels. By early afternoon *SC-1059* was moored at the Marine Railway, or slipway at Merrill Stevens.

By Thursday the 21st of December Lt. Tobin was able to report not only morning colors and crew muster, but that the men had resumed "daily work routine." After lunch Lieutenant Commanders Winslow and Falls paid a visit to *SC-1059* to inspect the ship. Early that afternoon the sub chaser left the dry dock and tied up alongside the machine shop, still at Merrill Stevents. The vessel was no longer in the emergency room, and her crew were home for Christmas. That evening colors were executed. So ends the wreck and salvage of *USS SC-1059*.

SC-1059 was decommissioned from the U.S. Navy on 14 May 1946 and transferred to the United States Maritime Commission. Little is known of the vessel's ultimate fate.

Charles A. Tobin excelled in civilian life. He obtained a degree in law from Boston College in 1949 and married Jane Herlihy two years later. By the early 1950's he had begun a 30-year career as an attorney with the Federal Trade Commission (FTC). Tobin rose from managing consumer protection concerns such as food labeling and funeral services to become Secretary of the FTC by the early 1970's. By the time he retired he had also served as acting Executive Director or an organization which in 2012 handled nearly half a million consumer complaints. He passed away in May of 2007, leaving three children, one of them also an attorney.

Modern Boats, 1990's to the Present

The third and final general category of mailboat is the modern type, defined as having at least one engine, being built of steel fairly recently in the US Gulf or Florida, and having cargo derricks or cranes on the forward decks, or roll-on / roll-off (ro-ro) capabilities for vehicles. There are numerous advantages of the modern type over its predecessors, the wooden and the European type. Wooden vessels were generally sail-powered, subject to the vagaries of wind, waves, and current to the degree that motor ships overcame those obstacles. Any wooden boat leaks, and wooden boats fitted with cantankerous machinery tended to leak a lot more. Also, wood is a lot less resistant to rot and reefs than steel is. Planks tend to break and it only takes a few of them to cause a sinking.

As for the European ships, they were designed for the rivers, canals and coasts of northern Europe, and as a result very long and thin, and tended to be deeper in draft than required for the Bahamas. They also had low deck-lines between the when houses aft and the bow, which could be swamped in the open waters of the southern Bahamas, damaging cargo and harming passengers. Finally, they tended to be single-engine, meaning that if something went wrong with one engine, the ship would be disabled. Single engine vessels are also more difficult to control in port and whilst docking.

The modern mailboat design can be traced to the mid-1980s and vessels like the North Cat Island Special and the Champion II, where were small, stout little ships, custom-built for the Bahamas mail, passenger and cargo trade. Roughly 75 feet long and only 6 feet deep, they were built of steel, under 100 tons, and powered as a general rule by twin diesel engines. Champion II's builder, Capt. Earnest Dean, admitted he built her small to get into the US market with less paperwork. Vessels like the Grand Master were built exclusively for the Bahamas market at almost twice the size – 214 tons, longer, wider, stronger and capable of withstanding bigger seas. For over 30 years this design has predominated, and makes up roughly half of the present fleet, although there were decades of change in the 70s to 90s during which all manner of craft – repurposed ferries, fishing vessels, offshore supply boats, landing craft, etc. were used.

Why is the modern mailboat so popular? It is strong, seaworthy, shallow, maneuverable, stable and thus comfortable, can work its own cargo, get into and out of hard-to-reach shallow docks, and if it goes aground on a reef, chances are (an many instances have proven) the steel hull will remain intact and the relatively flat bottom will keep it upright until it can be salvaged. The only disadvantage is that unlike the ro-ro variety, modern mailboats cannot simply motor nose-first to the shore – they require some kind of dock or at least another vessel to offload onto.

302

I thought this second-to-last feature would be one of the easiest to write – identify and describe some 20 vessels still sailing – but it is not. If you search online for a mailboat schedule (it is called the "inter-insular mail-boat schedule" in government parlance), the most recent one, on a government website, is a decade old and lists several vessels (Lady D, sank in 2014 and United Star sold to Honduras after a collision, and Bimini Mack, replaced by the Sherice M) no longer operating in the Bahamas.

Amazingly in this era of instant information, if one is planning a voyage on a mailboat, the best way to prepare is to visit the friendly dock master on Potter's Cay Dock – at the eastern end. The team there will cheerfully photocopy that week's actual schedule for you, for free. Armed with that information you should be able to locate the vessel/s of interest and if the boat is in, wander down to ask a few questions about schedules directly with the officers or crew. That way you are less likely to be disappointed by arriving long before a departure, or worse, after the boat has left.

Even after riding mailboats for some 35 years (we are planning a voyage to Ragged Island this August), and studying these sturdy craft from afar for the past five or so years, there is a vessel operating today that I know nothing about: the Lady Katherina. I cannot find a single image of her, and only gather that she has served Mangrove Cay, Moxey Town, and Lisbon Creek Andros for over a decade, and that the trip takes six hours and costs $45. Other boats serve Andros ports of Mangrove Cay, Fresh Creek, Smiths Bay, Kemps Bay, Long Bay and the Bluff.

Overall, there are nearly 50 ports in the archipelago, situated on some 20 of the larger islands which a fleet of around 20 mailboats serves today. From Bimini and Grand Bahama to the north to the many ports of Eluethera, Chub and Farmer's cays and Bullock's Harbour in the Berry Islands, several ports in Abaco, including Hard Bargain, Staniel Cay, Black Point, and other settlements in Exuma as well as Georgetown, each can expect a weekly or at least monthly mailboat call. Then Rum Cay and San Salvador, Abraham's Bay Mayaguana, the length of Long Island, Crooked and Acklins islands as well as Long or Fortune Cay between them, and Matthew Town, Inagua – are all covered, as is Duncan Town, Ragged Island.

The 20 or so work horses which accomplish the logistics of delivering people, goods, vehicles, vessels and creatures to and from the islands are similar but of course like their hybrid wooden and European predecessors, not the same. Almost half, or nine of these vessels are the modern ro-ro type popularized by landing craft in World War II and well suited to the shallow islands of the Bahamas due to their low draft and ability to dock, discharge, and load with minimum shore-side infrastructure; often a simple bull-dozed mound or earth would suffice for a ramp (as an additional advantage, the hull, or draft forward is about half as deep as the stern, which carries the engine and fuel and is thus a lot heavier).

The names of some of the new generation of ro-ro ships are Fiesta Mail (China-built and unique), Sea Spirit II (ex-United Spirit), Island Link, Lady Rosalind II, KCT and her substitute VI Nais, East Wind, and New G. The latter vessel was delivered to Bahamas for Capt. Tom Hanna in early 2015. The oldest in the present fleet is also the only holdover to wooden mailboats: the Current Pride. Though we have many photos of this vessel, I don't know when, where, or by whom she was built – presumably in north Eleuthera or Abaco in the 1960s or 1970s.

Are mailboats as essential and vibrant today as they have been for over 200 years? As vibrant as ever. To illustrate the point, if you were to spend a week "mailboat spotting" at Potter's Cay – the only place in the Bahamas where more than two congregate at a time - you would not be disappointed. On Monday you would see the Bahamas Daybreak III sail for North Eleuthera, then the (New) Eleuthera Express heading out for South Eleuthera, followed by the Captain Moxey that evening, serving South Andros. The Fiesta Mailboat would set off for Freeport at dusk, and before midnight the KCT or VI Nais push off for a long voyage to Acklins and Crooked islands.

On Tuesdays mid-day the Lady Rosalind heads for northern Andros, then Grand Master, under Captain Lance, doing what his father did, takes off for Georgetown mid-afternoon as well, followed soon after by either Captain Emmett or Island Link, for northern Long Island (Seymours, Deadmans Cay, Salt Pond). That very day Legacy takes an overnight passage to Abaco's capital and Hope Town and Green Turtle Cay. Captain C. heads for Ragged Island via several Exuma cays, and Captain Gurth Dean heads into the night for the Abaco islands via the Berries. The Lady Francis heads for San Salvador and Rum Cay, and Lady Mathilda for Mayaguana and Inagua. Lady Emerald sails for Smiths Bay Cay Island as well as San Sal and Rum Cay.

On Wednesdays the Bahamas Daybreak III has returned from south Eleuthera and heads for the northern portion of the island. The Fiesta Mailboat has likewise returned to Nassau and goes back to Freeport, as she will thrice weekly. Lady Rosalind heads west for north Andros later in the afternoon. The following evening – Thursdays – she if off again, this time for northern Cat Island – Arthur's Town, Dumfries, Orange Creek and Bennett's Harbour. That evening the Sherice M heads for Bimini via Cat Cay and Chub Cay in the Berry Islands. Current Pride makes for Hatchet Bay and the Bluff, Eleuthera, and the (New) Eleuthera Express under Captain Junior Pinder heads for nearby Spanish Wells and Harbour Island. Early – at 2 AM – the Lady Katherina heads for Mangrove Cay, Moxey Town and Lisbon Creek, Andros, arriving at dawn.

Fridays and the weekends things cool down on the docks as vessels come back to roost at base. At 10 am the Fiesta Mailboat returns to Freeport for the Taylor family of Mayaguana, often with a Bahamian band to entertain weekend passengers. That evening the Captain C returns, followed by the Captain Gurth Dean and 12 hours after she left the Fiesta again. Lady Francis folds its wings Friday morning, right after the Legacy returns from Abaco. On Saturday Lady Emerald returns from the southern islands, followed by the Lady Mathilda from even further afield in Inagua. The Daybreak comes back Sunday at 4 pm, preceded that morning by the Sherice M from Bimini. The (New) Eleuthera Express comes back just after noon, then the Fiesta. Finally, Lady Rosalind returns from Cat Island.

One defining feature of these myriad voyages is that you can rely on comfortable, if by no means luxurious, accommodation, running water, shared plumbing, three meals a day, good company, and by pretty much any standard, very reasonable rates of between $25 (Current Pride) and $90 (Lady Mathilda) per passage – not bad considering the distances traveled. But remember, don't rely on the internet, or even the papers to figure out mailboats: the real experts are the men and women operating them, and the real experience begins right under our noses – on Potter's Cay or the nearest government dock in the community you live in.

Roundup: Mailboats as a Living Bahamian Tradition

Bahamians are justifiably proud of their fleet of dozens of mailboats which connect the islands. Well, they should be. Since the inception of inter-island mail delivery, it has been a locally-sponsored and locally-developed trade. In 1803, world powers such as the United Kingdom, France, Germany, and the United States sent their mail and freight to the colony via a then-cosmopolitan, now nearly abandoned Fortune Island, or Long Cay, in the Crooked Island District. Larger, foreign-owned vessels generally brought mail and goods to Nassau from there and from ports in the US, Europe, Central and South America and Caribbean.

But then something new happened, locally built wooden sailing craft began carrying the mails and goods first between Fortune Island and the capital in Nassau (a considerable voyage), but then to nearby communities in North Eleuthera, Abaco, and so on. Soon farmers and fishermen came to rely upon this service to bring goods to market and return with the essential materials to enable them to expand their communities. As Fortune Island's demise has shown that without efficient trade communities die off: they lose their most important commodity – people – first. Imagine home-coming celebrations nowadays without mailboats to provide happy, affordable and sociable platforms for folks to go back to their roots?

In order to sustain the communities where their voting constituents resided and owned land, politicians and civil servants set about stabilizing trade with Nassau, which thus connected them with the wider world, its markets and transportation hubs. They agreed to subsidize the carriage of mail, and permitted the investors and owners of mailboats (many of them "mom and pop" business with the owner or his sons as captains), to profit from carriage of extra freight and passengers. The government also oversaw licensing and certification of vessels and officers and the allocation of routes and vessels to serve those routes. Given the inherent dangers of maritime navigation, the age of some of the vessels, and the costs in terms of time and capital of replacing mail boats, there has always been an informal system of standby, or replacement vessels to fill in. That system is illustrative of the interdependence and cooperation of mariners in this particular market.

The Bahama Islands require a well-adapted and large fleet of vessels to serve its many communities, particularly because the islands rank as one of the top archipelagos in the world. Bahamas is, according to Wikipedia, roughly in the top ten with some 3,000 cays or islands, behind Indonesia, Philippines, clusters of islands in Scandinavia, the UK, etc. We are the largest archipelago north of the Caribbean on this side of the Atlantic, as far as the Arctic. Our islands stand out from space. And to keep the roughly 35 districts together the commonwealth has devised a system of mailboats to supplant flights by calling at some 50 communities on over 20 islands. Since some of those communities have no regular air service, having a mailboat call, even every two weeks, is essential. After all, just having an airstrip isn't enough: on San Salvador I inquired why the only airplane on the runway had a wing missing, and was told the owner was so tired of folks demanding the use of his plane that he removed a wing!

These boats provide reliable contact, more or less weekly, with the capital, in a hub-and-spoke system. Importantly, mailboats are not exclusive – other freighters can ply their trade on unscheduled or private routes as they please. It is not a perfect system, in as much as everything must go through the capital, and islanders have historically complained that merchants in Nassau can be rapacious and impose usurious fees, etc. However, folks from far flung districts have also developed their own channels of trade, accommodation, and supply based on familial and long-standing relationships. Having mailboat owners and captains originate in the communities they serve has reinforced this tradition.

So mailboats have survived for over 200 years, the readers might say, but will they continue to survive? In my opinion, backed by nearly 30 years of seagoing or commercial maritime experience, yes, mailboats are here to stay. To put it simply, until they can fly petroleum in bulk lots, or pipe vegetables and concrete, the world will still need the reliable old freighters. We need only look a dozen years back, at the United Star versus Sea Hauler to realize that accidents will continue to happen. That case was particularly egregious because the officers had tools to avoid it – radar, radios. Nowadays the tools for collision avoidance are even better, however they are useless without a well-rested, trained and alert person operating them. Some 15 years ago I thought it was charming to be woken up by a mailboat's erratic motion, to wander into the bridge to find it abandoned, then voluntary take the helm, one captain to another, until the skipper returned from repairing machinery. As we all know now, there is nothing charming about a vessel without a lookout slamming into another one also steaming blind in the night.

As for the fall-out from the Sea Hauler/United Star collision, in which four Bahamians were killed and 25 injured, including an amputee, let's leave aside the contentious facts and look at the perception. To this day the official report is not readily available. Victims were left in the dark for months, then years. It is during times like those that citizens rely on their government for decisive, compassionate action. Yet families felt compelled to protest in the streets. The perception given was that authorities were hiding information and dragging their feet to compensate victim's families. And yet admiralty law is for the most part very settled and straightforward, is based on British common Law, with virtually every kind of maritime casualty has been adjudicated. Handing of this case illustrates how much we all stand to learn from the humble mail-boat.

We can also learn from how the recent sinking of the El Faro in Bahamian waters was handled: again, despite the many facts which appear to weigh against them, the ship owners and government regulators have been out in front of the media, settling quickly with family members, keeping the ball moving and the public informed. In today's multi-media information-driven world, where what even the disempowered say online can be empowering, perception is extremely important.

As for the future, it is virtually certain that other maritime fatalities will strike the mailboat fleet again. If we could outlaw shipwrecks, or car accidents, it would have been done. From casualties flow changes: after the cruise liner Yarmouth Castle caught fire en route to Nassau in November 1965 and 90 people perished, the Safety of Life at Sea (SOLAS) regulations were overhauled. As a leading flag state provider, with nearly 1,200 vessels registered to the Bahamas (6th in the world at 5% of the world fleet), the Bahamas has an especially high duty towards its domestic fleet, and has the specialized resources at its disposal to investigate and transparently report on casualties.

The Spanish government's mishandling of the $5 billion Bahamas-flagged Prestige oil spill beginning in 2002 cost them their jobs. A similar tanker spill from the oil terminals on New Providence or Grand Bahamas could be highly disruptive to tourism, fisheries, and the environment. When the Emerald Express was washed far ashore on Acklins by Hurricane Joaquin last year, there was fortunately no loss of life. Maritime crises are inevitable in a geographically delicate island nation through which major sea lanes pass, connecting oceans and continents. With the Panama Canal expanding this week, seaborne traffic will only increase.

What are the lessons that we can learn from mailboats? That adaptability to the local environment is key, that grafting foreign equipment to a new purpose in different lands can sometimes work quite well, but that ultimately the home-grown solutions prevail. That government and private investors can work together, so long as neither smothers the other. Entrepreneurialism and capitalism backed by government guarantees instills confidence by investors and captains in their vessels and businesses, and the local communities which are the end-users and beneficiaries. Wouldn't it be wonderful to develop a Bahamas-class vessel, based on what the owners and captains have learned? Even better, to have them manufactured, say at the Grand Bahama Shipyard, and exported?

Conclusion: Potter's Cay Dock and the Future

From looking at the press and applying other models, some basic truths seem to emerge about financing a sector like mailboats. As Captain Ernest Dean's early experience shows, insurance is very important – and expensive – as boats catch fire and sink, and sometimes persons are killed aboard them. They can also cause environmental damage far beyond their economic value. Any shipping or maritime endeavor is cyclical. While the government has sought to stabilize critical national infrastructure such as mailboats, it is impossible to iron out all the troughs and peaks in a global economy ruled by supply and demand. One example is fuel subsidies: neither the owners nor the sponsoring government will always be happy, with one side (say, the owners) claiming it is not enough, and the other (government) claiming at times it is too much – which at times like this with low fuel prices, can be true. But without a fuel subsidy community like Duncan Town Ragged Island or Port Nelson, Ragged Island, which don't have regular air service, would be effectively cut off.

Even if the owners operate a route at a loss (not good for anyone in the long term), they still need subsidies to call on those ports. Without them, they might go out of business. One technique is to peg the subsidy to a set price: fuel goes above that price and the government compensates on a percentage basis. Below that price, no subsidy is offered. As for freight and passenger rates, it is my understanding that these are also set by the government and standardized, enabling even those of modest means the opportunity to conduct business, obtain medical care, and see family and friends in Nassau and on the islands where they have people. If I were asked whether I would change the fuel subsidies or tariffs for cargo and passengers, I would suggest just leaving them alone.

Risk may be managed, not eliminated. The mailboat market place already has a high barrier to entry. The US is the preferred builder, and financing new vessels requires considerable up-front investment and risk. Because of their own subsidies, US shipyards tend to be very expensive when compared globally. The Bahamian investors who take those risks deserve to be rewarded. And the administrative burden of keeping vessels, crew, safety equipment and certifications up-to-date grows every year.

In conclusion, if there is one item this author and Nassuvian would advocate for, it would be wreck removal. It's not a particularly sexy topic when compared with the colorful vessels and ports, however it is nonetheless a critical one. We've talked about 200 or more vessels, but without a place to tie up in the capital, their cargo and people could not get ashore. I knew someone who abandoned an old car in the bush out west, only to be called by the police weeks later and politely asked to move it. But the same does not happen with vessels. Owners and their insurers may wrangle for so long that it costs more to remove a wreck than to abandon it. Then it becomes the government's problem, to attempt to adjudicate, to order removal, and in remove the wreck. On July 28th 2014 ZNS aired footage of the Lady D, a fairly modern (22-year-old) mailboat serving seven communities in Andros, sinking at its berth just east of the old PI Bridge. The channel is fairly shallow there, so most of the vessel is still above water and clearly visible. It has also blocked this invaluable bit of real estate for nearly two years. No one can claim ignorance of this blemish on our national image and trade.

In 2009 a Bahamian salvage company in Freeport I worked for at the time raised a similar-sized vessel which was completely submerged, also at a busy dock-face, in 4-6 hours. When the casualty occurred, I fail to understand how there were not sufficient crash pumps from other vessels or on shore. The fact is that if someone in authority puts their mind to it, they could have the Lady D's hull temporarily sealed, the water pumped out long enough for her to be towed to a nearby boat yard, where she could be hauled out of the water and out of the way of other mailboats, and the millions of tourists who see her annually from the bridges. Yes, the Lady D's removal will cost money. But the owners and insurers can be easily ascertained, and while they sort out those details, the boats would be out of harm's way on shore – perhaps sold to offset costs? Do it first and bill them later.

Potter's Cay is indisputably the capital of mailboats nationally – the only place they consistently congregate. Though it lies beneath bridges heavily trafficked by tourists and is passed hundreds of times a day by various vessels, many of them filled with tourists. Locals and tourists alike drive parallel to it in droves daily. Probably all Bahamians have at some point eaten seafood landed at Potter's Cay. Yet as a society, the island and its vital business is virtually invisible to many of us, perhaps even more so the younger generation.

Potter's Cay is .75 miles long and only 75 yards wide. Starting at the western end, there are the ro-ro mailboats and open-market ramp-style vessels, some of them owned and operated by Bahamas Ferries, serving most of the islands. Then the Fiesta Mailboat docks on the northwest tip, and beneath the Sir Sidney Poitier (western) bridge cluster a number of mid-size to large fishing boats. Then we have a travesty: a ship was abandoned right between the two bridges, taking up a huge area of roughly an acre which could easily be occupied by half a dozen other vessels, but it is now rendered useless. If Potter's Cay is to remain vibrant, relevant and picturesque, the hulk needs to be removed. Recycling of the steel could offset the cost.

East of the wreck, also littered by the hulks of Lady Tasha and other boats, lies a small fleet of what appear to be Haitian cargo boats. It seems these are what is left of the sailboat fleet which used to utilize the southeast corner of Arawak Cay. They are loaded to the gills with bicycles, mattresses, and other miscellaneous cargo, some of which litters the dockside. Recently the free access to walk around the island has been cut off by a fence erected by one of the warehouse operators. As a result, more junk is likely to clutter this area unless something is done. Moving east and out from under the original PI bridge, the wharf is dominated by mailboats of the modern type, lining the north pier to the northeast corner, which is home to a number of large, long, ro-ro type ramp boats. These also dominate the eastern jetty, which is hemmed in by a current-ripped reef marked by a rusting pole.

To the southeast of Potter's Cay a number of conventional modern mailboats line the wharf, then the wooden Current Pride, then an assortment of mid-size to small fishing vessels. The channel they must use, between private yacht slips to the south and the cay itself, is very narrow, sufficient but only barely. If a large yacht is berthed on the outside slip and two or more mailboats are docked side by side on the cay, passage is effectively blocked. The problem can be remedied by removing one of the yacht jetties, or prohibiting yachts from tying at the end, or mailboats from double-docking. On the other side of the causeway are more smallish fishing vessels, a number of them appearing to be no longer actively fishing. These lead to the dock where the Bo Hengy II and others dock.

This brings us to the land-side of the cay: there are two clusters of seemingly derelict containers, a larger one at the western end, between the new bridge and the ocean (I saw Capt. Tom Hanna and his team clearing some of these in March) – they take up parking spaces, and some are used for office and storage purposes. The others are scattered lightly in front of the fort at the eastern end, and some of them, too, are used for storage and office space by owners. Probably this space could be put to better use, and unused equipment cleared away to provide more parking for the many passengers on the dozens of vessels. Finally, there are the buildings: a dozen or so mailboat and passenger companies have set up make-shift retail offices in old containers and trailers, the largest of which is the cluster of trailers belonging to Bahamas Ferries. These facilities all offer critical services to passengers regarding tickets, scheduling, luggage, and freight.

The yellow government building to the east is a warehouse which seems to be clean and well run, and sells farm seed during the day. There are fences separating some of the waterfront from the causeway, but I am not aware of when the fences are closed, as mailboats leave at all hours. To the east are more parking spaces, neatly laid out, a cluster of semi-abandoned containers, then Bladen's Battery, built in the late 1780's and restored in 1949 and again in 1990, and largely eclipsed by commercial activity. Behind the large dock master's building is an enclosure on land containing dozens of small vessels, including regatta sloops.

Leaving aside the question of the condition and hygiene of the seafood stalls on the causeway (the acres of conch shells prevalent in the 1970s and 80s have been removed, and a good deal of the conch shack business has moved to Arawak Cay, along with container traffic), there arises the final issue of utilization of the

313

buildings between the bridges. Most of them appear to have very active tenants: rats. In the early 1990s my brothers and friends would stop in Big Daddy's daiquiri bar there in the evenings, and entertain ourselves by trying to hit the rats with empty bottles. In the afternoons it was a nice place to meet the mailboat skippers. At one point the Taiwanese government tried to farm shrimp there, and before that I recall seeing sea turtles splayed out, upside down, for sale. But nowadays, aside from some basic warehousing the buildings are mostly derelict and abandoned. Though forklifts busily inject some life, the overwhelming prospect of the area is of abandonment.

Potter's Cay is a major economic engine for locally grown produce, from frozen lobster tails from Spanish Wells and beyond to farmed goods, and unique Bahamian products like cascarilla from Acklins and Crooked. For the small and important few who remain behind on the home islands, raising families, crops, and maintaining churches, schools, post offices and clinics for future generations, not to mention manning the ballot boxes, it would seem to be in the government's best interests to invest in this incubator of progress. Errant vessel owners and their insurers should not be allowed to dump old steel in the waters of our nation's finest harbor, any more than the government permit a truck to be abandoned in Rawson's Square. Either end of Potter's Cay, while imperfectly maintained, exudes the crisp pace of inter-island trade and travel being conducted fairly and efficiently. Not so the middle sector. Without adequate dock front and a hygienic, safe platform for operators and passengers, this important commercial hub will remain handicapped. Certainly, tourists won't be attracted to it, which is a pity because Potter's Cay offers some of the most authentically Bahamian experiences – visually, historically, edible, and in terms of hands-on travel.

Potter's Cay should be the commonwealth's pride and joy, connecting the capital and its banking high-rises with Paradise Island, the cradle of our all-important tourism product. Like Prince George's Dock extending into the western harbor to accommodate cruise ships, Potter's Cay is home and haven for our island family and the captains and sailors who bring them to and from their communities. Yet new arrivals are greeted by a very slovenly core of Potter's Cay – one which could be invested in, reinvigorated, and turned around with a combination of capital and innovation. After all, Potter's Cay is not only situated in the center of the capital, but serves as the hub and spoke – the economic as well as social heart of the nation. We need to ensure it keeps pumping, keeping the furthest spokes on the hub connected with the capital.

While commerce by mailboat remains vibrant, we cannot allow distance from our nautical heritage to grow. Mailboats are more than a lively topic of historical interest – every few hours they sally forth with the government's steadying hand, to connect the people and islands of the Bahamas not just with each other, but the world economy.

Potlatch Survivors Bahamas WWII BHS Journal

S.S. *Potlatch* & Capt. John Joseph Lapoint:

The *Potlatch* was built as the *Narcissus* for the United States Shipping Board and launched in 1920. She was Moore Shipbuilding and Dry Dock Company of Oakland's 150th hull. The ship was 6,085 gross tons, 416.6 feet long, 53 feet wide and 26.6 feet deep. As the Narcissus she traded mostly trans-Atlantic from Europe and Russia to the US Gulf, then between 1930 and 1939 the ship was laid up in a cargo slump.

In 1940 the Weyerhaeuser Steamship Company of Tacoma, Washington purchased *Narcissus* and renamed her *Potlatch* after a lumber town which the firm had helped to establish in Utah. The name is originally Native American and refers to a tradition where warriors laid out their prized belongings and welcomed their neighbors to help themselves to them. Owner Frederick Weyerhaeuser joked that owning a shipping line felt like holding a *Potlatch*.

Originally *Potlatch* was envisioned to carry lumber from the Pacific Northwest to Baltimore, however with the escalation of the Second World War the ship was chartered to the US Maritime Commission. Under the agency of American Export Lines, she arrived in New York from India and Mozambique in October 1941. She was quickly loaded and turned around for Suez Egypt with government and military stores. She returned to New York on the 18th of April 1942 until her next voyage began on 10th June.

Potlatch's master during these voyages was Captain John Joseph "Jack" Lapoint was born in Haverstraw, New York in February, 1896. Twenty years later he married Marion Huntley in Cardiff, Wales, giving his occupation as a "seafaring carpenter" and his next of kin an aunt, Adelaide, in Fall River, Massachusetts. At the time of the *Potlatch's* final voyage, he had just skippered the same ship on a long voyage to and from New York, the Middle East, and India. One of his officers had succumbed to alcoholism, locked himself in the cabin, and died of its effects.

In New York the *Potlatch* didn't just load new cargo, it took on a fresh batch of young Navy Gunners (thirteen-week wonders), as well as mostly new merchant sailors and officers. Lieutenant Dorsey K. Lybrand led 15 other naval gunners and Captain Lapoint was responsible for 39 merchant sailors as well as all 55 persons on board. Henry Jensen, age 18, was a merchant sailor on board and David Parson, 65, the second steward. Estil Dempsey Ruggles and Jake Jatho of the Naval Armed Guard were only 17 and 16 respectively.

The Final Voyage:

On the 6th of June the US Coast Guard took a photograph of the *Potlatch* laden for her final voyage – visible on the fore deck are numerous tank trucks, which led to the misunderstanding that the ship carried military tanks, which it did not. On the 10th of June the ship cleared New York Harbor in a small convoy which had air escort. Because of engine troubles the ship had to pull into Lynnhaven, Norfolk, after a transit of the Delaware River and Chesapeake Bay. The convoy went on without them.

The ship had specific voyage instructions to sail to Suez via Trinidad and Cape Town. The ship didn't leave until the 21st of June. During the next week it would come close to a number of German and Italian submarines prowling the waters to the southeast: U-584, U-68, the Italian submarines Giuseppe Finzi, the Morosini, U-159, U-203, U-154, U-505, and U-504. Then on the 27th of June the German submarine U-153 caught up with *Potlatch* – its second Allied victim.

U-153 & Fregattenkapitän Wilfried Reichmann:

The motto of U-153 was "be bright, cheerful, and strike at them hard." The new submarine was known as "U-Axt" or U-Axe, as the symbol on the side of the conning tower was an axe on a Viking ship. Unfortunately for them, the only vessel they struck at the point of their Caribbean patrol was another German submarine: on 15 November 1941 during training U-153 rammed U-583. Both boats were intertwined with each other and plummeted to the depths of the Baltic Sea. At the last moment U-153 broke free and re surfaced, however all the men on the other sub drowned.

The incident shook up U-153's commander, *Fregattenkapitän* Wilfried Reichmann to the extent that he was hospitalized for weeks. Aged 36 at the time, Reichmann had risen through the ranks in officer roles aboard numerous surface vessels, including command of the escort ship *F8* and the sail training yacht *Asta*. He served from the Spanish Civil War to the Norwegian campaign, but never on submarines. Only one of his officers had been on a war patrol on a submarine – *Leutnant zur See* Eduard Thon, 24, the Second Watch Officer. His First Watch Officer, *OberLeutnant Zur See* Wolfgang Felsch, was 25.

U-153's patrol to the Caribbean began on the 6th of June, 1942, bound for Panama. Ten days later they missed sinking a large Allied ship, but on 25th their luck changed with the sinking of their first ship, the *Anglo-Canadian*, British flagged and 5, 268 gross tons. After the night-time attack the submariners turned on a searchlight at peril to themselves in order to assist survivors to make it into lifeboats. Then, at daylight on the 27th of June U-153 spotted a thick plume of exhaust emanating from the *Potlatch*.

Attack:

Potlatch was east of where she was routed by the navy to be: Captain Lapoint confided in US Merchant Marine Academy Cadet Michael Carbotti that by going east of the proscribed route he planned to outsmart the German attackers. It didn't work, only putting them further from land and salvation – the ship was 550 nautical miles east of Antigua and 1,100 miles to the Bahamas. At 3:52 pm a torpedo from U-153 slammed into the port stern of the *Potlatch*, blowing Oiler Adam Morris off the number four hatch, where he had been reclining in the afternoon sun.

317

The ship was mortally stricken and only had minutes afloat. Cargo was crashing around on deck as the ship shifted and began sinking by the stern. There was no time to aim and fire the guns. No SOS was sent, but Captain Lapoint managed to grab money from the ship's safe. Water and oil spouted from ruptured tanks. One man was crushed by trucks sliding down the deck, others were in shock and unsure of what to do and had to be pushed into a waiting lifeboat. Alfonso Delatorre had a badly injured leg but his shipmates helped him into the only undamaged boat. Basilios Paleologas was less fortunate – badly injured, he was thrown out of a lifeboat whose falls had been jammed and sucked into the hole made by the torpedo, never to be seen again. Overall, 49 men out of 55 made it into the water.

Captain Lapoint was thrashed through the rigging and derricks as the ship sank, finally surfacing with badly bruised ribs and coughing blood. His first act was to hand over command of the survivors to First Mate "Swede" Larsen, just in case. *Potlatch* sank in 5-6 minutes, leaving one lifeboat and four life rafts in various states of repair floating on the surface. U-153 weaved its way among the debris and survivors and armed Germans interrogated the Americans. Some of the life rings still read *Narcissus* so they wrote that down. When the merchant sailors would not tell them about the armament the Germans aimed their guns at them till, they spoke up.

The German interrogator – probably Felsch - asked why they only managed to get one lifeboat away. He seemed upset that they were so ill-equipped to survive, and gave them course and distance to land. He gave the men some cigarettes which were harsh to smoke, called "Good luck, gentleman" and saluted. The salute was returned and U-153 submerged and continued to its destiny (within weeks it was sunk by the US destroyer USS *Lansdowne* off Panama, with all hands lost).

Lifeboat Voyage:

So began a lifeboat voyage which would last 32 days, cover 1,100 miles, and cost the lives of two of the 49 men who set out. The sailors would also find themselves frustratingly close to salvation – the Caribbean Islands - but sail past and north of them for three weeks.

The lifeboat was made of metal and 26 feet long. It could accommodate 25 men comfortably; however, the *Potlatch* people were nearly double that number. So Lapoint ordered seven men each into two of the rafts, eight each into the other, and the lifeboat, which was equipped with a mast and sails, towed them. On the second day young Henry Jensen fell asleep and rolled off the raft – he was pulled back aboard. That night they abandoned the first raft and absorbed its people onto the others.

For navigation Captain Lapoint had neither sextant nor charts – all he had was a compass which deviated wildly to the north. As a result, the boats set a course to the west but were carried to the west north-west. The third day they rigged an awning for protection from the sun. The lifeboat had an 18-gallon drum of fresh water and a large quantity of pemmican, or meat paste, as well as malted milk tablets, biscuits and chocolate. Captain Lapoint issued orders as to rationing, but individual rafts set up their own system of rationing. Some of the men were able to catch fish and divided it up.

On the fourth day the second raft was abandoned and one of the men constructed a net using a bolt ring, to catch fish with. The following day two fish were caught. On the eighth day the two remaining rafts drifted free of the boat. A proposal to send the boat ahead for rescue and return with help was turned down by Captain Lapoint. In order to absorb more nutrients and fluids some of the men took to eating seaweed berries and bathing in the cool seawater.

Tysa Lifeboat Encounter:

On the tenth day of the lifeboat voyage Jensen noticed a speck on the horizon coming towards them. The *Potlatch* men succeeded in sending flares and attracting the attention of what turned out to be the lifeboat of the Dutch ship *Tysa*, which had been sunk by U-505 on the 29th of June. The boat was sailing at a fast clip under the command of Chief Officer Johan P. C. Roggeveen, who kept a careful log. He noted that the Dutchmen "Shouted to them the distance from land, that I should make a landfall on the following day and that I would report them."

The Americans for their part were dismayed when the Dutchmen sailed away without offering them food, water, or to alleviate the overcrowding by taking some of them in the larger lifeboat, which only had 30 or so men in it. Captain Lapoint also refused to believe that land was so nearby, though indeed the Tysa survivors landed in Anguilla two days later and reported their discovery to authorities. Probably the Dutch sailors were afraid that the *Potlatch* men might try to overwhelm their boat. With two rafts in tow, it may have been impossible for Lapoint to direct his flotilla to the south given the winds and currents.

On the 11th day of their ordeal the *Potlatch* men experienced their first bad weather – either a storm or the effects of a hurricane. They rode this out by constantly pumping the boat's bilges. When the weather cleared morale was still a concern. At least two men tried to kill themselves by jumping over – Dalbey the Radio Operator because he blamed himself for their predicament, having not sent an SOS. Both were dragged back on board and forcibly subdued. By the 15th day the food had run out and the men scavenged what they could from the sea in the form of fish, barnacles, and seaweed.

Lapoint remembered that one of the crew had ironed his shirts and paid him four dollars for the errand. There was a crew named John Miller whose nickname was "Stinky" who had become obsessed with catching fish. He was also drinking salt water, iodine, and licking bandages, becoming slowly made. When one of the men managed to drag a medium-sized shark aboard a raft by its tail, Miller wrestled with its head and was badly bitten on the arm. The shark got away.

Soon all but one raft was abandoned. By now the men were subsisting on a meagre water ration, milk tablets, and some 40 fish which they caught. By the 22nd day the fourth and final raft was cut free and all 49 men crammed into the lifeboat, barely able to move, including the fatally ill Miller, who was by now in a coma. He died at 5:00 am on the 18th of July and was buried at sea, Lapoint officiating. Later that day and then again, the next day the men sighted airplanes high in the sky overhead. They were either commercial craft going to North America or navy planes out looking for them, however they appear not to have seen the lifeboat, or mistaken it for a fishing vessel. The boat was then passing north of Puerto Rico.

Morale continued to fall, and the health of second cook Parson and the injured Delatorre concerned Captain Lapoint, who wrote: "Necessary to take more drastic measures. Quite a few are showing signs of weakening." On their 23rd day they sighted thousands of birds. Despite some windless days. Now the breeze picked up and they neared a line of clouds on the horizon. It turned out to be land – Great Inagua in the Bahamas. By 8:40 pm on the 23rd of July, the 25th day of their ordeal, the men wove through the reefs and landed. When Lieutenant Lybrand ordered plucky young Jatho to carry a lifejacket ashore, Jatho retorted "You carry it!" The men could hardly walk, their legs had atrophied. They slept on the beach, the galley staff making a fire for them.

Arrival in Inagua:

The men had covered 1,130 nautical miles, for an average speed of just under two knots. Over the next week they would navigate their way to three Bahamian island groups in their desperate search first for water and food, and then for human rescue. After two days of digging and searching, the men followed wild jackasses to a sulfuric fresh water spring and slaked their thirst. They collected conch and mussels from the beach and boiled large batches of stew. The weak and injured rested.

Lapoint and Lybrand hiked to the northeast tip of Inagua – they were unable to see the lighthouse on Matthew Town on the southwestern tip of the island. They could however see the Island of Little Inagua. They decided that as they could not find people they would set off for the next island. After two nights they did so by setting up a range guiding the men through the reefs. Roughly half of the men had to get out and push the boat full of injured and weak across the reefs. It was backbreaking work for the exhausted men.

The next day they landed on Little Inagua, where they found some abandoned shacks and an old canoe, but no people and only a trickle of water. After a night on the island, they set off to the north. What followed was two nights of foul weather and strong winds which sent water over the sides, soaking them. On the second night the men passed the Plana Cays. That day they had seen ships and planes, but were not rescued.

Arrival in Acklins:

Just after midnight on the 29th of July the men caught site of the Hell Gate Light at the northeast tip of Acklins Island, still in the Bahamas. Then David Parson died in the captain's arms – of exhaustion and exposure. It was a bittersweet moment for the 47 survivors. Lapoint wisely decided that it was too dangerous to approach the unknown shore at night and hove-to offshore until daylight. At dawn they shaped a course to the only dwellings visible, those at Pine Field.

Newton Williamson was a little boy of seven years old at the time who came running down to the water to greet the boatload of strange men who made their way to the beach below the small settlement. The adults were out working the fields, so you Remilda Williamson, his sister and the oldest of the group, cooked food for the men and sent one of the children to fetch the adults. Soon the Reverend Captain Samuel Collie and the local constable came up from Hard Hill to the south in their schooner named Go On. In this they transported the men and the body of Parson south to Hard Hill.

Lapoint was busy looking after his men. Several of them had to be carried over a mile to the local school house where the obtained shelter from the sun. Others had to crawl on their stomachs in the sand. Once there Lapoint sent word to the District Commissioner on Long Cay (Fortune Island), who got word of the men's plight to Nassau and made haste to their aid. The women and children of the community worked around the clock to nurture and feed the men, slowly easing their stomachs with a diet of broths and mush. Captain Lapoint purchased the entire stock of food and supplies, as well as all of the community's cigarettes.

Arrival in Nassau:

On the 31st of July, the 33rd of their ordeal, the men set off on the *Go On* for Fortune Island, sailing over the north end of Acklins and Crooked islands. That evening, just of Landrail Point and Bird Rock Light, a large power vessel loomed out of the dark and flashed "You are rescued!" It was *Vergemere IV*, built in the Bahamas by Standard Oil heiress and powerboat racer Marion "Joe" Carstairs. She whisked them all to Nassau, where they arrived at 5 pm the following day after 33 days. They were met on the dock by the Governor of the colony, the Duke of Windsor and his wife, Wallis Simpson, Duchess of Windsor and head of the Red Cross for the islands.

In Nassau several of the men were put under the care of Dr. John M. Cruikshank at the Bahamas General Hospital. The Naval Gunners were accommodated at the Victoria Hotel Annex for European staff. The officers were put up at various hotels including the Rozelda and Lucerne. Captain Lapoint and Lieutenant Lybrand were sent a chauffeured car which took them to Government House to meet the Windsors. The American Consul, John Dye, had the help of US Navy Liaison Lt. Aaron Bilgore in processing all the men and arranging a death certificate for Parson (Lapoint listed his relationship to deceased as "friend.")

In less than a week the 47 *Potlatch* survivors were flown out of Nassau on US Army Transport planes for Miami, where some of them recuperated further. Then they entrained for New York where they were interviewed by US Naval Intelligence and then given leave to visit their families. Most of them rejoined the US Navy or merchant marines to continue bringing the fight to the Axis.

A Humble Beginning Lyford Cay
International School (LCIS)

Lyford Cay International School can trace its origins to one man's fall from his horse. Early in 1954, the Canadian businessman, horse breeder and visionary Edward Plunket "EP" Taylor was riding his grey mare on the family estate named Windfields when the horse bucked, throwing Taylor onto the road and sending him to Toronto General Hospital for a month and a half. According to his biographer, Richard Rohmer, "It was during this recuperative period with little to do that he took a long, hard look at his own future and at the potential of Lyford Cay... 'I went there for reasons of my happiness and my health, and to make a contribution.'"

Shortly after getting out of hospital, Taylor and his wife Winnie returned to The Bahamas to stay with their friends the Allan Millers at Lyford Cay. He made an offer to Bahamian realtor Sir Harold Christie to buy all of the available land at Lyford Cay, which was still mostly swamp and mangrove. Musing on the reasons for the move, Taylor later said, "I've always found it difficult to refrain from embarking on a business venture which appears to be constructive, which would fill a need...Lyford Cay afforded the opportunity to lay out a perfectly planned community that would stand out for generations as a pleasant place in which to live."

The total land which EP Taylor purchased was about 2,800 acres. His accountant Don Prowse described Taylor viewing the property from a hill: "All I could see down there was mango [mangrove] swamp. He'd say, 'We'll put the golf course over there, the beach club will go there, and we'll have the first residential development over there.' He could see it. The place was transformed by his vision because he could see what most of us can't see. That's the nature of the man."

Of course, Taylor was not the first pioneer to visit The Bahamas – the Lucayans and Taino tribes first arrived around 700 AD, and Columbus landed in 1492. In 1648, William Sayle led the Eleutheran Adventurers to Eleuthera, and then in September 1785 Captain William Lyford Jr was granted 448 acres in what is now Lyford Cay for his service to the Loyalist cause as a ship's pilot in Savannah and St Augustine.

The origins of Lyford Cay School lay with EP Taylor's formation of the Lyford Cay Development Company in 1954, with the intention to carve one of the first and most exclusive international residential and seasonal communities. The area was to be gated in and include a golf course, marina, main club house with hotel-style rooms, club pool and beach, fire station, post office, roads, and so on. Taylor did not want to sell lots until the development was substantially complete; the golf course opened in 1958 and the marina opened in 1961. The main club opened at the end of 1959, and, by then, the club could boast 500 members. Almost all of the funding came from Taylor himself, and, until 1973, he owned roughly three quarters of the shares.

Lyford Cay School, now known as Lyford Cay International School, had humble beginnings in 1962 as a place where children of the staff of the club could receive an education for free, subsidized by their parents' employer. In the words Frances Millar, the wife of Tom Millar, first Headmaster, "We started with nine pupils and one building consisting of two rooms, toilet facilities, and a small staff room." Mrs. Millar described it as an "idyllic situation" which could "not last long." In the vernacular of the time her initial title was "Infant Mistress." She was a teacher who maintained "strict discipline [and] produced excellent results in a happy atmosphere," according an early yearbook.

The Millars brought their daughters Lesley and Gillian with them to The Bahamas. Their daughters have said that the family was living on the little island of Cumbrae on the west coast of Scotland when John Chaplin came from The Bahamas, where he was headmaster of St Andrew's School, to interview their father for the head role at Lyford Cay School. Mr. Millar accepted the job and they soon found themselves wearing woolen Scottish kilts in the tropical heat of Nassau.

In an interview, the women described their father as the "get up and go, joiner-in, do-this and do-that" type. He had a huge amount of charity: "Lyford Cay School was his life's passion, definitely," said his daughters.

In 1966, a schoolhouse was built. The following year, the fourth teacher joined the school, and construction of a second school house began.

The early 1970s were a time of upheaval then growth and stabilization for the school. Tom Millar died unexpectedly of a heart attack on 12 June 1971. As Mrs. Millar wrote in the school's first yearbook, "Such kindness and friendship were extended to me at that time. The School, or rather the children, gave me the will to continue." Her daughters observed that Mr. Millar's death "completely shook her to the core, but she stayed on to give her due."

These early, at times difficult, years set the stage for Lyford Cay School's tremendous development into what is now a leading educational institution in the Caribbean region. The school's perseverance has been the result of both passionate leadership over the years, as well as a thoughtful community that has grown alongside the school. Today, Lyford Cay International School and the vibrant community of Lyford Cay stand as testaments to EP Taylor's extraordinary vision all those years ago.

Struggle Towards Enforcing Justice, BHS Journal
The British Commission on Slave Trade from Africa, Havana, Cuba, 1824-1826 Case Studies of the Vessels *Palowna, & Orestes*

Despite the tremendous, and perhaps under documented loss of life among those Africans and Europeans undertaking the Middle Passage during the seminal 1820's, British anti-slavery forces were beginning to mobilize and gel, seeking and determining a pattern of naval and diplomatic action which would result in the most slave vessels apprehended and the most slaves manumitted. One mission, stationed in Spanish, and not British territory of Havana, Cuba, relied upon the Treaty of 1817 (in which Spain signed compliance with British laws against the trade of slaves) more than on actual cooperation in bringing justice to captured or guilty slave vessels.

In a rare dispatch of undisguised commendation (officially an "Approbation of Conduct"), Her Majesty's Foreign Secretary in London, George Canning, under whom the Havana mission worked, sent this brief message to his Commissioners there in July of 1826:

I approve of the unceasing watchfulness, which you exercise in inquiring into, and reporting upon, the Undertakings in African Slave trade, from and to the island of Cuba. Undertakings which... are not only as unremitting as ever, but are becoming still more undisguised, and continue in most instances unpunished, to the disgrace of the Island, and the apparent inefficiency of the Decrees of the Mother Country (England).

The role of British envoys in a colonial Spanish city such as Havana, where slavery was still in practice, was limited to diplomatic means based primarily upon naval accounts. Despite the formalities and constraints of law and diplomacy, they achieved during their fledgling years of monitoring slave trading through Havana limited success. Considering the prevailing circumstances, attitude, and difficulty to obtain, if not coerce. cooperation from their Spanish hosts and allies, it is impressive the success they did have. Examples demonstrated in the cases of the vessels *Orestes* and *Palowna* show, however, it was as often a case of wreck a grounding as capture on the high seas, which brought the desired emancipation of slaves.

The concept of slavers running themselves aground, while it may seem strange, was justified by Slave Trade laws allowing British vessels to board and capture others on the high seas, and not in the fortified harbor of, say, Havana. The traders could learn to use this to their advantage, relying upon those ashore (who might have a monetary interest in assisting them), and flee inland. In this way and others, some of the British regulations constricting the slaves of trade further endangered not only the vessels and crew, but the generally helpless, bound, and undernourished cargo of African slaves of all ages and both genders.

In October of 1823 representatives of the British Government committed to the cessation of the trade of slaves between Africa and the West Indies noted the departure from Havana, Cuba of the Spanish Brigantine *Orestes*, D. Zurbano, Master.[2] On the 20th of April, 1824, H. T. Kilbee, Her Majesty's Commissioner to Havana reported to his superior, Secretary Canning, in London, that "The Spanish Schooner Brig *Orestes*, Don Domingo Zurbano, Master, entered (Havana) in ballast, from St. Thomas (Sao Thome), on the Coast of Africa, on the 6th instant (of April, 1824)."

On the 13th of June, 1824, the *Orestes*, "a notorious slave trader" in the view of Kilbee, set sail from the port of Havana, "for the Coast of Africa".[4] This time the *Orestes* was captained not by Don Zurbano, but a Master named as G. F. Vega.

On the 20th July 1825, *Orestes*, with Don Doze Ramon Mutio as Master, departed Havana for the coast of Africa; a cast deep in the supply of slaves, and equally thick in monitoring British vessels. The *Orestes* arrived in Africa during September of that year, and lingered until a sufficient cargo of African slaves could be amassed without harassment by patrolling naval vessels.

On 10th of January, after more than three months on the coast during which "she had been visited by one of His Majesty's Cruizers," the Mate related how "her whole cargo, amounting to 285 (slaves), was shipped in 5 hours"[6] an incredibly short time to stow that many people for up to two months. On this voyage, after years of close monitoring and frequent dispatches between Havana, Cuba, and British Commissioners in Sierra Leone, the Brig *Orestes* would run afoul of those who wished 'in interrupt her trade - a trade in human cargo.

The *Orestes* set off immediately from West Africa, bound back to Havana. Five weeks later she was given chase by, and evaded, two British Schooners. During the voyage, between 22 and 25 of the Africans aboard perished. The British ships left off the chase for fear of running aground in the in famously shallow waters of the Bahamas. The desperate *Orestes,* however, struck aground at night near the Grass-Cut Keys, on the Grand Bahama Bank, on the 28th of February 1826. Within two days, those slaves that had survived were left to drown by all "White men", including the Captain, (Don Doze Ramon Mutio, "who died shortly after"), within days of their running aground.

In a letter written aboard H.M.S. Isis in Port Jamaica, by Vice Admiral Sir L. *W.* Halsted, K. B., Halsted informs J. W. Croker that "Lieutenant Bennett, commanding His Majesty s schooner *Speedwell,* has reported his having fallen in with the wreck of the Spanish Slave Brigantine *Orestes,* from the coast of Africa, and took from it 238 negroes, near the Grass Cut Keys, in the Gulf of Providence, on the 5th of March, in 1826."

Lt. Bennett discovered 238 surviving Africans ("besides several dead Africans") when he boarded the stricken vessel three days after it ran aground. When landed in Havana harbor, in accordance 'with the Treaty of 1817, "The Negroes (were) consequently declared to be free from ail slavery and captivity, to the number of 212...", and the vessel "declared to be a good and lawful Prize" by a Mixed British and Spanish Commission on March15, 1826.

By the standards of the day, in which a great disparity often lay between the law against the trace in slaves and the reality of their demand, if not profit, the 212 surviving slaves, of a cargo of 285 persons, were relatively fortunate in their manumission. In arriving in what to them would be an almost entirely new world, they were at least spared the immediate enslavement and grueling labor, which a crop such as sugar demands of its harvest.

The circumstances of being a freed slave in a slave society still rife with enslavers, smugglers, and privateers is hardly a joyous one (Kilbee would later propose the exportation of freed slaves to Europe as a more humane expedient than their remaining in

Cuba), but it was in the eyes of most reformers of the time, far superior to arriving in the 'New World' condemned a slave. Having survived the fatiguing Middle Passage between slave depots on West Africa and the West Indies was an advantage enough in a land where their labor of Africans, and no longer weaker European indentured labor, was so much in demand as in Cuba.

Slaves who survived the Middle Passage and found themselves recipients of 'freedom' (from men similar to those who enslaved them) did so as a result of the increasing surveillance and interference of the slave trade. These mandates the British government and its dominant Royal Navy, were beginning, or rather trying, to enforce. During this politically volatile time, each emancipation was an affirmation of good to reformers and abolitionists; it was one step further from an absolutely slave society.

Less than a month after the rescue of these 212 from aboard the *Orestes,* for example, 165 slaves aboard the brigantine *Palowna* suffered the *very* fate from which the *Orestes* victims had been rescued. On the night of 28th April, 1826, the *Palowna*, arriving in the West Indies like the *Orestes,* from Africa, "struck on a rock, rounded off, and sunk immediately."

Lieutenant A. B. Lowe, commander of H.M. Schooner Union, came upon the *Palowna* (which "did not once show its colors", identifying her nationality) where she had sunk on shoals fringing the Grand Bahama Bank. The Eulogy of these 166 souls is summed up in Lowe's letter to Commander Hobson, dated Crooked Island, Bahamas, June 22, 1826: "...the captain, two men and the informant secured the boat and were the only persons saved." A report from Halsted in Jamaica of 4 August confirms that R. W. Eliot, merchant of Nassau, Bahamas, "informed him that 20 bodies of Negroes, in a state of nudity, were found by a [New] Providence wrecker, washed up on the Orange Keys."

In conflicts of interest between British agents against slavers and those Cubans who may have supported it or profited from it, the British found themselves pushed to the perimeter of political spheres; forced to watch, frustrated, as the slaves were smuggled ashore in Cuba. At times, though rarely, they were able to bestow emancipation upon their new charges; the enslaved people of

Africa, as their guardians on an outermost fringe of their naval empire.

It seems that for all practical purposes, the only hope that the British had of preventing the sale of and giving the emancipation of was to capture them alive, on tin high seas, and later to win legal jurisdiction over them in a potentially hostile town.

Though their task was by no means an easy one (and harassment of slavers admittedly may have heightened some of the dangers and discomfitures of an already torturous Middle Passage) the British did manage a medium of success manumitting slaves brought illegally into Cuba. The 1825 annual report sent by Her Majesty's Commissioners to Cuba to Secretary Canning features "Copies of the register of the Slaves Emancipated by Decrees of the Mixed Commission. (BPP. V.11, p.117). This brief dispatch ascertains that between 17th December 1825, and 30th June 1826, no fewer than 445 slaves were Emancipated in Havana: 175 from the *Magico,* 58 from the *Fingal* and 212 from the *Orestes*

As their superior, Secretary George Canning would concur; it was a relatively successful start to the year, during years that the slave trade seemed to be escalating. Not even tightened the burning of baracoons or the tightening of blockades off West Africa coagulated the human hemorrhage out of Africa during this time and through the 1840's. In emancipating these 445 slaves, however, it is note-worthy that the British had as their ally the dangerous shoals, against which, two of the three vessels dashed themselves.

Within the safely Spanish harbor of Havana, the British lived and worked among a governing body, which proved its generally reluctant to cease the slave trade, immoral or otherwise, which benefited them and their colleagues. The challenge which the British undertook of enforcing treaties long since agreed upon (but rarely put into action in Havana) became the greatest professional task of British diplomats and naval commanders on and around Cuba.

It is striking, in reviewing dozens of cases of human rights abuses in Spanish Cuba, but just as much so in British Jamaica or other European colonies in the Caribbean, how great a part the concepts of reputation, of pride, name, and social standing play in the determination of justice on a local level.

Often, only with the interference of an objective tribunal or outside judiciary is any semblance of justice enabled to be enacted upon offenders resident in a closely-bound community such as Havana in 1826 is reported to have been. It is this unpopular role of interventionist, which the British were cast to play in Cuba at that time. It is understandable that they were received with formal reception and a general lack of heartfelt, cooperation.

The legal wrangling around these cases, precipitated in part by the instances *Orestes,* and *Palowna*, would ensnarl not only British and Spanish factions in Havana, but also the international governments of those nations. Meanwhile, the commissioners in Havana held a front line against slavery in Cuba, which remained a bastion slave-dependent colony in the New World.

The legal aspects of what the British were attempting to do were often the very obstacles to be worked around, and there are many instances given in the British Parliamentary Papers on the Slave Trade of British emissaries using restraint rather than aggression it their attempts to condemn vessels suspected of even known to be trading slaves

The real problem for Macleay and his entourage was not gathering sufficient evidence, but rather having Her Catholick Majesty's government in Havana "put the laws into execution." (ibid.) As if the language, police force, demand for labor, and general attitude, as reported, being against them weren't enough, it was made painfully evident to the sailors and Commissioners, still out against other slavers, that Time, on top of it all, seemed to be against them.

On 2nd September 1826, Macleay, "with the greatest sorrow," described to Canning how

Lieutenant Smith and all the crew of His Majesty's Schooner *Magpie*, except two, perished at Sea, close off Havana, on the 27th ultimo, owing to the Vessel being upset in a squall; this melancholy subject has been a general subject of conversation for some days past in the city... (Ibid. p.124).

Emotionally the death of these young men in the seas just outside the harbor (added to the developing vanity of their having pursued the Minerva within Havana harbor to reach a bureaucratic or diplomatic, stalemate), appears to have been a watershed British progress towards condemning the Minerva and emancipating her cargo of slaves. Shortly after the *Magpie* mishap, the Spanish Captain-General summoned the dead crew to testify in an almost mocking way, provoking Macleay's testy reply that "the melancholy fate has been known for several days, and is so much to be deplorable." (Ibid. p.132).

Within the Captain-General, Francisco Dionisio Vives, ended one of his correspondences to Macleay with this rebuff: "...your functions are clearly marked out; I hope that hereafter you will confine yourself strictly to them." (Ibid., 132). The relationship between British and their Spanish ally/hosts seems not always to have been characterized by willing cooperation and profession of common interest, in a sense this delicate balance deteriorated under the strain of the *Minerva* affair. One of Madeay's greatest fear's, partly realized, was that the scenes of January 1825, with respect to the *Magico* which Mr. Kilbee has set so fully before His Majesty's Government, were about to be repeated, with the important difference, indeed, that the facts here were as notorious as noon-day, and the principal actors Persons in Authority on the Island (Ibid.).

Commissioner Macleay forewarned that Spanish failure to assist the British, not only on the deck-level, but in the courts and governments, would hurt the entire British effort against slaving in the region. Macleay expressed in terms of how a slaver or smuggler might view Havana (and Cuba in general) after the downturn in their efforts to tighten control of the harbor:

I do not, I confess, anticipate otherwise than the acquittal of the *Minerva,* in which case the Havana will appear to the Slave-traders to be at once the safest and most profitable Port for their Vessels to enter (BPP, V.11, p.124).

A series of pardons against Spanish slavers using Havana in the space of only months, in a town where such decisions are felt personally, could only have been a severe blow to the British movement to abolish the trade in slaves not only between West Africa and the West Indies, but also between the island colonies of the Caribbean and West Indies. Their campaign could only take an upturn after these series of legal blows, and the British abolition movement would gain its fighting arm most effectively on the high seas, off the coast of Africa and the West Indies respectively.

Bibliography

Canoe, Captain Theodore, with Brantz Mayer (1928): *Adventures of* An African 1928, pp.269-270

Davis, D. Brion: *Slavery and Human Progress,* Oxford University Press

Great Britain, *Parliamentary Papers* 1825 VOL XXVII, Irish University Press Series: "Correspondence with British Commissioners and with Foreign Powers Relative to the Slave Trade [Class A and Class B]," *Slave Trade* 10, Shannon, Ireland. 1969: "Havana," Noon 63-103, pp.63-161

Great Britain, *Parliamentary Papers* 1826 VOL XXIX Irish University Press Series of *British Parliamentary Papers:* "Correspondence with British Commissioners and with Foreign Powers Relative to the Slave Trade [Class A and Class E]," *Slave Trade* 10, Shannon, Ireland, 1969

Great Britain, *Parliamentary Papers* 1,826-7 VOL XXVI, Irish University Press Series of *British Parliamentary Papers:* "Correspondence with British Commissioners and with Foreign Powers Relative to the Slave Trade [Class A and Class B]," *Slave Trade* 11, Shannon, Ireland, 1969: "Havana," No.s 61- 93, pp.97-151

Great Britain, *Parliamentary Papers* 1828 (542) VOL XXVI, Irish University Press Series of *British Parliamentary Papers:* "Correspondence with British Commissioners and with Foreign Powers Relative to the Slave Trade [Class A and Class B] *Slave Trade* 11, Shannon, Ireland, 1969

Klien, Herbert S.: *African Slavery in Latin America and the Caribbean,* Oxford University Press

World War I and the Bahamas: Defender Stephen A. Dillet

On the 22nd of March 1915 the *New York Times* reported that Abaco captain Beecham Roy Russell had discovered and salvaged the pinnace, or small boat, belonging to the German cruiser

Karlsruhe. The German ship had been surprised by British warships in the Bahamas north of San Salvador while replenishing another German raider during the early days of World War I. Aged 21 at the time, Captain Russell was the son of William Clifton and Ann Louise (Curry) Russell of Abaco. He as 5'8" tall, had a ruddy complexion, brown eyes and a crop of red hair. Presumably he was out in the wide Atlantic fishing when he encountered the small vessel, which the Trade Winds had carried northwest from San Salvador, tied a line to it and claimed 100% ownership by virtue of towing it into Hope Town's protected harbor.

The *Karslruhe* was a 6,000-ton, 466-foot light cruiser of the *Karslruhe* class in the German Imperial Navy under the command of *Fregattenkapitän* Erich Köhler. Completed only in January 1914, the ship could achieve 28.5 knots (about 32 mph), which was faster than her nemeses, British cruisers. Her first mission was to patrol the Caribbean, where she arrived in July of 1914, mere weeks before the outbreak of World War I. While arming the passenger liner SS *Kronprinz Wilhelm* near San Salvador on August 6th, both ships were surprised by the British, and the *Karlsruhe* managed to escape by dint of her speed – and abandoning the pinnace. Karlsruhe's gunners managed to strike HMS *Bristol* twice. After the Bahamas the ship operated off Brazil then Barbados, which is where in early November 1914 the *Karlsruhe* blew up internally, killing most of the 373 men aboard. A nearby German coal ship took the few survivors back to Germany the following month.

SMS *Karlsruhe* under way with steam emanating from two of four stacks.

The author and editors at the *New York Times* optimistically opined that the salvage of the pinnace was "evidence that the cruiser has been lost," which was unfounded. Russell sold the little vessel to a wealthy American visitor, who had it taken to the capital, where it was re-purposed by the Porcupine Club shuttling well-heeled guests across Nassau Harbor for years. The Porcupine Club itself was repurposed first as Club Med and then later for worker's accommodation at Atlantis resort. Russell went on to marry Sarah Lottie Roberts in 1921, but after the death of both of her twins a year later she herself died soon thereafter. Two years later he married Daisy Doris Johnson. By 1934 he was an official for the government. He lived until 1970, dying in Florida.

A near-miss by the substantial ship *Karslruhe* in Bahamian waters was exactly the kind of chivalrous challenged the stoked captain and patriot Stephen A. Dillet. The progeny of a long line of distinguished civil servants, Captain Dillet strove to organize a navy of sorts to protect the colony. His colleagues at the *Nassau Tribune* attributed many talents to Dillet in an article of 1930: "....writer who wielded a trenchant pen, an orator and a politician. He was a temperance reformer and a musician."

Stephen Albert Dillet was born in August of 1845 to Stephen and Flora (Spence) Dillet of Nassau. His father is said to have been the son of a French army officer, Etienne Dillet and Hester Argo, his mother, who accompanied him from Haiti to Nassau with his two brothers. In 1833 Dillet became the first man of color elected to represent the Town of Nassau, an election he won seven times. He became Post Master General in 1851 and Inspector of the Police. He also served as Coroner to the colony, Vestryman at Christ Church Cathedral, and a leading Free Mason.

At the Boy's Central School young Stephen rose from age six to 12 to be head of his class. Given to rising through the ranks, by age 15 he was a postal clerk then apprenticed at sea aboard the Lighthouse Tender *Georgia*, in around 1861, during the American Civil War. Known for his punctuality and precision, he proved himself adept navigationally and within a decade, at age 23, was the Acting Deputy Inspector of Lighthouses. Then he was made First Officer of the Lighthouse Tender *Richmond* until 1871, following which he resigned from the Imperial Lighthouse Service to work overseas.

Returning to Nassau three years later, he spent the next 18 years as mate aboard the Richmond until the ship was scrapped. He sailed for the United Kingdom, commissioned and took over the new Steam Ship *Richmond*, and returned to the Bahamas in command of her. When in 1906 *Richmond* the second was also condemned he joined the tender SS *Carnavon* at age 61 until 1910 when he was pensioned out of the lighthouse service due to his age. As he approached his seventies WWI enveloped the Bahamas, and greybeard Dillet was appointed to the Executive body of the War Relief Committee.

Dillet was a member of the Recruiting Committee for volunteers from Bahamas to Europe for WWI. With characteristic enthusiasm he accompanied new recruits as far as Kingston Jamaica, in one instance even commanding the ship, the schooner *Kate Sturrup*. Here is an account of their sending-off from the *Nassau Tribune* of Thursday May 10, 1916:

"His Excellency the Governor made a short pithy speech which was greatly appreciated. No time was then lost in getting the men on to the "Zellers" and the "Kate Sturrup." Soon the tug "Colonia" had the two vessels in tow. The Police Band discoursed a variety of music in fine style from the deck of the "Colonia" while she was towing the "Zellers" and the "Kate Sturrup," and when a rag time item was on, many people, both on the boats and on the land, swayed themselves to the time thereof in rhythmic fashion. Those who witnessed the scene will not easily forget it, and many who would scorn to weep loudly found a strange choking sensation at the throat as this new body of soldiers left our shore.... ...Those of the contingent who sailed on the "Zellers" were under the care of Capt. Cole, while Capt. Dillet had the control of those who embarked on the "Kate Sturrup."

As early as September 26, 1914 Dillet was actively recruiting volunteers for His Majesty's Navy, according to the Tribune of that date. His goal was not just to export talent to the waters of Europe, but to protect the local waters of the colony during a time of attack. The presence of the *Karlsruhe* and *Kronprinz Wilhelm* in Bahamian waters, an affront to British sovereignty which was successfully countermanded by Rear Admirals Christopher Craddock and Archibald Stoddart, who lead five cruiser squadrons, one of which with HMS *Suffolk* and HMS *Bristol* chased the Germans away in August 1914.

The departure of these squadrons back to Europe left a vacuum which Dillet tried to fill. His extensive experience in leadership since a young age, his straddling racial communities, and the family's history of public service, bolstered by his specific knowledge of seamanship, mastery of vessels, supply of various lighthouses and the archipelago itself made Dillet uniquely qualified to lead the waterborne defense of the Bahamas, come what may. It was no fault of his own – perhaps even to his credit – that no sea battles occurred there during the conflict, which increasingly became a myopic stalemate between entrenched armies.

Not only was there a fear that German surface raiders might return to the Bahamas, but concerns that German submarines might attack were very real as well. This was underscored by the arrival of Norwegian merchant sailors after two weeks on the inhospitable sea at the islands of Turks & Caicos adjoining the Bahamas. The *Stifinder* was a steel bark on a voyage from New York to Freemantle Australia with drums of petroleum when it was intercepted and sunk roughly 1,000 miles east of New York on October 13th, 1918 by U-152 under Adolf Franz. Whilst 10 crew made it to New Jersey, the other boat with Captain Gustave Bjorckman and seven sailors spent fifteen days covering 1,500 miles in harsh conditions, landing at Grand Turk, Turks & Caicos on the 5th of November. This once more brought the war to Bahamas' doorstep.

His colleagues at the *Tribune* has this tribute for Dillet during this time: "For many months during the First World War, Dillet was "Admiral" of the fleet which searched Bahamian waters for suspected submarine bases and men-o-war. He was on duty on board the Flagship *Coraline* when that vessel was blown up off Grand Bahama. As a result of this calamity he lost one of his eyes." The motor vessel *Coraline* was built in 1915 at the Symonette Shipyards in Nassau and Hog Island. She was 13 net tons, had a 30 horsepower engine, was built of wood, and was just 37 feet long, 12.3 feet wide and 4.6 feet deep.

Perhaps not surprisingly, Dillet was also a prolific writer actively contributing to a number of publications, including not just the *Tribune*, which he edited whilst the full-time editor holidayed in Canada, but also the *Nassau Guardian*, *Nassau Times*, the *Strombus*, *Freeman*, and *Watchman*. He was a contributor the *Tribune* for many years, and editor of the *Freeman* and *Watchman*. Dillet was actively involved in leading a number of honorable societies within the Bahamas during his life. He and his wife

Elizabeth Rae (who he married in 1868) had three children; Elizabeth Stuart, Lillian Clarke and Stephen Argo Dillet.

A citation for The Kamalamee Organization, which honors everyday people who changed the Bahamas, recognizes Dillet thus: "This August man known to many people as "Captain Dillet, Brother Dillet, Admiral and Our Grand Old Man" departed this life on 19 November 1930. He was buried at sea with all the pomp and ceremony due to the man who had been "a familiar figure in the life of the colony for many years ... a character in the history of these islands... well known to several generations of Bahamians."

Bernews Book Promotion U-Boats Off Bermuda

Eric Wiberg, the writer of the book "U-Boats Off Bermuda," will attend a book signing event tomorrow [April 5] at the National Library, starting at 6.00pm.

An excerpt from the book's introduction says, "During World War Two Bermuda not only sent forth convoys, escorts, and aviators to attack or evade submarines, it also welcomed over twelve hundred survivors from wrecked merchant marine, Royal Canadian Navy, and US Navy survivors to its shores.

"There are also fifteen sailors buried in Bermuda between 1940 and 1944, perished in accidents aboard eleven Allied ships. Overall, nearly 4,657 Allied sailors were thrown into the ocean by German or Italian submarine attack around Bermuda.

"Of those, 1,208 or roughly a quarter perished, the balance finding safety ashore, mostly by drifting for days in lifeboats and being rescued, but some of them by being retrieved from the water by Bermuda-based aircraft.

"This is the story of the nearly 100 Allied ships which deposited hapless and distressed mariners ashore in Bermuda between 1939 and 1945, particularly those whose ships were sunk by German U-boats and a lone Italian submarine. There were nearly eighty merchant marine ships sent to the bottom by U-boats in a 450-mile radius around the island.

"They represent nearly half a million tons of shipping destroyed or attacked—474,795 gross registered tons. About a dozen voyages were destined for Bermuda or originated there, and their loss, particularly of passenger ships, was keenly felt by the island's population. Bermudians were forced to realize that despite their relative proximity to the mainland of America, they were in many ways cut off by sea.

"Some vessels like the merchant ship Anna and its escort the irascible US Navy tug USS Owl encountered the enemy more than once, as did seasoned aviators based in Bermuda who managed to sink two German subs. One of the pilots, killed in action weeks later in Europe, never received the recognition due him until this study.

"When the Germans found their targets at Cape Hatteras— nicknamed Torpedo Junction – tapering off they intentionally moved their depredations east towards Bermuda, to catch vessels using that route to avoid the lethal capes, keeping the Allies tasked with hunting them perennially off balance.

"This is not a study of the social or political or even military situation on Bermuda itself in World War Two—there are others including Jonathan Land Evans who have covered that topic in great detail. In this study Bermuda is seen as a pivotal hub around the activities of over 200 vessels—submarines and merchant ships—revolved.

"One could even think of Bermuda as a rescue ship—a highly welcome destination and landing spot for desperate survivors cast into the North Atlantic and its often-cold waters. Most of them were quickly packed off to serve on other vessels in other theaters of the war, also fraught with danger. For most of them, their cherished days in Bermuda were uniquely restful ones.

"There are many tempting distractions from the core story of U-boats versus merchant ships in and around Bermuda in World War Two. There were the early convoys which sent forth the famously brave men of the escort Jervis Bay, attacks by breakout German commerce raiders to the east, the story of accelerated construction of naval air stations and a NOB, or Naval Operating Base in Bermuda, the arrival of Sir Winston Churchill or the Duke and Duchess of Windsor in transit, or the capture of suspected spies on merchant ships, the harboring of the captured and highly secret U-505 on the island, the enabling of a small army of censors, and the utilization of six French submarines as well as eight Italian submarines for use as testing by some 500 Allied ships in Bermuda and the mainland.

"But they all lead away from the core tale, which is submarines and their victims off the island, and resultant arrival on it.

"It is precisely because of the relative invisibility of these victims—the fact that the attacks all occurred hundreds of miles from land and were unseen by anyone except the participants—that the author strives to have these stories heard.

"That men and women of all races and religions—crew from the Far East and India, passengers from Europe, and North and South America, made it ashore in Bermuda is extraordinary. A coterie of women who ran various benevolent organizations graciously opened their homes to the survivors, as did hoteliers and the indefatigable Dickie Tucker, who founded both the Bermuda Sailors' Home as well as the Guild of the Holy Compassion. This is their story.

"U-boats off Bermuda deals also with U-boat attacks and survivor stories from Bahamas and New England. In that sense, Bermuda is pivotal. The area covered herein is roughly 400,000 square nautical miles, and since the Bahamas area covered one million, there is some overlap in vessels. However, aside from survivors who found themselves taken from Bermuda to New England, there is little overlap with New England.

"Canada, New York, Cape Hatteras, the Gulf of Mexico, and the Caribbean are not covered because other authors have already ably done so. By contrast, the topic of the war in Bermudian waters has not been addressed, and nor was it likely to be.

"The reasons this story has not been told are manifold: we do not tend to move activities which were far beyond our horizon of sight and knowledge into the forefront unless it is done for us; the loss of half a million tons of shipping and over 2,000 Allied sailors represented a black eye for the Allies; Bermuda was essentially 'out there'—a colony of Great Britain, not a country of its own, distant and afar from any neighbors; and finally, the story of the German and Italian exploits have been unheralded for the simple reason that for a time it represented an Allied loss, and to the victor goes the privilege, generally, of telling the tale.

"This particular tale will remain no longer omitted or overlooked, and this book aspires to add another 400,000 square miles to the vast and yet growing lexicon of World War Two.

"The goal of this book is to both inform and entertain, and perhaps to inspire empathy not only for the mostly civilian victims of Axis submarine attack, but also for the indubitably brave Axis submariners who were attacked with increasing and fatal ferocity towards the end of the war. Without U-boats attacking, there would be no stories of stoic Allied response and survival. The German and Italian stories bear telling.

"There were 143 Axis submarine patrols to the area resulting in attacks on eighty Allied vessels, including one naval ship [USS Gannet]. The most intense period of attacks was between January and August 1942, and the German offensives during this period were named Operation Drumbeat [Paukenschlag] and Operation New Land [Neuland].

"One of the submarines was Italian and sailed for the Betasom Flotilla, a joint venture between the Germans and Italians based in Bordeaux, France. U-505 was not on a patrol when it came to Bermuda in June 1944; it had been captured and was taken to the island in secrecy for analysis.

"Operation Paukenshlag [literally translated as timpani beat, or drumbeat], was ordered by Adolf Hitler shortly after Germany declared war on the United States on 11 December 1941 [in the immediate aftermath of the attacks on Pearl Harbor by Japan]. In order to reach the US coast off New England, New York, the Virginia Capes, and Cape Hatteras, the most direct route took the submarines through the Bermuda region.

"This applied to their return voyages to bases mostly in France as well. En route to and from the US, the subs, of course, continued to sink lone shipping targets. Overall, these attacks were devastating on the largely undefended US coastline: 609 ships of 3.1 million tons—roughly 25 percent of all Allied merchant ship losses in the war—were sunk at a cost of twenty-two Axis U-boat losses.

"In the Bermuda region, eighty ships were lost at a cost of two enemy submarines [U-158 and U-84]. The first wave of Drumbeat boats—the larger Type IXs—departed France on 18 December

1941, and arrived off Bermuda starting on 20 January 1942. During a few weeks, Hardegen in U-123 sank seven ships, Kals in U-130 took six, Zapp in U-66 five, Bleichrodt in U-109 four and Folkers in U-125 sank a single ship.

"There were five waves of Operation Drumbeat. Operation New Land, which followed, was aimed more to the south and the Caribbean but the U-boats still skirted Bermuda. These included the smaller, more maneuverable Type VII submarines. Looking at a composite chart of all Axis submarine patrols around Bermuda, it is clear that most of them were heading to or from Cape Hatteras, the Straits of Florida, the Windward Passage, the Bahamas, and Caribbean.

"Patrols to the Bermuda area lasted for thirty-two months, from January 1942 to August 1944, with 11 months in that period during which no patrols had begun. The first patrol to the Bermuda region began on 20 January 1942, and the last patrol began 24 August 1944.

"There was only one day—2 March 1942—where four submarines entered the region on the same day. There were five on 8 February 1942, 21 March 1942, 11 April 1942, 17 April 1942, and 9 July 1942, when three subs entered on one day. Subs entered the region in pairs on nineteen occasions. The busiest single month for patrol commencement was April 1942, with twenty-five patrols begun that month—almost one a day."

"The most active single day was 28 April 1942, during which there were no fewer than fourteen Axis submarines patrolling the waters around Bermuda.

"Who were these submariners who attacked the vulnerable underbelly of the new world so persistently, and then dispersed for other more fruitful waters—like the Bauxite route of north-eastern South America—as quickly as they arrived? The average commander departed and returned to France, spend just over one week in aggregate in Bermudian waters per petrol, was thirty years of age, and sank an impressive ten ships of 50,000 gross tons.

"It is not surprising that German submarine commanders boasted of working for the largest ship-scrapping effort in the history of the world. The longest patrol in the area around

Bermuda was by Hans-Ludwig Witt in U-129 and lasted twenty-four days. There were three patrols—by U-84, U-509, and U-156—which were merely dips into the region for a day or so.

"There were six patrols that lasted over twenty days, twenty-three that lasted from eleven to nineteen days, and nine that lasted ten days. A dozen patrols spent nine and eight days in the area, six spent seven days, fourteen spent six days, fourteen spent five days, twenty-three spent four days, fourteen spent three days, six spent two days, and three spent a single day there.

"There were only two U-boat commanders who patrolled the Bermuda region three times; Horst Uphoff in U-84, who was sunk by Allied aircraft south of Bermuda on 7 August 1943; and Reinhard Suhren [known as 'Teddy' to his colleagues], in U-564. Aside from those two, there were twenty-nine skippers who made two patrols to the Bermuda region, among whom Erwin Rostin in U-158 and his crew, who were lost west of Bermuda on 30 June 1942, also to Allied aircraft based in Bermuda.

"There were seventy-eight commanders who made one patrol to Bermuda, plus U-505, which was under the command of the US Navy when it arrived in Bermuda in June 1944. Overall, there were 108 individual U-boat commanders who led 143 patrols, indicating that thirty-five submarines came back for multiple patrols.

"The ranks used to categorize U-boat commanders were those they attained at the end of their careers. There were seventy-one commanders with the rank of Kapitänleutnant and forty-eight who were ranked Korvettenkapitän. Eleven attained the rank of Oberleutnant zur See and one of Oberleutnant zur See [R]. Nine were Fregattenkapitän and only one [Heinz-Ehler Beucke] was Kapitän zur See.

"Di Cossato, the only Italian commander, was ranked Capitano di Corvetta. Erich Topp in [among others] U-552 sank the most ships during his overall career; thirty-five ships for 197,460 tons, followed by Heinrich Lehmann-Willenbrock in U-96 who sank twenty-seven ships of 194,989 tons. Georg Lassen of U-160 sank twenty-six of 156,082, followed by Heinrich Bleichrodt of U-109 who sank twenty-four ships of 151,260 tons.

"At the other end of the spectrum, Rupprecht Stock in U-214 sank only a single ship of 200 tons, and twelve other skippers did not sink any ships at all over the course of their careers.

"Certain commanders achieved multiple attacks in the Bermuda region in 1942–1944. Di Cossato of the Enrico *Tazzoli*, Scholtz of U-108, Hardegen of U-123, and Schnee of U-201 all attacked five ships. Bleichrodt in U-109 and Rostin of U-158 attacked four each in the region, and the following each attacked three ships: Von Bülow of U-404, Witt in U-129, Rasch in U-106, Feiler in U-653, Forster in U-654, and Flachsenberg in U-71.

"These skippers each claimed attacks on two ships: Schuch in U-105, Linder in U-202, Würdemann in U-506, Suhren in U-564, Hirsacker in U-572, and Markworth in U-66. The most decorated commander to have patrolled Bermuda was Reinhard "Teddy" Suhren, with the Knight's Cross with Oak Leaves and Crossed Swords with the War Merit Cross 2nd Class with Swords added in 1944 and the U-Boat War Badge with Diamonds in March 1942.

"Erich Topp of U-552 also earned the Knight's Cross with Oak Leaves and Crossed Swords and the U-Boat War Badge with Diamonds. Otto von Bülow of U-404 also received the Knight's Cross with Oak Leaves, as well as the U-Boat War Badge with Diamonds and the War Merit Cross 2nd Class with Swords, very similar to Suhren's but without the Crossed Swords to the Knight's Cross.

"On the Italian side, Carlo Fecia di Cossato of the Enrico *Tazzoli* was awarded their armed service's highest decoration: a Gold Medal of Military Valor as well as two silver medals for bravery. He also had an Italian Navy submarine named after him in 1980. Kurt Diggins, German commander of U-458 was awarded the Italian medal in Bronze for Military Valor.

"Overall, sixty-one out of the skippers of 143 patrols were awarded Knight's Cross in some iteration, and forty received no decorations over their career. The balance received a variety of awards and additions to the Knight's Cross, including Wounded Badge in Silver with U-Boat Front Clasp, Iron Cross First Class, U-Boat War Badge 1939, Iron Cross 2nd Class, and German Cross in Gold.

"Overwhelmingly, most of the boats—sixty-eight out of 143—were Type VIIC, followed by the Type IXC, of which there were forty-two. There were thirteen IXB, eight IXC/40, and six VIIB and three VIID types. There were three milk cow-type tanker subs of the XIV type and one Italian of the *Calvi* Class.

"Overall, there were eight classifications of sub; however, three were iterations of the VII type [seventy-seven overall] and three types of the IX class [sixty-three overall]. There were four U-boats that returned for three patrols to the Bermuda area: U-84, U-98, U-129, and U-564.

"It is noteworthy that the submarines did not necessarily have the same commanders for each patrol. There were sixty-three U-boats that returned to the region twice, and sixty-nine for whom there were only single patrols to the area.

"There was a total of nine different flotillas represented by the submarines which attacked the region. However, membership in a flotilla did not necessarily determine which ports the subs sailed to or from, as they moved from base to base, flotilla to flotilla, and repositioned.

"Members of the tenth Flotilla, for example, sailed from Saint Nazaire, Lorient, Kiel, Helgoland, Kristiansand, Lorient, and La Pallice. There were forty-one submarines in the 2nd Flotilla, twenty-five in the 1st, twenty-three in the 10th, and twenty in the 7th. The 3rd Flotilla was represented by eighteen U-boats, the 6th Flotilla by seven, the 9th by five, and the 12th by two—the tanker boats.

"The lone Italian submarine in the region sailed for the Betasom Flotilla based in Bordeaux, France ['Beta' is for Bordeaux and 'Som' for Sommergibili, the Italian word for submarine].

"Most of the Axis submarines which patrolled Bermuda—fifty-two out of 143—left from Lorient. Thirty-one departed from St. Nazaire, also in France, and twenty-nine from Brest. A further thirteen left from La Pallice [near La Rochelle] and two departed from Bordeaux.

"A dozen departed from Kiel in Germany, two from the island base of Helgoland [Heligoland in Danish], and two left from Kristiansand in Norway, using their patrol to the Americas to reposition from the Baltic to French ports. Lorient was the lead port for the U-boats to return to after their patrols, with fifty-four submarines going there, followed by thirty to St. Nazaire, and twenty-three to Brest. There were nineteen U-boats sunk or captured.

"La Pallice had thirteen U-boats return there following Bermuda patrols, Flensburg two, Bordeaux two, and El Ferrol [in neutral Spain] one. U-505 was captured on the high seas in the North Atlantic away from Bermuda but taken to the island, and two submarines—U-158 and U-84—were sunk near Bermuda. Three subs were sunk in the Bay of Biscay en route to France, three off Cape Hatteras, and one each off Panama, Virginia, Key West, New Orleans, the Azores, Cuba, Haiti, and Halifax.

"The age ranges of the commanders of submarine patrols around Bermuda were between twenty-three [Offermann and Carlsen] and forty-seven [Wolfbauer, who had fought in World War One]. There were sixty-three commanders killed in the line of duty or otherwise—one committed suicide rather than face execution, and another dove from the conning tower and struck a saddle tank.

"This study does not account for whether commanders became Prisoners of War during or after the conflict, only whether they survived the war. Perhaps the most striking statistic is that there are estimated to be, at the time of writing in May 2017, eleven commanders who are still alive.

"They are: Carlsen, Petersen, Lauterbach-Emden, Stock, Markworth, Wissmann, Wintermeyer, Hardegen, Siegmann, Geissler, Schulze, Schutze, and Borchert. It is well known that the Axis submariners, particularly German U-boat officers and sailors, suffered death rates of roughly 66 percent over the war—the highest such ratio experienced on either side by any branch of the services.

"This compares with the merchant mariner's death rate of 25 percent in Bermuda. If one compares apples to apples, only two out of 143 Axis submarines were sunk, and thus only a small fraction of their mariners actually perished in the Bermuda sphere; rather, most of them were killed while positioning to or from the Bermuda region or on later patrols.

LCIS In Adolescence

Early Beginnings

The early years of LCIS under its first principal, Mr. Tom Millar, were a period of endless spontaneity. School life was colorful, enhanced by animals including a goat in a petting zoo, and a duck that occasionally laid eggs. One memorable Christmas, dressed as Santa and perched on the back of a pickup truck on which a convenient piano had been installed, he accompanied the students as they travelled around Lyford Cay, serenading the residents with holiday carols. Millar's impromptu Christmas cheer was typical of how the school's administrators dealt with new situations: with pluck and aplomb. This improvisational spirit lasted until Mr. Millar's death in 1972 and was continued, to some degree by his widow, Frances, and a series of committed and passionate teachers who found themselves at the helm of the school.

By its 15th year, the school had organically grown from its original nine students, receiving new pupils into the original building which was located adjacent to the headmaster's house. Tuition remained low, $150 per term, as the school served a revolving roster of expatriate workers for the developer's Lyford Cay Company and residents wintering in The Bahamas.

An Awkward Adolescence

Mrs. Veronica Campbell joined Lyford Cay School as a teacher in 1981, later stepping up to serve as headmistress. She quickly found herself balancing daily budget hurdles with a larger vision for the school, all while providing the best experiences possible for each student. She founded some of the schools most enduring traditions: the house colors; out-island field trips; events such as Founders Day; and the introduction of a scholarship programme for Bahamian students.

While the school was more integrated than others on the island, it struggled for a sense of community. Some students were there only seasonally. Others were from families who only worked for the development company for a few years. Still others drove into Lyford Cay, from Nassau and beyond. While built to serve the neighborhood, it was not always easy to create cohesion with its migratory and disparate members.

Enrollment declined. Students transferred to other local institutions or to boarding schools abroad. There were even rumors of bussing the remaining Lyford Cay School students "out east" to St. Andrew's while the school was "wound up." By 1985, the Founder's Day event, typically a lively festival of family, pets and races, was small and subdued. The school's longest-serving employee, Ms. Dala McKinney-Smith, recollects that the school seemed in dire risk of closing.

While the school was now independent of EP Taylor's original development company, they still owed annual rent that rose steadily on the back of a 12-year lease, from $27,000 to $40,000. With this tremendous drain on the school's budget, tuition revenue could not keep up with expenses. The operating budget often fell into deficit and was filled by passing a hat. Rooms were not air-conditioned and rains made miniature ponds on the fields. One of the Tomlinson boys recalls making model planes out of shingles that fell from the roofs of school buildings.

Lyford Cay School had to adapt to survive for the long term or risk sinking back into the bush and swampland on which it was built. The school needed to redefine its mission and shore up its foundations. School leadership needed outside guidance and assistance. The days when teachers or spouses became principals gave way to administrators having to act as financial and strategic planners. The dwindling enrollment and target community compelled the school to refocus its vision. Lyford Cay School would repurpose itself as school not only for families who used the school as an amenity but also for families who lived on the island year-round.

The school needed to reinvent itself.

Working Through Challenges

By 1991, Lyford Cay School was on the brink of financial failure. Fortunately, two families, Mr. & Mrs. Clarence Dauphinot and Mr. & Mrs. Michael Dingman, were committed to finding a solution. Leading a team of committed parents and community experts, urgent corrective actions were implemented. Saving the school from demolition, they incorporated the school as an independent, not-for-profit organization, successfully negotiated the purchase of the land on which the school now stands and stipulated that this property would remain a school in perpetuity. With this new stable foundation, Lyford Cay School was assured a future.

After August 10, 1993, when the school was incorporated and all assets were purchased, the new entity no longer had to pay rent and the Lyford Cay Company was freed of any school liabilities. As the school adapted to its new structure, the board began to look further forward, asking how Lyford Cay should evolve and even set out to develop an endowment.

In 1994, leadership of over 100 students and 16 staff passed to Ms. Mary Guthrie. Originally from the UK, Ms. Guthrie had lived and taught in Australia, Qatar and Papua New Guinea, before being lured back to the Bahamas in 1991, first to teach and then to lead the school. While the school was again promoting a vibrant educator into the role of school leader, there was now an infrastructure and volunteer team in place to offer support. Educators could, with smiles on their faces, focus on the students while the myriad administrative tasks were supported by industry experts, procedures and policies.

Under its new structure and leadership, the school had a significant growth spurt. The staff more than doubled, from 13 to 30. The Early Learning Centre was added, welcoming students as young as three. Parents and community members supported fundraising for new buildings, which meant that Grades 1-6 could each have their own classroom. The campus also saw a new library, administration building and innovative art studio. To further enhance athletic opportunities, the school negotiated a lease to use the sports fields behind St. Paul's Church just outside the gates. Most importantly, the years of tumult ended and the school did not lose a single student nor shingle.

Like Mrs. Guthrie, students arrived from all over the world, creating a vibrant blend of local and global cultures that enhanced the student experience. The transition of Lyford Cay School to an international school was an important priority. A 1994 Campaign Booklet states: "The diversity of the school, its students, its staff and the many countries with which the school has connections, requires that the school's vision of education take a global perspective." The school soon found itself capitalizing on this international fusion and providing an education that would help students succeed on the global stage academically, personally and professionally.

The Roots of New Growth

As the larger economy blossomed, a new demographic of young families looking to settle on New Providence sought the best education available to their children. In the late '90s, Western New Providence had its own growth spurt when the adult children of residents began to move home. The Lyford Cay School, Club and community grew side by side. The school worked hard to keep ahead of the shift to younger families in and outside the club, and branded itself as an engine for community development, and a place where locals could experience a world-class education without having to leave home. The intimate size of the school was itself a draw for families all over the island.

To achieve its potential, the school board, staff and administrators worked to further expand the size and diversity of the student body and the scope of its offerings. They set a goal to double the student body and become a community of more than half Bahamians. The school grew its reach, adding Grade 9 in 1998. And the world was put within the hands of the students as they welcomed visits from a Maasai warrior from Kenya, anthropologist Jane Goodall, a U.S. president and Apollo astronaut Tom Stafford.

In 1998, Lyford Cay School received additional accreditation from the European Council of International Schools and the New England Association of Schools and Colleges. Parents appreciated European and American validation of the systems and curriculum. The school benefited from the standards and accountability that accreditation provided.

Shortly thereafter, Lyford Cay School began its multi-year journey to officially become Lyford Cay *International* School. The board pursued International Baccalaureate accreditation, earning authorization to use the Middle Years Programme curriculum in 2003, followed by the Diploma Programme in 2004. This effort was supported by families, local organizations, outside board members and donors, all of whom saw the benefits of being able to meet the expectations of a growing international community. Hardworking volunteers, leaders and staff at the school had, over the years, reinvented Lyford Cay to a stand-alone, self-financing entity that used its international features to develop its programme and community.

Today, there are more computers than goats, and the swimming pool has replaced the persistent puddles. While EP Taylor left us in 1989, the school has continued to be guided by the vision of the community developer, who 55 years ago, looked across a swamp and saw the future. Parents, fundraisers, educators, volunteers, religious ministers, corporate citizens, friends of Taylor, all invested in this vision to make sure the children were happy, the books were balanced, the plans strategic and the roof tiles intact. This community of support carried the school through its sometimes-awkward adolescence so it could realize its founder's vision, creating an entirely new world in which to set the LCIS student and faculty experience: this one entirely of their own making.

U-Boats Off New England

Between January 12th 1942 and up to May 5, 1945 there were 72 German submarine, or U-boat patrols off the coast of New England. The area is defined by a line from the Maine/Canada border in the Bay of Fundy southeast past Yarmouth, Nova Scotia, out several hundred miles into the Atlantic, and from Montauk Light in the south also out to sea. It does not include the upper reaches of the Bay of Fundy, eastern Nova Scotia, or Long Island or Long Island Sound. It does include the coasts of Rhode Island, Massachusetts, New Hampshire, and Maine. There were important US Navy bases in Newport and Portsmouth (near Kittery, Maine) at the time, a number of U-boats surrendering to the latter port in 1945 after Victory in Europe, or VE Day.

New England thus sustained a near continuous assault by U-boats, lasting from a few weeks after Adolf Hitler declared war on the United States on 11 December, 1941, right up to the very end, when U-853's brazen commander attacked and sank the ship

Black Point off Point Judith, Rhode Island within a week of Germany's capitulation. No Italian or Japanese submarines invaded these waters during this time; however, a dozen or so captured French and Italian submarines were used for training from New London and nearby Bermuda. Out of the 72 submarines which patrolled the area roughly 10% of them were sunk during the patrol – U-701, U-215, U-869, U-550, U-866, U-857, and U-853. A further five of them surrendered, either in Portsmouth NH (U-1228, U-805, U-873, and U-234) or in Lewes, Delaware (U-858).

In round terms, on average only every other submarine managed to sink an Allied ship, and for every three ships a German submarine was sunk. These were altogether not spectacular results in the Germany's favor, provided that their objective was for each submarine to sink several ships on each patrol and thus win the tonnage war. The protracted Battle of the Atlantic was the longest in history, by which Germany aimed to bleed US supplies to a trickle and thus starve their nemeses Great Britain and Russia into submission. As we shall see, though their flank was initially insufficiently protected, the Allies were able to muster adequate defenses and actually, utilizing air power, go on the offensive against the U-boat menace. By then saboteurs had been landed in Amagansett, Long Island and Frenchman's Bay, Maine and 30 ships – merchant and military alike – had been sent to the bottom.

There were 22 months – during a period of 77 months – that U-boats patrolled off the New England coast, coming within sight of Cape Cod, Nantucket, Block Island, and the US mainland in Rhode Island and Maine. U-123 under the indefatigable (and still living) Reinhard Hardegen began the offensive on January 12th, 1942. He was followed by seven other boats that month. In February only three boats arrived as part of Operation *Pauckenshlag*, or Drumbeat, followed by eight in March and April respectively. Eleven U-boats arrived in May of 1942, and seven the following month, with only three in June. To end 1942 only U-86 entered in August, U-455 in September, and two U-boats in November. 1942 was to be the busiest year of the war for attacks, at least until the spring of 1945 when the Germans counter-attacked the region.

1943 was not a particularly active year, as many boats moved to the Caribbean and Africa or Indian Oceans, and in Black May of that year the Allies finally struck a decisive blow against the wolf-packs hounding the convoys from Halifax to the UK. There were two patrols in April 1943, one in May, and two in August. In 1944 there were only single patrols for the following months: February, April, May, June, September, and November. Then there is a remarkable uptick in attacks for 1945: one in March, three in 1944, and an impressive five in May, as Hitler and *GrossAdmiral* Donitz flung all their newest technologies and remaining seamen against their enemy the US in a desperate gambit. They lost, and in 1945 three subs were sunk off the US coast and five boats surrendered.

The overwhelming majority of Allied ships sunk of New England in World War II – 26 out of 30 - were during 1942. This was achieved by 52 U-boat patrols to the region, although admittedly the objectives of some submarines were the approaches to New York, and other simply probed south of Halifax and north of Hatteras and Bermuda. In 1943 there were five U-boat patrols off New England which accounted for no ships sunk. Six patrols in 1944 resulted in two Allied losses, and nine patrols in 1945 saw two ships sunk, one of them the US Navy patrol craft USS PE-56 (USS *Eagle*), in the Gulf of Maine. During the period of maximum effort, when the US military was largely off balance in early 1942 and focusing on avenging Pearl Harbor in the Pacific, the returns for the Germans were predictably the greatest, and diminished thereafter. The Allies instigated convoys, submarine hunter-killer groups in mid-Atlantic cutting off floating U-boat tankers, more efficient decoding and dissemination of decrypted German signals intelligence, and a concerted and continuous air presence over the coast, as well as yachts assigned as picket boats and beefed-up destroyer and blimp patrols and Coast Guard presence.

The *Norness* was the first ship sunk, south of Rhode Island on the 14th of February 1942, by Hardegen in U-123. A week later the *Alexandra Hoegh* was sent to the bottom by U-130 in roughly the same position. The *Thirlby*, attacked by U-109, followed two days later. On the 17th of March U-71 sank the *Ranja* and five days later

U-373 dispatched the *Thursobank*. On the 29th of March U-571 destroyed the *Hertford* and the 8th of April saw U-84 sink the *Nemanja*. *West Imboden* succumbed to U-752 on the 21st of April, followed a week later by the *Taborfjell*, at the hands of U-576. In May seven ships were sunk: the schooner *Angelus* by U-161, *Fort Qu'Appelle* by U-135, *Skottland, Fort Binger*, and *Plow City* by U-588 within a week of each other, *Zurichmoor* and *Liverpool Packet* by U-432.

June of 1942 was a devastating month for the Allies off New England, with a record nine ships attacked and sunk by seven German subs. They were the *John A. Poor* (U-510), *Berganger* (U-578), *Mattawin* (U-553) and the fishing vessel *Ben & Josephine* and *Malayan Prince* by U-432. These depredations were followed by the loss of the Lark to U-107, *Cherokee* and *Port Nicholson* by U-87 on the same day off Cape Cod (the *Port Nicholson* has been said to have contained millions in bullion), and the *Moldanger* to U-404. The following month, July, saw only the *Lucille M.* sunk – by U-89. In 1944 there were two ship sunk: *Pan Pennsylvania* by U-550, which was quickly avenged by the sinking of the submarine 70 miles south of Nantucket in April (it was discovered in 2012), and the *Cornwallis* by U-1230 in December. 1945 saw the USS *Eagle* sunk off Maine in April (the loss, to a mine, was attributed by the navy to a boiler explosion until recently), and the *Black Point* off Rhode Island – both by U-853, whose commander was hell-bent on risky destruction. His revenge was meted out to him in a determined counter-attack which sent the U-boat to the bottom off Block Island: one of the German sailors was buried with honors in Newport, and the sub's propellers rested outside the Inn at Castle Hill for decades.

Since the landing of saboteurs on Long Island and in Canada did not occur in New England, they are not germane to this study, however the November 29th 1944 insertion of an American double-agent and his German colleague are. U-1230 had two sailors row Erich Gimpel (the German) and William Curtis Colepaugh (the American, an MIT drop-out from Niantic CT), ashore in a snow storm in Frenchman's Bay. They used German sausages to quiet barking dogs and made their way to Portland, then Boston and finally New York, where Colepaugh betrayed

Gimpel. They were each severely sentenced and survived the war. It is believed that the dirigible *K-14* salvaged in Southwest Harbor Maine riddled with bullets from a German submarine, but the US Navy denies a connection, saying its loss was due to pilot error.

There were numerous instances of exceptional bravery off the harsh winter-bounded coastline of New England during the war. One of the picket boats, *Zaida*, was dismasted and pushed to sea off Nantucket resulted in the largest air-sea rescue mission to date, until the men were located alive of the Virginia Capes three weeks and 3,100 miles later. The servicemen of the US Coast Guard Cutter *General Green* (WPC 140) came to the rescue of survivors of the ships *Polyphemus* and *Norland* (the latter ships' men having been rescued by the former before the *Polyphemus* was itself sunk. Not only did the *General Greene* take the exhausted and cold men (it was May) to Nantucket, but it also transported other survivors to Newport for debriefing and repatriation. The other vessels involved in saving the men from these two ships were the Portuguese steamers *Maria Amelia* and *Mirandella* and the US fishing vessels *Hunting-Sanford* and the *Alpha & Estelle*.

Overall, the story of Allied ship sunk by double the number of German submarines off New England is a chronicle of hardship on both sides, and courage and fortitude particularly among those cast into the harsh winter seas. Surprisingly, given the coverage that New York, Cape Hatteras, the US Gulf and the Caribbean have received, there is no single book devoted to the battle zone which was New England for three and a half years. With the help of archives such as those on offer by the SSHSA in Warwick, continued research will allow these dramatic and wrenching stories to be told.

Swedish Bahamian in Azores, *A Praca Magazine*

Being of Swedish descent and raised in the Bahamas, naturally one would not think I might have much connection with Portugal and the Azores. Yet in less than five decades my father settled in a ranchero named *Palmeiras* outside Sao Paolo (mid-1960s), named his house in Nassau Bahamas *Palmeiras* when he said the ranchero, and I ended up traveling to mainland Portugal with a tiny rental car in college to buy pottery for our sister's wedding (1992), then sailing to Horta from Bermuda (2000), studying law in Lisbon (2003), and returning to tour several of the lovely Azores on my own by ferry.

Given the short nature of this essay, I wish to share a paragraph each on the pottery trip and the first Azorean voyage. The pottery trip arose from my father trying to save money. He saves up every airline mile, and offered my older brother John and me tickets from Boston, where we were both students, to Lisbon, if we would rent a car, drive to Coimbra, buy a complete set of 8-piece ceramic dining set with hand-painted floral pattern, package it carefully, and hand-carry it via Boston back home to Nassau in time for my sister's wedding to a Swede.

Of Course, we did! With a sleeping back in a tent and a $19-d-day tiny Yugo car with stick-shift that only he knew how to drive, we took about 5 nights during a cold November Thanksgiving holiday, and within half an hour of landing in Lisbon (via Nice France on Delta) we were speeding through roundabouts in Lisbon aiming for the coast! That night we found a coastal fishing village near Nuovo Porto (Newport), and pitched our tent, sleeping comfortably with the breaking waves nearby. We went to one of the lighthouses on a peninsula which must have been Peniche, took many photos including a black cat under a fishing boat in the old stone harbor. We went to the citadel city of Coimbra, and capped off our outward trip by getting completely lost around Oporto - we must have gone over the bridge in rush hour traffic ten times and finally a restaurant let us use the phone.

A friend of our sister's showed us the family distillery in Oporto - he was a bit nervous about our visit it turned out! We have a lovely time, drove to Coimbra where negotiating a lumpsum purchase, shipment, and payment using a dozen methods and currencies was fine, and capped it off with a long morning at the "*legendary Coconuts*" nightclub (now Casa do Marquês) overlooking Cascais - for starters, dozens of exotic persons were dancing in cages. The day before our flight we took in the beach and café scene of Estoril and maritime museums of Lisbon, returning to college with a lot more baggage then when we left - all for less than $250 each.

The voyage in 2000 to Horta is easier to tell. When I stepped ashore in Bermuda from a well-known racing sailboat, I was not looking forward to the comparatively short trip back to Newport with little pay - I had been doing Bermuda voyages for over a decade and was single and restless. My yacht delivery company was always quietest in mid-summer, so when friend introduced me to another captain a few minutes after I landed on the dock, and he (Mick, an Australian chef) offered me a ride to the Channel Islands off France on a small boat but good pay, I naturally said "Yes!"

The very next morning I took a bus to the other end of Bermuda, sent some postcards, told my parents but sent no other emails, and joined the boat. It was over two weeks before we sighted lovely Horta for the first time. During that time, we grew lots of facial hair, broke the plumbing and fixed it numerous times, caught lots of Dorado and tuna (sushi!), ate over 100 cans of Progresso soup, and experienced the calmest, longest spell I've ever known in 75,000 miles at sea on over 100 vessels. So lazy were we getting that Mick unplugged the Autopilot. One day a young born-again-Christian crew dropped a huge copy of Dostoevsy's book Crime and Punishment on the skipper's head through the hatch and I waited for the cat-o-nine-tails, but Mick was gracious about it. We found lots of turtles on the surface, seaweed, wood and other things floating (flotsam, from land and jetsam, jettisoned off ships as well). We sent an email ahead to friends on land via radio to the NY State training ship Empire State. It was a good trip.

Horta and Faial were magical. Again, I was very lucky. At that time, before big changes only 3 years later with the EU and global prosperity, it seemed to me that so much was affordable. I took out 200 Euros but in 4 nights of generous socializing and a scooter rental never spent all of it. We had delicious squid, painted a (not very creative) sign about our boot *Maruti* on the wall, and I was able to meet a lovely sailing lass from Nova Scotia who was on a boat full of men, one of them the skipper, her father. They invited me to tour the island on scooters and we went to beaches, the old volcano, and several farms. We loved it and I later studied the dream of having a farm in the Azores which I could visit a month a year (still a dream 20 years later). I even learned of direct summer flights from Providence, and I did return to Azores 3 years later.

We were invited into homes, and treated like long-lost family at Peter's Port which is unique to me in the very elegant and old-world way they welcome sailors, as comrades with a hot drink and conversation, not a row of shot glasses, which you find some places in the Caribbean. My funniest, admittedly rather silly memory was the morning I was forced (for the only time in my life) to flee the hotel in a castle in central Horta harbour, by dangling off the balcony, dropping into the garden, running to and down a spiraling staircase and out into the "*Praca*" below into the public streets and for the yacht *Maruti*! You can imagine that in that context I was a bit relieved to have cut the mooring lines and headed towards Europe, though everything was taken in good stride and we have all remained in contact.

LCIS Evolves

The late 80s and early 90s were a period of very significant changes and expansion for the Lyford Cay School. With tremendous support, the school had become a stand-alone institution within the Lyford Cay community, independent of the Club, developer and Property Owners Association. It had grown from a one-room pink schoolhouse centered around a leaking headmaster's cottage to the 1980s campus which was bursting at the seams with students. Saved from demolition in the early 90s through the incorporation and asset purchase led by the Dingman and Dauphinot families, the school was growing into its expanding footprint and mission. More change was still to come as the school evolved to meet the changing and growing demographics of the island in the late 90s and early 2000s.

In the late 90s under the guidance of Headmistress Mary Guthrie, the school expanded its offerings to include middle school grades which attracted many local students. In addition, alumni who had been compelled to study abroad from young ages bucked the trend, returning to Nassau and keeping their children on the island for their schooling. The student body, which numbered only 100 in 1994, had doubled in 1997 with the addition of Grade 9. The faculty grew from 16 to 30.

The Bahamas and Lyford Cay were also growing as a whole. Renowned as a place for the world's cosmopolitan set to stay, visit, or keep their money, Nassau began attracting new residents and investors from around the world. Top-tier financial, legal and career opportunities became available to parents and alumni right outside the gates and the demographics shifted from a migratory, short-term expatriate model to include more families who were full-time citizens and residents.

In order to keep up with this new demographic, school governance knew that it was time to expand. The late Mr. Yves Lourdin was one of the visionaries who helped to guide this transition in the late 90's in his role as chair of the LCIS Board and subsequently as a Governor. Fellow board member and parent, Mr. Peter Vlasov, commented on Mr. Lourdin's impact at this time, "As Chairman of Pictet Bank, Yves knew that in order for the country to continue to grow economically, the school would have to keep up with the world and become a legitimate international school." As the new millennium approached, the community was on the cusp of the next point in its evolution.

The school leadership and community, consisting of parents and some alumni, set about to meet the world that was arriving on its doorstep. Determined not to let the school be defined by the walls of the gated community around them, they set about a quest to reach for international standards in education and achieve recognition well beyond New Providence. Becoming an "International School," went far beyond the diverse global school it already was.

Board members scoured the planet for skilled change agents and world-class administrators who had literally written the code for the emerging international school criteria and, with the introduction of International Baccalaureate (IB) curriculum models, change was afoot. In 2000, a new Principal was appointed, Mr. Thomas Schädler who was recruited from the International School of Stuttgart, and the multi-year application to the acclaimed IB Organization had begun. He brought the stringent standards he was accustomed to in Europe and Asia to marry with the Lyford Cay "island" style.

The school had become one of the first institutions in the Caribbean to be recognized by the European Council of International Schools, the New England Association of Schools and Colleges, and the Council of International Schools. Pets on campus became things of the past, as international norms for safety were adopted and procedures were standardized as part of the various international school accreditation processes.

The IB Middle Years Programme was the first to be authorized in 2003 followed shortly by the Diploma Programme in 2004. This made the school an all-age school with students from Nursery to Grade 12. The school celebrated its first graduating class in June 2006.

Subsequent headmaster, Paul Lieblich (2005–2008), noted that his predecessor "left me a school that was running quite smoothly." On his arrival, he expanded on the recent authorizations to offer the IB curriculums in the secondary school. "We started with a name change to Lyford Cay International School and then to get the school fully accredited by IB by expanding their curriculum to the youngest children. Part of what I was brought in to do was modernizing the curriculum. My having helped to co-author and co-found the Primary Years Programme (PYP) may have helped. PYP learning is based on the student doing inquiry, finding out. The student is learning and collecting information, then they're constructing meaning, they're constructing knowledge." At the time, adding the PYP made LCIS the only school in the Bahamas and one of a handful worldwide to offer all three components of the IB.

Along with curriculum standardization and external accountability, IB accreditation brought openness and ability to interact in the global educational marketplace in new ways. Former student Michele Cove (1971-1978), a board chair and parent, said that the board chose the IB after researching different types of curriculum and came to the conclusion that "for our students who would be going all over the world, the IB would be the best education that we could possibly provide for the kids."

Guidelines for accreditation also meant a lot of expectations. Alessandra Holowesko who was Chair of the Board, a Board Member and parent from 2002-2018 reflects on the school's continued and continuing efforts to reach its highest potential with academics, a diverse student body, systems and facilities. "LCIS is a national resource. Obviously, we've evolved. We've had to institutionalize." She continues, "One of the things that we kept hearing when we were accredited was that we lacked some basic pillars and policies. So, there were some tough periods, because change, by definition, is challenging even if you know it's the right thing. I'm hopeful that it ushered an era of positive change that it is an iteration of what others had done before us to keep the school on a launching pad to bigger and greater things."

With these improvements, the parents of students who did not have the income or inclination to send their children to overseas schools now had a viable option for their children. There was only one issue: persistent space constraints. Former headmistress Mrs. Campbell reflects that as far back as the 80s, the school was affected by business growth when hotels were being developed in Cable Beach. " People liked the small classes, but we didn't have the small classes in every grade. You could be as high as the sky with your education, but if you don't have facilities to give it to them with, they're not going to get it." Lieblich remembers limited facilities affecting the school's potential in his day as well. "I could see right away that the facilities that we had at Lyford Cay were a wonderful environment for primary school, but if we're really going to be serious about secondary school, we were going to have to build a proper secondary school facility."

A committed group of parents and corporate partners donated a large Apple, single-integrated computer and IT internet system, and the former school hall was converted to a facility to house classes for the upper grades. The school also expanded its sports regimen and added programmers and academic classes to retain local talent until it was time for college. This included formalizing an agreement with the Catholic Bishop of the Bahamas to rent space for school sports teams to utilize the St. Paul's Church grounds, the building of a 25m swimming pool and the clearing of land adjacent to the pool to put in a first-class field for all sports. Vlasov is also excited about the school's evolution continuing in the present day, noting the additional resources and space of the new campus: "When you have a proper campus as we will have, it'll make this a lot easier to really develop proper varsity teams."

The theme of growth still influences LCIS today. The school continues its journey to meet the growing needs of a student body and community of locals and expatriates who are attracted to the school because of its reputation for continuous evolution and commitment to excellence. LCIS has earned its way, through several extremely thorough vetting processes, to international recognition, achieving the most with its little footprint. In doing so it may have lost some of its improvisational charm and a pet goat or two. However, strength has remained as the footing of the constant ambition to give students in The Bahamas an education that can stand up to their peers around the world. And the buildings, including those at the new state of the art Upper School campus, still remain pink.

Foreword to Johnson Book *Bahama Tales*

"One theme running through the stories, anecdotes, and truisms of Bill Johnson's new book Bahama Tales is that the author is sharing his life with the reader. Despite all the life-threatening adventures he undertook ashore and afloat from Port-de-Paix to the Cuban mountains to Androsian bights, he survived to tell them. Perhaps no one is as surprised that he survived as William Johnson, Jr.–known to me while growing up as Uncle Bill. Innumerable boys have sat on the pierheads, or on hilltops, and gazed out at seas and valleys that were metaphors for their future. Many have vowed, as Black Mike did in one of the stories, to venture forth, to control his destiny and alter his life's path. Many, however, do not.

As demonstrated in this book, a worthy successor to his Bahamian Sailing Craft, Johnson shares his knowledge on everything from herbal remedies, storm anticipation, water-making, and finding a place of Zen by building a home with one's own hands and interacting with wildlife around us. Bill Johnson is above all a communicator. He does more than promise, he delivers. As a former student of marine biology and keen listener, he has honed his craft for over half a century.

He writes, draws and paints exceptionally well. He achieved a trifecta that few do, by living out the lifeline, then passing it on in words and images. It is noteworthy that his work and perhaps even the craft of wooden boat building fell from the general public's focus. They were revived. In 1993, for example, I sailed a wooden ketch from Panama to New Zealand because the owner did not trust the shipwrights of Europe and the Americas to refit her properly. Yet in the Galapagos, as in the Nassau of my childhood, they were still building wooden sailing craft on the harbor and in driveways on Shirley Street. Now, the Haitian trading sloops of the 1980s and 1990s, Bahamian spongers and fishing smacks have largely vanished from our conscience and from the waterfront, supplanted by ubiquitous fiberglass motorboats. Thanks in part to enthusiasts like Johnson, there has been a significant blossoming of interest in and funding for wooden boat building and maintenance, leading to a new generation of shipwrights.

Bill Johnson is that rare man of action, of sensitivity, able to retain vast depths of detailed knowledge and then relay it. He and a friend were marlinspike sailors, paid to perform hands-on traditional sailing work for yachtsmen and others. Johnson served the US in Korea. He fought Batista in Cuba under Che Guevarra. His family knew racial ostracism first-hand: his beloved maternal grandfather Poppa Neil (Neil Campbell) was half Scots and half Cree Indian, raised in Tennessee, who had the audacity to elope with a full-blooded white girl, and was as a consequence run out on a rail. Johnson makes it clear that he associated with the highest and the lowest, with night workers and the homeless who slept aboard boats in the yard. Johnson and his characters, perhaps honed by the severity of the Great Depression, show benevolence and acceptance of the less fortunate:

In the chapter "The Blue and the Green," Johnson relates that "They were the night people who came at dark to sleep in the empty smack boats and cook on the pitch-pot fires.... 'They're good people,' [the yard manager] said knowingly. 'They're good luck for us here in the yard.'" Johnson has inspired young writers and artists and craftsmen. He was generous with guidance. For one, he has been an immense inspiration to me over nearly 40 years, encouraging me to compose half a dozen books dealing with Bahamian maritime and educational history. He made time to nurture and encourage, sending letters and critiques since before I was a teen. He is also modest about his work–my mother showed him a lovely window view he painted in Exuma years before.

Running his fingers over the brushstrokes, he exclaimed that he did not recall painting it. The theme of listening pervades this book. In the chapter "Childhood in Nassau" he tells of ".... sitting on the seawall pretending to fish and listening to the patrons telling stories [and how] .... a sightless black boy came to the Prince George bar every morning, led there by a family member." That would be Blind Blake. What a pair: a little white boy with ears wide open saving up his stories sitting on a dock beside a poor black boy who could not see but who turned to song to express himself, covering similar material such as the heartbreak of shipwreck. Johnson's work has echoes of other masters as well, from Ernest Hemingway's The Old Man and the Sea to Winslow Homer's watercolor After the Hurricane which could as easily depict Johnson's story about Robert Barr in the chapter called "Seaman." Johnson shares in words what Ruth Rodriguez preserved of Abaco boatbuilding and craftmanship in Out Island Portraits. Johnson has dedicated much of his life to passing onto the present audience what he learned in the past, often a hard way, and lived largely frugally for it, like Father Jerome Hawes in his hermitage on Mount Alvernia Cat Island, who Johnson cites in Bahama Tales.

In his chapter "Generations" is Johnson perhaps ruminating over his own active life when he writes of this exchange across generations? A grandfather explains to a boy that the boy's father "wasn't an idle dreamer; he was a doer and an innovative creator. He caroused a lot to satisfy his carnal obsessions but he left a mark upon the world, that's for sure." Bill Johnson is an extraordinary individual. He has proven himself fiercely determined to live, record and retain a seagoing culture and way of life now kept alive and afloat by vibrant Family Island Regattas. He chose to furrow a modest path, largely away from the limelight, keeping the public informed, crossing not just the Nassau bar outbound numerous times under sail and sheathed only in a thin wooden hull, with no engine; he also crossed the color bar as well as social and class barriers. He was an artist who walked the walk, choosing to keep the company of craftsmen and storytellers on the waterfronts from Port-de-Paix to Cuba, Andros and Ragged Island.

In Bahama Tales Uncle Bill Johnson relays a lifetime of hard-won knowledge and stories which blend the practical with the mysterious. We should enjoy what we learn in these pages. We should learn from them, emulate, and share them. In doing so, we preserve some of the Bahamas' maritime and cultural heritage for other generations, as Johnson so eloquently has within these pages. Eric Wiberg Boston, August, 2019"

TCI In WWII Vineland Survivors Part II

In the Fall 2019 issue of *Astrolabe*, the author detailed the sinking of the Canadian dry-bulk ship *Vineland*, on April 20, 1942 by the German submarine U-154 while it was roughly 90 miles north of North Caicos. The survivors voyaged in three lifeboats until they were picked up by fishermen in the Caicos sloop Emily Conway and towed to Chalk Sound, Providenciales. The story continues as follows . . .

Vineland survivors were initially taken to tiny Salt Cay by fishermen, and hosted by the leading Harriott family and in other homes for several days. After supplies became taxed the men were moved a short distance north, where they staying in guest houses awaiting a north-bound ship. Their erstwhile hosts, the Harriotts, accompanied them to Grand Turk to ensure their onward passage.

The White House on Salt Cay is still owned by descendants of Daniel Harriott. The Harriott family, along with other families who could, took in Vineland survivors until they could be transported back to the United States.

The Harriotts originally emigrated from Bermuda in the 1830s and with profits from salt harvests built the largest building on Salt Cay, wedged between the salt pans and the ocean. Named the White House, it still stands today. Family lore has been well kept by Georgina Dunn Belk. She shared family anecdotes about Captain Ralph Williams and the *Vineland* crew. Her aunt writes that "as children, we saw evidence of the torpedoing of ships by the German submarines when some of the survivors of a torpedoed merchant ship were brought to East Harbour by fishermen who discovered them drifting in lifeboats. Our family, along with other families who could, took them in until they could be transported back to the United States." One of the *Vineland* survivors says that "on Grand Turk the women made clothes for some of us."

Life on shore was bleak, but not as bad as for others surviving wartime winter in Canada: "Ships from the [Canadian] Maritimes had even poorer food to feed the crew and for them a meal ashore at the White House, where [the hostess] would have a chicken killed for them as honored guests, was memorable." The Islanders had become, by necessity, adept at scavenging the bounty of wartime submarine attacks. "Essentially, anything that floated ended up on a beach, and Turks Islanders would come to the door of the White House selling items they had found including life boats, life rafts, oil drums, ropes and tarps, timber and furniture. But the most treasured finds were the crates of dried tinned food, so when large tins of white powder washed up the beach [we] brought it from the salvager. It has the appearance and consistency of porridge. Cooked and eaten for breakfast, it had the consistency of glue but was more or less edible."

One of the Harriotts continues: "We had five seamen in our home from the sunken British merchant ship with supplies that left New York for South America to pick up raw rubber. The rescued men were picked up one afternoon by our fishermen. (Daddy told us later that the men were covered in oil and some were burned quite badly). Five of them were settled into our home after Cleo and I had gone to bed. We didn't know about our guests until we came down the next morning for breakfast and there they were at the dining room table with my father and mother having their morning tea." She continued: "Our torpedoed British seamen stayed with us and the other families four or five days until a ship came for them. We borrowed additional cots from family, and they took over our bedroom upstairs, and we moved into our parent's room and slept on the floor."

Presumably the officers stayed at the White House. Eight of the men were later accommodated at the Louise Ariza boarding house in Grand Turk. Osvaldo Ariza remembers that his mother "put up survivors there" and that "most were Canadian." He remembers hearing that a young boy from the ship said he had been torpedoed three times, and that Captain Williams was fond of telling local school children that the "**V**" in Vineland stood for Victory. Another of Mrs. Ariza's sons remembers one of the cooks aboard the *Vineland*, a man named Hutter. The Arizas and Mr. Hutter remained in contact for years after the war.

During their stay in Grand Turk, Captain Williams managed to get word through to the Naval Officer in Charge in Trinidad. Through that channel, the British Admiralty in Jamaica learned that *Vineland* had been lost. After thirteen days on Grand Turk, or about May 10, a Dutch inter-island passenger ship took them to Curaçao. Their farewell was poignant and a community event. One of the Harriotts recounts how "When arrangements were made for them to return on a ship that came to pick them up, Daddy, Cleo and I went down to the waterfront where all the survivors had congregated, as did most of the men of the island. They were loaded into small boats and taken out to the ship ... and they were returned to the United States where they were to be assigned to another ship carrying supplies to England."

Despite nearly being torpedoed a second time, they made it and were given "shaving equipment, suits, socks, underwear, you name it. And they even gave us money to spend," wrote Mess Boy Ralph Kelly. The harrowing repatriation of *Vineland*'s men was not over. After less than a week in Curaçao they boarded a German-built, Dutch-run ship laden with ammunition, bound to Halifax. Fortunately for all involved, it was an uneventful voyage of fourteen days during which "everybody was scared stiff" wrote Kelly. They didn't arrive back until early June, over six weeks after their torpedoing.

That autumn Ralph Kelly joined the Royal Canadian Navy. He and his brother Captain Charlie remained admired fixtures in the Nova Scotia maritime community. On the same patrol, U-154 sank five ships worth 28,715 tons. Aged 34 at the time (he would live to 1992 and the age of 84), German Commander Walther Kölle "made his career" in a single patrol through the Bahamas. Having earlier survived the scuttling of the *Graf Spee* off Uruguay, he surrendered command of U-154 to Heinrich Shuch after his third patrol, and moved ashore.

Coronavirus Quarantine Story 1 Anthology 2020

Date: March 25 to May 5, 2020
Geographic Location: Maidstone Lake, Vermont
Contributor's name: Eric & Felix Wiberg, of Boston

On learning that my former spouse had caught COVID-19 and also losing a job as a boat captain in Boston, I loaded my Subaru Outback with survival food and equipment, and shared it with friends. A boarding school friend asked: where will you go? Well, although I'd been to Maine, Vermont and New Hampshire looking for a place to escape to and shelter our son from COVID-19, I had neither a place nor a budget, and hotels were closing.

For five weeks we stayed in my friend's lake cabin, mostly carrying our own water for cooking and toilets from a spring. We shopped weekly – our only outing – then every 2-3 weeks after angry locals put up signs saying "Flatties Go Home" and flipped us the bird the store parking lots since we had Massachusetts license plates.

We took long walks and saw fresh moose tracks and were viewed generally with suspicion by anyone we encountered. The only person to introduce themselves to us was a boiler repairman and a man looking for two lost dogs. Felix did remote learning; it was frustrating for him. We worked together on creating new meals, had a freezer full of drinks and meats.

After a while we wore down; a good friend from boarding school lost her husband to COVID-19, they had 2 daughters. The condition of his mom did not improve. We worried a lot.

Finally, one day he had a meltdown over school frustration. We hadn't had resupplies for weeks. The crayfish in the lake were not biting our own chicken in a trap. We did launch a paddle boat and tried to break the ice. Folks called to us from other cabins, but we didn't understand.

We both collapsed in tears and agreed to get the hell out. Since no one had collected garbage for 5 weeks, we strapped 13 bags of it on the roof of the car with a quilt over it and drove to Boston. Suddenly the neighbors noticed us and started driving and walking by a lot more – for the first time. They had called each other to find out who was staying there.

We drove out, not stopping till Boston - over 3 hours. His mom was waiting in her mom's driveway to wave to each other. I went to Boston, meaning I would not be able to see him for weeks. He was and is a trooper.

We are all still here, after over a month in the Northeast Kingdom, Vermont, which didn't have a single COVID-19 case while we there. Our effort to play basketball on an outdoor court at the local school was rebuffed. We could see Canada outside our window. The nearest paved road was over 7 miles. If a delivery truck drove to the lake you could hear it for miles, the ruts and holes on the mud road made it leap so high!

Funnily, we would gladly go back.

Worldly to World Class Lyford Pendragon LCIS History

Growing hand-in-hand with the Lyford Cay community and New Providence, Lyford Cay International School has since burgeoned into something far more cosmopolitan than what the original staff and students may have imagined at that time. Not all grand concepts are flourishing over half a century later, yet Lyford Cay International School and the club are thriving. By adding protocols to passion, Lyford Cay International School has grown into a world-class institution, buttressed by many cultures. The school has achieved the hallmarks of recognition - and of success - from its peers in The Bahamas and internationally with accreditation, and have defended its successes in successive audits.

The expansion period of Lyford Cay International School's history between the fall of 2008 and 2020 is remarkable for its stability of leadership, with the longest-serving principal, Dr. Stacey Bobo, handing over the reins after 11 years to a returning administrator, teacher and parent, Mr. David Mindorff. During her years of service, former principal Dr. Bobo left an indelible imprint on the school. Dr. Bobo, characteristic of a Lyford Cay International School principal, had brought both passion and geographically broad experience to the school to help it reach the next rung.

Dr. Bobo was recruited to focus on the crucial steps of continued accreditation, as well as to develop policies and procedures to further elevate the school, and bring best practices and leadership on education trends to the school and country. She came from the Miami and Los Angeles public school systems, noting that "I wanted to be the head of a high school. So, this-was my opportunity to be international, and the head of a high school, and explore the International Baccalaureate." She adds that upon visiting she was quickly smitten: "Lyford Cay was pretty similar to my school in LA, needing to just be restructured. It's like a little jewel in the West, like the Lyford song."

Dr. Bobo most fondly remembers seeing the 'Lyford Lyfer' photos with students as they grew from their first years of enrollment as a toddler into a high school graduate. "Lyford Cay

International School offers world-class curriculums and programmers," she said. "The preparation the school provides for university and life is unmatched." Under Dr. Bobo, the school grew up like its Lyfers.

Dr. Bobo is very candid about the pitfalls she stumbled upon, and is also glowing in praise for those who helped her and the school. By lending leadership and continuing the trend of board members with financial expertise, Mr. Stephen Holowesko and Mr. Sean Farrington alleviated a great burden. Mr. Frèdèric Bournas as assistant principal, Mr. David Mindorff as an implementer of IB programmers, and Mr. Leiblich before them, all helped to both establish and maintain the school's stellar academic standing, which parents not only expected but demanded.

In 2012, Dr. Bobo assembled a team to present a proposal to the board regarding campus expansion, updating the plan to meet facilities demands and expansion plans which had been in the works for almost a decade. "Working together, and of course keeping the IB programme as the forefront, we started really working on that...The board was really exploring all the options of land and where they could get land from, and they were able to find some land. Obviously, we kept it very quiet. And they were able to find it, fundraise for it, and pay for it by the time we announced it." The next phase in growth would now begin.

Over this past decade, while faculty balanced the daily emphasis on delivering a superb education with the longer-term accreditation process, the board and other school leaders implemented an even farther-reaching plan to construct a new campus for the Secondary School adjacent to the St. Paul's Church. With stronger systems and protocols in place, the school could look forward and outward for growth and secure the physical space needed to both permit expanding to meet demand and also to fulfil the growing vision for students.

Meanwhile a strong and flourishing board of directors and board of governors developed. Alumni Bruce Fernie recalls how he joined in about 2013 - he later became a co-Chair. "I was on the development committee for at least two or three years before they asked me to join the board. I remember distinctly how I first got involved with it. It was a phone call from Alessandra Holowesko that I couldn't clearly hear: it kept cutting in and out and I wasn't exactly sure what I was agreeing to. If somebody's asking you to do something as a volunteer, something to do with school, I've got to say yes." He also recalls how "my mother made a blue cardboard hat for me. This tall hat that I had to wear for the Christmas pageant. All I had to do was go, "Rum-Pa-Pum-Pum," you know? Everyone was thinking I should go, "Dun-da-dun-dun," a few times. That was a good memory. I remember when they built the auditorium, which is now the high school building." Now he is part of helping build a new campus for the school!

With the leadership turnover from Dr. Bobo to Mr. Mindorff, the returning teacher and IB specialist, brought a deep understanding of the school and its constituents as well as new experiences which would influence the school's upward trajectory. Principal David Mindorff was head of the LCIS secondary school for four years before going to lead a private school in China. Originally Canadian, he has also worked in Scotland, Canada, Hungary, and Romania. It took Thomas Stadtler extending the invitation twice before the Mindorff family returned; Mrs. Michele Mindorff works at the school and their four sons are attending or have graduated from LCIS. ".....I enjoy living here and I really like this school. The school is very well led by the board, which is comprised of solid, long-term volunteers. I also really enjoy seeing alumni who have children in school, and am very pleased that we exist to give parents that opportunity."

Mr. Mindorff's specialization is the International Baccalaureate (IB) program, about which he says: "Some expatriate global nomads of the 1960s felt that an education is for preparation for the workplace, and to prepare you to make a contribution, with international mindedness a cornerstone. An IB education both facilitates geographic mobility on the presumption of character education." With only 25% of some 10,000 international schools achieving equivalent approval levels to LCIS, it is clear that the commitment to continuous improvement is a strategy consistently achieved. After the initial sprint was won, Lyford Cay International School is now prevailing on the marathon stretch as well.

Mindorff adds that "We are a US Department of State Office of Overseas Schools-endorsed institution and one of about 37 schools in the world to have all four IB programmers. This is just the beginning. We have successfully completed the first level of the application procedure to join the prestigious Round Square network of independent schools which will benefit the students with new programmers and resources, but also cement the school's position within the leadership ranks of an elite educational landscape."

In order to sustain itself and fulfil its mandates and promises, the school had to expand its footprint. Lyford Cay International School's need to develop its facilities to support the development of opportunities for students made the decision to purchase land and build a new campus for the Secondary School a necessity. As board co-chair Mr. Bryan Glinton put it, "We had not just the opportunity, but the *need*, to develop the leading academic primary and secondary school in the Caribbean, and to provide our students with the most challenging and transformative experience possible."

In 2014, the board and school administrators formulated a new strategic vision to physically transform Lyford Cay International School. With thorough preparation, guidance from local and international architectural firms, and philanthropic support, an inspiring master plan was presented. In early 2016, after careful vetting, the Board of Directors approved not only the new secondary school campus but also a renovated lower school campus.

With expansion providing facilities unmatched in the region, students would now have access to spaces that matched and facilitated the school's high-quality programmers, with purpose-built science and robotics labs, a multi-discipline art studio, maker space, and performance studio, all on the doorstep of the St. Paul's field already leased by the school and with acres of land and a master plan to guide the continued build-out of athletic, academic and other facilities. "The new secondary school campus will allow Lyford Cay International School to teach academics in ways that only the world's top boarding schools now achieve and will give the school state-of-the-art language labs and art rooms," observed Assistant Principal Mr. Bournas.

Concurrently, the school continued to develop the skilled and visionary board which had already brought it so much stability and growth. One hallmark of a strong Board of Directors is that a group of people have enough in common, yet distinct skills, that together provide the school with global, local and professional perspectives. For example, a school board could include educators, finance specialists, lawyers, entrepreneurs, parents, club residents, religious leaders, and specialists in diverse fields including marine science or construction. By its very nature, a board is a collaborative group, with staggered terms, encouraging close cooperation. Just as a board acts independently, that team is being observed and reacted to by other groups, be they administrative leadership of the school, or a board of governors, who might be a layer removed from the action but still contributing.

As many board members and governors are parents of children at Lyford Cay International School, the team can carefully balance the decision-making process of the school with the pulse felt from the classroom and community. They also watch over the financial valves and levers to ensure the school is prudent in financial commitments. Yet, there was also a concomitant need to expand and to take a level of financial risk to do so; their job was to strike that balance for the benefits of the students.

Students will not have to go far to find their new, 17.5-acre campus. Mr. Basil Goulandris, a board governor and father of four Lyford Cay International School students, commented on the interdependence of the school and the community which it serves: "The success of the school has enriched our familial community, and we all have a vested interest in developing a well-rounded and sustainable community." The school has always had value to the students, the families, the community, local businesses and the nation, but that value proposition has been elevated to new heights with the building of its new campus atop the hill near St. Paul's.

While the school developed, implemented and approved it's high-level academic, artistic and athletic offering, it provided a level of learning for a symbiotic global clientele. Lyford Cay International School's mandate is less like a diploma, which can become static, and more like a license, or the many different professional seals of approval, which require constant training, preparation, upkeep and proof of success to be renewed. Mirroring the values of the International Baccalaureate, the school's leadership has thoughtfully chosen this position of constant reflection and evolution, and all who join the institution in that mission must upkeep it rigorously and continuously.

Lyford Cay International School is a community school; but the communities it serves and creates are uniquely local, then national, and global at the same time. Just as mangroves provide a sheltered environment for all manner of marine life to grow and develop skills before entering the ocean, Lyford Cay International School is a natural place to keep learning; somewhere that young talent is nurtured then released into larger communities. Lyford Cay International School now finds itself growing into a new home a bit like a conch, with a lovely, new, appropriately pink shell. With the new campus to move into, one can only imagine the exciting new developments waiting to be accomplished in its 6th decade as the school fulfils its promise to provide a world-class experience for its students and their families, whether they are from right down the road or across the globe.

As the school, and the world it expands into, seeks an equitable and inspiring balance in its student body, course offerings, and opportunities for exploration, education, and inquisitiveness, it is helpful for the community to reflect on what has constituted a balance in the past. In the outset, the first classes were composed entirely of the children of staff at the Lyford Cay Club, including landscapers and Club chairs. Then, what might be called snow-birds added their children, but not year-round. And expatriates with homes west of Cable Beach. Then children from other communities, followed by a reverse flow outwards - to bigger schools in Nassau and overseas. The Early Learning Centre then an upper school were both added so that finally there were Lyfers, as those so admired by Dr. Bobo.

Then the children of alumni enrolled, and bankers from overseas, many of whom made the most of Lyford Cay

International School to settle down, raise families, and stay for the duration. Diversity is so many things, whether financial, geographical, including diversity of thought, appearance, language, and culture. It includes every person affiliated with the school; students, teachers and administrators to board members and governors. Because it permeates ideas, conversations, and is expressed in the arts, music and academia, diversity is fun precisely because it *isn't* easy to quantify. A school which fought so hard and for so long to afford to expand, to build itself out, to diversify its offerings in an increasingly limited footprint, is now, for the first time, having to bifurcate: to split into two campuses, two age subsets, two layers of maturity.

It will be up to the primary campus to feed the newer one, infuse it with inspiring new persons, students, leaders, teachers, and ideas and skills, in sport, in culture, in intellect. And above all the sense of fun, of celebration, the willingness to express charm through wit that a small, supporting, tight-knit and tolerant community provides its members, must be retained. Board member Mr. Vlasov dressing as a janitor, Mr. Millar tickling the piano keys from atop a truck, Mrs. Nelson leading a mother duck and its chicks around the puddles and Mrs. Campbell learning to tackle other campus wildlife, all form an enjoyable daisy chain of lightheartedness which has helped Lyford Cay International School to bridge the Clifton Canal to the gate campus, and now to the new upper school.

Truly, 2020 onwards will be a time in which everyone has enough pasture on which to graze their intellectual and sporting appetites. For the first time since its earliest years, the school has not just one, but two campuses to grow into together. With so many of the hindrances removed, everyone can buckle down to and focus on learning about and adapting to a world in radical flux, in which it is not a luxury but an imperative that all its inhabitants learn to cohabit and collaborate together. Lyford Cay International School and the visionaries who have led it have always been thought-leaders in internationalism. Acceptance and togetherness remain as important as ever as the community strives towards its next major milepost: its diamond jubilee of 75 years.

In 2020, Lyford Cay International School approaches its sixth decade with new leadership; a headmaster who also helped lead the school in earlier times. Mr. Mindorff arrives atop a mountain of planning and work which led to the ribbon-cutting of the extraordinary new campus, which itself has room to grow. With a global pandemic reshaping the ways we are educated and interact with each other and borders closed, our minds are forced to open to new realities. We must all face a sometimes-jarring awareness of the depth of injustices and inequalities suffered by friends and neighbors on a daily basis. Debate seems riven by vast schisms rather than just polite differences. As we thread these uncharted reefs, the emerging generation of Lyfers must not only *face* a new world, but construct one. The result will be the creation of today's students, for there is no manual for these layers of crises.

As we have seen in this history, though, the new generation never acts alone. Mr. Taylor and Mr. Christie emerged from a war-town world which took the lives of 2% of all humans. The Millars and others planted, nurtured and watered the seed of an institution, and ensured that it grew into a sapling. As that small tree teetered from the blast of successive financial hurricanes, the Dingmans, Dauphinots and others held the tree upright, replanted it, and supported it, day and night. Aided by a diverse staff, board, administration, parents and alumni, the school has truly taken root. It stands today not only as an island-wide, national and regional institution but as a school of truly international reputation and accreditation. Like any tree, there are rings in its trunk showing that some years, where the circles are close together, were very lean indeed, and others, with rings wider apart, were times with water aplenty and expansion afoot.

Perhaps the most fitting tree to compare Lyford Cay International School with is the national tree of The Bahamas; the durable *lignum vitae*, which means, literally, *wood of life*. This is the tree chosen in the school's alumni generations garden. Every time a former student of Lyford Cay International School becomes a parent, they plant a tree in the garden, and currently there are 18 trees and families with trees in this lovely grove. It has been central to the economy of The Bahamas since May of 1650, when William Sayle and the Eleutheran Adventurers helped save

Harvard College by shipping ten tons of it and braziletto wood to Boston, and it became the college's second-largest gift. The tree appears crouched, poised for anything, enabling it to survive myriad hurricanes. Known for its versatility of uses, *lignum vitae* has been used to extend Pete Seeger's banjo, is in the belaying pins on the USS *Constitution*, and the shaft bearings of the polar submarine USS *Pampanito*, Master clockmaker John Harrison helped to determine Longitude with it, enabling more voyages from the UK to the Americas. *Lignum vitae* appears in calypso songs by Trinidadian Sam Manning in the 1920s, and *Love in the Time of Cholera*, by Gabriel García Márquez, in 1985, and the Merlin's wand in *The Once and Future King* was made of the wood.

Like *lignum vitae*, the students who have entered Lyford Cay International School since the 1950's have not only the grace and elegance, but they graduate with the inherent strength of the tree. Alumni globally have proven that when encouraged and prepared by a community strengthened by those before it, the students emerge capable of contributing to the larger world in multifarious ways, across a wide spectrum from academically inquisitive to scientific and sporting. The resilience which Lyford Cay International School's demanding curriculum and challenging process inculcate in those accepted to study there has ably equipped graduates. The school has produced and continues to develop students of the highest caliber. Equipped with an extraordinary new campus, these graduates who will contribute significantly to the third generation of the school.

To understand the future of Lyford Cay International School, it might be worth considering what the alumni are doing and where, globally, they are transferring their skills. Interviews for this book over six years took place on a construction site in Malaysia, a high school campus in the United Arab Emirates, an art gallery in Cable Beach, dive shop on Harbour Island, a school in Australia, the plush carpeted floor of a club overlooking Central Park, and in private homes in Switzerland, Nassau, of course Lyford Cay, and hotels in Boston and beyond. Lyford Cay's alumni are adjusting to a wildly unpredictable pandemic which is equally redolent of opportunities. The importance of collaboration has never been more key while at the same time more challenging.

Mr. Mindorff provides his perspective on the school bridging into a new era with a new campus, saying the school will be connected with old fashioned foot traffic, as well as modern social networking. He appreciates the school's tradition of having Founder's Day, meaning E. P. Taylor, with the apostrophe in front of the "S," becoming Founders' Day with the apostrophe after the "S:" "I think that that's a great change." He sees the future in the students, which the school hopes to expand to 600 in years ahead, leading the way to a rapidly evolving western community. He emphasizes the community's "...connectedness to our alumni. It is key they know that when you attend LCIS for a range of years, that makes you an alumnus, just as much as if you graduated from high school or been a *Lyfer*. Someone who left our school takes the values that we've inculcated to a new place."

These alumni will harness what they learned at Lyford Cay International School, and what they are continuously learning, to not only share it far and wide, astride and beyond the 27,000 or so miles around the Earth. Not only that, but they and their children, like the Hawksbill turtles close to extinction when the school was founded, have rebounded, and return just a few times in their lifetimes to plant future generations.

Looking into the future, Principal Mindorff sees a community with fewer boundaries, with more space to grow, physically, musically, linguistically, athletically with court sports, and multi-nationally. "Rather than being an isolated school, we will take our message to inspire excellence, and make it more international. LCIS will be far more active seven days a week, and contribute to life in the west, as a community-based school. We will be a green school, and contribute to the pedestrianism of the west: we will be two campuses with one school, in the heart of a larger community." Going forward, LCIS's expansion will allow the community to expand.

TCI Astrolabe: Fauna in the Bahamas in WWII

What is remarkable about the sinking and the loss of the *Fauna* off the Turks & Caicos Islands is that her destination *was* the TCI, and her survivors spent nearly three weeks essentially circumnavigating the Islands in a lifeboat and a local sailboat over the course of an impressive 300 miles!

The *Fauna* was a Dutch 1,272-ton steamship constructed in 1912 by Rijkee and Company, N.V. of Rotterdam. Her only owners were the KNSM, or Royal Dutch Steamship Company, of Amsterdam. By 1942, long after the Netherlands were overrun by the Germans, the firm was being operated out of 25 Broadway in New York City. Her dimensions were 262 feet long, 36 feet wide and 16 feet deep. An 800-i.h.p. triple-expansion engine drove a four-bladed propeller which boosted the ship at 9.5 knots.

Fauna was a small ship whose cargo reflected her size. She carried 5 barrels of gasoline and 15 barrels of kerosene (presumably for the generators on the small island of Grand Turk where there was a salt works), and a full general cargo including matches, cement, machinery and flour. The 20 barrels of gasoline and kerosene were stowed on deck. The master was also entrusted by the British with 22 bags of mail plus 1 bag of registered mail.

A crew of 29 men was under the command of Captain Jacob den Heyer, a Dutchman. Four of the crew were British, including a 42-year-old "servant" named John White; Othniel Dickenson, aged 46, sailor; Ben Eve, 49, sailor' and Sam Sanny, a fireman, 25, of 92 Atlantic Avenue, Brooklyn, New York. Of the 25 Dutch men on board, 2 of them were gunners manning a 3-inch gun aft: Wilhelm Johann Kervezee, aged 29, and Tonnis Bierling, aged 42. Some of the crew helped man the guns as well.

The *Fauna* left New York on May 6, 1942 destined for Grand Turk, followed by a stop in Port au Prince, Haiti, where she was to deliver some Lend-Lease cargo. The ship was under orders of the British Naval Control and took some 11 days to cover roughly 1,300 miles. She was less than a day from her destination on May

17 when she was found and intercepted by U-558 under Günther Krech in the Caicos Passage.

The position of the subsequent attack was 22.00ºN (or 22.10ºN) by 72.35ºW (or 72.30ºW) which is east of Mayaguana Island, Bahamas, west of Caicos Island, and just 10 miles or so north of Northwest Point, Providenciales, in the Turks & Caicos. The passage is some 30 miles wide at this point. The Captain described it as "very narrow (about 10 miles), and ... not generally used as a shipping lane or route." This is an unusual statement given that the *Fauna* was, according to the position given, in the Caicos Passage, a deep, wide shipping channel commonly used to gain access between the Windward Passage and the open Atlantic Ocean. Captain den Heyer may simply have been referring to the ship's proximity to land, which was only 10 miles.

At seven minutes before midnight the men on watch were no doubt anticipating their eminent relief from duty. The ship's course was east–northeast and speed ten knots. It was a clear night with a slight swell and no wind to speak of. Without the moon, visibility was one to one-and-a-half miles. There were three lookouts on station, one on the forecastle up forward, one manning the gun aft, and a third on the bridge.

Günther Krech began his first patrol into The Bahamas area aboard the U-558 on May 15. The *Fauna* was struck in a channel so narrow—only ten miles wide—that the survivors supposed that the sub must have been waiting there for resupply. Krech was tracking the *Fauna* from seaward, or the ship's port side to the north. Suddenly a single torpedo pierced the merchant ship's Number Two cargo hold, roughly two feet below the water line. The explosion ignited the cargo of matches stowed there. The large hole blown in the *Fauna*'s side immediately flooded the number two and soon after the number one cargo hold, then the engine and boiler rooms. Hatch covers from both holds were blown into the air, the radio shack and the ladder to the bridge were destroyed and the port-side motorboats were knocked clear of the ship. There was no opportunity to send a radio distress message or to man and train the guns.

Given the circumstances, the men behaved with restraint commended by Captain den Heyer, particularly Third Mate Jan Noordveld, Third Engineer Jan Rab, sailors Nicholaas Plugge and Maarten de Jong, and Wilhelm Johann Kervezee, a gunner, who "stayed on board to see everything clear" and in doing so perished. Soon the *Fauna* was listing to starboard at an alarming 26º, then 30º. The men on watch grabbed personal papers and some cash and made their escape. Within ten minutes, 27 men had leapt into the water or clambered into the only remaining lifeboat—the one from starboard. Just before midnight, and only five minutes after the attack, the men in the water saw U-558 approaching from the starboard beam. Krech brought the submarine to within three quarters of a mile, kept it darkened and circled the bow of the stricken ship. When U-558 made it to the port quarter, aft of the beam, it switched on its searchlight to help the men in the water make it to the boat.

Then the sub circled the lifeboat and asked for the name, tonnage and destination. One officer came down to the deck to do the questioning, which he did in English. Den Heyer responded in German, but still there was a misunderstanding about the spelling of the *Fauna*, and the Germans ended up writing "*Towa*" instead of the correct name. After this brief interrogation the sub motored through the wreckage and then set off in a northeasterly direction, submerging as it did so at five minutes after midnight, twelve minutes after the attack.

As the lifeboat set about gathering survivors from the water, *Fauna* performed a death-roll. A heavy explosion rocked the ship, on which six men remained—this was possibly a boiler exploding when the sea water hit it. At first the ship stayed on course, but then it veered to starboard. Finally, after roughly 50 minutes, at 43 minutes past midnight on May 18, the *Fauna* rolled over to port, the side with a gaping hole in it, and sank quickly. The Germans did not attempt to board the blazing wreck. Of the six men who remained on board, four of them—Noorduelt, Rab, Plugge, and de Jong—managed to escape and swim to the lifeboat. Keverzee, of the Royal Dutch Navy, who had been born in Rotterdam on August 22, 1912 and was 29 years old, drowned, as did G. C. van Baardwyk, aged 40, a trimmer from the engine room. Both men were seen on deck by their crewmates just before the sinking. Captain den Heyer observed, "It is believed they went back below, and were trapped."

Once they had collected all 27 survivors, the men set out for the nearest land. Strictly speaking this would have been Northwest Point, Providenciales, however winds and currents pushed the lifeboat west and south. As a result, they managed to make landfall on the unpopulated island of West Caicos, at 11:00 AM on Monday, May 18. There appears to have been a settlement named Yankee Town near Lake Catherine, but den Heyer and his men "found no people there."

The same day, the lifeboats set off to the north, and after 14 miles they rounded Northwest Point and headed southeast, looking for signs of habitation. While they were underway, the boats were discovered by two local fishing boats. Captain Ralph A. Ewing, owner and skipper of the schooner *Sister E.* (also known as *The Sisters*), was the first one back to shore at 1:00 AM on Tuesday, May 19. The local craft, weighing 10 tons and built in Blue Hills in 1922, was loaded with roughly half of the *Fauna* crew.

According to historian Kendall Butler, "the Ewing family was prominent in High Rock, Blue Hills, Providenciales. Hilly Arthur Ewing [was a] boat builder." Doris Ewing was nine years old at the time and remembers her father Captain William Ewing returning to Blue Hills aboard his boat *The Flirt*, with the balance of *Fauna*'s survivors. She says that "the boats used to go down by Inagua and the Caicos Passage to look for food and clothes floating in the sea that came from torpedoed ships." In this instance the Islanders discovered more than they expected in the jetsam of war.

The men were found in poor condition—cut up and bruised—and several of them were naked and covered in oil. The children were kept at a discrete distance from them. Captain Ralph enlisted the help of his wife to clean them up, and they would have enlisted the help of the island midwife, who was the senior caregiver in the community. Doris Ewing relates that her "mother and aunts and other men and women, from North-side, bandaged them up and fed them." Local historian Sherlin Williams relates that "The midwife was the only healthcare giver to be found in each of the three settlements . . . No young women in the entire island during those days would have been allowed to be exposed to naked men. Only mature persons in age bracket of the wives of boat owners, whose children were already grown, would have been in direct contact in their condition."

General Greene

From all the vessels sunk by German U-boats in the North Atlantic during World War II, 649 Allied sailors were rescued and landed in 16 ports in New England. While more of these survivors were landed in Boston than in other ports (268), it was Nantucket that received more survivors than any other port in southern New England, well ahead of Newport (36), New Bedford (27), and Woods Hole (23). The ninety merchant sailors landed at Nantucket all arrived over two weeks in the spring of 1942, rescued by the U.S. Coast Guard from four [doomed?] merchant ships. Because of the exigencies of war, these men mostly arrived on island in darkness and were given round-the-clock security details, but they were warmly welcomed by the islanders during their brief stays before being whisked to Newport by the US Coast Guard Cutter *General Greene*. Among the rescued were thirty-three Chinese men and ten British West Africans. Ivy-League volunteers with the American Field Service who ran the lifeboats like yachts. Some Nantucketers remember seeing them shuffling through town, and a steward named Woyle remained in the hospital.

Although few American civilians appreciated it at the time, the lightship *Nantucket*, stationed 40 miles southeast of Nantucket, was like a lamp attracting both Allied mariners and their predators. German U-boats struck Allied shipping hard in this vulnerable area beginning in 1942 continuing until driven to other waters by intense U.S. naval and air countermeasures like air cover and more surface defences and convoying Nantucket was a lifering for friends afloat when they were cast adrift, but for the balance of the were they were never sunk at such high rates as mid-1942. The plucky naval vessel which habitually towed the empty Allied lifeboats back to port under was led by Lieutenant (jg) P. F. Shea of New York. A US Coast Guard cutter under navy control, it was named *General Greene* and Lt. Arthur Gibbs, whose younger brother Maurice caught glimpses of survivors on the island, served aboard her that year. Just a week before the first survivors were landed, three vessels from Nantucket's Coast Guard Auxiliary and their crews were taken into the Coast Guard Reserve. The vessels were the *Dancing Lady, Alice A.*, and *Squam*, and the men, led by George Andrews, commander; H. Brooks Walker, vice-commander; and Charles Whelden, junior vice-commander; were Balfour Yerxa, Everett Chapel, Arthur McCleave, Manuel Reis, Irving Bartlett, and Hollis Burchell. Overall there were four Coast Guard station on Nantucket at Brant Point, Coskata, Madaket, and Surfside. Protecting the island's shores was an island-wide effort, touching everyone, everything and everywhere.

The British motor ship *Peisander* was torpedoed and sunk southeast of Nantucket by U-653 under Gerhard Feiler on 17 May 1942. Days later, a wary Allied ship named *Plow City* approached the captain's lifeboat, fled, and was quickly sunk by U-588 under Victor Vogel. Then the British shp *Baron Semple* offered to take the men from two of the three *Peisander* boats, but the shipwrecked sailors voted against being cramped passengers to South Africa in favor of a chance at adventure in sailing to America. It was "...a decision which surprised everyone aboard the steamship." Harvard Professor Stilgoe in his study of lifeboats relates how at 3 a.m. on 24 May "....an able-bodied seaman... heard what he thought might be a cow mooing. He woke Frank Brown, ...commanding the boat, who soon discovered the sound to be that of surf breaking on Nantucket Island beaches. A few hours later, trailing a pail astern on a line to slow their progress through the surf, the castaways aboard the double-ended life-boat arrived on the sand unharmed after six days...."

Brown's boat, with 23 men spent from dawn to just after mid-day slowly being pushed westwards along the coast until they arrived off Madaket, and landed at about 1 p.m. Boat Six with 20 men under engineer John Wilson, 40, followed close behind. They were picked up at 1.30 p.m. and towed by *CGR 37*, then quickly handed over to the motor-lifeboat *CGR 3828* based at Madaket. Together, the rescue boats towed the first two lifeboats and 43 survivors, to Brant Point Coast Guard Station, arriving at 5.40 p.m. The Red Cross, already busy with injuries sustained by a large influx of servicemen, met the *Peisander* survivors, and they "were taken to Bennett Hall, where they received medical attention, food and clothing. Most of them were suffering from exhaustion, and needed rest and refreshment only, but three were taken to Nantucket Hospital for special care, x-rays, etc."

At 9 a.m. on 24 May the 18 men in Boat Two under Captain Shaw heard breakers on the port bow. Deducing they had drifted south onto Nantucket Shoals, Shaw shaped a course northeast for eight miles. At 5 p.m. two planes saw them and circled around the lifeboat. The fog set in thickly, then darkness. At 1.40 p.m. the cutter *General Greene* was ordered from Newport to their aid and pulled into Nantucket Harbor for a few hours that night, until 3 a.m. At daylight on 25 May the planes returned and dropped supplies in two packets of First Aid, tomato juice, American pemmican, or meat paste of Native American origin, and chocolate. Second steward Doyle could only swallow liquids, his teeth had become so painfully bad. Shaw kept some of the boat's emergency rations and complained that even his dog would not eat them!

Finally, the fog cleared and they were discovered by *General Greene* at 9.45. a.m. on the 25th *En route*, the rescuers attacked a suspected U-boat. Given the shallow water (the lifeboat was at anchor) it could not have been a U-boat. The depth-charges most likely bounced off the sea-floor and lifted the cutter's stern over ten feet out of the water, causing Shea to consider abandoning ship. The *Peisander* men were then picked up at 10.45 a.m. Shaw said they "were treated very well... and those who required medical treatment were attended to." A *Greene* officer said "some of them were in poor condition and had to be assisted from the lifeboat." Just 54 minutes after arriving at Brant Point at 4.06 p.m. the *Greene* "un-moored and stood away from dock. Received two life boats for transportation." Sixty *Peisander* men and three boats landed in Newport.

Only British Second Steward Leonard Woyle, 37, was put ashore for hospitalization. The poor fellow had lost his false teeth overboard in the attack. When provided a complete set by the Red Cross, he wrote them a grateful letter from New York. Headquarters also commended the Nantucket branch. Woyle later took a ferry to the mainland. Captain Shaw was proud of the derring-do of his men in the other boats in refusing the *Baron Semple*. As with *Plow City* and *Polyphemus*, rescuing ships were often quickly sunk themselves. In November that year he was honored with a King's Commendation for "...brave conduct when their ships encountered enemy ships, submarines, aircraft or mines."

The Norwegian motor tanker *Norland* was attacked and sunk after a fight with U-108 under Klaus Scholtz east of Bermuda on 20 May, 1942. Another Allied ship, the large passenger liner *Polyphemus* rescued 14 survivors of the *Norland* before it too was sunk on 27 May by August Rehwinkel in U-578. *Polyphemus'* Boat Three held seven *Polyphemus* and three *Norland* men under Dutch Third Officer Jan Dykdrenth. Germans had a stronger presence off the US coast at the time, and two U-boats provided aid to the men in the lifeboat before they reached shore. Dietrich Borchert on U-566 gave the men water, a course to Nantucket, his last name, and the chance to stretch their legs and walk the U-boat's deck. The following day U-593 under Gerd Kelbling logged that a "life boat cutter with sail from Dutch *Polyphemus* passed. A can of bread and a flask of rum [was] handed over." They were 35 miles off Siasconset and it was very rough.

On 4 June the *Greene* raced from Newport looking for *Polyphemus* survivors. At 5.45 p.m. on the 5th they found Boat Three, assisted them aboard and brought they and their boat to Brant Point. Robert Mooney relates how "the Red Cross called for volunteers, and scores of nurses and volunteers responded to help out. This ...left a lasting memory with all who attended them." Mooney knew whereof he spoke; his father was the island's police chief and mother head of the Red Cross. The men spent the weekend in Bennett Hall, and on "Sunday, all ten men filed into the

Congregational Church to morning service through the door connecting with Bennett Hall, thus keeping within bounds. In the afternoon they were taken, still carefully guarded, to a baseball game which they thoroughly enjoyed."

One must assume that "keeping within bounds" and "still carefully guarded" refer to military security precautions: they were all Allies, three Dutch officers, a British radio operator, three Chinese crew, (one from Canton the other from Shanghai), two Scottish teenagers (both named Campbell) and a 22-year-old Scottish Ordinary Seaman. A curious boy named Maurice Gibbs tried to see more of the survivors, however they were kept quite sequestered. "Although townspeople were asked, and did, respond quickly with clothing and bedding, the survivors were kept somewhat isolated. I do remember my mother taking what little we could give [to them]. However, she only went to the door of Bennett Hall." *Norland* survivors were interviewed by US Navy officials, but were so confused over both submarine attacks that they "were... often mixing the details" off different attacks. Today this might be attributed to post-traumatic stress disorder, or PTSD.

On 31 May the British ship *Mattawin* under Captain Charles Sweeny, 47, passed Nantucket *en route* from New York to Cape Town, and passed *Nantucket Lightship* at dawn, as instructed. After dropping the pilot, a US plane circled overhead, then that night U-553 under Karl Thurmann sank her. The men sent SOS messages which both German and US navies received. Boat Three held 19 men under Third Officer Geoffrey Griffiths, 20, which was left behind as 52 of their shipmates were rescued by steamships or landed at Nauset. After a week adrift, on 6 June the indefatigable *Greene* was sent to a spot where a plane had dropped food to about 20 men in a lifeboat off Nantucket, but blimp *K-3* lost contact in the all-enshrouding fog.

The survivors were discovered southeast of George's Bank just after 10 a.m. on Sunday 7 June. Less than half an hour later the boat was alongside and all 19 Allies were taken aboard, with their names and ranks recorded. The *Greene* was back under way for Nantucket before 11 a.m., and arrived at Steamship Wharf just after midnight. The *Mattawin* men were not permitted ashore,

389

since a few hours later, at 5.25 a.m., the seven *Polyphemus* and three *Norland* survivors padded down the empty wharf to board the *Greene*. They were all bound for the navy base in Newport.

This group of 29 men covered the widest cross-section of Allies who landed on Nantucket. There were 15 merchant crew and a British gunner from the *Mattawin*. The three American AFS volunteers were Edward LeBoutillier, Ronald Gubelman (MIT, 1922), and Coffin Colket Wilson, III. Seven of the men were from British West Africa, including Johah Peter of Monrovia, 25, who suffered a head wound when thrown into the sea from his lookout perch in the attack, and Captain Kwesi Blankson, 26, cleaner, from the Gold Coast. They hailed from Australia, Canada, China, Gold Coast, Guinea-Bissau, Liberia, Netherlands, Nigeria, Sierra Leone, UK, and the US. Shea noted with satisfaction that "this accounts for all the *Mattawin* lifeboats known to have been launched." The survivors were very pleased to learn that all of their shipmates had also made it ashore, many on nearby Cape Cod.

By the evening of its return to Newport the *Greene* was on to its next assignment, standing by *Empire Woodcock*, disabled off Brenton Reef. There would be no more Nantucket rescues for her during the war. The following day Lieutenant Shea was sent for inpatient treatment at Naval Hospital Newport, reasons not given. He had done stellar duty.

Though it is clear that by providing escorts and regulating their movements carefully, islanders (or at least the military) were wary of their foreign guests, the seagoing people who populate Nantucket were quick to aid distressed colleagues from the waves. Without hesitation they scoured their thin cupboards and threadbare drawers to provide for the transients. This enabled the mariners, whose skills were much in demand, to return to their jobs in the hiring halls of various ports and on the bridges and in the pantries and engine-rooms of Allied ships. There they took the war to the enemy, one ball-bearing and cup of flour at a time.

Through their humanity and unspoken empathy, the skilled mariners who pulled them ashore on Nantucket using tiny dories and large cutters also provided the survivors with something intangible – dignity - during an ignoble episode. For the survivors, it was a traumatic time: identities were mix-mashed, and foe (not friend) popped out of the depths multiple times - some *Norland* men witnessed four or more U-boats between sinking and shore. Not only were the officials ashore confused, but survivors themselves were. For a brief time, the world could see how Nantucket laid out its welcome for men of eleven nationalities from five continents. As Mooney put it, "....our shoal waters permit so few of these disasters to come to us. But if and when they come, we are ready to meet them."

No other US community had spent so many years voyaging amongst foreign lands from the Arctic to the tropics, and working hand-in-hand with polyglot mariners than Nantucketers did in the global whaling and sealing voyages of the 1700s and 1800s. In the spring of 1942 Nantucket townsfolk and beachcombers alike drew on their cosmopolitan outlook and bedrock faith, using it to benefit strangers on their shore. While it is true none of the Allied survivors filled a grave or a baby's crib as a result of their visit, for a while Nantucket's proud elbow jutting into the North Atlantic provided just the roost for desperate sailors to latch onto with the help of the island's life-savers and the Coast Guard. That was enough to save nearly a hundred lives, allowing them to keep fighting the Battle of the Atlantic, the longest continuously fought engagement.

Story of The *Gertrude H.*, Tulip Tree Publications Semifinalist honors, 2020, Stories That Need to Be Told

I was a yacht captain in my early 30's in Rhode Island when a stranger called; said he'd heard I was the man for a job in the Dutch Antilles. I'd just returned to Newport from half a decade in the Asia-Pacific. My main gig was helping people who owned sailboats but didn't have a lot of experience or time. They would pay me on short notice to do anything from shift the boat across a harbor or from one to another, and crewing and sailing large yachts thousands of miles. Ironically, summer was my quietest time. Most owners are so determined to just enjoy their boat without interference that they refused to call for help in July and August. So I was idle.

The local lobsterman was named Ted, also single and in his 30's. We hadn't met, and I didn't know him; I had only fished commercially one day – in Maine – and it was not a success (I talked too much to be invited back). Ted said he had an unusual project. His ex-girlfriend owned and lived aboard a boat in Aruba that had a broken motor. She need help sailing it back to Newport, or at least to the United States. The problem was that all her money and effort was tied up in a drunk abusive local man considered her boyfriend. After several weeks intervening with her family and Ted, even after I coached her on how to sail out of port without a motor, we all realized that the dreadful situation was not going to change, so long as he demanded everything she had – and continued to receive it. Stockholm Syndrome was beyond my job description. We all realized that even my sneaking in the take the boat back didn't solve issues like her repatriation, and the underlying issues. In fact, it might leave her homeless and more vulnerable.

Towards the end of August, Ted called again, this time tacitly agreeing that she had wasted my time and expertise with no reward. As a compromise, Ted offered that if I showed up the next day – my birthday – at 4.30 am and fished lobster offshore till late night, he would pay me handsomely, and our ledger made clean. I agreed.

Before sunrise, I parked my Block-Island-bought rusted junker of a car at the fish piers, and met with some young men. One of my crew had on his ankle a wide metal probational tracking bracelet for child support (he was just out of Rogers High School), and others were more seasoned. It took about 3 hours to get offshore. As a kind of guest, while the others slept, on the trip out and back I was expected to entertain the captain, help keep him awake. The day's fishing was characterized by excellent weather, a bite by a lobster to my finger (my role was bander), and lots of very loud music, fast-moving lines, traps, hooks, tattoos, cigarettes, hosing the deck, and spinning motor drums with lots of pressure on them, and swearing. Then, about sunset, we headed back to port without injury or damaging too much tackle.

An hour into the 3-hour trip to Newport, it was about 9 pm. I was tired and running out of stories and questions, I took a risk with my new companion, and asked him why his boat was named *Gertrude H.*? The inference was that, given we were both young and single, why didn't he consider a spicier name more apt to attract the ladies? I settled in as he launched into the story of the *Gertrude H.*, straight from Ted, her captain and owner.

On or about August 31, 1954, in what may have been Hurricane Carol (700 buildings and 17 persons lost in Rhode Island), the US Coast Guard Station Castle Hill, in Newport, sent out an all-persons broadcast, essentially stating:

"Calling all stations, from Point Judith to Sakonnett and Gay Head to Nantucket: All seaborn vessels are to seek shelter ashore immediately. A storm, the speed and ferocity of which was not anticipated, is upon us. The Coast Guard is unable to deploy its boats to rescue you. Repeat: seek the nearest and best shelter, and remain there. God speed, and good luck. This is the Coast Guard standing by."

Something like that. The call was made un the clear, so that anyone with a radio could hear it, and any boat which could hear it headed for port, or bay, or beach. That was about 3 pm.

Hours passed.

About 9 pm, with the full impact of the hurricane enveloping them, there came a scratchy, but audible radio transmission on the same frequency. Like that by the Coast Guard, it was addressed to no one in particular, and everyone at the same time; it was personal, in an impersonal way.

"This is the *Margaret M.*, the *Margaret M.* We are south of the Sakonnett River, and there's no way we can make it to port. Tom and I are going to head for Second Beach, and try to land there. Figure we'll get to the middle of it about midnight. *Margaret M.*, over and out."

Those that heard it could only have thought:

"There's the voices of dead men talking. They don't stand a chance in a 38-foot wooden fishing boat, with all that gear, lines and traps, on that mile-long beach. If they make it to the surf line, the boat will implode onto them, or tangle them up and crush them on they way in. They are doomed, plain and simple, and must have known it when sending that plaintive message."

393

Hours went by.

About 11.30 pm *Margaret M.* with skipper Zane and mate Tom, entered wide Sachuest Bay, towards Second Beach, on the southeast corner of Aquidneck Island, on which Newport sits.

They made it most of the way up the bay, almost to the surf line in fact, when the hull of the *Margaret M.* first hit the shallow sand of the bottom. It was a very high tide, with massive rollers for waves, and though Zane and Tom, resignedly waited to be crushed, the hull held. Gradually, they bumped towards the beach as one unit.

It was just before midnight.

Soon the decision loomed: leap and risk being drowned in the surging waves, or stay on the boat and hope to see sunrise unbroken, un-mangled and alive.

They didn't have to decide.

With no warning, two large, white lights flashed on in the dunes ahead and above. Soon, above the howling wind in the rigging which blew sand in clouds inland, the men could hear a jerking, clunking, mechanical noise. It was like a beast dragging metal blocks across a padded floor: slowly and awkwardly.

Puffs of black smoke raced past the lights, which also jerked up and down, but remained above the fray, equidistant from each other. Knowing it was not the sound marine diesels make, Zane and Tom guessed that it was the sound of a tractor, as on that uninhabited stretch there were no other boats, trucks, or trains. They were in the navel of a crescent of miles of untrammeled dunes. The lights and the noise lurched down the beach from above, crossing an apron of sand hundreds of feet wide, towards them. Soon it reached the frothy white bands of the surf.

Cupping a hand to his mouth, holding his flannel winter hat on the other hand, his whitish hair whipping forward, Zane leaned over the swinging bow and yelled:

"Who goes there? What are ye?"

The tractor swooped into the surf line and turned sharp left. In what moonlight there was, this exposed the two large wide rubber rear tires, and a bowl of a metal seat. Thereupon perched a thin, wispy, white-clad figure, right hands on the long metal levers, left upon the wheel. As soon as the bow of the *Margaret M.* was aligned with the tires of the tractor, and not before, came a high, level and determined call that reached Zane and Tom.

"It's Gertrude, Zane! Now get off the boat, and hook the chain to it, quick-like!"

And he did; Zane leapt off the bow, ran to stern of the tractor, and hooked that chain into the nose ring on the front of the *Margaret M.* that was sunk deep through the hull for just such emergencies.

And once they did, Zane's wife Gertrude set that tractor in gear – the tractor she ran down to the neighboring farm to borrow in nothing but a night gown and a winter coat. She then drove the same tractor through the farms of Middletown to the back of the dunes of Second Beach and found her husband, his mate, and their boat, upon which the family so depended.

She pulled that *Margaret M.* briskly, if jerkily, all the way out of the surf, propeller through the sand and all, into the base of the dunes, saving the lobster boat from certain destruction.

So Zane had a new name for her.

......Steering the wheel of the *Gertrude H.*, that August night in 2000, towards a birthday party which I had missed (and smelled far too bait-fishy for anyway), Ted said to me without looking over:

"And that is how this boat got her mane, and not anybody's going to change it. Not even the person who buys it from me."

And they haven't. She lies in Newport still.

I understood.

Not only did I understand, but the story makes me cry every time I tell it.

You see, as a young teen, I went to a boarding school overlooking Second Beach. And for two years I was somewhere I couldn't escape from, but wanted desperately to. I needed, I called for, I so wanted an angel to find me, to throw the big lights on, and make the monsters go away, to illuminate my fears, banish my darkness with lights, with power, with decisiveness.

That person was my mother.

Only, my *Gertrude H.* never arrived.

395

Coronavirus Journal Entry 2 Anthology

Date: Monday, 21 September, 2020

Place: Eagle Hill, East Boston

Weather: temperature high 50's, bit overcast, fall in New England

Events: A bit of a scramble from 6.30 am to get our 13-year old out of bed and fed with some Corn Flakes and fresh water, but we managed to get he, the book bag, a warm shirt, long pants, a pair of faded Vans lace-less sneakers in the Subaru Outback with a kayak rack and up 40 minutes to his school on the border of Beverly and Manchester by the Sea, North Shore. On the drive back I diverted to Nahant and took a look at the tip of that peninsula, where Northeastern University has a marine lab in complex of naval defense towers and tunnels (I used my training in maritime law to ensure I adhered to most of the relevant laws for a pleasant coastal walk and was not bothered or ticketed!)

Events in Boston: A car carrier ship left Charlestown and since we live in the loft of the old schoolhouse with amazing views from Boston Harbour Islands to Everett, I filmed its departure for Haiti with used cars and posted it on Instagram, Twitter, Facebook, and Linked-in. Fun! It was my first Korean car carrier and had the name "*Asian Lady.*"

Edited a 1,000-page encyclopedic history of Bahamas in World War II, which is a 11-year slog but we are a few days from publishing. Tomorrow I'm going camping at Miles Standish State Forest with my girlfriend, so I wanted to be up to speed and send my editor in Quetta, Pakistan, who is drying out from floods, my draft.

"Bought" an inflatable Avon Dinghy, about 25 years old, from the side of the street (put $50 in the mailbox) to encourage our son to get out more, and so I put that in the back of girlfriend's car to Charge Pond and its maiden voyage

Wanted to visit my favorite statue ever, of Harvard and Oxford professor Samuel Elliot Morison on Commonwealth Ave, go to my favorite sushi place on Newbury Street near the bookstore, and return a WWII-era book about a lifeboat survivor which I used on a recent book SEA STORIES, however I'll wait till my book is printed to return the Athenaeum's book with 'interest,' and frankly it's difficult to get son and girlfriend to venture out into public a lot during the pandemic.

Applied to help promote a maritime museum online

Learned that a water taxi outfit I worked in 2019 and 2020 is closing up till next March, which seems sad and a bit fearful to me for the future.

Called my Mum and Dad in the Bahamas, they are happy to have each other but are tried much by severe lockdowns there and not able to see grandchildren much. Also chatted on Wassapp with brothers and sister and longtime family friends; mostly silly banter about kids, spouses, gossip, politics and human-interest news and advice.

Corresponded with our host / hotelier on Cuttyhunk about internet access and food as we will have to be self-sufficient on our private writer's retreat there in October.

Learned that after 30 years of publishing books, booklets, articles, I was nominated for both semifinal and quarterfinals for a short story I wrote one afternoon and submitted, several typo-s.

Approved final drafts on cover and interior for two other books, TRAVEL DIARIES, and SCARS, which will all be published on the same day, this week or next for over 2,750 pages! Phew!

MAILBOATS OF THE BAHAMAS is being laid out by a friend of a friend, but she feels the photos from 200 years or so will never be good enough and I agree, so off to my team in Pakistan to lay it out.

Negotiated a parking spot outdoors but on premises at the large airy school house for my girlfriend, which will be nice in the snow.

My 23-year-old nephew in Sweden and godson is keen to return to New York City for work so I've introduced him to some folks who may be able to help, and am 100% certain he will honor the introductions and follow up.

His Mum met our son after school – he spends weekdays with her, closer to home.

That's it! I'm also pretty lazy and go to bed about 9 pm, and spent other time trying to collect payment, and sent a 33-page proposal to a shipping entrepreneur about ghost writing his book and a salvage expert about restoring an antique yacht. And I tried to remember to eat and drink more than just coffee, and watch a bit of Rowan Atkinson, Stephen Fry, and Hugh Laurie in BLACKADDER for a laugh before going to bed, and lay off the WWII and WWI tragedies.

Good night, Boston!

Initiation & Mirror

At the last, when you have sailed long and far enough, you come to understand that the sea is everything. It is calm and restless, stormy and laughing, many-hued and one-hued, and one-colored, salty and fresh, warm and cold, an enemy and a friend, a help and a hindrance, a tragedy and a jest. Everything! Sufficient for every mood, for every dream, for every hope, for every sorrow. It will give you health and it will break you. It will teach you strength and turn your courage to water....

And so in your youth, when the bridge-watch comes, you regard that sea which took your boyhood and gave you a certain wisdom and joy, warily, as a fencer regards his foe. And something of the mystery, something of the wonder, something of the clean, innocent and sincere love you gave to deep-water goes slowly away, never to return.

From *Way for a Sailor*! Albert Richard Wetjen (1900-1948), British-American merchant mariner and author. From *The Oxford Book of the Sea*, Jonathan Raban, editor, Oxford University Press, 1993, pages 396-398.

Joseph Conrad was born Józef Teodor Konrad Korzeniowski in what is now the Ukraine in 1857 a Russian subject in what became Poland, and died in Kent, England as a British subject in 1924. Along with Jack Kerouac, whose first language was French, Conrad is notable as an Anglophile author in English whose mother tongue was Polish. He is known as one of the finest modernist novelists of the 19th Century, having published over 20 novels, dozens of short stories, and over a dozen essays.

Conrad is remarkable for the nautical realism, rich description, and technical accuracy blended with a sense for portraying the fantastic in the weather, in maritime mistake, and in human characters such as *Lord Jim*. He portrayed a major colonial and then global expansion and interactions 'twixt traders and sailors in the Atlantic and Indian and Pacific oceans and the South China Sea. If there were a comparison with a character on a tramp steamer in the Far East by William Somerset Maugham, Conrad would have been more than the narrator; he would also have been the captain.

While a success as an officer in the French and British merchant marine, and as a writer, Conrad was also moody, at times lonely and morose. As a consequence, at age 20 he shot himself in the chest with a revolver in Marseilles, France, largely due to worries about finances. But for continued intervention and support by his Polish uncle Tadeusz Bobrowski, the Conrad's already turbulent life of global voyages would have doubtlessly been even more unstable and dangerous.

Many members of the New York Yacht Cub will be familiar with Conrad's writing already, having at a minimum read a book or two of his before college and during university. Being sailors, members will have been imbued with a knowledge of his skill as a mariner and someone who almost sensually portrayed the dank jungles of the Far East in books like *Lord Jim* and the intrigue and mystery of going up river in *The Heart of Darkness*, which morphed into Francis Ford Coppola's 1970s epic *Apocalypse Now*, and his wife's documentary *Hearts of Darkness* about the madness of making the film.

In mid-2020, as COVID-19 cut most of us off from the shelves of Conrad on 44th Street and the Library at Harbour Court, I took as keen an interest as anyone in trying to help members to engage with the club in new and novel ways. I was asked to contribute a book review to the Library Committee, on which I have been honored to serve for some years. The club has given me much to learn from, and a safe haven to shelter in during winters and economic blasts, and I am happy to oblige and do what I can. After all, I launched one of my maritime history books there, and have had the privilege to present on a book or two as well. In fact, several of the books I've published have been researched and written in both club houses. So here we are!

How does this relate, and how is this review organized? A gentleman who frequented the Harvard Club beside the NYYC from the 1940s to the 1970s as a managing partner of Reid & Priest, purchased the 1925 leather bound, gold-embossed Doubleday edition of *The Mirror of the Sea* by Joseph Conrad. His name was Ralph Manewal McDermid and his daughter Jane worked across the street from the club at *The New Yorker* in the early 1960's. She cherished the book, and on his graduation from college she gave this treasure to her son – your author. The cover of this book is on the title page of this essay, and the original sits in front of me as I type. It is propped near a window overlooking the Bunker Hill Monument in Boston from East Boston, across the harbor I spent the winter as captain of passenger boats, often taking fresh arrivals from Logan International Airport downtown.

The parallels between the revered Conrad and my modest efforts to keep up with him are few, but can be briefly brush-stroked. I was mate across the Atlantic at age 21, then watch captain on an aluminum Frers-50 racing sloop on the Marion to Bermuda Race, right after college, and rose to first command from Galapagos to New Zealand of a leaking wooden 68-footer at age 23. I know the loneliness of being separated from ones mates, having survived 16 minutes in the water in an afternoon snowstorm, farm from land and having watched the yacht I had so recently commanded sail out of sight.

By coincidence, the wrecked ship central to the core story is a "Danish brig homeward bound from the West Indies." In 2003, as law school ended for the year, I was hired to fly from Newport to St. Martin and deliver Bristol 57' sloop to Sag Harbour. On the leg from Bermuda we went through over 50 knots of gales trying to enter the Gulf Stream, and unbeknownst to me our South African crew had a strong bond with an audacious and tenacious young Danish skipper. He was running a slight and fast stripped-down 40-foot-or-so racing sloop named *X-Base* for X-Yachts. And damn if that boat was not always at our side as we emerged from gales, storms, fog, rain, all of it – we were his insurance policy and they never gave in! At one point they came along side and threw some birthday cake onto our deck, everyone doing over 7 knots under sail. I marveled at and admired that Danish captain as the young Third Officer Conrad did the Danish ship master who survived the sinking brig, as they all sculled back to the ship that evening. In 2000 the 1936 classic Camper & Nicholson *Stiarna* sank under our feet, aflame, north of Trinidad, thankfully east of Venezuela. I was hit by a Thai long-boat off Rai Lay, and was malnourished when the freezer broke on the first week of a 21-day trans-Atlantic passage in severe weather, Bermuda to Belgium. Like many readers had a few other unpleasant experiences due to the ocean, failures of equipment, and people – more often than not me. I've been so scared at times across some 125 boats and 75,000 nautical miles that I'd frankly rather not say – but Conrad more comfortable sharing his misgivings, and lays his out for all of us to appreciate, respect, and relate to, whether we admit it or not.

So, let's all enjoy parsing his words and mine with a sprinkling of criticism or critical thinking, pretend we are young again and going to the aid or wrecked wretches. Here is how this is organized:

Part I - *Initiation*, in *Mirror of the Sea* discussed.

Part II – Conrad's appearing in my logs & diaries, his writing influencing mine.

There is of course a brief *Introduction, Conclusion* and *Further Reading* each. *Enjoy!*

In late August, 23-year-old 1880 Joseph Conrad enlisted as third mate on an iron clipper ship, the *Loch Etive*. The next day the ship left London, arriving in Sydney in late November. The return voyage began in January of 1881. In his 1905 retrospective of insights gained from sea experience named *The Mirror of the Sea* Conrad describes for the readers his ship's rescue of a doomed Danish brigantine overtaken by a hurricane between the West Indies and Europe and adrift with nine men for over three weeks (the exact days are left a bit in doubt as the Danish captain is told the actual date and falls silent). The *Loch Etive* arrived in London late in April, roughly four months after leaving Australia.

401

The vignette known as *Initiation* is one of the coming-of-age stories which Conrad shares. To set the stage, he wrote how he "felt its dread for the first time in mid-Atlantic one day, many years ago, when we took off the crew of a Danish brig homeward bound from the West Indies." Peter Villiers, in *Joseph Conrad, Master Mariner*, begins by assuming the incident occurred in 1881 aboard *Loch Etive*, but concludes it is an amalgam of several incidents, possibly the wrecked *Able Seaman* in 1879, rescued by the *Duke of Southerland* off Canada (pages 37-43). Conrad himself prefers to leave his novels vague and imprecise in origin, as Villiers notes; "...he heartily disliked too close an attention being paid to the origins of his writings." Conrad wrote directly to an inquisitive fan that "It is a strange fate that everything I have, of set artistic purpose, labored to leave indefinite, suggestive.... Should have that light turned on it and its insignificance... for any fool to comment upon." (Villiers, pp.42-43, Curle, Richard (ed.) *Conrad to a Friend: 150 Selected Letters to Richard Curle*, Sampson, Low, Marston & Co., London, 1928, ibid.)

Conrad speaks of men's working relationship with vessels as being driven by a pride of endurance, which I find is true of offshore voyages, and races. He observes that the anthropomorphism which men and women apply to machines or animals fails in their interactions with the sea, which "has no generosity. No display of manly qualities - courage, hardihood, endurance, faithfulness - has ever been known to touch its irresponsible consciousness of power." Humans "cannot brook the slightest appearance of defiance," without incurring its wrath, since the sea "is always stealthily ready for a drowning. The most amazing wonder of the deep is its unfathomable cruelty."

We readers recognize that this will be no ordinary evening in the doldrums, or after a storm, when the lookout on Conrad's ship is so alarmed at the sight of living bodies on the wreck that they shout on with "a most extraordinary voice - a voice never heard before in our ship; the amazing voice of a stranger." The once-mighty rescue ship – and its crew – become reduced to drifting "silent and white as a ghost, towards her mutilated and wounded sister, come upon at the point of death in the sunlit haze of a calm day at sea." Already the reader and narrator drift into a surreal world of phantasm, with dusk's onset blurring life and death, afloat and sunk....

Conrad is a junior officer at the time – entirely the point of the story, and as he become master of a small row boat, he realizes that "It takes many lessons to make a real seaman." Rescue boats race towards the sinking hulk. "The issue of our enterprise hung on a hair above that abyss of waters which will not give up its dead till the Day of Judgment. It was a race of two ship's boats matched against Death for a prize of nine men's lives, and Death had a long start. ...Already, her bulwarks were gone fore and aft, and one saw her bare deck low-lying like a raft and swept clean of boats."

Then, as launch captain to brig's captain, Conrad prepares to receive his counterpart, with he and the reader perhaps expecting a salute, tip of hat, or handing of ceremonial sword. As is was, there was no *Captain Sorensen, I presume* heroic Victorian flourish, rather "....the captain... literally let himself fall into my arms." No bugles and cavalry charge there. In fact, the participants note that "it had been a weirdly silent rescue - a rescue without a hail, without a single uttered word, without a gesture or a sign, without a conscious exchange of glances." Rather, the surviving nine mariners could not take their eyes of the pumps until one final order was given to cease, and then they stood, without caps, with the salt drying gray in the wrinkles and folds of their hairy, haggard faces, blinking stupidly at us their red eyelids, they made a bolt away from the handles, tottering and jostling against each other, and positively flung themselves over upon our very heads. The clatter they made tumbling into the boats had an extraordinarily destructive effect upon the illusion of tragic dignity our self-esteem had thrown over the contests of mankind with the sea.

The narrator relates the devastating effect this had on him, as though an acolyte become swiftly an atheist, or at least an agnostic.

On that exquisite day of gently breathing peace and veiled sunshine perished my romantic love ....the cynical indifference of the sea to the merits of human suffering and courage, laid bare in this ridiculous, panic-tainted performance extorted from the dire extremity of nine good and honorable seamen, revolted me. I saw the duplicity of the sea's most tender mood. It was so because it could not help itself, but the awed respect of the early days was gone. I felt ready to smile bitterly at its enchanting charm and glare viciously at its furies. In a moment, before we shoved off, I had looked coolly at the life of my choice. Its illusions were gone, but its fascination remained. I had become a seaman at last.

The captain of the sinking brigantine explained to Conrad, in the thwarts of the rescue boat on its way to the new mothership, that "the ships they sighted failed to make them out, the leak gained upon them slowly, and the seas had left them nothing to make a raft of. It was very hard to see ship after ship pass by at a distance, as if everybody had agreed that we must be left to drown." The rescuers have narrower recollection of the rescue, which took an hour or so, than the survivors, who were adrift nearly a month after a hurricane. Conrad describes that even in retirement, "I remember the dark-brown feet, hands, and faces of two of these men whose hearts had been broken by the sea. They were lying very still on their sides on the bottom boards between the thwarts, curled up like dogs.

Suddenly, with no word spoken, the brig's captain emits a groan, and Conrad loses command of his boat to his Scandinavian stranger: "....after a glance over his shoulder, [he] stood up with a low exclamation, my men feathered their oars instinctively, without an order, and the boat lost her way." Then "... he pointed a denunciatory finger at the immense tranquility of the ocean. .....the amazing energy of his immobilized gesture made my heart beat faster with the anticipation of something monstrous... the stillness around us became crushing."

Brilliantly, Conrad makes his men, perhaps even the readers witnessing, complicit in what happens next, as the surge of the swell destined to condemn the Danish brig to the depths passes beneath the mother ship and the launch, lifting them all up, even for just a moment, informing them of its inevitable intent...

For a moment the succession of silky undulations ran on innocently. I saw each of them swell up the misty line of the horizon, far, far away beyond the derelict brig, and, the next moment, with a slight friendly toss of our boat, it had passed under us and was gone. The lulling cadence of the rise and fall, the invariable gentleness of this irresistible force, the great charm of the deep waters, warmed my breast deliciously, like the subtle poison of a love-potion. ...As if at a given signal, the run of the smooth undulations seemed checked suddenly around the brig.

This description is extraordinarily accurate, in my experience. As a new captain of a historic yacht which caught fire, I watched I dismay from a Trinidadian Coast Guard cutter as the wooden, oil-soaked vessel, freshly loaded the night before with 72 gallons of diesel in bladders, became engulfed in flames leaping higher than the cotton sails and booms. We men who had swum to the safety of another boat waited for the diesel to explode, but nothing but a "poof" emitted: grey steam and hot air. Then the water tanks when. And finally, when the moment arrived and the fire had eaten like leprosy from one side right through to the other so that we could see gaping, smile-like holes in the 64-year-old hull, after the mast had toppled onto itself like a broken matchstick, all of us hats off an in awe, the owner's recent baby imperceptibly rose to the top of a whale-back, silky smooth swell, and every so gently and almost silently was enveloped in the forever embrace of the ocean.

The boat sank 134 feet down into the seas over which German U-boats had ferociously fought the US and UN navies in The Bocas, or Mouth of the Dragon. It was all so oily, silent, anti-climactic, sorrowful or even wan, drained of emotion. It was so actual and matter-of-fact, like the sliding of a corpse off a tray from under a flag, anchor chain on ankles, into the depth. It just happens. The absence of a stunning sensation is in itself a bit stunning. Watch these on the internet, and you will notice – that ships and yachts often do go out with a whimper, a whisper, a puff of air. In my case since I had three months of belongings on board, the coast guard RIB found pieces of my grandfather's nautical tie, of an old Oxford shirt, and the boat's charred life-ring with its name. The owner quickly went on to own *Columbia*.

And then, the *coup-de-grâce*, as the narrator related how by a strange optical delusion the whole sea appeared to rise upon her in one overwhelming heave of its silky surface, where in one spot a smother of foam broke out ferociously. And then the effort subsided. It was all over, and the smooth swell ran on as before from the horizon in uninterrupted cadence of motion, passing under us with a slight friendly toss of our boat. Far away, where the brig had been, an angry white stain, undulating on the surface of steely-gray waters, shot with gleams of green, diminished swiftly, without a hiss, like a patch of pure snow melting in the sun.

Following this stark experience, the young officer forever changed by them relates his new perspective of his host, livelihood, and adversary. The sunken brig, ne notes as he watches the devastated Danish master, "...had lived, he had loved her; she had suffered, and he was glad she was at rest." Conrad ruminates on the future for he and his own men as they fall under the shadow cast by their home'

Ships are all right." They are. They who live with the sea have got to hold by that creed first and last; and it came to me, as I glanced at him sideways, that some men were not altogether unworthy in honor and conscience to pronounce the funereal eulogium of a ship. This smile of the worthy descendant of the most ancient sea-folk [Danes], whose audacity and hardihood had left no trace of greatness and glory upon the waters, completed the cycle of my initiation [into] the sea, which has betrayed so many ships, so many proud men, so many towering ambitions of fame, power, wealth, greatness!

Being welcomed by cheering shipmates and congratulated, even backhandedly by a wizened captain of his ship, Conrad ensures the survivors make it to the deck of his ship and then the author ruminates.

It was not for [my Captain] to discern upon me the marks of my recent initiation. And yet I was not exactly the same youngster who had taken the boat away - all impatience for a race against death, with the prize of nine men's lives at the end. Already I looked with other eyes upon the sea. I knew it capable of betraying the generous ardor of youth as implacably as, indifferent to evil and good. ....My conception of its magnanimous greatness was gone. And I looked upon the true sea - the sea that plays with men till their hearts are broken, and wears stout ships to death. Open to all and faithful to none, it exercises its fascination for the undoing of the best.

Part II Conrad's writing & influence in my logs & diaries:

406

The somewhat absorbent effect of reading *Initiation* on an aspiring and ambitious young sailor reminds me of a winter day in the southern hemisphere, on the commercial fishing dock in the village of Oban, on Halfmoon Bay, Stewart Island, at 47 degrees south in the Roaring Forties. I was 24 and finishing a memoir of sailing to New Zealand, and while waiting for new typewriter ribbons to arrive on the ferry from Invercargill, I struck up a conversation with an older fisherman. He was chewing something and in a philosophical mood – I'd lived on the island about three months and was considered OK to speak to, I guess. He spread his arm across the entire horizon in a sweeping grand gesture on that steel gray cold, still afternoon and said to me:

"My son is in construction. He takes me to Dunedin and Invercargill and Christ Church and shows me all the buildings he's helped to put up. When he comes here to Stewart Island and I want show him what I have to show after more than five decades of fishing these waters, this is all that I have. There's not one damn thing to show him for all that work. The sea hasn't noticed me."

Next, we look at the dozen or more times that Conrad's works, thoughts and experiences have bled into my personal diaries and voyage logs over more than 30 years. They are pulled from a 750-page compendium of 55 diaries largely collated and in one of the alcoves of the 44th Street clubhouse last year – the one nearest the new *Tenacious* model, which is fitting as I sailed and raced her as War Baby from 1991 to 2001, and remember RAF veteran Charlie Berry being up to his chest in water in that cockpit when rounding Portland Bill, UK, in the summer of my 21st years. These diary entries are meant to show how reading Conrad interwove with my own coming-of-age as a sailor.....

On August 22, 1987, I was a week from turning 17 when I wrote that on a flight, "a lady who sat next to me for three hours Miami to New York finally asked me, *Can I buy that when it's a novel*? See, I'd been writing in my diary for hour after hour! *Live by the pen, die by the pen. Come home wearing your mainsail or in it*, said Saint George's teacher and sailing coach T. J. B., who had been my Junior Varsity sailing coach. In 1990 or 1991, I saw Coach B. crushed, broken, sobbing uncontrollably after their sailboat was dismasted racing to Bermuda and moments after days of living hell and a tow, he made it to the payphone booth (where I was also calling my parents), and called his. It was like a Joseph Conrad short story from *The Mirror of the Sea*, the single text which most impresses me with its saltiness, as the film *White Squall*, about the loss of the training ship *Albatross* does as well, with Jeff Bridges and an amazing soundtrack of the ocean under way. The experience helped teach me that can still deal with reality while accepting the romantic."

On the 3rd of July, 1989, I was 18 and in that wild summer between six years of boarding school and four of university. I had the good fortune to sail as boat boy on the Marion-Bermuda Race, then the voyage back to Newport, with some trepidation, since the tanker *World Prodigy* had spilled some 300,000 of fuel oil on Brenton Reef the previous week:

I dreamt of being under blocks, crushing me, of a freight ship sending me adrift, of poems. I feel like Joseph Conrad. Tom, studying marine biology at URI, saw a whale last night. This is the offshore sailing I've dreamt about for years! No more school poems of and yearning for the sea! This he real thing. Circa 1,500 nautical miles; almost enough from Newfoundland to Ireland (trans-Atlantic). Now I can wear red shorts or even pants. It's much more casual sailing back to Newport than racing down to Bermuda. Fine people. ....The others tell sailing stories about big racing boats; Maxis or ones I've seen, like *Stars and Stripes* in 1983, *Grey Goose, Shamrock IV*. D.G., who has been a bosun's mate on many a square-rigger, tells of a ship's officer ordering a cadet up rigging then stepping away from spot "x." A minute later, the sailor's knife plummeted to that spot! Two days later, I wrote: "I'm going crazy. Four-plus days, and we're only halfway there. Newport, with its women, cigarettes, relative freedom, and old and new friends, seems very inviting. I'm reading Graham Greene's *A Burnt-out Case*, about a madman in an African leper colony, like Joseph Conrad's *Heart of Darkness*, V. S. Naipaul's *Bend in the River*, and three other Graham Greene books; *Power and the Glory, Our Man on Havana,* and *The Quiet American*. So far, I only vaguely like Durrell's *Bitter Lemons*. Scene opens with crew boating up a river while smoking and drinking. There in Sargasso Sea. This drives me mad....."

408

A month or so later I enrolled in Boston College as an English Major, joined the big boat sailing team (really contributing nothing to it, sadly), and the first day of summer I set off sailing; after Freshman year I bicycled to Newport, caught a boat back from Bermuda Race, then another to Europe. The next summer I blindly caught a one-way ticket to Antigua and found a boat to Belgium where I could join *War Baby* ex-*Tenacious*, then attend Oxford. During this time, I was submitting stories of voyages to Bermuda, on the Australian tall ship *Young Endeavour* in Bahamas, and *Chebec* across the North Atlantic to the school paper in Boston, *The Nassau Tribune*, and *What's on Bahamas*, and the St. George's School *Bulletin*. As a result of these forays, I became a journalist for a while, covering everything from robberies at the local store to a coup in Haiti, a struggle for LGBTQ tolerance and round-the-world yacht races, allowing me to meet participants in the BOC Challenge and even Florence Arthaud.

During this stint I attended a lecture on Graham Greene given by his most assiduous biographer (Boston College, holds much of Greene's papers). His name is Norman Sherry, and he published *Conrad's Eastern World*, and *Conrad's Western World* in the 1970's, one colorful illustrated edition of which was gifted to me to read during three years helping to operate a commercial fleet of tankers from Singapore. It was ideal, and I still have it. Sherry also completed a monumental three-volume biography entitled *The Life of Graham Greene*; he is funny, and no slouch. So, I faced the world empowered by the words of Greene, the humor of Sherry, the adventurism and skill of Conrad, the socially skewering wordsmithing of Somerset Maugham, and a bit of the inaccessibility of Lawrence Durrell and the sardonic humor and sly British wit of Evelyn Waugh, who might have been mistaken for an effete artiste were it not for his having participated as a soldier in numerous World War II campaigns, from Scandinavia to the Med, as well as West Africa. Overall, being able to meet one of Conrad's biographers brought me a step close to him, and to his worldly travels.

Years later, on August 25, 1993, two days before my 23rd birthday, and after graduating from college in Boston, I set off for a career at sea, and wrote: "Books I recently read: *Looking for a*

Ship, John McPhee, *Lord Jim*, by Joseph Conrad, *Voyage, a Novel of 1896* and *Wanderer*, by Sterling Hayden, *Alive!*, the story of Chilean air crash victims and survivors; cannibalism, *North by Northeast*, by Ray Ellis and Walter Cronkite, *Islands of Maine*, by Bill Caldwell, *The Sufferings of Young Werther*, by Goethe, and *Mutiny on the Bounty*, by Nordhoff and Hall, two Americans living in Tahiti, in French Polynesia."

A month later, the final Conrad entry of my youth; on September 26, 1993, a Sunday at 9 pm, I was a crew with a young couple in command and a friendly former naval officer from New Bedford, also very nice. We were between Newport and the Bahamas on a 60-foot sloop, emerging from a crappy first half and into a sunny second one:

The current is against us in the Gulf Stream, north-northwest at about four knots. Bimini is visible, despite being low and flat. It is clear, calm, humid, hot. We decided over our evening beer together that we would bypass rushing for Bimini tonight in favor of delaying all night, arriving early morning one week after departure from Newport. The captain's plan is to anchor outside in deeper water in order to do work like refitting the boat and general cleanup as needed.

This may determine whether I stay on board for the trip down-island to the U.S. Virgin Islands and Antigua or not; it is something I could easily do by flying from Nassau to Fort Lauderdale, and I could use the money. Meanwhile I think after six to seven days of confinement, calm, torpor, languishing and its corrosive toll, I'll feel a bit the butt of ill-humor, but it's all well. We'll see, right? What awaits me in Florida? Other deliveries south? The fabled ultimate role: ascending to the industry throne of captaincy? 9:30 pm. Bimini is only 30 nautical miles, or eight hours away. We are still bucking the Gulf Stream, that hot river of water which is about three feet higher and several degrees hotter than the water either side of it. Joseph Conrad wrote *A Personal Record*, a wonderful work about being a professional merchant marine officer. This diary or log is the personal record of mine. Simultaneously, I am keeping a voyage log of *Jadeante*'s passage south from Newport to Miami initially bound for my home port of Lyford Cay, Nassau, and now via Bimini, Berry Islands, Bahamas, and Fort Lauderdale. I say *personal record* because, from this afternoon, I'll play closer attention to the personal aspects of this voyage, and the crew who initiate and carry it out. I have learned that as our character roles settle down into an established pattern of sorts, I find the evidence of alchemy unsettling.

Another Diary entry for Friday, August 18, 1994, after arriving by sea in New Zealand, reads: "....Ho Chi Minh City, which makes me think of the film *Apocalypse Now*, based on regicide and Conrad's *Heart of Darkness*...." This is due to my final paper for documentary film in college was based on the influence of Conrad in *Apocalypse Now*. I considered much of my assumption of first command and subsequent travels in the light of Condrad-esque perception, coloring it with the wide-eyed gone-more-cynical outlook which this story in particular encapsulates so well. And I don't see it translating to other professions as easily. Had those nine men on the Danish brig lost their fight at the pumps, going up and down like an eternal, infernal pump trolly or railway handcar, they would have been lost forever, with no remains to make it into the local church. Just the vast heaving surface of the sea, over 139 million square miles just of the salty stuff.

Conclusion:

From my early teens to the daunting, scary yet emboldening assumption of my first command, trans-ocean, at age 23, I have always felt that Joseph Conrad has been by my side to guide and support me. Like some of my other heroes, including Sterling Hayden, Felix von Luckner, and Samuel Eliot Morison, Conrad went out and *did it* first. It is extraordinary for someone to write such lovely, evocative prose about the ocean we all so deeply cherish. What I admire and respect about these men, and others including Albert Richard Wetjen, is that they often quit reputable schooling and families to experience the hard knocks of an ocean-going global life first-hand, before they share their perspectives as writers.

One thing which is clear to me from all this, and may be to you, the fellow reader, is that references to Conrad, comparisons, thoughts, memories of he and his writing and the high bar of example he set for me, depression and self-doubt and all – are things I've not only literally carried around with me most of my life, but interwoven and used it as well. Conrad is not passive. You breath, fear, see, and sweat or tremble right alongside him.

And now I return to him – to Conrad – as I do when I sit at the feet of the statue of Admiral Samuel Morison on Commonwealth Avenue in Boston. I do so at the start of my second half-century, chastened, hardened to the sea perhaps, as scared of the sea as ever, and as the account in *Initiation* makes clear, wiser, less bedazzled, better prepared and with fewer expectations and almost none of the rose-tinted innocence left. Having known true terror alone at watch at sea, fumbling for the emergency cockpit fog horn before realizing it won't cure me of the terrors, I have some round to Conrad's view that almost anyone can be brave. It takes someone who has been terrified to go back to sea afterwards that constitutes more than just wisdom. I think it constitutes bravery, which is made more by the underlying terror.

Though in this instance Conrad shows us how a shipwreck can end, the truth is that in many instances, no one is left to relate how their shipwreck ended.

Thank you, Captain Conrad.

Bahamas in World War II

"Nothing happened in the Bahamas during World War II."

Hearing this extraordinary assertion from an erudite colleague in a bookstore in Nassau over a decade ago, as I began amassing over 50 three-ring folders of research for what became *U-Boats in the Bahamas*, I decided that, however mundane, thankless, and costly the process, I would have to literally set the record straight. So, I raced home, and that weekend wrote this book to share the millions of things that did happen in the then-British-colony of the Bahamas from 1939 to 1945 (actually, it took more like 550 weekends). What better way to do so than to use the actual war diaries of both belligerents; German and Italians in submarines and for the mainly British and US allies, logs detailing merchant ships, bomber planes, many warships, but mostly destroyers and sub-chasers, convoys and airships?

We must put the impact of World War II on the Bahamas in perspective. At one extreme is denial; saying that nothing of consequence happened. In the middle is the approach most often taken; to focus on several events which helped define a nascent nation, namely, and in no particular order, The Project, which brought work to thousands of Bahamian laborers, The Riot, which sewed the bloody seeds of a labor movement which would later help propel the black majority to power after the war, The Windsors; the Duke and Duchess, who brought international media attention and 'glamour' to the colony, The Contract, which brought exposure and income to poorer, mostly black Bahamians, what I will call The Trial, a sensation following the brutal tar-and-feather, slash-and-burn murder of the colony's most influential man, Sir Harry Oakes, while his family waited for him at The Willows, their home in Bar Harbor, Maine, and finally The Airports; fittingly named Oakes Field and Windsor Field, along with others built in Exuma, on San Salvador and the Turks & Caicos, which permitted the Bahamas to conveniently capitalize on a post-war tourism boom which has supported it for 8 decades since.

One could over state it, as in the assertion on Wikipedia that "During World War II, the Allies centered their flight training and antisubmarine operations for the Caribbean in the Bahamas." The word "centered" may be strong, but between Canadian and US factories, Nassau provided a vastly more efficient means of delivery for thousands of aircraft bound to Africa and beyond. Yes, there were also major bases in Trinidad, Panama and beyond, but Bahamas was critical for providing airways safe from winter weather and more experienced *Luftwaffe* pilots in which 5,000 or so men became certified in bombing techniques which flattened Europe and bombed U-boats. Here is an assertion which would seem extraordinary were it not written in 1955, 9 years after the RAF left, by A. Deans Peggs, Ph.D., Head Master of Government High School, Nassau, in his *Short History of the Bahamas*:

With the outbreak of war in 1939, memories of the last war caused Bahamians to fear the worst. With the entry of the United States into the war [1941], the tourist traffic virtually ceased. *The colony was saved from depression, however, by the construction of a Royal Air Force* [author italics] training station and Ferry Command base. ...Consequently, what might have been a severe depression as in the First World War became a period of great prosperity, with the Colony's revenue exceedingly even the peak of the bootlegging years.

Here are some facts which will surprise even many of us from the Bahamas:

$62 million in USD equivalent to 2020 rates was spent locally to build the bases under the Lend-Lease Agreement of 1941: per the National Archives, 1943 GBP629,978 on labor by contractors, and GBP250,000 on local merchants ($44.46 M + $17.65 M = $62.1 M).

25% of the population of New Providence during the war were RAF and other personnel, basis the New Providence population in 1943 was 29,391 persons (per the Van Voast-American Museum of Natural History Bahama Islands Expedition), and at least 8,000 RAF soldiers and nurses stayed on New Providence. With 3,000 permanent staff on one base alone, 5,000 trainees, 2,000 flights through on a different base where aviators all stayed at the Royal Victoria (3,000 of them named herein), yet no names from Canadian and US Navy units and bases, almost certainly the number would top 10,000, or more than a third of all persons living around the capital.

Windsor Field was 1.33 miles long: 7,000' X 150', with another runway 5,000' X 150'. Oakes Field was over a mile long, at 6,000' X 150' wide, with another runway 5,000' X 150', and both were capable of operating at night as well as in various wind conditions, with numerous hangars and tie-down arrangements. During hurricanes they evacuated to West Palm Beach or Cuba.

The Red Cross and War Materials Committee managed not only to provide entertainment, hospitality and distraction for the aviators, but also to bury the many who died and keep their graves honorably with the IODE decades after the war ended. The Red Cross in 1943 sent 2,140 boxes with 22,835 hand-collected and hand-packed items to the UK.

Much is made of the Gallant Five and the hundreds of Bahamians who volunteered and served for the UK, but also Canada, the US, and other services, many with distinction. Yet in Nassau, Rosemary Kelly was the first Bahamian to volunteer for the military, as did Ann Wanklyn, Rosalie Knowles, Jean Sweeting,

Winks Brownrigg, Joan Winders, Mary Brown, and Peggy Hilton, all of whom served in the RAF Women's Auxiliary Air Force, or WAAF.

Not only did Terese Stratton lead the Red Cross branch in Nassau, reporting to the Duchess of Windsor, her daughter Joan served in the WAAF and her son left Queens College to fly against Germany in the RAF, was shot down, and killed. While hundreds of men left the colony for the war, many more remained behind, performing key security functions such as guarding the sprawling bases and protecting Clifton Pier's vital fuel depot, who deep-water tankers threaded past the more than dozen German and Italian submarines which transited just north of Nassau using the Northeast and Northwest Providence Channels.

As with any story which was banned from the public for over 30 years in the national archives thousands of miles from Nassau, a degree of fantasy was allowed to supplant reality: the Hemingway fiction of U-boat commanders landing in the Bahamas pushed out the hard facts that 112 submarines indeed invaded, but never had to land. Ditto rumors of Fifth Columns operating out of Darby Cay, Exumas, Little Harbour, Abaco, even Hog Island, opposite Nassau. One rumor, finally dismissed along with all the others in the esteemed 2011 *Bahamas Handbook*, was that a German submarine was supplied with fuel and other items at a submarine "pen" or just offshore Hog Island. Besides the fact that this grossly insults the patriotism of Bahamians by suggesting they participated in treason, it is also an affront to the British and Bahamian servicemen protecting the population at the time. Of course, even though the operation would have required the illegal accrual, storage, shuttling, and transfer to U-boat on the high seas requiring at least 100 persons and many months of preparation, not witness ever reported hundreds of tons of rationed, high grade diesel being loaded into a submarine. At any time during the war. Anywhere in the Bahamas. Because the Germans did not require help to sink some 130 ships; they had each other, Italians, and resupply ships and submarines of their own and made more economical use of the diesel and electric engines – German engines – than the Allies gave them credit for until after the war.

Admittedly, Wenner-Gren and the Duke seemed made for each

other; The Duke and Duchess were enamored of people with money and large yachts; Simpson witnessed many air crashes as the wife of a US Air Force officer, and preferred to travel by sea. Wenner-Gren literally owned the Bank of the Bahamas, as well as *Southern Cross*, the largest yacht in the world at the time. Their palatial homes overlooked each other across narrow Nassau Harbour. The down-side to their affinity for each other was that the Duke was also caught on camera being chummy towards Adolf Hitler in Germany (something which mortified Churchill and most allies), and Wenner-Gren had tried to appease the British by befriending Hermann Göring, with whom he had Swedish connection; Wenner-Gren's sister and Göring's Swedish wife Karin were friendly. When both men ended in Nassau during the war (the Swede by choice, the British former King forced there from Lisbon by an irate Prime Minister), it was Wenner-Gren who took the fall by being black-listed; the Duke got to keep his job as well, until he that that up as well.

Interestingly, another leading ally who lost his job through appeasement had spent six years in Bahamas: Neville Chamberlain, British Prime Minister from 1937 to 1940, who infamously uttered "peace in our time" after meeting Hitler. At age 21 Neville and his brother were sent to Andros, Bahamas (there is one of similar ship in Greece), because the Governor to the Bahamas, Sir Ambrose Shea, convinced their spendthrift father, Joseph, Secretary of State for the Colonies, that they could make a fortune in sisal (aka agave) on Andros. Early in 1891 the duo leased 26,000 acres (40.6 square miles), in North Andros, improved infrastructure, reduced drinking, set up a banking system, and ultimately lost $8 million USD in today's currencies. Neville returned to the UK after nearly 7 years in the Bahamas early in 1897, successfully built ship cabins, and rose to political heights. Wenner-Gren, who also thought he could make peace, but was dismissed precisely because he actually had no sway over Germans, nor were treasonous acts proven, himself invested in North Andros, starting in the early 1950s with the Andros Bahamas Development Company and the development of Andros Town, which within a decade was chosen as the site of the US Navy Atlantic Undersea Test and Evaluation Center (AUTEC), abutting

416

Fresh Creek, in 1959.

Rather than being recognized for saving survivors of the *Athenia*, or founding the Wenner-Gren Foundation (which fizzled when he was blacklisted first by the US, then the British), or his having created a "canal to nowhere" project for the governor to help him out of a pickle by providing work for angry labor following the completion of the bases and a shortage of work and wages, Wenner-Gren was maligned and effectively banished to Mexico for the duration of the war, following which he returned, and the canal he envisioned became the backbone of the Atlantis pool system. With the benefit of hindsight, by banishing him to appease their American allies, the British probably did Wenner-Gren a favor, sparing him the ignoble fate of another uber-wealthy outside with wartime power and influence in the colony, Sir Harry Oakes, whose wartime murderers have never been caught or even named. He has, however, been rehabilitated in Sweden and beyond, with he and Electrolux being recognized as an early proponent of globalism (*Wenner-Gren International Symposium; Reality and Myth: A Symposium on Axel Wenner-Gren*, Luciak, Ilja, Daneholt, Bertil, *The Life of Axel Wenner-Gren*, 2012, and Leifland, Leif, *The Blacklisting of Axel Wenner-Gren*, Stockholm, 1989).

A U-boat commander, Herbert A. Werner, wrote me and flatly dismissed the notion of German sailors landing in the Bahamas, though during the war two companies were sent to protect the Duke of Windsor, who quit his job as Governor before the war ended. His wife, Wallis Simpson, Duchess of Windsor's worked with the Red Cross, forcing a canteen serving alcohol to open against the wishes of many locally, has been overshowed. Even today, deep suspicions of her southern racism continue, to the extent that after a decade of attempting to post a small sign in Nassau commemorating her reception of hundreds of allied mariners in World War II, and repeatedly flying to and entering meetings empty of people, I just gave up.

Her husband, The Duke of Windsor, is often credited with nobly seeing the war through as Governor of the Bahamas; Craton writes "The Duke and Duchess left The Bahamas in May 1945 immediately after the war in Europe was over. The Duke turned down (as he was probably expected to) the only alternative post he was offered, the Governorship of Bermuda. (*A-Z*, p.396). Bahamian serviceman Jack Lowe from Abaco noted how with the presence of the Duke and Duchess, "the Bahamas came into the international limelight [when] he agreed to be Governor of our small colony of 65,000 people," (*My Life*, p.95), giving the tenure as lasting until "May, 1945." These give a misleading impression that Windsor somehow served his term and finished the job, while neither are correct.

While technically they remained in the colony for just over a day in May, the Duke quit just under 2 months before VE-Day, stopped work in April, and left the colony months before the war ended; it was scramble to fill his place, and it was only achieved by taking an able administrator from Bermuda, just barely in time (two weeks) before the war ended, and while the RAF activities at No. 113 (Transport) Wing were still in full swing, with many official events and funerals and economic transitional activities to oversee, including which loyal Caribbean, Central and South American nations were worthy of the millions of pounds of military equipment after the submarines withdrew their barbs. Up to September 1944, that year alone the Bahamas we besieged by U-boats numbered U-518 (twice), U-154, U-170, U-218, U-541, and U-539. The threat was real and immediate, with gunfights taking place with Bahamas-based aircraft, as German used the same tactics as the US: attacking the most vulnerable areas.

The fact is that, just as he abdicated as King Edward VIII after 326 days on 10 December, 1936, so, too did HRH the Duke of Windsor quit his role as Governor of the Bahamas before World War II ended, in fact before even Victory in Europe (VE) Day. Windsor resigned on the March 16, 1945, roughly two months before Germany fell. The year before, the man who had loaned them the Chateau in which they were married in 1937, Charles Eugène Bedaux, killed himself in a Miami jail overseen by the FBI, where US forces in Algeria apprehended, he and his son building a pipeline for the Germans.

The Duke's replacement was brought in from Bermuda, and did not assume the Governorship until July 28, 1945, close to 5 months after the Duke resigned. Governor William Lindsay Murphy vacated his role as Colonial Secretary of Bermuda to become Governor of the Bahamas, following postings in Sri Lanka and before another to Rhodesia. The father of an Irish poet, he oversaw the opening of the Lerner Marine Laboratory in Bimini. Murphy was transported by the RAF in the Bahamas half a dozen times, however none before July, 28, 1945. The Duke bid adieu to the Bahamas Legislature on April 3, and the Executive Council on 25 April. As Bloch, their apologist, writes; "the Duke of Windsor formally ceased to be Governor of the Bahamas on 30 April, 1945, the day Hitler committed suicide. He and the Duchess sailed without ceremony on 3 May, the day Lord Louis Mountbatten entered Rangoon." (Bloch, p.356).

The Windsors did stay in the Bahamas until May, leaving on May 2, a week before VE-Day on 8 May, and 3.5 months before VJ Day and the end of the war on August 15, 1945. Both of them embarked on the *Jean Brillant*, and the RAF assigned the specific B24 with tail number NT, which, per the daily diary, went "airborne from Windsor Field to escort ferry *Jean Brillant* with HRH, the Duke and Duchess of Windsor on their journey to Miami. Landed back after duty completion on 3rd day." The Windsors were joined by 19-year-old Bahamian valet Sydney Johnson. The same aircraft was deployed the next day: "B24 NT airborne, 2nd day from Windsor Field to escort the ferry *Jean Brillant* with HRH, the Duke and Duchess of Windsor journey to Miami." Although the Duchess had already effectively moved to Baltimore with her Aunt Bessie, she returned to Nassau, and the Windsors; "slipped away from Nassau at dawn" to visit friends in Palm Beach, Florida.

One wonders the soldiers and aviators and sailors at the RAF bases on New Providence and scattered throughout the islands would have thought had they known that their most senior leader and erstwhile king had retreated with less than a week left in the war in Europe, months before a replacement had arrived from overseas (Murphy from Bermuda on 28 July). The Windsors headed for the cocktail circuit in monied Palm Beach, awaiting their return to Europe from exile five years earlier. They were to remain in the social orbit for the balance of their lives, no job deemed satisfactory to him being offered to the Duke and none taken up. Years of effort to access his correspondence with the Colonial Office in London led vaguely to an archive in Windsor

Palace which is inaccessible to the public. The Duke came back to the Bahamas for golf – his wife did not return (Turnquest, p.153).

Between July and September, 1944, the RAF flew around an Acting Governor while the Windsors were off-island. Then in spring 1945 they had to improvise again. For example, parades to celebrate VE Day by the RAF and other units had to substitute in VIPs to "take the salute," no doubt throwing off protocol in a leadership vacuum. Officially, the Duke rationalized that, since his main job was to help the colony get through the war, he could not also be expected to help it get through the post-war phase as well, so better to hand it of before them. However, it came as a surprise to all. Michael Bloch, the Windsor's devoted biographer, gives an explanation where others have not. Four days after resigning, the Duke confided to newspaper magnate Roy Howard, in a March 19, 1945 letter, that "....I see no reason why I should continue to rot indefinitely on a semi-tropical island or accept some other exiling job, just because the British may not offer me a worthwhile appointment." (*The Duke of Windsor's War*, p.351). From the horse's mouth, as they say.

Craton was correct to add that "The Windsors lent glamour to the local social scene, especially among the well-heeled tourists who continued to flock to the islands....". And Lowe goes on to say how "the war years proved beneficial to our economy. Many rich Europeans took shelter in Nassau. Employment opportunities increased with the expansion of Oakes Airfield, and in the construction of a new air base at Windsor Field. Nassau became an Air Force town. Thousands of uniformed men from the Royal Air Force, Royal Canadian Air Force, and the United States Army Air Force mingled downtown. Some attended churches and found friends in hospitable families. After the war servicemen spread great reports of the Bahamas' beauty, and their return visits with family members boosted the tourism that steadily grew." (*My Life*, p.95)

The facts are that without World War II and the RAF and US Navy in the Bahamas, these are the likely outcomes:

- No building and employment boom
- No 25% to 30% surge in the capital's population
- No Riot

- No Contract
- No Windsors
- No Airports to start a post-war tourism boom with after the war
- No RAF and Prospect Hospital
- No Belmont School
- No wrecks, graves on 3+ islands, boat bases, airplane dive-sites, archaeological finds
- No exposure to the greater world from both military and labor participants.

Whether the Oakes saga might have played out, the fact it happened in 1943 made it inexorably linked to the war years, ditto any intrigue surrounding Wenner-Gren. *U-Boats in the Bahamas* confirmed that axis powers sent 112 submarines into the million-mile region bounded by Savannah, Bermuda, Anegada, Havana, and Key West. *U-Boats off Bermuda* delved further into the anti-submarine efforts of US Navy and RAF aircraft. What emerged was a significant battlefield, with some 2,000 killed in the line of duty on both sides, over 140 vessels lost to war-related causes as well as hundreds of airplanes; the Bahamas alone lost close to 200 aviators, none to enemy action except Isadore Stressel of the airship *K-74* off Cay Sal Bank in July of 1943.

Tens of thousands of merchants and allied naval ships transited the region, manned by millions of personnel. 700,000 tons of that shipping was sent to the bottom. At least 30 allied military units, most of them RAF, others US, and manned by servicemen from the empire and the world are listed below:

1. Bahamas Defense Company (BDC), North Caribbean Force, aka the Bahamas Battalion. Oct. 1942-1945. Under Major Rutherford, Capt. Lightbourn, Adjutant in Aug. 1943, and Lt. Roberts in Feb., 1944. May 1944 Lt. Wenzel Granger, Battalion served Italy, Egypt.
2. Bahamas Air Service Squadron, Jan. 1944 with 100 "colored troops" at Oakes Field, New Providence, Fl. Lt. Cullum
3. Volunteer Defense Force, 1939-1945, Nassau & Family Islands, protected installations.
4. Bahamas Batmen Establishment, Oakes Field. Authorized

by the RAF Delegation Washington in July, 1944

5. Garrison of Pictou Highlanders (Company), Nassau (Canadians, protecting Governor)

6. Garrison of Veterans Guard of Canada, Nassau (mission to protect Government House)

7. Queen's Own Cameron Highlanders, reopened and occupied Fort Montagu Hotel, 1942

8. US Army Engineering Department, subcontracted Pleasantville, Inc. of USA to build both Oakes Field in Grants Town and Windsor Field, in the Pine Barrens out west.

9. RAF No. 1318 (Communications) Flight, formed Nassau, 1944, disbanded, June, 1946.

10. RAF Ferry Training Flight, under No. 111OTU, formed in Nassau in 1942/3 and disbanded on August 3, 1942, becoming 3 Ferry Crew Pool, part of Service Aircrew Pool, Dorval.

11. RAF 7 Ferry Crew Pool, Attached to RAF No. 113 Transport Wing, Oakes Field

12. RAF 7 Ferry Unit, No. 113 Transport Wing, Oakes Field, formed July 5th, 1944 in Nassau, from parts of 3 Ferry Crew Pool, Reykjavik and Dorval (itself from Nassau to August 3, 1943), from Jan. 1945 to disbanding in Nassau on 1 Oct. 1945

13. RAF No. 7 Aircraft Preparation Unit was formed in Nassau on 5 July, 1944 from Transatlantic Aircraft Preparation & Despatch Unit (AP&DU), within No. 45 Group, and disbanded on 1 Oct. 1945.

14. RAF 88 Terminal Staging Post (TSP), Attached to No. 113 Transport Wing, Oakes Field. To avoid confusion, references in the diaries to No. 80 SP Amphibious was in Bermuda, No. 82 SP was in New Jersey, No. 83 SP in Gander, Canada, No. 89 SP in Jamaica, No. 90 in Ascension, No.95 SP was in Trinidad at Piarco Field, No. 96 SP was at Borinquen Field, Puerto Rico, No. 97 SP was in Miami, No. 98 SP was in Natal, No. 99 was in Belem, Brazil.

15. RAF No. 111 (Coastal) Operational Training Unit (OTU), RAF, Windsor (Main) Field, Nassau. Formed 20 Aug. 1942, at Oakes Field, to train general reconnaissance crew on

US-built aircraft, using 35 Mitchells, 29 Liberators, and 3 amphibious aircraft. Worked with US Navy and US Army Air Force against Axis submarines. On 25 July 1945 planes flew to Lossiemouth UK, completed by 1 Sept. 1945. "One of the largest in the Empire."

16. RAF No. 18 Group, supported No. 111 OTU with 25 Liberator VIII and 7 Wellington XIII/XIV bombers, also left Oakes Field on 12 Sept. 1945 for Lossiemouth, UK
17. RAF No. 113 (HQ, South Atlantic) Wing (Transport Command), RAF Oakes Field, (HQ No. 45 (Atlantic Transport) Group Dorval, Canada, Nassau on 15 Feb. 1943, "to control ferrying operations over the South Atlantic." On 11 Mar.1943 named No. 113 (Transport) Wing, on 3 July, 1945 became No. 88 Terminal Staging Post
18. RAF No. 45 (Transport) Wing disbanded Nassau 15 June,1946, and Dorval 29 Sep., 1946
19. RAF No. 250 Air-Sea Rescue Unit, Harbour Island ASR Aircraft Search and Rescue marine base, Dunmore Town, Eleuthera
20. RAF No. 250 Air-Sea Rescue Unit, Lyford Cay ASR Aircraft Search and Rescue marine base, western New Providence
21. RAF No. 250 Air-Sea Rescue Unit, Montagu Bay ASR Aircraft Search and Rescue marine base, northeastern Nassau
22. Princess Mary's Royal Air Force Nursing Service, 6 at a time at the RAF Hospital
23. RAF Out Island Commission, Jan., 1944 to recruit Bahamians to RAF, Bahamas Defense Company, Bahamas Air Service Squadron
24. RAF San Salvador Signals Detachment, amphibious, providing navigational aid to transport aircraft on long-distance flights. Cockburn Town, San Salvador
25. RAF Station Hospital, Skyline Drive, Prospect Ridge, Lake Cunningham, between fields
26. RAF Station Military Band (subset of No. 111 O.T.U.)
27. Main Field (later Windsor Field, built after Satellite, Oakes Field), west New Providence
28. Satellite Field (later Oakes Field, before Main, Windsor

Field), southern New Providence

29. US Navy Amphibious aircraft base, George Town, southern Exuma Islands
30. US Navy OSS Maritime Unit, Groups I on, Underwater Training, Underwater Demolition Team UDT 10, and others, trained by Navy SEALS, UK's Office of Strategic Services, and others. Salt Cay, northeast of Hog Island and Athol Island, Nassau, for 1 year, 1944.
31. W.A.A.F., Women's Auxiliary Air Force; recruited in Bahamas, trained in Jamaica
32. West Indian Auxiliary Territorial Service (ATS), 1943-1945), a female branch of the British Army. Vernell Albury, Earl Grant, Sybil Lightbourn, Shirley Wright, and Zoe Cumberbatch went to Jamaica to train and serve, from secretarial to manning AA-guns.

Note: One cannot include, nor ignore, all who served. Some added names of Bahamians who served are Basil Johnson, Rudolph Pyfrom, Lt. Augustus Roberts, Capt. Reney, Major d'Arcy Rutherford, Lt. David smith, Lt. William Pemberton, Kendal Isaacs, Fane Solomon, Benson McDermott, and W/O Norman F. Aranha, a gunner on RAF Liberators; any omissions are regretted.

The US Navy built is its amphibious aircraft base as well as an airstrip at Georgetown, Exuma, as part of the Destroyers for Bases Agreement of 1940. They also had a consular official, naval attaché (US Consul John W. Dye and USN Lt. (jg) Aaron Bilgore), and air liaison in Nassau for most of the war, with aircraft and pilots ebbing and flowing as needed; USN planes would land on search and rescue missions and stay for weeks. Similarly, British Staging Posts and Terminal Staging Posts sprung up on other island, like Trinidad, and within existing bases, such as No. 88 TSP at No. 113 Transport Wing, Nassau, and, is believed, in the southern Bahamas as relay stations, perhaps attached to the San Salvador bases. These also ebbed and flowed with the exigencies of war, with occasional glimpses caught as personnel were recorded transferring between bases.

Looking at the wartime contributions of the RAF alone, many Bahamians and students of World War II generally are unaware (in part due to these records only becoming available in the

1970s), of the scale and magnitude of their operations. Here are highlights. The RAF:

- Built two large airfields in Nassau and smaller bases on other islands
- Maintained a permanent staff of 3,000 over nearly 3 years; with churn over 7,000
- Hired thousands of locals over the years to build bases, join contingents, etc.
- Ferried over 2,000 aircraft – most of them large bombers requiring 11 men each
- Trained over 5,000 airmen in aviation warfare, bombing, anti-submarine, etc.
- Built out infrastructure including roads, hangars, hospital, chapel, cemetery.
- Developed and trained an RAF Choir, football teams, a rugby team, and so on
- Recreated at the Nassau Sailing Club, RAF Seafarer's Club, contributed to ZNS Radio, made their own magazine *The Liberator*, frequented the IODE café in the Masonic Hall, the Bahamian Club, the Canadian YMCA, Emerald Beach Club at Cable Beach, Hobby Horse race track, the Royal Victoria Hotel, the Fort Montagu Beach Hotel, British Colonial, Windsor, and Rozelda hotels, went deep-sea fishing on the yacht *Opitsa*, and conducted parades by marching to town and back for church, memorial services.
- Flew to the rescue of numerous civilian and commercial vessels including ferries and mailboats, and overdue yachts.
- Rescued fellow airmen, or retrieved their remains, or identifying evidence.
- Buried over 80 comrades in Nassau and commemorated over 100 others missing.
- The main aircraft they flew, trained and ferried were land-based bombers, including Mitchells, Baltimores, Mosquitoes, Liberators, and many others including fighters and amphibious craft.

In her memoir *The Windsors I Knew*, based on her experiences as the Duchess' Private Secretary from 1940-1944, Jean D.

425

Hardcastle-Taylor relates how the influx of over 2,500 laborers from Out Islands into the communities of Grants Town, Bain Town, Fort Hill, Kemp Road, Fox Hill, McCullough Corner, Mackey Street, and Johnson Road (Turnquest, 72), as well as the thousands of RAF, US military, and civilian construction onto the bases, created "the water problem facing Nassau: The sudden increase in our population brought about by the arrival of evacuees from England [20] and troop and Air Force activities here had given the island a water problem" (p.36, notes). When Hardcastle-Taylor identified and proffered the services of a highly experienced Scottish engineer with experience in catchments and aquifers and water farming, the introduction fizzled over discussions of whether they were Bahamian, white, or black, and why white policemen could not be brought in to police white areas, as in Bermuda, and so forth.

On a more substantive level, Hardcastle-Taylor gives the back-story of the United Services Canteen in the iconic estate known as the Bahamian Club, which in recent decades has forlornly peered over the brush at The Fish Fry at Arawak Cay, flanked by Fort Charlotte, the Bahamas Humane Society, and Ardastra Gardens.

One of the Duchess of Windsor's greatest successes in the Bahamas was her United Services Canteen in Nassau, a place where the forces could spend their leisurely hours. The canteen was located in the famous and fashionable Bahamian Club, owned by Mr. Frederick Sigrist [Sopwith's partner and British aviation pioneer], who lived partly in ...the Bahamas. ...The Duchess planned the arrangements for the canteen directly with the RAF staff, and spent many hours superintending the alterations and decorations (*The Windsors I Knew*, p.70)

She described who renovations were made by the American airport construction firm Pleasantville Constructors, and underwritten by marquee names such as Sir Harry Oakes, Lord Nuffield (inventor of the Morris Mini), Rogers', Davis,' Bush, et. al. The canteen was run by Nassuvian Miss Bessie Armoury, and were separate from the RAF Officer's Club and those of the US military, and the IODE Canteen in the Masonic Lodge on Bay Street. The grand opening took place on December 24, 1942 and throughout its existence, by all accounts it was a joyous and lively place. They building even had its own Military Police presence. (*The Windsors I Knew*, p.70-71)

Since the pivotal military tenant, change-agent, and employer in the Bahamas was the Operational (Coastal) Training Unit No. 111 (aka 111OTU), a short synopsis of its history is appropriate. The unit was formed at Oakes Field on August 20th, 1942, and "its main mission was to train crews for maritime patrol service (for Coastal Command, as well as ACSEA), on aircraft supplied by the USA according to the Lend-Lease Act." (text by S.C.L., RAAF, father to aviation historian Robert Livingston, of Brisbane, who kindly shared it in 2020). As soon as training started in November of 1942, the newer, larger Windsor Field opened, which hosted "C" Squadron's Liberators, with Squadron A and Squadron B, using twin-engine B-24 Mitchell Liberators aircraft staying behind at Oakes, at least until No. 113 Transport Wing arrived from Canada the following year. The first Liberators for training arrived at Nassau on 28 February, 1943, eventually tolling 29 during 1943, or more than one fortnightly.

Equipment is technical. Each plane was named, starting with a base identifier of the letters L, M, or N, and the letter after that being specific to the craft, as in LA, LB, and LC up to LX3. Fifteen of the new Liberators were described as GR fitted with Mk. V, and ASG-3 radar sets, and a further 8 were "Dumbo" fitted, with ASG-1 radar. Yes 6 more were type III, and 8 more were fitted with Mk. VI and allocated after April of 1944, with 16 more GR M. VIII's in 1945; many were fitted with Leigh Lights behind their engines. The two-letter combinations assigned to No. 111 OTU aircraft were H3 and X3 in 1942 to 1945, with 3G used later. As you will see specific aircraft numbers in training and the annals of wrecks and deaths will include, in order of delivery:

A Squadron: B-24 Mitchell I FK179 AR, from August, 1942 to July, 1945

C Squadron: B-24 Mitchell II FR378 CL, from August, 1942 to July, 1945

F Squadron: B-24 Mitchell II FW150 FP, from August, 1942 to July, 1945

J Squadron: B-24 Mitchell III KJ671 JZ, from August, 1942 to July, 1945

L Squadron: Liberator III FL993 L & Liberator V BZ806 LU, August, 1942 to July, 1945

M Squadron: Liberator V BZ810 MA, BZ811 MB, from August, 1942 to July, 1945

N Squadron: Liberator VI EV896 NA & KH262 NH, from August, 1942 to July, 1945

X3 Squadron: Liberator VIII KK333 X3-C & Wellington XIV PG183 X3-CC, '44-July, 1945

Other aircraft identified specifically include Mk. VI EV880 NC, Liberator GR Mk. V's BZ808 LY, BZ722 LK, BZ813, BZ812 MC, and BZ744 LL. Sadly both BZ746 LM and Liberator B MK III FL994 LA collided mid-air while approaching Windsor Field on 23 February, 1945. A Halifax III, VI RG386 D, and possibly other types may have been utilized. A Grumman Goose on loan from the US Navy was active in the Bahamas which may have been Goose I FP742 and FP740. Although it is possible that one-off anomalies of aircraft types used Nassau as a layover or waystation, and those were recorded in the ORBs or base diaries, the core aircraft for the training unit were Liberators and B24 Mitchells. The countries of different services used different names for the same aircraft, just as the Japanese World War II aircraft Mitsubishi A6M was simply called "Zero" by its adversaries. A B24 Mitchell was also known as a Liberator, a Baltimore to the British is a Martin A-30 to the US, a Catalina is a PBY, or a Consolidated, Dakotas can also be a C-47 Skytrain, a Mariner is also known as a PBM, and a Liberator can be a Consolidated B-24; and this is a simplification of how complex it can be.

These more than 20 aircraft were used to train the following "classes" at Nassau:

- 202 Advanced Flying School
- 205 Advanced Flying School
- 206 Advanced Flying School
- 215 Advanced Flying School
- Central Flying School
- 102 Flying Refresher School
- 1 Flying Training School
- 3 Flying Training School

- 6 Flying Training School
- 7 Flying Training School
- 22 Flying Training School
- 9 Advanced Flying Training School
- 22 Service Flying Training School

A lesser-known fact was that as soon as they graduated from the course, the 5,000 students then delivered aircraft over the South Atlantic towards the Middle East, and were expected to join combat units. After VE-Day, Liberators and Mitchells went back to USA and the balance of RAF aviators and aircraft returned to the UK, via Bermuda and Canada, starting 23 July, 1945. They were all delivered to RAF Lossiemouth in Scotland by 29 August, 1945, with the arrival of the last 18 Liberator. By the 1st of September, No. 111 OTU had handed over Oakes Field, and on the 12th Oakes Field and some aircraft for transport and conversion purposes were handed over to RAF 113 Transport Wing, which remained through much of 1946. By the 21st of May, 1946 No. 111 Coastal OTU was officially disbanded.

The genesis of the No. 113 Transport Wing, which was created beneath NO. 45 (Air Transport) Group with HQ in Dorval airfield near Montreal, and which shared the base with No. 88 RAF TSP (Terminal Staging Post), lay with the July 1940 creation of AFTERO, the Atlantic Ferry Organization. Its purpose was to move aircraft from the US factories to the UK battlefields before the US entered the war in December, 1940, and after. No. 113 Wing arrived after No. 111OTU and stayed later. They arrived first on 22 February, 1943, opened in March of 1943, and closed completely on 31 May, 1946. Their purpose first and foremost was the safe delivery of over 2,000 aircraft from North America to theaters of war in North Africa, Europe, and the Middle East via the Caribbean, South America, Ascension Island, and Africa. Without Nassau a lynchpin providing access to the vital South Atlantic route would have not gotten, to use a pun, off the ground, and a vastly more perilous, though shorter route via the North Atlantic would have constrained the throughput of aircraft at critical times to Tunisia to Rangoon.

Aircraft used by No. 113 and its affiliated Communications Squadron included:

- Liberator II AL504
- Ventura V JS955
- Hudson III, IIIA, VI FH315
- Spartan 7W KD10
- Dakota III FL528
- Catalina IIIA FP530
- Norseman FR406
- Baltimore IIIA, IV FA114
- Marauder III FB455

So, who were the people covered herein, who operated all of the military and civilian equipment? Roughly 6,000 German and Italian submariners attacked, some repeatedly, and some submarines repeatedly. Roughly 10,000 British and allied servicemen and women are estimated to have rotated through several RAF bases and posts in the Bahamas, with thousands more from the US Navy in Exuma and Nassau. The figures for the allied merchant marine that were actually attacked were 5,844 sailors, gunners and passengers on the ships, of whom 1,323 were killed in or after the attacks, and 4,613 survived, of whom 321 made it to shore in the Bahamas or Turks and Caicos.

The names, ranks, vessels, and where possible dates of all 1,915 personnel killed in the line of duty are listed herein; 1,323 allied merchant mariners, 183 RAF aviators, 254 US Navy personnel, and 155 German sailors. Also 2,399 persons listed in the diaries of No. 111 O.T.U. and 369 in those of No. 113 Transport Wing, are included, for a total of 4,683 persons named.

Regarding convoys, 200 of them specifically to and from the Bahamas, calling mostly at Nassau or a smattering in Exuma, are listed. In the channels through and around the Bahamas but not to the colony, 2,756 convoys are listed with dates of arrival and departure and from, and to where. If each of those convoys included an average of 5 merchant vessels and 2 naval escorts, that would equate to 19,292 allied vessels in convoys. The fact is that many convoys had more ships, and some had none, and were cancelled. They were to act like escalators: a reliable convenient way for ships to assemble, board and move regularly up the coast, from one place to another; in laden, back empty. If 20,000 ships convoys (some ships many times), and a very rough guestimate of

15,000 ships sailed independently, particularly during over 2.5 years between September, 1939 and May, 1942 when a state of war existed yet no convoys had begun in the area, and each ship carried an average of 40 persons, that would mean roughly 1.4 million allied merchant mariners, plus some Germans, early in the war, returning from the Caribbean to Germany. Added to these are British, US, and other naval and even army armed guards to fire weapons against U-boats and try to defend the merchant ships from attacks by German raider ships, Italian and German submarines, and the *Luftwaffe*, where they operated.

The fact is that determining precisely how many ships entered a million-square-mile body of ocean during wartime is impossible: it would require studying on the records of every port from 80 years ago, starting with knowing which ports to search. It would require not train-spotting, but equivocates better to setting up next to a major highway and trying to count traffic both ways, over a period of over five years, by vehicle type. So although the number, including ship sailing inbound independently from all over the world, continuously, to all US and Canadian east coast ports, is almost certainly much higher, this author posits that at least 1.4 million allied merchant sailors traversed the Bahamas and surrounding water, and with military personnel from all sides added, the figure is sure to exceed 2 million.

While it is impossible to pinpoint exactly how many allied service personnel entered the region in transit and on anti-submarine and convoy escort missions from over 140 air, naval, rescue, supply, refuel, airship and other bases in and around the Bahamas, it is safe to say that there were hundreds of thousands involved from base construction to manning, administration, maintenance and direct military operations, which resulted in the destruction of three German U-boats, which simply means *under-sea-boat* in German. So, including the rim of nations which supplied airfields and naval bases to the west, south, southeast and northeast (Florida, Cuba, Haiti and the Dominican Republic, Puerto Rico, other Caribbean islands down to Trinidad, and Bermuda), and all servicemen on the water and the air, it is easy to estimate that well over 2 million persons participated in this theater and contributed to an ultimate allied victory. While 25%

of mariners on ships struck by U-boats, on average, perished, 2,000 overall deaths out of some 2 million is a vastly lower death rate, though of course that would matter not to families of the killed.

Axis submarines seeking to sever the Achilles heel of allied supply lines, destroyed or attacked 690,928 gross registered tons of allied shipping in this region alone, including many of the most valuable tankers and ore carriers. Over a third of allied losses globally were in the Americas in early 1942. Literally millions of tons of shipping passed through the region; particularly as certain ship types are well suited to ply much of the same routes most of their working lives, such as the bauxite route for aluminum and tanker trades into specific ports where there are refineries and tank farms. Some ports have facilities to receive gypsum, dolomite, aragonite, cement, chrome ore, refined or crude petroleum, acids, frozen meats, or livestock on the hoof, and others do not. So many ships, like the submarines, returned multiple times.

Unfortunately, even a study which tries to be as comprehensive as this does, cannot include every contributor. Ironically, since it was a colony and the invaders and many of the defenders were imported from Europe, and most of the Bahamian servicemen were sent to Europe or abroad, the vast majority of the participants named and detailed in this study are non-Bahamian Europeans. However, back then, Bahamians were also British subjects, so it was literally a different world, and the world war, which cost the lives of 3% of the planet's inhabitants, was all-consuming.

Since it is important to recognize all participants, if only once or twice, here are groups from, or based in the Bahamas whose hard-won contributions deserve mention:

- Bahamian contingents raised and sent overseas such as
  o Caribbean Regiment and any other allied branch (not a focus here)
  o RAF trainees at OTU 111
  o RAF "batmen," or servants, at OTU 111
- Labor for the construction of Oakes Field (aka Satellite Field)

- Labor for the construction Windsor Field (aka Main Field)
- Labor to construct and maintain bases in Exuma (USN), and San Salvador (RAF)
- The many grassroots I.O.D.E. volunteers who set up canteens and worked with the Red Cross, the Masonic Lodge/s, and on drives to procure all manner of useful donations for the war effort, from bandages to scrap metal to recreational rooms.
- The Red Cross, run in the Bahamas by the Duchess of Windsor, who inherited the role from Lady Dundas, the wife of the previous governor, founder of the branch.
- Civil Defense forces, some of whom patrolled the Montagu Foreshore
- Civil Servants sent by the colonial British government on postings that include teachers, engineers, technicians, doctors and many other administrative roles.
- Finally, there were unusual participants who nevertheless required the government's attention, including French escapees from the penal colony on Devil's Island off French Guyana. After the Germans took over much of France, the prison complex was largely abandoned, leaving thousands of desperate criminals on a diaspora for freedom anywhere they would be accepted; ideally via the US back to France by way of the U.K. to join General de Gaulle.
- The military police and local, as well as British, police sent to maintain order, who found themselves amidst two of the country's defining moments; deadly labor riots relating to wage differences between the US and British for work on the air fields, and the murder of Sir Harry Oakes, unsolved nearly 80 years later.
- US forces built an airstrip on South Caicos in 1944 for a short-lived base, locals manned an anti-aircraft battery on Grand Turk, in 1942 Cable & Wireless connected with the Dominican Republic and Jamaica, an RAF bomber crashed in the islands, and 2 ships arriving and one departing were sunk.

What does this study miss, or fail to capture? In the interest of managing expectations and equanimity with the reader, the following are not covered well herein:

- Bahamian politics, social events, and national, rather than international events
- Non-military activities, including cultural, inter-island transport
- The US Navy amphibious base in Exuma is covered through the daily diary of the parent organization, the Gulf Sea Frontier. Only passing photos, convoy, and other flight activities between Nassau and Exuma are covered, as the base diary was not obtained or used
- US Navy, US Air Force, US Civil Air Patrol (CAP), USN Airships, or Blimps, US Army, and even US fleet deployments, including aircraft carriers, cruisers, battleships, destroyers, are covered only insomuch as they were used in tandem with, rescued, convoyed with, and interacted in any way with, forces actively protecting the Bahamas, like the RAF and USN fliers.
- Florida, Cuba, Puerto Rico and the dozen other locations manning over 130 bases large and small cannot be adequately covered individually in a book this size. The Bahamas are the central focus of this work from the outset to the conclusion, so only a fraction of activities in other areas are covered. That said, the extensive data on 3,898 ships and 2,956 convoys, plus the interweaving Gulf Sea Frontier Diaries, and those of the two major RAF bases in the Bahamas, do succeed in providing much of the interplay between the areas, without trying to name each person, plane, and activity in the other regions.
- Bermuda, being small with very detailed aviation and naval records, and exclusively occupying a large swathe of ocean with frequent contact with the Bahamas, is an exception, in that its World War II activities to its south are covered.

Although at the outset of this book the goal was to be about events not people, and data not personalities, because the diaries for both RAF bases include VIPs and persons of global impact, from royalty to entrepreneurs, Peruvian pilots to French penal colony escapees, and a young man daydreaming out of a bus window who lost his arm, as well as nurses and technicians, and an accountant sent to Harbour Island to investigate "a claim for compensation submitted by the owner of The Little Boarding House, in which personnel of Air Sea Rescue were billeted during 1943 to 1945." So, the exclusionary net was opened a bit to include 2,768 persons welcomed aboard or working at the RAF bases, in the hopes that locals and family of servicemen alike will make a connection. Not every discovery will be enjoyed; as new aircraft such as the Mosquito were being rolled out, trainees had to test them, with they themselves flying them for the first time. One poor fellow is recorded having damaged two of them in back-to-back days; however, he emerged uninjured from both episodes.

Despite its many failings, the pages ahead do actually contain a bit of local color; brushes with Bahamian ships and shipyards and shipwrights and merchants, like the entrepreneurial family who leased out their van to the base when wheels were rare. Many of Nassau's hotels are cited, even in passing, as are spots like Whale Cay, where Marion aka Joe Carstairs held court, and remote Bahamian spots like Cay Sal Bank, Cay Lobos opposite Cuba, Mira Por Vos Passage and Hogsty Reef, and Mayaguana and Ragged Island, where a battle with a U-boat took place in which 3 allied ships where hit. During the war, for example, The Little Boarding House was the island's only hotel, owned by Ms. Marion Johnson and Ms. Hattie Thompson, who managed the blue shingled building on the corner of Murray Street (named for John Murray, 4th Earl of Dunmore, governor of the Bahamas from 1787 to 1796, for whom the town is named), and Bay Street. Ms. Johnson was then headmistress of the Harbour Island primary school.

One quickly learns that not all official correspondence need be tedious. Take these two back-to-back entries, post-war, in the No. 113 Transport Wing diary: "Major J.U. Moorhead, representing the U.S. War Department, visited this Unit with instructions that all Post Engineers activities cease forthwith and withdraw U.S. Corps of Engineers detachment by 31st March, 1946. [*Next entry*]: Vital services of US Post Engineers Department taken on to RAF civilian payroll." Officers read about a crash in Yundum, outside Banjul,

435

the capital of The Gambia, who had taken off from Nassau. And during the war we learn that "one German prisoner under armed escort passed through in transit from Jamaica to Canada. He was accommodated at Fort Charlotte Barracks and proceeded to Dorval next day." It seems a page from the Governor Sir Woodes Rogers in the early 1700's since enemy prisoners were housed under guard at Fort Charlotte, overlooking Nassau Harbour (as a footnote, efforts are still underway to locate Roger's 1732 grave in Nassau).

During the war cooperative behavior which would seem unthinkable a few months after it, in the Cold War, flourished. Under Batista, Cuba was a major supporter of the US and allied effort generally, and the US provided vessels and aircraft for Cuba's many air bases and cooperation. Once Castro took over, it was as though Cuba had not sunk U-176 or helped the war effort at all. During the war the US provided its allies with much equipment, including for Arctic Convoys and the Soviet Air Force and Navy. So, occasional flotillas or military convoys of Russian assault boats, whether under command of US or Soviet forces was not clear, transited the Bahamas and escorted convoys. A little tugboat being carried on a larger freighter popped free when the freighter was sunk, only to be sunk by a befuddled German U-boat crew who found the *Letetia Porter* floating with no evidence of ever been crewed. Many more stories, of men on the *Potlatch* missing the entire Antilles islands, being rejected by a sailing boat, finding Inagua but no people, donkeys, but having no ability to kill and eat them, and other Norwegian captains refusing aid in favor of sailing to shore themselves, occur throughout.

One local character based in Nassau was nicknamed *The Last Schoonerman*; Capt. Lou Kenedy lost his schooner *Wawaloam* to a U-boat between Barbados and Nova Scotia, insisted the U-boat skipper tow him to shore, and when rescued, insisted that the Irish ship deliver his crew to a Canadian warship to expedite their arriving at a destination of their choice. Among other odd side-effects of war, rather than let the Germans know they had invented radar, the RAF put out fake news stories that they were instead feeding their pilots extra doses of Vitamin A, enabling them to see better and thus find U-boats from planes without radar. This drove public demand for Vitamin A up, and since shark liver oil is a source, the shark fishery in Green Turtle Cay, Abaco, skyrocketed and was sustained throughout the war, according to the Albert Lowe Museum.

Following the war, US and British officials deepened commercial ties with countries like Uruguay, Peru, and Argentina, hosting Mr. Dodero of Dodero Airlines, Argentina; perhaps, as the allies sold Liberty Ships as cheap surplus after the war, some aircraft were being sold commercially – or militarily. The evacuation of thousands of serviceman and aircraft during several hurricanes were done with admirable, well, military precision. Locals were employed in various functions including transport and baggage details. Extra defenses were in place on the anniversary of the labor riots. Parades continued right through Victory Japan, or VE and into the final departure at the second half of 1946.

Every year, special ceremonies were held to honour the RAF Ensign in Christ Church, the fallen dead-on Remembrance Day at the Cenotaph, those comrades who lay at the RAF Cemetery, still as lovely as ever thanks to the efforts of IODE volunteers. When a cook drowned in an off-duty sailing accident, he was buried "with full military honours." Local troops, referred to as colored at the time, were assigned to guard a vital fuel depot and defend Clifton Pier following a fire and reduction in available guards from overseas. A truck clipped the tail of a large transport plane one night, and the driver did not confess, so a senior official was held up for days. The Royal Victoria, Windsor Hotel, Rozelda, Montagu Beach, and many others are cited, as is the Jungle Club.

The extraordinary case of British evacuee children who spent almost the entire war in Nassau illustrates how difficult it can be to separate pure military from civilian activities. I learned of these students by speaking with Alan Heald, a radio operator aboard the British tanker *Athelqueen*, which was torpedoed off Abaco in early March 1942. Heald and almost all his colleagues survived being sunk, and then accidentally rammed by the colorful Italian commander Count Carlo Fecia di Cossato in the R.Smg. *Enrico Tazzoli*. Then several British sailors drowned trying to swim from the outer reef to Hope Town, Abaco, and the remaining survivors were taken to Nassau by yacht-turned-mailboat the *Content S.*, once the pride of the New York Yacht Club, then owned by local businessman Richard Sawyer.

The British sailors lay over in Nassau to recuperate and await another ship back to the UK via the US and Halifax. During that time, they visited the churches, theatres, clubs, canteens, beaches, forts, and other attractions. Heald, who was taught how to plait palm fronds in Abaco and danced on a balcony with the daughter of an ice-factory owning family named Farrington, told me of the pleasure he took of interacting with the friendly teachers and volunteers who would cheering up a small group of evacuee students. They were well looked after, as Sir Harry Oakes provided his four-storied, 18th-century Clerihew House on Bay Street for their campus, and the Duke and Duchess of Windsor visited them, and included them in a Christmas feast at Government House their first year, in 1940.

So, how did the students find their way to Nassau? In short, the headmaster, Max de Wharton Burr, befriended Harry Oakes in the 1920's and was invited to send children to Nassau, whence the American-Canadian gold magnate had decamped, having purchased a lake believed to have been drained of gold; Oakes emptied the lake and became one of the richest men in the empire on the gold he found under it. The voyages out of the UK were short-lived and fraught with very real danger. Between 12 and 24 August, 1940 a party of 16 students (the only three girls were sisters), from Belmont School, a British preparatory school in West Sussex, and four adult escorts and teachers, successfully crossed the North Atlantic from Liverpool. From the decks of the British SS *Orduna*, the children witnessed some of the six ships (of 50 in the convoy) being sunk by U-boats, despite an escort of four destroyers, it was a traumatic voyage, at least until the party arrived safely in Bermuda.

Despite the Lend-Lease Act, in late 1940, the Panama Treaty established a neutrality zone essentially connecting Halifax, Bermuda, Antigua, and Trinidad, beyond which German and Italian submarines did not penetrate until early 1942. The near-miss on the way out and the tragedy of the British SS *City of Benares*, sunk by Heinrich Bleichrodt in U-48 a few weeks later, which killed 77 of 90 evacuee children and 260 out of 407 total persons on board, caused Winston Churchill to cancel the Children's Overseas Reception Board (CORB) evacuation plan as a result of outcry by parents as well as the public. So, being unable to sail back home, the Belmont School pupils became long-term inhabitants of the Bahamas for most of the war, and part of the community. The students performed in the Christ Church Choir, practised First Aid, performed water sports, and drama, among many activities.

The teaching staff were drawn from the island and included Kenneth Brown, an announcer on Radio Nassau; Father Holmes, a local priest later to become a bishop; Baroness Anna Trolle, a Swede, and Mrs. Marcelle Goldsmith, mother of Teddy and Jimmie (later Sir James), who joined the school as pupils. As the school history relates, "Belmont became very popular with the local residents, the numbers rising to 36 boys and 16 girls, ...and close to 100 by the end of the year. These included the ADC to the Governor's children, Sir Harry Oakes's two sons and a daughter, and Norman Solomon, whose uncle, Sir Kenneth Solomon, was Speaker of the Bahamian House of Assembly." The children of prominent families, British and Bahamian, attended, including Richard Coulson, Peter and Diane Christie, Hubert Hauck, Roy Solomon (who served), David Donald, and Gale Kelly.

As a postscript, what became known as Belmont Bahamas repatriated its original students and instructors by ship, air, and train. The trip from Nassau to Miami, New York, New Orleans to Lisbon on the neutral SS *Magallanes*, and via British Short Sunderland Flying Boat to Foynes in Ireland, and Northolt, England, concluded safely at Lichfield, Staffordshire, England, on March 2, 1944. Their arrival; and survival, was chronicled in both the *Daily Gleaner* in Jamaica, and the *London Evening News*. Belmont Bahamas student James Goldsmith dropped out of Eton, became an industrialist, then a Member of the European Parliament for France in the EU. He and his family are larger-than-life; his son ran for Mayor of London, losing to Sadiq Khan, and daughter Jemima Marcelle married Imran Khan, the world-renown cricketer who would later be elected leader of Pakistan.

Alan Heald, the radio operator who survived the torpedoing of the *Athelqueen* and the loss of shipmates on a reef at night, would not discuss the balance of his voyage with this author, or indeed with his own family. The nearest one can surmise is that before he arrived home, two other ships were shot out from him. As a result of undisclosed traumas, he was categorized DMS, for Distressed Marchant Sailor, deemed unfit for sea, and provided work in a factory assembling and repairing radio sets. He retired to Preston, near Liverpool and never shared the details of the other traumas.

To illustrate how the RAF structured its various units and sub-units, like the marching band, the chaplaincy, the medics, transport, marine, and many other units including mail, mortuary, accident investigation, legal for courts martial, and to publish *The Liberator* weekly magazine, this passage from the No. 111 O.T.U. Operational Record Books from February 1, 1944, should be instructive:

Introduction of Bahamas Air Service Squadron: The unit was formed upon the Station for the recruitment of colored troops. The unit was to have been called the "Native Detachment." This name was changed to the Bahamas Air Service Squadron for the purpose of recruiting. The recruiting appeal was augmented by a short talk by the Officer Commanding No. 111 OTU, over the local Radio Station. The number [of recruits] who reported on the 10th of January 1944 was 104. There were only 2 absentees. The Officer Commanding the Squadron, Flight Lieutenant Cullum and the Adjutant Flying Officer Evans, instructed the recruits on their obligations upon joining the RAF.

The men were quartered in a self-contained unit. NCO's [non-commissioned officers] from both the RAF and the Bahamas Defense Company have been seconded to the unit for the purpose of instructing the recruits in foot and arms drill. As yet [Feb. 1, 1944] only foot drill has been given to the recruits. An Out Island Commission composed of Officer Commanding, the Adjutant, and a medical officer from the Station Hospital made a tour of the islands for the purpose of recruiting men for the Squadron. The commission set sail on the 28 Jan. 1944.

On 29 Jan. 1944 the Squadron was represented by a flight of men at the Dedication Parade for the RAF Ensign at Nassau

Cathedral. After the parade to the Cathedral the Flight took part in the march past HRH the Governor, who took a salute, supported by the Officer Commanding troops in the Bahamas, Captain R. N. Waite.

It is fascinating that the RAF were both flat-footed (intending to name a new unit "Native Detachment,") and also media-astute: they recruited via radio programs and sent fairly high-ranking RAF officers in uniforms aboard sleek modern aircraft to remote airfields to recruit impressionable young men who were perhaps looking for a way to reach the larger world: they offered a patriotic and respectable way for them to leave home in wartime. At the same time, it is clear that the recruits were in a "self-contained" unit; in other words, they were segregated. To provide further context, British and allied servicemen were prohibited under penalty of courts-martial of visiting Nassau's over-the-hill communities, particularly night clubs and so forth; again, the enforcement of a *de-facto* color bar.

Courts-martial cases in the record books were focused mainly on adjudicating young men for going AWOL, stealing equipment or trucks, driving drunkenly or recklessly, being caught in forbidden night spots at forbidden hours, breaking and entering, theft of property, and participating in fights. Punishments usually consisted of confinement for a period of weeks or months. They were dealt with quickly, and often quite severely. Other committees were set up to investigate crashes, damage, wrecks, accidents, and airborne fatalities.

Often VIP officers were flown in from Canada, Trinidad, Bermuda, the US or beyond to officiate and inspect, everything from technical aspects to engineering, and some foreign dignitaries were hosted on the way from South American countries to Washington DC, and smaller bases had their soccer teams flown in for friendly matches. On special days like the King's Birthday or VE and VJ days, the bases were closed to all but essential personnel and extra fleets of busses were provided for trips to town and the beach. On Christmas Eve the officers broke protocol by waiting on serving the enlisted men dinner; an especially popular occasion.

The focus of this study is to faithfully record what actually happened, when, by whom caused, and upon whom the effect was felt. Readers seeking overall strategic views and sweeping opinions, or analyses of tactics and strategy, or post-war assessment, will not find it in these pages. The goal of this book is very simple: to bring the often hard-to-access original raw data concerning day-to-day events of a tucked-away-seeming, yet geographical lynch-pin of a colony to life in a synthesized and readable way. It is as much written by the participants themselves, in their action and words, as by any modern writer, and indeed whole sections of the No. 111 OTU are typed verbatim from the base diaries, or Operational Record Books (ORBs).

While the scope is ambitious, the goal is simply to bring a period of a small colony's history to light, and place it alongside other critical epochs in the Bahamas over 500-year-history. The Bahamas found itself from early 1942 onwards straddling three major conduits of oil and supplies from the Western Hemisphere to the UK: the Windward Passage from the Venezuelan oil fields and Guyanese ore deposits from which metals were made. Ships also utilized the Caicos Passage, Turks Island Passage, Mayaguana Passage, Crooked Island Passage, Old Bahama Channel, Santaren Channel, Mira Por Vos Passage, Passage, Nicholas Channel and others to vulnerably thread their way through Bahamas with shallow reefs on both sides.

The oil patch in the US Gulf, particularly Galveston and Houston, utilizing the Straits of Florida, which rides the Gulf Stream northwards around Maravilla Bank and Walker's Cay above Grand Bahama, and the Northwest Providence Channel from Bimini to the Berry Islands south of Grand Bahama, and the Northeast Providence Channel, passing between southern Abaco and North Eleuthera at Spanish Wells and Harbour Island, once the colony's capital. Both allied merchant ships and German U-boats accessed the Straits of Florida and the wide North Atlantic using these routes, which were later heavily convoyed.

It is hoped that this *Daily Diary Section*, with its dozens of supporting charts and data, will be a starting point for further research into exactly who undertook those actions and what greater outcome resulted therefrom. This is the only reference book detailed exactly what happened in Bahamas during the war, in the air, on the surface of the sea, and below it. The overall area is massive, with 90% of it beyond Bahamas' boundaries; the archipelago was a strategic choke point. You can think of the archipelago straddling a divining rod, or Y-shaped trading route: the left leg is the Gulf of Mexico, the right leg is the ore and oil route from South America, and after they join above the Bahamas from the Straits of Florida, ships headed up the stem towards the Halifax convoy assembly point prior to heading east across the Atlantic to the UK.

This unique study covers every relevant day from leading up to formal initiation of war in September 1939 to May 1945, and through to the end of 1945 to include VJ-Day and the closure of most bases. It includes details of:

- all attacks on allied merchant ships in the area
- all U-Boat patrols by both 5 Italian submarines & 107 German missions
- all convoy transits, including convoy and ship names, dates and ports
- air traffic from RAF air bases and overlapping USN operations in the same area
- transcription from USN Gulf Sea Frontier diaries of daily maps and entries detailing US air squadrons, convoys Miami-Nassau, all of the Straits of Florida.

The progeny of this book has been manifold, but on a visit to the Bahamas National Archives, I was given a short pamphlet covering resources for both world wars, about five pages long, as the bulk of their holdings on the topic. I found that exemplary history books covering the Bahamas devoted mere sentences to the military aspects of World War II: a passing reference to "the contract," to HRH The Governor and Wallis Simpson, the riots, or to the distant threat of U-boats and local contributions to the war effort; much of which on foreign fields.

Then, starting in 2009, I personally stumbled upon two massive troves of data in outside DC and London: the Gulf Sea Frontier Diaries in the US National Archives and Records Administration (NARA) and the complete daily war diaries (ORB's or Operational Record Books) of the RAF No. 111 O.T.U. and RAF No. 113 (Transport) Wing, both based in Nassau in the war. I was determined that students, researchers, visitors, and World War II devotees around the globe will no longer have to hunt overseas in order to learn what happened in and around the Bahamas from 1939 to 1945.

Amazingly, huge data clusters were only discovered in the months leading up to publication: the entire base diary for No. 113 Transport Wing RAF had be obtained in London and typed from scratch by a dedicated team overseas. Books on aviation history focusing on Bermuda, on USN aircraft losses, Banana River and Morrison Field aviation histories, on Puerto Rican and Cuban military history (the latter not celebrated as it was under Batista, not Castro), barely arrived in time. Then the COVID-19 shutdowns began, and I decided that 11 years is enough: that this would not continue to be a never-ending project, and if there were missed threads, like getting all the original *The Liberator* magazines from Canberra or London or Nassau, that could be done by other enthusiasts, the principle being that *a bird in the hand*.....

So now, with the publication of this hybrid chronology, encyclopedia, time-line and database, the veil is pierced. I am more messenger and project manager than author. This is not the *final* word on the topic so much as I hope it will be a *first* word, for others to grasp and follow up on. May it be a modest foundation, the function of a building which most persons using it don't see; for students and others to hang their aspirations and accomplishments on going forward. One aspect about which this author found not a shred about, is the concept of war babies; not one case of them, despite some 10,000 men making up a third of the population for years. For not a single child to have been borne of these circumstances must make it unique!

Since this book is data-driven, it may come off seeming heavy on fact. While every effort has been made to merge information and condense it into readable, palatable bits. In the pages ahead readers are able to study a chart, then easily flip a few pages to read the actual data underlying the outlay of symbols on that chart, and from there take in photos and scale-models of silhouettes showing aircraft, naval, and merchant vessels to clarify.

There is no index, because this book *is* an index. If you are looking for long and florid narrative, descriptive sentences, there aren't many. If, as reader, you revel in finding mistakes and errors, you will probably find hundreds of them, particularly as the book is being rushed to press at the outset of a global pandemic. However, rest assured that if you are willing to stick with this book, you will also find thousands, if not hundreds of thousands of details, facts, and minutiae which this author hopes will motivate and inspire authors and researchers going forward. Nothing could please me more than to have a new author utilize this one and for she or him to create a better one, in a direction they prefer.

Readers of this book will likely have very specific targets, like the bomber pilots and submariners detailed herein. The audience will likely be a global, polyglot, dedicated and small cabal of individuals. The importance of this book is to assert, almost on a basic, baseline level, that *very much happened* in the Bahamas during World War II. This book should illustrate through contemporary accounts by participants in virtually real time, that the residents of the colony should be proud of their islands' daily battle to fend off an often-superior enemy, and to hold up a bulwark of freedom and democracy at the footstep of our ally, the United States.

Many Allied pilots sallied forth in planes from New Providence and other bases, from Florida to Bermuda to Trinidad and Puerto Rico or Cuba, and never returned. Thousands of Allied merchant sailors perished in or near our waters, as did 155 German officers and men in three submarines, the sailor from a US Navy airship, and hundreds of their colleagues killed in a hurricane (the destroyer USS *Warrington*), or the friendly fire of a minefield in Key West (USS *Sturtevant*). This is not only their story – it is our story.

In the face of considerable death, there was also new life borne of these interactions: Jack Lowe, Bahamian serviceman from Abaco who moved to Nassau to contribute to the war effort, writes of the understandable outcomes of Nassau having, as he put it in his memoir ...become an Air Force Town... some found friends in hospitable families. Jack Joudrey, stationed in Nassau for a year

445

with the Royal Canadian Air Force, lived at the Fort Montagu Hotel. He met our sister Eulah at the Paris Ship downtown. Often Jack came into the shop, attracted to the beauty and fragrance of Eulah. Jack Joudrey left Nassau, survived the horrors of air battle in Europe, and was later honored with war medals. Eulah and Jack corresponded until their marriage in 1946. They lived in his birthplace, Nova Scotia. A number of other Bahamian women married servicemen at the same time. Some relocated in England, the United States, and Canada. Our cousin Joyce Russell married a Canadian and they lived in Toronto (*My Life*, p.95-96).

Another RAF officer, Harold Woodman, married Bahamian wife LaGloria Maria Pyfrom, and a number his colleagues returned to run Bahamas Airways: W/C Eric H. Coleman, formerly officer in charge of the base became the first Director of Civil Aviation in May of 1946, and F/L Wilfred "Tubby" Welch joined BAL in 1951 (Aranha, p.81). A young American personal secretary to the Duchess of Windsor, Jean Wallace Drewes met and married Brian Hardcastle-Taylor and married at Government House on December 31, 1943.

Before we take off on this story together, a personal vignette. In the late 1970s my brothers John and James and I explored, as boys are wont to do, many square miles of forests, swamps, and lakes around our home on Skyline Drive. The remains of the RAF Hospital started half a mile southeast of our home, between Sanford Drive, on which the Duke and Duchess of Windsor lived, at Sigrist House (named for Fred Sigrist, who with Tom Sopwith who lived down the road across from the present Prime Minister's office, created Sopwith Aviation, and the wildly successful Sopwith Camel aircraft, among others). The RAF Hospital was intentionally placed on a ridge so that patients would have fresh breezes, and between the Oakes Field and Windsor Field, where the 3,000 or more residents were likely to take ill or be injured.

When the RAF Station Hospital was completed on 21 March, 1943, its leader, Dr. R. H. Pratt, had fallen ill, and so Dr. C. R. McLaughlin assumed command. Sadly, this was not uncommon, with SMO Dr. Bell being hospitalized there and senior base commanders (OinC, for Officer in Charge), including the first, John Alexander took seriously ill and was replaced, underscoring the need for good care. The Senior Medical Officers (SMO) for the hospital included Dr. Rassin, Dr. Lockhart-Mummery, Dr. Pearce, Dr. Lyons, and Dr. Primrose, Group Surgeon Dr. Luth, and Dr. Hughes. The Chief Medical Officer for the colony was Dr. John Merrill Cruikshank. They were all ably supported by half-a-dozen matrons and nurses from the Princess Mary's Royal Air Force Nursing Service, or PM RAFNS, founded in 1918 by Dame Joanna Cruickshank, DBE, RRC, British Army and RAF Matron-in-Chief.

Of these doctors, Dr. Rassin returned to the Bahamas and created Doctor's Hospital on Collins Avenue and Shirley Street, Dr. Cruikshank oversaw the stabilization of two starving survivors from the *Anglo-Saxon*, a ship shelled by a German raider named *Widder*. The men, Tapscott and Widdicombe, arrived on Eleuthera in October, 1940 after 70 days and 2,300 miles in a lifeboat, now at the Imperial War Museum in London. Cruikshank became Chief Medical Officer of Fiji and British possessions in the Pacific. Dr. Lyons went to the aid of the survivors of the *O. A. Knudsen* in Cross Harbour, Abaco, in March, 1942 aboard the Carl and Richard Sawyer-owned mailboat *Content S.* The medical community as a whole tended to 255 allied survivors of German and Italian submarines in Nassau in 1942.

What remains of the RAF Hospital? Between 1947 and 1953 the Bahamian government leased and reactivated it while the Bahamas General Hospital was being constructed. During those 6 or more years it was known as Prospect Hospital, and many patients were treated with a new cure for tuberculosis. Prospect Hospital accommodated 160 patients in general wards in five pavilions, with maternity, children's tuberculosis, and a private ward (Munnings, p.83). As children we found dozens of concrete or wooden and stucco buildings intact, in tidy rows, many of the roofs still on them. There was a main avenue with perhaps a dozen yellow-colored buildings perhaps 20-feet-square on each side. These were presumably accommodations either for staff or patients, or both. Different out-buildings, for food preparation, waste disposal, guards, and so forth, including a dispensary with many shelves, could be found. There was little glass; the windows were louvered to allow air and sunlight in. My two main recollections were of thousands of discarded vials of morphine, empty, and fascinating medicinal bottles, which had survived where wood had rotted and metal rusted.

As for today, should one wish to find remnants, there is good news. First, none of the base hospital became the BahaMar Golf Course. As a major development began, I visited a small building on a bluff which is still shown on online satellite maps. Broadly, the base is bounded by Stanford Drive to the north, Skyline Heights Drive to the west, Ficus Drive and Prospect Lane to the south, and Prospect Ridge Road to the east. More precisely, the line between the back of Bahamas Red Cross and the imposing old gate at Tiger Findlayson's old Star Acres estate covers the focal area, at the highest point.

The highest probability of finding actual ruins is 100 feet before where Prospect Ridge Road meets the JFK Drive roundabout. I was fortunate to discover an outbuilding intact around 2009, and kept a beautiful window shutter which must have been made of the finest woods and been impervious to termites and so forth, as even the green paint was intact. Inland, or west of there is a square structure. If that is not the old building, you should find traces in that vicinity. Much more dubious is to try walking the neighborhood and asking residents if they recall anything. Though heavily developed, the area has about 15% vacant lots, some of which might harbor some archaeological gems; I do not, however suggest you tell residents that you are simply looking for vials of old drugs!

Resources on this topic include *Westward: The Walk of a Bahamian Doctor,* by Dr. Harold Munnings, Jr., which covers the colorful and moving history of modern medicine in the Bahamas. *Artist on His Island, A Study in Self Reliance*, by sculptor Randolph W. Johnston, published in 1975, makes a specific reference to traveling from Little Harbour, Abaco, to the hospital on Prospect Ridge in the 1950s. Also, reading accounts of travel by mailboat, references are made by Bahamians to the hospital, with one gentleman saying he was born there after the war. It would seem a lovely and low-cost thing to erect a placard for visitors and locals alike to the RAF Hospital, which served so many people so well and for so long.

For many months after the war, the RAF and USN continued to help Bahamian vessels and persons in distress, just as locals helped find and rescue survivors of many air crashes. In February, 1946 local recipient of the Distinguished Flying Cross for leading bombers in combat over France, Squadron Leader Lester Brown was sent to the Pine Ridge Lumber Camp, in Grand Bahama to save lives. A railway engine boiler had exploded, killing four men, and injuring four others, one of whom had lost a limb. Assisted by aviators Nay and Miles, and joined by SMO Dr. Lockhart-Mummery, they raced in a large amphibious Grumman Goose on loan from the US. As the base diary reads: "Plasma was administered to one of the injured, who had lost an arm as a result of the explosion, but he died on the airfield."

Among the first Bahamians to volunteer, Brown was one of the Gallant Five, including Fane Solomon, John Maura, John Maillis and Ivor Thompson. The month before the Grumman was sent by the Colonial Secretary to race to bring back a "serious ambulance case" in Cherokee Sound. The 2010 census for the community shows 169 persons live in Cherokee Sound, and the dock is so shallow that vessels have to anchor off and shuttle in. At the time even that was cut off from decent roads. Earlier in the war, Captain Granville Bethel of that port made lemonade from lemons when he salvaged the lifeboat from the Norwegian tanker *O. A. Knudsen* and converted it to a whale-bottomed miniature mailboat to help his neighbors in equally isolated Crossing Rocks nearby. The name Captain Bethel christened his unusual craft with? *Beluga*. And a beach to the south, at Cross Harbour, has been known as Olaus Johansen Beach, since his grave was found there in 2015. Another flight was sent to Mangrove Cay, Andros, for an urgent medical evacuation.

Regarding RAF airplane crashes, with the exception of New Providence, north Andros is where most of the planes that were found ended up. Most of the planes of course simply went missing at sea, with, if fortunate, a self-inflating dinghy to mark the spot, but rarely any bodies. Thousands of hours were flown by aviators seeking lost and missing comrades; a lonely, frustrating duty often turning up patches of seaweed thought to be oil, and wooden wreckage actually from boats, but at times tail numbers and in one case off Booby Rocks, wreckage visible in less than 20 feet of water.

One does not have to look far for evidence of massive engineering structures begun during World War II: that National Stadium sits on what was Oakes, or Satellite Field, Atlantis is astride the can which Axel Wenner-Gren funded on the island he then owned, to appease justifiably upset labor, and the government, Windsor Field is now the country's main commercial artery and primary airport, the US Navy facilities in Georgetown became Exuma's main airport, Morrison Field is now Palm Beach International Airport, and so on. While the Montagu Beach Hotel, Royal Victoria's main buildings, Rozelda and others are gone, as is Symonette's shipyard, many other structures such as the Windsor Hotel and the footprint of Clerihew House and many other edifices can still be found. *Reminiscing: Memories of old Nassau,* by Valeria Moseley Moss and Ronald G. Lightbourn describe what has been lost and preserved.

Skin-diving and SCUBA enthusiasts will be interested to learn from obscure and declassified records just how many RAF and other planes crashed; this study found at least 75 accidents, involving over 300 persons. They planes came down at places like Soldier Road, within a mile or two miles of the Lyndon Pindling International Airport, 400 yards from Balmoral Island, then North Cay, in eight feet of water (my brothers and I dove that one in the 1970s and 1980s), and another large bomber of Simms Point, Goulding Cay, near Lyford Cay where rescue boats where kept; two bodies were recovered. Another plane landed on rocks near Bannerman Town Eleuthera, and another was visible in the sand off Acklins. One plane was salvaged from a lake on New Providence; however, it is thought to have wrecked after the war. A chart herein shows the dozens of air wrecks on New Providence, some along major roads, though most like most ruins burned and were scattered by the accidents and pillaging. Still, there must be much for the archaeologist in these pages.

Importantly many, presumably hundreds, of nurses, ranked as Sisters, Matrons, and the like, rotated through No. 111 OTU. These are virtually the only women, aside from heads of the Red Cross and IODE and spouses and family of VIPs such as governors, HRH

Princess Alice, traveling with her husband, the Earl of Athlone. The most senior woman VIP who arrived as a guest of the RAF was Squadron Officer Lady Bowhill, wife of Air Chief Marshal Bowhill, who adroitly predicted the position of the *Bismark*, allowing British aircraft to find, disable, and sink it. There were many interesting VIP's transiting both RAF bases in Bahamas, on their way to and from many air bases along the entire eastern seaboard, particularly Morrison Field, now Palm Beach International Airport, Key West, Norfolk, Elizabeth City, and beyond.

In Canada, flights often included Dorval near Montreal as well as Gander, and Halifax. Island ports of call included Bermuda, Borinquen on Puerto Rico, Guantanamo on Cuba, Jamaica, St. Vincent, Piarco Field on Trinidad, Ascension in the South Atlantic, and emergency landing strips in between, of which many were built during the war, creating tourism access following it. On mainland South America planes called and fueled at Georgetown, British Guyana (Demerara) and Belem, Brazil. The landing fields in Africa are too numerous to list here, but the primary ones were Accra, Ghana, in West Africa, Khartoum in Sudan, north-eastern Africa, and fields in South Africa.

It was not uncommon for the base diaries to record sanguine notes about pilots setting off for Cairo, Egypt, or making an emergency landing near Ascension and being rescued, or landing on a desert strip in West Africa. And there are tantalizing details like local pilot, Squadron Leader D. Lester Brown earning a medal for service in Burma. There are many references to Mid-East, and one can surmise that the aircraft passing through Nassau made it as far as India and Myanmar and probably supported the critical supply lines over almost impassable mountains known as *The Hump*, as the India-China Ferry by air was known, crossing the southern Himalayas. So, the Bahamas can lay claim to having helped push the Allies over The Hump in World War II. On top of this, "World War II changed aviation in The Bahamas. Many Bahamians who volunteered for service with allied air forces pursued careers in civil aviation on their return," (Cleare, History of Tourism in the Bahamas, p.89). Examples of those who contributed after the war include former RAF Ferry Command pilot Colyn Rees, Lambert Albury, Bobby Hall, Jack Graham (ex-FRAF), and Sid Larkin, to name a few.

Continuing the vignette with another, towards the coast, friends including Colin Green and Paul Bowers were fond of looking for turtles and exploring the woods, lakes and ponds behind the Westward Villas Subdivision at Cable Beach. Colin lived on Yorkshire Street, and Paul on Hampshire Street. Once, while exploring the road which connects them, in the lot on the southeast corner of Eton Avenue and Hampshire Street, we discovered an aircraft bomb which was almost like a funny cartoon, tear-drop shape, with the round fins at the back. It was small, metal, about two feet long, and painted a durable white, as it showed no rust streaks. It was light and looked merely decorative, with no detonation function.

We assumed at the time, and I believe to this day, that in the 1940s an RAF pilot jettisoned that very bomblet into a then-uninhabited forest for practice, or for a lark, and that we had the fortune to find it. In these pages we learn that the RAF participated in a show to impress Bahamians, whereby the Police indicated an area for an RAF plane overflying to bomb, with dud bombs like the one we found, being dropped at the parade ground at Fort Charlotte. As they hit, "fake" explosions with dust and a loud noise were set off from the ground, as though the bomb blew up. Of course, my friends and I had no idea what happened to it, and indeed it would have been less popular for us to have walked around the community with a bomb than the usual spears for fishing with. We left it where it was, and perhaps some treasure hunter will find it and marvel at what a story it must have told, as we did.

On a local scale, this is the story of how that bomb ended up in our neighborhood. The story populates as quickly as it folded, and it is unlikely that the Bahamas will play so central a role in global military events for some time. The author has never been in any military or police, or on the staff of any university or government library or archive, nor is he an aviation historian. As well as being a point-person on a global team, he's what has become of a wide-eyed child who wanted to know what happened in his neighborhood in the most encompassing war ever; needing to

452

know why there was a plane on the reef, an aerial bomb in the back yard, and vials of morphine across the street. Having found out; he determined to share what he learned.

I hope that you enjoy, and share in some of that wonderment here.

TCI in World War II: SS *Fauna*, Part II

In Blue Hills they appear to have traded the life boat for a local sailing boat, or perhaps they bought or chartered the boat. In any event they set of later that day for a longer voyage – to South Caicos Island. Unless they took the shallower inland route, this would have meant a voyage of twenty miles to the north tip of North Caicos, then a voyage of 35 miles down the windward coasts of North, Middle and East Caicos. After two days, in daylight on the 21st of May, they reached Cockburn Harbor, South Caicos, which is also known as East Harbor.

The men remained on South Caicos for a week. During that time three of them – Third Engineer Rab, 25, who had an injured leg, Third Mate Noordveld, aged 21, who was burned, and Oiler Johannes Stroomberg, 46, who had a cut foot, were treated for their wounds. After a period of recuperation, the men all set off again on about the 27th of May for Cockburn Town, Grand Turk, which was their original destination. Again, the three injured men were treated, and again they opted to remain and recover for a week. On or about the 3rd of June 25 of the survivors set off for Cape Haitian, a port city on the northwest coast of Haiti separated from Grand Turk by 115 miles of open ocean. Two men, Othniel Dickenson, 46, and Ben Eve, 49 both British sailors, opted to remain behind in the British West Indies islands. Perhaps they didn't feel up to another open boat voyage. It is not clear whether they used the same local sailing craft or obtained transit on another vessel, but probably the latter, which would have been safer. Taking another ship to Haiti would help explain the wait of a week as well, since they would have been reliant on another skipper's schedule.

Once they landed in Cape Haitian and reported their predicament, the men were provided with transportation by automobile to the capital, Port-au-Prince. Captain den Heyer was debriefed by the US Naval Attaché in Port au Prince. From there they were given another ride to the city of Saint Marc. This meant a car journey over the mountains of at least 75 miles and many hours, much as the survivors of the *Tonsbergfjord* and *Montevideo* had endured together two months earlier. Again, two men opted to remain behind: a Dutch Fireman named Francisca, aged 40, and the English "Servant" John White, aged 42, stayed in Port au Prince. On the 11th of June 1942 the 23 remaining men, still led by Captain den Heyer, boarded the ship Gatun bound for New Orleans, where they arrived on the 20th of May. The refrigerated steamship *Gatun* was built in 1926. She was owned and operated by the Standard Fruit and Steamship Company and her master at the time was Captain MacLean. Aside from employment carrying bananas from Haiti and other islands to home base in New Orleans she was utilized by the US Army during the war. Presumably the Gatun was convoyed to New Orleans via Guantanamo and Key West.

On arrival in New Orleans Captain den Heyer was interviewed by W. S. Hogg of the US Navy. He then proceeded post-haste to New York, in order to report on the loss of his ship to the owners there. Presumably the remaining 21 Dutch crew were re-assigned to other Dutch vessels by the Dutch consulate, and Sam Sanny, the English Fireman, made it home to his wife Cornelia in Brooklyn.

U-558 followed a pattern of light success in its eight-day transit of the Bahamas area followed by heavy losses inflicted in a different zone (in this case the Caribbean) and a further ship bagged on the return voyage. The submarine also attacked and sank the HMS *Bedfordshire* (FY 141) on 12 May, off Cape Hatteras, then after the *Fauna* the Canadian *Troisdoc*, damaged to the *William Boyce Thompson*, and the sinking of the *Beatrice* and *Jack* in the Caribbean and the *Triton* on the way home – northeast of the Caribbean on 2nd June. The total tonnage for the patrol was 19,301 in seven ships.

Krech was amongst the first U-boat skippers to utilize the Mona Passage between Hispaniola (the Dominican Republic) and Puerto Rico, which he did on 29th May. Over the next four days he steamed northeast until the sub left the region north of St. Martin on the 1st of June 1942 bound for Brest where the boat was based with the First Flotilla. On the return trip U-558 again refueled from U-459, this time in mid-June west of the Azores. It returned to Brest on the 21st of June 1942 (Wynn, Vol. 2, p.33).

Günther Krech, 27 at the time, became one of the better-known U-boat skippers of the war, made famous in part by his over twenty ships and over 100,000 tons sunk and his activity off the American coast. He is also remarkable for his youth and early recognition: he earned the Knights Cross shortly after this patrol four days before his 28th Birthday on 17 September 1942. In April 1941 he had achieved the rank of *Kapitänleutnant*. On 20 July 1943 U-558 was sunk by Allied aircraft in the Bay of Biscay, with Krech and four others surviving and being kept in captivity by the Allies during the balance of the war and sometime thereafter.

Günther Krech survived and lived until age 85, not passing away until June 2000. A member of the crew of 1933, he had served in the Luftwaffe for four years before returning to the U-boat arm in November 1939 and serving under Schepke in U-100. He was the officer to commission U-558.

Over ten patrols of 437 days Krech sank 17 ships of 93,186 tons, the HMS *Bedfordshire* (the British officers and crew of which are buried on Cape Hatteras) and damaged two others for 15,070 as well as effectively destroying a further ship of 6,672 tons.

Sources & Copyright Holders

1. "Education", Yearbook, Lyford Cay School, later LCIS, Nassau, NP Bahamas, 15-Apr-1976, Bahamas.
2. "At the Farm", Yearbook, Lyford Cay School, later LCIS, Nassau, NP Bahamas, 15-Apr-1977, Bahamas.
3. "Tall Tales of Eric Wiberg", Yearbook, Lyford Cay School, later LCIS, Nassau, NP Bahamas, 15-Apr-1979, Bahamas.
4. "Stuff", Yearbook, St. Andrew's School, Class 6 Harding, Nassau, NP, 15-May-1981, Bahamas.
5. "The Straw Market", The Outlook, student anthology, Eaglebrook School, Old Deerfield, MA, 15-Apr-1984, USA.
6. "A Day at Sea", The Outlook, student anthology, Eaglebrook School, Old Deerfield, MA, 15-Apr-1984, USA.
7. "One Rainy Day", The Outlook, student anthology, Eaglebrook School, Old Deerfield, MA, 15-Apr-1986, USA.
8. "Coastline", Poetry Fest Annual Anthology, Governor's Academy, Byfield, MA, 15-Apr-1987, USA.
9. "Big, Dead, Headless", The Red & White Newspaper, St. George's School, Middletown, RI, 9-Oct-1987, USA.
10. "Swedish Countryside", The Dragon, anthology, St. George's School, Middletown, RI, 15-Dec-1987, USA.
11. "Quotes", The Dragon, anthology, St. George's School, Middletown, RI, 15-Dec-1987, USA.
12. "Whittemore-Wiberg Water Wonders", The Red & White Newspaper, St. George's School, Middletown, RI, 19-Feb-1988, USA.
13. "Memories of WWI", Poetry Fest Annual Anthology, Governor's Academy, Byfield, MA, 15-Apr-1988, USA.
14. "Evenings", The Dragon, anthology, St. George's School, Middletown, RI, 15-Apr-1988, USA.
15. "The Boot", The Dragon, anthology, St. George's School, Middletown, RI, 15-Apr-1988, USA.
16. "Excerpts from Chapel Dreams", The Dragon, anthology, St. George's School, Middletown, RI, 15-Apr-1988, USA.

17. "Ignorance Epigram", The Dragon, anthology, St. George's School, Middletown, RI, 15-Apr-1988, USA.
18. "A Swimming Paragraph", The Lance, yearbook, St. George's School, Middletown, RI, 15-May-1988, USA.
19. "Sinking Sailors", The Dragon, anthology, St. George's School, Middletown, RI, 15-Dec-1988, USA.
20. "That Day", The Dragon, anthology, St. George's School, Middletown, RI, 15-Dec-1988, USA.
21. "Egyptian Adventure", The Red & White Newspaper, St. George's School, Middletown, RI, 15-Feb-1989, USA.
22. "Alexander the Great East of Indus: 327-325 BC", The Concord Review of History, Concord, MA, 15-Mar-1989, USA.
23. "Curtains", Poetry Fest Annual Anthology, Governor's Academy, Byfield, MA, 15-Apr-1989, USA.
24. "For Kerouac", The Dragon, anthology, St. George's School, Middletown, RI, 1-May-1989, USA.
25. "Untitled", The Dragon, anthology, St. George's School, Middletown, RI, 1-May-1989, USA.
26. "Weebs' Final Adieu", The Red & White Newspaper, St. George's School, Middletown, RI, 2-Jun-1989, USA.
27. "A Summer Under Sail for Eric", The Nassau Tribune, Nassau, NP, 15-Aug-1989, Bahamas.
28. "Memorial Orchestrated", The Heights newspaper, Boston College, Chestnut Hill, MA, 11-Dec-1989, USA.
29. "Armed Robbery Occurs at Local Li'l Peach", The Heights newspaper, Boston College, Chestnut Hill, MA, 24-Sep-1990, USA.
30. "Faculty Discusses U.S. in the Middle East", The Heights newspaper, Boston College, Chestnut Hill, MA, 1-Oct-1990, USA.
31. "Sailing Devotee Shares His Love of Sport", The Heights newspaper, Boston College, Chestnut Hill, MA, 1-Oct-1990, USA.
32. "BC Unable to Hold Mass Audubon Society Conference", The Heights newspaper, Boston College, Chestnut Hill, MA, 29-Oct-1990, USA.

33. "International Influence of Sailing: Commentary", The Heights newspaper, Boston College, Chestnut Hill, MA, 13-Nov-1990, USA.

34. "An Appreciation: Durrell", The Heights newspaper, Boston College, Chestnut Hill, MA, 3-Dec-1990, USA.

35. "Government Blamed for Inner City Violence", The Heights newspaper, Boston College, Chestnut Hill, MA, 3-Dec-1990, USA.

36. "BC Recognizes the Seriousness of AIDS", The Heights newspaper, Boston College, Chestnut Hill, MA, 10-Dec-1990, USA.

37. "Youngest Singlehanded Circumnavigator Speaks", The Heights newspaper, Boston College, Chestnut Hill, MA, 28-Jan-1991, USA.

38. "Students Lend a Hand in Ecuador and Haiti", The Heights newspaper, Boston College, Chestnut Hill, MA, 4-Feb-1991, USA.

39. "Democratic President Elected in Haiti", The Heights newspaper, Boston College, Chestnut Hill, MA, 19-Feb-1991, USA.

40. "Sandel Argues for 'Substantial Moral Discourse'", The Heights newspaper, Boston College, Chestnut Hill, MA, 25-Feb-1991, USA.

41. "CBS POW's Return from Iraq", The Heights newspaper, Boston College, Chestnut Hill, MA, 18-Mar-1991, USA.

42. "Consuls' Night Opens Doors to Students", The Heights newspaper, Boston College, Chestnut Hill, MA, 25-Mar-1991, USA.

43. "Earth Week Plans Underway on Campus", The Heights newspaper, Boston College, Chestnut Hill, MA, 8-Apr-1991, USA.

44. "Frenchman Wins 1990-'91 Sailing Challenge", The Heights newspaper, Boston College, Chestnut Hill, MA, 29-Apr-1991, USA.

45. "Log of Yacht Chebec's Trans-Atlantic Voyage [Duplicate, Manchester College Oxford, 1992, & BC Stylus, 1993]", The Bulletin, annual magazine of St. George's School, Middletown, RI, 15-May-1992, USA.

46. "Chebec's trans-Atlantic Voyage [Duplicate, Bulletin, 1992, BC Stylus, 1993]", The Mancunian,magazine of Harris-Manchester College, Oxford University, 15-May-1992, UK.

47. "Australian Tall Ship Welcomes Bahamian", The Nassau Tribune, Nassau, NP, 20-Aug-1992, Bahamas.

48. "Harbor Island Visitor Gives First-Hand Account of Storm", The Nassau Tribune, Nassau, NP, 26-Aug-1992, Bahamas.

49. "BC Student Meets Hurricane Andrew in the Bahamas", The Heights newspaper, Boston College, Chestnut Hill, MA, 8-Sep-1992, USA.

50. "BC Admissions Thrives Despite Recession", The Heights newspaper, Boston College, Chestnut Hill, MA, 8-Sep-1992, USA.

51. "Editorial on the L.A. Riots [Missing]", The Bridge, pop-up publication, Boston College, Chestnut Hill, MA, 15-Oct-1992, USA.

52. "Studying Abroad Proves Valuable to Students", The Heights newspaper, Boston College, Chestnut Hill, MA, 19-Oct-1992, USA.

53. "Eric's Guide to Jitneys", What's On Bahamas, Nassau, NP, 15-Jan-1993, Bahamas.

54. "Eric's Guide to Mailboats, with Schedule", What's On Bahamas, Nassau, NP, 15-Jan-1993, Bahamas.

55. "Eric's Guide to the Paradise Island Ferry", What's On Bahamas, Nassau, NP, 15-Jan-1993, Bahamas.

56. "Harbour Island Recovers from Hurricane Andrew", The Nassau Tribune, Nassau, NP, 17-Jan-1993, Bahamas.

57. "Log of Chebec's Trans-Atlantic Voyage [Duplicate, Bulletin, 1992, Manchester College Oxford, 1992]", The Stylus, literary magazine of Boston College, Chestnut Hill, MA, 15-May-1993, USA.

58. "23-Year Old Skippers 70' Sailing Yacht Across Pacific, Part I", What's On Bahamas, Nassau, NP, 15-Jan-1995, Bahamas.

59. "Nassuvian Skippers Sailing Yacht, Part II", What's On Bahamas, Nassau, NP, 15-Feb-1995, Bahamas.

60. "A Review of Riddle of the Sands by Erskine Childers: Review", Newport This Week, Newport, RI, 1-Oct-1998, USA.

61. "A Delivery Skipper Sees His Lifetime in 16 Minutes", Cruising World Magazine, Middletown, RI, 1-Oct-2000, USA.

62. "Law Student Sinks Yacht:Stiarna, Part I", The Docket, Roger Williams University School of Law, Bristol, RI, 15-Feb-2002, USA.

63. "Sinking Loss of Yacht Stiarna, Part II", The Docket, Roger Williams University School of Law, Bristol, RI, 15-Feb-2003, USA.

64. "Sinking Loss of Yacht Stiarna, Part III", The Docket, Roger Williams University School of Law, Bristol, RI, 15-Apr-2003, USA.

65. "Advice to Owners at Eleuthera Island Shores", Newsletter, Eleuthera Island Shores Property Owner's Association, Cocoa Beach, FL, 15-Jun-2007, USA.

66. "U-Boats in the Bahamas in WWII", The Bahamas Handbook, Depuch Publications, Nassau, NP, 1-Jan-2011, Bahamas.

67. "Wartime Stories Of Derring-Do 2011", Bahamas Handbook and Businessman's Manual, 1-Jan-2011, .

68. "WWII U-Boats Attack Three Ships off Abaco", The Abaconian, Marsh Harbour, Great Abaco, 15-May-2012, Bahamas.

69. "U-128's Attack on Tanker O. A. Knudsen, Abaco", Schooner Bay Mainsheet, Great Abaco, Nassau NP, 15-Aug-2012, Bahamas.

70. "U-Boats in Bahamas: Local Witness and Two Graves", The Nassau Tribune, Nassau, NP, 15-Nov-2013, Bahamas.

71. "Sir Augustus J. Adderley & the S/V Emma Tuttle", The Bahamas Handbook, Depuch Publications, Nassau, NP, 1-Jan-2015, Bahamas.

72. "Historia del Sumergible U153, 1939-1942 (Wilfried Reichmann, Cuatro Víctimas y su Pérdida) [In Spanish]", U-Historia.com, Dani Janer Åkerberg, editor, 15-Jan-2015, Spain.

73. "Young Man & the Sea, Alumnus", PenDragon, annual magazine of Lyford Cay International School, aka LCIS, Nassau, NP, 15-May-2015, Bahamas.
74. "U-Boats in the Bahamas & Bermuda", PowerShips, magazine of Steamship Historical Society of America, Warwick, RI, 15-Jun-2015, USA.
75. "War in Paradise, the Bahamas in WWII", Oxford Today, magazine of Oxford University, Oxford, Oxfordshire, UK,, 15-Aug-2015, UK.
76. "U-Boats off Bermuda, Part I: Axis Submarine Activities", BerNews, Bermudian news service, Hamilton, HM, 8-Oct-2015, Bermuda.
77. "U-Boats off Bermuda, Part II: Survivors Landed in Bermuda", BerNews, Bermudian news service, Hamilton, HM, 1-Nov-2015, Bermuda.
78. "U-Boats off Bermuda, Part III: Survivors and Bermudians", BerNews, Bermudian news service, Hamilton, HM, 9-Nov-2015, Bermuda.
79. "U-Boats off Bermuda, Part IV: Bermudians as an Aviation Outpost ", BerNews, Bermudian news service, Hamilton, HM, 1-Dec-2015, Bermuda.
80. "USS YP-453, ex-Yacht Pleiades: Narrative of History & Wartime Loss, 1928-1943", David Wright, Manager, Yard & District Craft Archives, Navsource.org, 24-Feb-2016, USA.
81. "Mailboats: Introduction, background, motives", The Nassau Tribune, Nassau, NP, 24-Mar-2016, Bahamas.
82. "History of Mailboats from 1804", The Nassau Tribune, Nassau, NP, 1-Apr-2016, Bahamas.
83. "Mailboats of and to Abaco", The Nassau Tribune, Nassau, NP, 8-Apr-2016, Bahamas.
84. "Mailboat Service to Eleuthera", The Nassau Tribune, Nassau, NP, 15-Apr-2016, Bahamas.
85. "Mailboats to Northern Islands", The Nassau Tribune, Nassau, NP, 22-Apr-2016, Bahamas.
86. "Mailboats to Southern Islands", The Nassau Tribune, Nassau, NP, 29-Apr-2016, Bahamas.
87. "Roberts Family Mailboat Dynasty", The Nassau Tribune, Nassau, NP, 6-May-2016, Bahamas.

88. "Taylor Family Mailboat Dynasty", The Nassau Tribune, Nassau, NP, 13-May-2016, Bahamas.

89. "History of Tractor Tugs", Marine Technology, newsletter, Society Naval Architects & Marine Engineers, Providence, RI, 15-May-2016, USA.

90. "History of Horses in the Bahamas", PenDragon, magazine, Lyford Cay International School, Nassau, NP, 15-May-2016, Bahamas.

91. "Dean Family Mailboat Dynasty", The Nassau Tribune, Nassau, NP, 20-May-2016, Bahamas.

92. "Hanna Family Mailboat Dynasty ", The Nassau Tribune, Nassau, NP, 27-May-2016, Bahamas.

93. "Wooden Mailboats, to the 1960s", The Nassau Tribune, Nassau, NP, 10-Jun-2016, Bahamas.

94. "History of Mailboats of the Bahamas: 200 vessels over 200 years.", PowerShips, magazine of Steamship Historical Society of America, Warwick, RI, 15-Jun-2016, USA.

95. "European Mailboats, to the 1990s", The Nassau Tribune, Nassau, NP, 17-Jun-2016, Bahamas.

96. "The Grounding and Salvage of USS SC-1059 in Bahamas", David Wright, Manager, Yard & District Craft Archives, Navsource.org, 24-Jun-2016, USA.

97. "Modern Mailboats, from the 1990s", The Nassau Tribune, Nassau, NP, 24-Jun-2016, Bahamas.

98. "Roundup: Mailboat as a Living Tradition", The Nassau Tribune, Nassau, NP, 1-Jul-2016, Bahamas.

99. "Conclusion, Potter's Cay Dock, the Future ", The Nassau Tribune, Nassau, NP, 8-Jul-2016, Bahamas.

100. "SS Potlatch Survivors' Voyage Through Bahamas", Journal of the Bahamas Historical Society, BHS, Nassau, NP, 15-Dec-2016, Bahamas.

101. "A Humble Beginning, History, LCIS 1960s to early 1980s", PenDragon, magazine of Lyford Cay International School, Nassau, NP, 15-May-2017, Bahamas.

102. "McAllister Philadelphia Hosts VIPs, Head of MARAD", At the Helm, newsletter of McAllister Towing, New York, NY, 15-Dec-2017, USA.

103. "Struggle Towards Enforcing Justice: The British Commission on Slave Trade, Havana 1824-26", Journal of the Bahamas Historical Society, BHS, Nassau, NP, 15-Dec-2017, Bahamas.
104. "WWI and the Bahamas: Defender Capt. Stephen Albert Dillett", The Bahamas Handbook, Depuch Publications, Nassau, NP, 1-Jan-2018, Bahamas.
105. "Book Signing of U-Boats off Bermuda by author", BerNews, Bermudian news service, Hamilton, HM, 15-Apr-2018, Bermuda.
106. "LCIS in its Adolescence, History from Late 1970s to the 1990s", PenDragon, magazine of Lyford Cay International School, Nassau, NP, 15-May-2018, Bahamas.
107. "U-Boats off New England 1942-1945", PowerShips, magazine of Steamship Historical Society of America, Warwick, RI, 15-Jun-2018, USA.
108. "Re-Floating Bulk Carrier Sarocha Naree", At the Helm, newsletter of McAllister Towing, New York, NY, 15-Jul-2018, USA.
109. "Tugs Iona & Buckley Rescue Asphalt Tanker Feng Huang Ao, with M. Hwang", At the Helm, newsletter of McAllister Towing, New York, NY, 15-Jul-2018, USA.
110. "ISM/ISO 9001 Audit, with M. Hwang", At the Helm, newsletter, McAllister Towing, New York, NY, 15-Jul-2018, USA.
111. "Azores from a Swedish-Bahamian Sailor", Magazine A Praça, Azores & Bristol, RI, USA, 1-May-2019, Portugal.
112. "LCIS Evolves; School History from the New Millenium", PenDragon, magazine of Lyford Cay International School, Nassau, NP, 15-May-2019, Bahamas.
113. "Foreword", Bahama Tales, by William Johnson, Jr., 15-Aug-2019, USA.
114. "TCI in World War I and World War II", Astrolabe, newsletter Turks & Caicos Museum, in Times of the Islands, Providenciales, TCI, 15-Sep-2019, Turks & Caicos.
115. "Survivors of U-Boats in the TCI, Part II", Astrolabe, newsletter Turks & Caicos Museum, in Times

of the Islands, Providenciales, TCI, 30-Dec-2019, Turks & Caicos.

116. "Coronavirus Quarantine Diary, Maidstone Lake, Vermont, March 25-May 5, 2020", COVID-19 Anthology Book, Compiled, Edited by Claire Cabot, Beverly, MA, 5-May-2020, USA.

117. "From Worldly to World-Class, School History from 2008-2020", PenDragon,magazine, Lyford Cay International School, Nassau, NP, 15-May-2020, Bahamas.

118. "TCI in World War II: The Fauna, Part I, 1942", Astrolabe, newsletter Turks & Caicos Museum, in Times of the Islands, Providenciales, TCI, 15-Jun-2020, Turks & Caicos.

119. "USCGC General Greene's WW2 Rescues at Nantucket", PowerShips, magazine of Steamship Historical Society of America, Warwick, RI, 15-Jun-2020, USA.

120. "The Story of the Gertrude H.", Stories that Need to be Told Contest, Tulip Tree Publishing, Boulder, CO, 1-Sep-2020, USA.

121. "Coronavirus Quarantine Diary, Eagle Hill, East Boston", COVID-19 Anthology Book, Compiled, Edited by Claire Cabot, Beverly, MA, 21-Sep-2020, USA.

122. "Initiation, The Mirror of the Sea, by Joseph Conrad, Retrospective and Book Review for the NYYC", New York Yacht Club Member Newsletter, New York, NY, 27-Nov-2020, USA.

123. "Bahamas in World War II: RAF & Overview", Journal of the Bahamas Historical Society, BHS, Nassau, NP, 1-Dec-2020, Bahamas.

124. "TCI in World War II: The Fauna, Part II, 1942", Astrolabe, newsletter Turks & Caicos Museum, in Times of the Islands, Providenciales, TCI, 30-Dec-2020, Turks & Caicos.

* 9 7 8 0 9 8 4 3 9 9 8 6 4 *